THE LAST
AMATEURS

ALSO BY JOHN FEINSTEIN

The Majors

A March to Madness

A Civil War

A Good Walk Spoiled

Play Ball

Hard Courts

Forever's Team

A Season Inside

A Season on the Brink

Running Mates
(A Mystery)

Winter Games
(A Mystery)

THE LAST AMATEURS

*Playing for Glory and
Honor in Division I
College Basketball*

John Feinstein

Little, Brown and Company
Boston   New York   London

First Edition

ISBN 0-316-27701-0
LCCN 00-105890

10 9 8 7 6 5 4 3 2 1
Q-FF

Designed by Stratford Publishing Services, Inc.

Printed in the United States of America

This is for
Ethan Samuel Sattler and
Matthew Richman Feinstein,
with love to their parents

TO PLAY THE GAME IS GREAT . . .

TO WIN THE GAME IS GREATER . . .

BUT TO LOVE THE GAME IS THE GREATEST OF ALL . . .

— *Plaque in the lobby of the Philadelphia Palestra*

CONTENTS

THE PATRIOT LEAGUE

Bucknell University, Lewisburg, Pennsylvania

Colgate University, Hamilton, New York

College of the Holy Cross, Worcester, Massachusetts

Lafayette College, Easton, Pennsylvania

Lehigh University, Bethlehem, Pennsylvania

U.S. Military Academy, West Point, New York

U.S. Naval Academy, Annapolis, Maryland

INTRODUCTION

AS has often been the case in my career, this book took form when I wasn't looking for a book to write. And, as has been the case just as often, it took a while for me to figure out just how to go about doing it.

In March of 1995 my boss for life, George Solomon, asked me to cover an NCAA Tournament subregional in Dayton, Ohio, for the *Washington Post.* At the time, I didn't work for the *Post,* but that has never really mattered when it comes to my relationship with George. I've always said we do our work best together when we aren't working together.

I agreed to go. I have fond memories of Dayton, having covered a number of NCAA subregionals there through the years and because I first met longtime Dayton Coach Don Donoher and his wife, Sonia, as a kid in New York in 1968 when Dayton won the NIT. Even though Don had retired, I knew I would get a chance to see them.

George wanted me in Dayton for two reasons: he needed someone there who could write a column and he needed the University of Virginia covered. On the first day of the tournament, I did both: I wrote a column about Miami of Ohio's upset of Arizona and then wrote a game story on Virginia's victory over Nicholls State. It was about 6:30 by the time I finished the Virginia story. The evening doubleheader was scheduled to start in a little more than an hour. Since the first game was a virtual walkover — top-seeded Kansas against number sixteen Colgate — my plan was to go out and get a good dinner, then come back near the end of the first game (just in case someone from Kansas broke a leg and I had to write about it) and then stay for the second game between Michigan and Western Kentucky.

The arena was empty as I packed up my computer, the afternoon crowd having been cleared out, the evening crowd not having been allowed in yet. I had been writing on press row because I've always enjoyed the feel of an empty arena, especially when the alternative is a smoke-filled press room. Walking toward the ramp that led to the parking lot, I spotted a familiar figure sitting all alone on one of the team benches.

It was Jack Bruen, someone I had known for years, dating back to his days as the coach at Catholic University in Washington. Bruen had always been one of my favorite people in the coaching business; someone who loved the game and took it seriously but never seemed to take himself seriously. He had left Washington in 1989 to take over Colgate's reeling program and now, in his sixth season, he had the school in the NCAA Tournament for the first time in history.

I walked over to say hello, wondering what exactly Bruen was doing sitting on the bench in the empty arena. After we shook hands and exchanged small talk I jokingly asked him if he was hoping the game might start before Kansas arrived if he commandeered the bench early enough.

Bruen laughed. "I've been in this sport all my life," he said. "Just being here tonight really is a dream come true for me. It's the same for the kids. At our level, getting to play in this tournament against a team like Kansas, we have to pinch ourselves to believe it." He smiled. "I know what's probably going to happen once the game starts. I just wanted to come out here by myself for a little while and soak the whole thing in, you know, being in the moment or whatever it is they call it."

By the time Bruen finished talking, my plans for the evening had changed. I would get something to eat in the press room and then watch Colgate play Kansas; watch Bruen and his kids in their moment. Maybe there was a column in it, maybe there wasn't. But I figured it was worth watching — at least for as long as Colgate kept the game respectable.

I ended up watching the entire forty minutes. That was how long Colgate kept the game respectable. Kansas kept trying to make a big run to put the Red Raiders away and couldn't. A tough little kid named Tucker Neale buried one 3 after another from the perimeter and Adonal Foyle, the gifted six-ten freshman who had been recruited by all the big-name schools a year earlier, wouldn't let Kansas dominate inside. Foyle fouled out with just under two minutes left. Kansas led by 8. As he walked to the bench, Kansas Coach Roy Williams walked down from his bench and onto the court to shake his hand.

It ended 82-68, but the Kansas players all knew they had been in a real basketball game. When the buzzer sounded, I looked behind me for Mark Murphy, Colgate's athletic director. Murphy was another erstwhile Washingtonian, having played defensive back for the Washington Redskins for nine years after graduating from Colgate in 1977.

I walked over to congratulate Murphy on his team's effort. His eyes were glistening with pride. "It's just hard for people to understand what it means for us to compete like that," he said. "Except for Adonal, there's not a kid on our team who will ever even think about playing in the NBA. There probably isn't a guy on the Kansas team who *won't* think about playing in the NBA."

He was, of course, 100 percent accurate. Foyle is the only player in the Patriot League's ten-year history to play in the NBA. For the rest of the Colgate players, just as for Bruen, that night was a memory they would cherish for as long as they lived.

They weren't alone. I walked away from that night thinking that the kids from Colgate, corny as it sounded, were what college sports are *supposed* to be about.

Needless to say, they aren't close to what college sports is truly about. College basketball today is about colleges chasing millions — no, billions — of dollars; it's about a win-at-all-costs mentality that more often than not starts in the president's office and works down; alumni and fans who could care less what a school's graduation rate is as long as they're winning championships; illegal payoffs that go way beyond what is reported because they are so hard to prove; academic fraud that only occasionally comes to light; and pampered players who expect everyone to kiss their butt twenty-four hours a day because that's the way their lives have been since the day their talent was discovered.

I have a memory of an NCAA Tournament regional several years ago. Two players from a top-seeded team had been asked by a local radio station if they could come by their hotel after practice for a brief interview. The station sent a limo to pick up the players and their sports information director. When the players arrived, an eager producer rushed up to greet them. Did they want something to eat? Drink? And, by the way, we had T-shirts made up for the regional, how many would you each like to take with you?

One of the players looked disdainfully down at the producer and said, "Haven't you got any hats? CBS gave us hats."

The only reason I don't name the school and the player is that the same thing could easily happen with any team, any school, almost any player. The mentality of entitlement that exists in college basketball today is mind-boggling.

Every time I sit in an NCAA Tournament press conference and hear the moderator — under orders from the NCAA — ask if there are questions for the "student-athletes," I want to jump up and ask them exactly what they have done to be students while the multibillion extravaganza known as March Madness has been going on. Been to class lately, Mr. Student-Athlete? Did you bring any books on the trip with you? Tell me, what are your plans for the day you can't play basketball anymore? The answers in, I would say, about 90 percent of the cases would be: No; why would I do that? and, Be a TV commentator, that's national TV, none of that local stuff.

Fast forward a little more than four years from Dayton in 1995 to Teaneck, New Jersey, on a warm July day on the campus of Fairleigh Dickinson University in 1999. In the interim, I had written two books involving college athletes. The first one was about the Army-Navy football rivalry. In researching that book, I had worked with kids who knew they were not going to be pro football players; who played because they loved to play, because they loved being a part of the team. I had never enjoyed writing a book more. The second had been on ACC basketball. The focus was on the nine coaches but, naturally,

I spent a good deal of time around the players. I didn't dislike them, in fact I liked a few of them — notably Tim Duncan — quite a lot. But my overall feeling being around them was that almost all of them were pros-in-training. Some went to class, some graduated. (The ACC's overall graduation rate for basketball players in the 1990s was 49 percent.) But almost all of them looked at college as little more than a stepping-stone to playing professionally. If not (God forbid) at the NBA level, then certainly overseas. My guess is that among the slightly more than one hundred scholarship players in the ACC that year (or any given year) at least ninety were counting on basketball as their way of making a living.

There's nothing wrong with that. But it hardly qualifies them to be called "student-athletes." I vividly remember hearing one ACC coach angrily lecture a player during a game because he appeared tired. "You spent too damn much time studying this week!" he yelled, completely serious. I am not implying that ACC coaches or other big-time coaches actively discourage their players from studying or going to class. But I *am* implying that you better believe basketball comes first. At the best places, school is worked in as often as is possible.

I was in Teaneck on that July day, at one of those summer meat markets posing as a basketball camp, to talk to some coaches about participating in a charity tournament in Washington. The coaches were there to watch top players perform and to make sure the top players saw them watching them perform. I had seen this show before. All I wanted to do was find the coaches I needed to talk to and pitch them on bringing their teams to the tournament.

Inevitably, I found myself sitting with different coaches while they watched games. Just as inevitably, several players caught my eye. As much as I may dislike the summer basketball culture, I still like basketball and, like any fan, when I see a good player, I'm curious about him.

So, as the afternoon wore on, I occasionally inquired about players. Here, verbatim, are some of the answers I got:

"Can't touch him, his boards are brutal."

"Already got an agent."

"The bidding's too high for us."

"Going straight to the NBA."

I'm not claiming any of this is new, but it hit me that afternoon that the bad guys seem to have taken control of the big-time game. Everyone has to deal with the sneaker company sleazebags and the street agents and the AAU coaches and, the newest phenomenon, the guys dealing players under the guise of "financial advisor." I'm not just talking the so-called outlaw schools, I'm talking everyone and anyone who dreams of the Final Four or, for that matter, the Sweet Sixteen.

I got up to walk outside and get some fresh air — literally and figuratively. Walking into the lobby, I encountered Don DeVoe, the coach at Navy, and Emmett Davis, his long-time assistant who had moved on a year earlier to become the coach at Colgate. I was a little surprised to see them because the kind of "student-athlete" performing inside rarely landed at Navy or Colgate.

"Generally speaking, you're right," DeVoe said. "But there's always a couple that are good students. Right now, there's not a kid in there thinking about Navy or Colgate. But as time passes, they might not have as many options as they're thinking they have now."

DeVoe had seen the big-time side of the game for a long while, coaching at Virginia Tech and Wyoming and Tennessee. He'd had success at all three places but seemed quite happy at Navy in the relative boondocks of college hoops. "I may not have great talent, but I've had great kids," he said. "They're fun to coach and they're the kind of people I'll be proud to say I worked with someday." He smiled. "Not too many guys walk out of the Naval Academy with entourages."

Davis laughed and briefly told a story about a Colgate kid who had given up basketball a couple of years earlier because he needed extra study time to try to qualify for a Rhodes Scholarship. His Rhodes essay had been about the pain of giving up basketball. He was leaving for Oxford in a month.

The two coaches walked into the gym to look for a diamond in the cesspool. I walked outside, my mind racing. "Wouldn't it be fun," I thought, "to write a book about the kind of kids DeVoe and Davis coached?" I didn't know a lot about the Patriot League, only that it consisted of seven academically oriented schools: Army, Navy, Colgate, Holy Cross, Lafayette, Lehigh, and Bucknell. I knew the league had been formed on the Ivy League concept that all scholarships should be based on financial need, not athletic ability. I knew that only because I remembered Fordham's basketball team leaving the league a few years earlier because it couldn't live with that concept any longer.

I walked around the parking lot for a few more minutes. I was now trying to anticipate the questions I knew people would ask about the book. The first would be "You want to write about *who?*" The second would be "What's a Patriot League?" The third one would be legitimate: "If you want to do a book on true student-athletes, why not the Ivy League?"

"Maybe," I thought, "I should do the Ivy League." After all, that was the league in Division I college basketball that best combined athletics and academics. But I was looking for ball players who worked in virtual obscurity. Princeton and Penn simply didn't fit that description. They were too good. Princeton had been a number four seed in the NCAA Tournament in 1998 and had beaten UCLA, the defending national champion, in 1996. Penn had been a play or two from advancing to the Sweet Sixteen in 1994 before losing to Florida, a team that reached the Final Four that year. The two schools also produced NBA players on a semiregular basis — not to mention ex–NBA stars running for president.

There was another problem with the Ivy League: Princeton and Penn won the league title almost every year. In the thirty-one years since my then-beloved Columbia Lions, led by Jim McMillan, Heyward Dotson, and the immortal Roger Walaszek, won the Ivy League championship and advanced to the Sweet Sixteen, someone other than Princeton or Penn has won the league exactly three times. The Ivy League is also one of two conferences in Divison I (the Pacific-10 is the other) that doesn't have a conference tournament. When only one team is going to represent a conference in postseason play, there is a natural drama to those three days in March that decide a team's fate. In ten years, the Patriot League has never had a second team invited to either the NCAA or even the NIT. One team goes, everyone else sits home and watches. In the Ivy League, the runner-up — Princeton or Penn — often gets an NIT bid.

Having decided that the Patriot League was more of a dramatic setting than the Ivy League, I then wondered if I should consider a book on basketball in Division III. After all, that is college athletics in its absolute purest form. No one on scholarship, no one at the games, almost no travel during the season, kids not good enough (most of the time) to get a Division I or Division II scholarship, who play at the Division III level for no reason other than to play.

I rejected that idea because I wanted to be a little closer to the spotlight, to work with kids who got a peek at the other side — through recruiting, through regular season games where they were fed to big-time teams in order to let their school cash a check, through those forty minutes of fame one school gets each year in the NCAAs.

I walked back into the gym convinced my gut was right. A book on the Patriot League. A book on kids who could play, but wouldn't get rich playing. A book on kids who had stories to tell and would tell them in complete sentences. A book on kids who would be more than happy with a T-shirt. A book that would allow me to be around college basketball without feeling as if I needed a three-hour shower every time I walked out of an arena.

There was some danger in taking on such a project. What if the kids didn't turn out to be as smart and unspoiled as I thought they would be? That concern was laid to rest on my first trip to each school. My winter is perhaps best summed up by a conversation I had in the Lafayette locker room in early February. The Leopards had just won a tense game against Bucknell, hanging on for a 75-73 victory when Bucknell's Valter Karavanic rimmed a 3-pointer at the buzzer.

I had already made a note to myself during the game that eight of the ten starters had GPAs of 3.0 or better, led by Karavanic, a GTE Academic All-American who carried a 3.8 in electrical engineering. A high GPA may indicate only book smarts or good work habits. It doesn't define a person. Even so, at a time when entire leagues may not have eight players with 3.0 GPAs, it was an impressive statistic, especially given that these were two good basketball teams.

When the game ended, I spent some time in each locker room. As the Lafayette locker room emptied, I found myself sitting with junior point guard Tim Bieg and sophomores Reggie Guy and Brian Burke.

I can't remember who brought it up, but one of the players looked at me and said, "So, were you surprised that [John] McCain beat [George W.] Bush that badly last night?"

The next fifteen minutes were spent discussing the New Hampshire primary and its ramifications. As we talked it occurred to me that this conversation wasn't likely to be taking place in locker rooms in the ACC, the Big Ten, the Big East, or any of the other glamour leagues around the country.

Unless of course Bush or McCain could shoot the 3.

THE LAST
AMATEURS

1

ONE SHINING MOMENT

ON a frigid March day, in the quiet of a near-empty field house, the members of the Lafayette College basketball team went through the routine one last time. For four days they had prepared and re-prepared and prepared again to play Temple in the opening round of the NCAA basketball tournament. In all, there may not have been a soul outside of the twenty people inside the Canisius College gym that morning who gave them any chance to win the game. Temple was ranked fifth nationally and many were picking the Owls to reach the Final Four. They were the number two seed in the Eastern Regional.

Lafayette was the number fifteen seed. According to the computer rankings that the tournament selection committee uses as a guide in seeding the sixty-four-team field, it was the 126th-ranked team in the country. Among the thousands filling out brackets in office pools, the number of people picking Lafayette to win the game could probably be counted on one hand — with fingers to spare.

Temple's most impressive victory of the season had been an upset of top-ranked Cincinnati — at Cincinnati — on national television in February. Lafayette's most impressive victory of the season had been a 26-point rout of 131st-ranked Navy in the Patriot League Tournament championship game a week earlier. That victory had put the Leopards into the NCAA Tournament and created the matchup with the powerful Owls.

But in the small Canisius gym, the notion that tiny Lafayette could upset Temple was a living, breathing thing. The players and coaches understood their role in the grand scheme of the event. They were supposed to be fodder. A day earlier in the Buffalo newspaper they had read a story in which Ian Eagle, who would do play-by-play on the game for CBS, had explained that he would do extra research for the Temple-Lafayette game because there was a good chance he would need a lot of fill material once Temple pulled away.

Their coach, Fran O'Hanlon, whose soft-spoken manner hid a deep-seated competitive streak, had reminded them again and again that, as good as Temple was, as much as he respected Coach John Chaney, they were beatable. It would not be easy, but it was far from impossible.

"Remember one thing," O'Hanlon told his players during a brief break in the pregame workout. "No one will work harder than you. No one will want to win more than you. No one deserves to be here more than you."

They looked him right in the eye as he spoke, his voice, as always, just loud enough to be heard. They nodded in agreement. There would be close to 20,000 people in the Marine Midland Arena that afternoon. Only twice all season — at a tournament in New Mexico — had they played in an arena that seated more than 10,000 people. Those games had been played before a lot more empty seats than people. Now, they would be playing in a huge, packed arena. The CBS telecast would only go to a small portion of the country unless Lafayette was in a position to win. Then, a producer in New York would order a switch flipped and the entire country would be watching Lafayette.

It was a quiet practice. There was very little of the usual joking and ribbing. The previous day, several players had received prank phone calls in their hotel rooms from someone claiming to be a reporter from the *Buffalo News*. The consensus was that the prankster had been Brian Ehlers, the two-time Patriot League player of the year whose deadpan manner belied a mischievous streak. But that time had now passed. In a few minutes, they would leave the empty gym behind. The packed arena and the Owls loomed.

When he had put them through their final paces, going over Temple's personnel one last time, walking through the offensive sets they would use against Temple's infamous matchup zone defense, reminding them again and again how important communication would be from the game's first minute, O'Hanlon called them all to the center jump circle.

"Okay, guys," he said, his voice soft as ever, but filled with the firmness all the players understood to mean he wanted complete attention. "There's nothing they're going to do we haven't prepared for. You know that. We just have to be ready to play from the first minute. Not the fifth or the tenth, the first. Everybody understand?"

They all nodded. They all understood. There was no margin for error in this game. They had developed a penchant early in the season for dropping behind teams in the early minutes of games. Most of the time, they had been able to recover because they were a smart, experienced team that didn't panic. Against a team like Temple all the smarts and experience in the world wouldn't be enough if they fell into an early hole.

O'Hanlon held their gaze for a moment, then stepped into the middle of the circle with his hand in the air. "Okay then, let's get it in."

They all stepped into the circle, surrounding him, each with his right arm in the air, leaning against one another with the natural closeness that comes with being a team. "On three," O'Hanlon said. They waited three counts and then, as one, said simply, "Leopards!" the word bouncing off the empty gym's walls.

As they separated and began making their way to the benches where the sweats lay that they would put on before venturing into the subfreezing Buffalo morning, Rob Worthington, a six-six sophomore from St. Paul, Minnesota, the youngest of the five starters, looked at Alan Childs, the team's faculty representative, and Dawn Schleiden, the trainer, with a gleam in his eyes. Pointing to the clock on the wall that read a few minutes before eleven o'clock, he said, "Four hours until we shock the world."

They had to wait an extra fifteen minutes. O'Hanlon had gone through his pregame talk, trying to time it so that his last words would be spoken just as the first game of the afternoon double-header was ending. Locker room number six in the Marine Midland Arena, the one that had "LAFAYETTE" printed in large blue letters on the door, was about five times the size of the locker room the players dressed in at home. In one corner was a television set. When O'Hanlon finished, someone turned the TV on to check the status of the Oregon–Seton Hall game. There were less than ten seconds left and Seton Hall had the ball, trailing by 2. The players watched in silence, wanting to know if the game was going to end or go to overtime.

It went to overtime. A Seton Hall senior named Rimas Kaukenas hit a short jumper just before time expired. The noise from the arena could be heard through the television and through the back wall of the locker room, since the playing floor was no more than fifty feet beyond the wall. The players, all of them standing in anticipation of taking the floor to warm up, sat down, knowing they would have to wait out the extra five minutes.

O'Hanlon grimaced for a moment. The only thing worse than waiting for a game to start, especially a big game, is waiting an extra fifteen minutes for a game to start. "Relax, fellas," he said. "Watch the overtime."

Then he walked down the hall and out to the court to watch from there. Players are always looser when their coach isn't in the room. O'Hanlon had been a player long enough to remember that. So, he gave them some extra space. As the overtime clock wound under a minute, he turned to walk back to the locker room. At the entrance to the hallway where the locker rooms were located, a security guard stopped him.

"Sir, I need to see your pin."

At the NCAA Tournament, each member of a team's official party is given a lapel pin — a new one with a different color for each day — that grants him access to the locker room area. O'Hanlon had stuck his in his pocket. Now he fished through his pockets for it, even as someone was explaining to the security guard who O'Hanlon was. Finally, O'Hanlon produced the pin. The security guard was less than impressed.

"You're supposed to be wearing it," he said.

O'Hanlon said nothing, although a number of different responses crossed his mind. Once he was safely in the hallway he smiled and said, "I'll bet John Chaney doesn't need his pin."

By the time he reached the locker room, the clock was under ten seconds again. This time Seton Hall had the ball, down by 1. Point guard Shaheen Holloway sprinted the length of the court, ducked between defenders and threw a desperate shot toward the rim. The ball kissed high off the glass and dropped through the net. The cheers came out of the TV and through the wall again. Seton Hall had won, 71-70.

The television was shut off as soon as the buzzer sounded, and the players gathered around O'Hanlon. "This is a day we're all going to remember the rest of our lives," he said. "Let's make it a special memory."

They formed their huddle around the coach one more time, said the Lord's Prayer, and then walked down the hallway and into the bright lights of the massive arena. They took the floor at almost the same instant that Temple did, each school's pep band trying to drown the other out. It is a rule of basketball that you don't stop and watch your opponents during warm-ups, but every once in a while there was a stolen glance, a quick look. What the Leopards saw wasn't so much scary as sobering. Even in their warm-ups, the Owls looked huge.

Suddenly, Stefan Ciosici, Lafayette's six-eleven, 260-pound center — nicknamed "Boogie" by his teammates because "he's bigger than the boogie man" — didn't look quite so huge. Not when Temple trotted out Ron Rollerson, at six-ten and at least 300 pounds, as well as six-ten, 250 Lamont Barnes and six-ten, 250 Kevin Lyde. Worthington would be the second biggest Lafayette starter at six-six, 215.

Size doesn't always guarantee success in basketball, but Temple had the whole package: size, quickness, experience, and shooters. The players had known that on Sunday night when they had gathered to watch the pairings announced on CBS, but now they could see it firsthand. They had known this would not be easy; now they could see exactly why.

Even so, they weren't intimidated. They had been in the NCAA Tournament a year earlier and faced another number two seed, Miami. For twenty-five minutes, they had hung with the Hurricanes, until their size and strength wore them down; the final score had been 75-54. They had played good teams during the season just past: Georgia Tech, Villanova, Penn, Princeton — all on the road. They had beaten Princeton in overtime. They had lost in the final seconds to Villanova and Penn. They had hung close to Georgia Tech before losing by 11. They knew Temple was better than any of those teams. But this was March. They were better now than they had been early in the season. And this was a neutral court, a court where they assumed — hoped — the crowd would be for them if the game stayed close because they were such overwhelming underdogs.

It was 3:15 in the afternoon when they walked onto the court for tip-off. They were listed as a 21-point underdog. That was fine with them. They were ready to shock the world.

At a couple of minutes after four, they made the walk back down the hallway. This time, no one asked O'Hanlon for his pin. His response if he had been stopped might not have been as calm as it had been earlier.

The halftime score was 38-20. Lafayette had the 20. O'Hanlon didn't even feel as if his team had played poorly. It had simply been overmatched. Lafayette's only realistic hope had been to catch Temple on a day when its outside shooters were off the mark. Mark Karcher, their top 3-point shooter, had started the game by making three shots from beyond the arc. The half had ended with Quincy Wadley making an off-balance jumper as time expired. O'Hanlon slumped against a wall outside the door to the locker room and said to his three assistant coaches, "Boy, they've really made some shots."

Deep down, he knew the dream had died during the first twenty minutes. But he couldn't admit that to himself and he certainly couldn't admit that to his players. He walked into the locker room and there they were, slumped in their chairs, staring at the floor. "Get your heads up," he said. "This game's not over."

They picked their heads up and listened as he explained what had to be done to turn the game around. "One possession at a time," he said. "There are no eighteen-point possessions. Just go from offense to defense and work hard at both ends of the floor. There's no reason to panic." He repeated himself, to reassure them and to reassure himself: "The game's not even close to being over."

They went back on the floor and gave O'Hanlon everything they had to give. Five minutes into the second half they had chipped away and cut the margin to 45-31. Ciosici yanked down a rebound and flipped an outlet pass to Tim Bieg, the baby-faced point guard who other Patriot League coaches often described as Lafayette's most important player. Bieg, who had been recruited by three Ivy League schools for baseball but not basketball, pushed the ball into the front-court and found Tyson Whitfield, the team's best 3-point shooter, open in the corner.

Whitfield releases his shot so quickly he is one of a very small hand-ful of Patriot League players who occasionally draw the attention of pro scouts. His range is beyond the NBA 3-point line. Now, he lined up a shot from the corner as the coterie of Lafayette fans sitting opposite the bench came out of their seats in anticipation. They had seen Whitfield bury big shots from long range throughout the season and, as he released the shot, a glimmer of hope ran through them. If the shot went down and the margin went to 11, maybe they could get it into single digits and maybe Temple would start to get tight. . . .

The hope lasted for as long as the ball was airborne. The shot clanged off the back rim and was rebounded by Rollerson, even as Lafayette's sixth man, Brian Burke, tried to somehow climb over him to get at the ball. Later, O'Hanlon would remember the moment vividly because it symbolized the entire afternoon, the 185-pound Burke trying to get over Rollerson, who looked a lot closer to 350 pounds than the 290 Temple admitted to. "Brian looked like a racing stripe on his back," O'Hanlon said.

Rollerson shed Burke like a raindrop, quickly got the ball into the hands of All-American point guard Pepe Sanchez, who found a streaking Barnes for a layup even though Whitfield had raced back to try to cut him off. It was one of fifteen assists for Sanchez and it started a brutally efficient 11-4 run over the next three minutes. Sud-denly, what could have been an 11-point deficit had become 21. The Lafayette bench, always alive with encouragement for those on the floor, was almost silent. Everyone knew that the world would not be shocked on this day.

With 4:09 left, Ciosici, who had battled foul problems throughout his career, fouled out. He had come all the way back from major knee surgery to be the MVP of the Patriot League Tournament seven days earlier, but none of that was on his mind as he came to the bench. He didn't hear the cheers of the Lafayette fans or see them all standing to thank him for his efforts. O'Hanlon gave him a hug, then kneeled in front of him as he sat, head in his hands, on the bench.

"Hey, Stef," he said. "You've fouled out before. No big deal." He smiled, a life-goes-on smile. Ciosici wasn't quite ready for it. All he could think was that this was the end after five years of working to become a basketball player. Five years of work, of learning to sound like an American and think like one. All those painful hours of rehab after the knee surgery. It wasn't supposed to end sitting on the bench, fouled out in a one-sided game.

With 1:26 to go, O'Hanlon took Ehlers out. Once again, the Lafayette fans came to their feet. One by one his teammates greeted Ehlers. His expression never changed, but the emotion he felt was apparent. When he got to Ciosici, the hug was a little longer, the two seniors understanding that this was the end of a long road they had traveled together. Ehlers clung to a comforting thought: it had to end sooner or later. Thank goodness it's ending in the NCAA Tournament.

At that moment, it was difficult for most of the players to feel anything but disappointment. They had thought the result was going to be different. They had truly believed they could stand in with a team filled with future pros and somehow make it a game. The cheers of their fans, their friends, even their families, meant little as the clock wound toward zero. O'Hanlon had told them over and over that the goal was not to participate, but to compete. They hadn't made the trip to Buffalo to participate. They had come to compete. A final score of 73-47 was not what they had in mind.

And so, after they had gone through the ritual postgame handshakes with the Temple players, when they walked off the court and saw their school president, Arthur Rothkopf, waiting to congratulate each one of them, it didn't feel right. They had lost, hadn't they? The game hadn't been close. Ian Eagle had undoubtedly used all of his fill material. But there was Rothkopf, hand extended, thanking each one of them as they left the court.

Age and perspective allowed Rothkopf to understand what the players couldn't understand in those first few minutes of defeat. He knew exactly what their back-to-back conference championships had meant to the school, to the students, the faculty, and the alumni. He knew that the forty-six victories in two seasons had been accomplished without selling out academically, that four of the team's five starters had grade point averages of 3.0 or higher, that the four seniors would all graduate with degrees they had earned — not degrees that had been gift-wrapped for them to ensure that they stuck around to keep winning basketball games. He knew that these players would look back fondly on their college days, that basketball would always be important to them, but that their futures would be as doctors and lawyers and writers and artists and CEOs. Maybe one or two would coach basketball and that was fine, too.

That was why Rothkopf felt so proud. That was why he said thank you. To him, 73-47 was nothing more than a footnote. As a coach, O'Hanlon had to tell his players that participating was not enough. As a college president, Rothkopf understood that participating was, in fact, plenty. They had been out there, in the arena, as Teddy Roosevelt once said. They were battered now and beaten, but they had been *there*, in the arena, with the future pros. The day before, a reporter from ABC News had told someone from Temple that Lafayette had a team GPA of 3.0. What, she wondered, was Temple's team GPA? "No comment," was the answer.

In the quiet of the locker room, O'Hanlon told his players how he felt now that it was over. "No one from Lafayette will ever forget this team," he said. "You should feel proud of what you did for the school, proud of the way you approached every game and every day of practice. I know it hurts now, but you did everything you possibly could, gave everything you had every single day. No coach can ask for more than that."

Then he pulled them all into the middle of the room one more time. They put their hands in and O'Hanlon said, "Lafayette, loud and proud."

"LAFAYETTE!" they shouted, hanging on to the moment for an extra second or two.

Loud and proud.

With good reason.

2

"OTHERS WILL FOLLOW ..."

LAFAYETTE'S NCAA Tournament experience was not all that different from most of the teams who participated in the event. After all, half of the sixty-four-team field lost in the first round and forty-eight of the sixty-four teams were gone by the end of the first weekend. Those who made it to the second and third weekends were almost always power schools, the kind who had virtually unlimited basketball budgets, coaches who made more money than anyone else on the college payroll, and rosters filled with players whose post-college plans were pretty much focused on three letters: N-B-A.

"Let's be realistic," Fran O'Hanlon said when the season was over and the fantasies of early March had been put aside. "At our level, making the NCAA Tournament is like reaching the Final Four. To win a game would be like winning the national championship."

Especially when one considers the fact that the NCAA Tournament committee automatically buries teams from smaller conferences, like the Patriot League, at the bottom of the bracket. That means the Patriot League representative is always going to play a power team, one of the top seeds in the tournament. It is a little like sending David out to face Goliath without his slingshot.

"The hardest thing is to remember that the other team is a college team, too," Navy's Sitapha Savane said. "I remember in 1998 when we played North Carolina in the first round, we were all *fans* of North

Carolina. We watched them play on TV all the time. When we walked out to start the game, I didn't know whether I should shake hands with [national player of the year] Antawn Jamison or ask him for an autograph."

That's the rub when college students find themselves in a game against TV stars. And that's what happens when the Patriot League ventures into the multibillion-dollar industry that is the NCAA Tournament. Temple appeared on network television or national cable television fifteen times in 1999–2000. Lafayette did so twice — in the Patriot League championship game and the Temple game. The 1998 North Carolina team that Navy played made twenty-four national TV appearances. Its first *practice* was on ESPN.

Lafayette was the tenth basketball champion of the Patriot League. The loss to Temple was the tenth first-round loss for the Patriot League representative in the NCAA Tournament. Only once had the margin of defeat been less than ten points, a 68-59 Connecticut victory over Colgate in 1996. All of which surprised no one in the Patriot League. Winning national championships has never been what the league is about.

As has so often been the case in college athletics, the Patriot League came about because of football. In the early 1980s, the presidents of the eight Ivy League schools, having agreed to expand their football schedules to ten games in 1980, were concerned about who they could play their three nonconference games against on a regular basis. They didn't want to play too far "up" — and have their players beaten to a pulp by teams that averaged 300 pounds a man across the offensive line — and they didn't want to play too many teams that wouldn't challenge them either.

A vice president at Princeton named Tony Maruca was assigned by the Ivy presidents the task of finding a group of schools for the Ivies to play against on a year-in, year-out basis. After a couple of false starts, Maruca made contact with Father John Brooks, the president of Holy Cross, and Peter Likens, the president of Lehigh.

Holy Cross was a superb school academically, but it also had a big-time sports program. It had always played good football and it had

been a national power in basketball, winning the NCAA championship in 1947 and the NIT — when the NIT still mattered — in
1954. Boston Celtics Hall of Famers Bob Cousy and Tom Heinsohn
were counted among their alumni.

Nonetheless, Brooks was intrigued by what Maruca was proposing:
a conglomerate of schools that would band together in a league of
their own and play their nonconference games against the Ivy League
schools. In order to make the deal work, though, the new league's
schools would have to follow the Ivy League model: no athletic scholarships. Athletes would be treated like other students. If they had
financial need, they would receive financial aid. But being a great
quarterback would not guarantee you a full scholarship.

Brooks knew that such a move would set off a firestorm at Holy
Cross. But that notion didn't intimidate him. (Under the definitions
of *crusty* and *feisty* in the dictionary, one might find a picture of
Brooks.) What's more, he was convinced it was the right thing to do.
Now seventy-seven and retired as school president since 1994, but
still a professor and a vice president for development, Brooks works
in an office adorned with sports memorabilia: headlines from the
Boston Globe on the day after Holy Cross's last victory over Boston
College in football; a photo of the football stadium on a sunny day
with a sellout crowd in attendance. He is a real live fan, a regular at
Holy Cross athletic events. But he says he never believed in athletic
scholarships.

"In an ideal world, we'd scholarship all the students, but we don't
have that kind of money and never will," he said, his voice rich with
the tones of a man who has spent his life in New England. "I've never
believed that a basketball player or a football player is any more
deserving of a scholarship than a chemistry whiz or a talented cellist.
It's just not right. I have friends at other schools who talk about the
money it can bring to a school, but at what price? Most schools *don't*
make money off their scholarship athletes. Those that do have to sell
their souls to do it. And anyone who tells you different is fooling
themselves."

Brooks, Likens, and Maruca ended up recruiting four other schools
to join their new league: Bucknell, Colgate, Lafayette, and Davidson.
William and Mary was set to become the new league's seventh team,

but a hue and cry from alumni over the notion of dropping athletic scholarships forced a rethinking of the school's position.

The six schools, under the name "Colonial Athletic League," began competing in 1986, playing four nonconference games each against Ivy League schools. As in the Ivy League, there was no commissioner, just an executive director who reported directly to the presidents. "The idea from day one was that the league would be built on three premises," Brooks said. "Presidential control, a real academic index that would be adhered to, and need-based scholarships."

The Academic Index — or AI as it is known within the league — is a combination of a student's grade point average and SAT or ACT scores. The presidents agreed to share with one another the AI for all their athletes and agreed that if a school accepted a student whose AI fell well below the AI of the student body, it would be forced to defend that acceptance to the satisfaction of the other presidents.

"Every once in a while there was someone who raised an eyebrow, and there was usually a reason why he had been accepted," Brooks said. "But it never got out of hand. It was one here, one there, more often than not a minority student who the school felt had the potential to do well academically."

The AIs of the athletes were tracked by the presidents throughout their time at each school. If a pattern developed where a particular school seemed to be losing a number of athletes prior to graduation or where a dropoff in the AI was noticed, it was brought up to the president involved. "It didn't really happen very often," Brooks said. "Making the AIs public to one another was a good way of keeping everyone in line."

What's more, the schools involved were all academic-minded. The average SAT score within the student body for Patriot League schools ranges from the mid-1200s to the low 1300s. Rarely does an athlete in the league fall below 1000, and they usually have strong GPAs as a balance. Even then, they are considered high risk.

Almost from day one, the league presidents were searching for additional members. Within two years, Davidson had dropped out of the league. Being in a northeastern-based league was difficult for a school in North Carolina and the school didn't want to give up scholarships in basketball if and when the league expanded to include basketball. A committee of three was formed to seek other schools, with the notion that the conference could not survive in a football-only mode. Brooks, Colgate president Fred Dunlap, and Alan Childs, a psychology professor at Lafayette who had been hired as the league's first executive director, were given the assignment of finding new members.

Fordham was interested in joining, especially if the league also included basketball. Athletic Director Frank McLaughlin did not feel that the Metro Atlantic Athletic Conference was right for his school and told the search committee that he suspected the people at Army felt the same way and encouraged them to approach Army.

Army was looking for a new league for its basketball team, but had absolutely no intention of dropping from Division I-A in football to the Colonial League's Division I-AA. At first Brooks was adamant that Army drop to I-AA in football. Childs and Dunlap eventually talked him into softening his position.

"Father Brooks has strong feelings on everything," said Childs, who still teaches at Lafayette but long ago left league administration behind. "He didn't think there was any reason to compromise on any of the principles the league was founded on. But what he figured out fairly quickly was that some compromise was better than not having a league at all."

Bringing Army into the league was going to change the dynamic under any circumstances, since all 4,000 cadets are on scholarship — government scholarships. Brooks and company were able to deal with that notion for three reasons: like the other schools in the league, all the students at West Point were treated identically in terms of financial aid; Army was academically comparable to the rest of the league's schools; and, perhaps most important, the five-year postgraduate military commitment made it just as impossible for Army to recruit future NBA or NFL players as the other schools.

During the course of the negotiations with Army, David Palmer, the superintendent, and Carl Ullrich, the athletic director, brought Navy into the mix. Army and Navy don't like to make too many decisions without consulting each other — although Army did recently join a football conference without Navy — and Ullrich knew that Jack Lengyel, his counterpart at Navy, was looking for a way out of the Colonial Athletic Association in basketball.

When all was said and done, Fordham, Army, and Navy joined and the Patriot League was launched in 1990. The name was changed from Colonial Athletic League because the Colonial Athletic Association threatened to sue, and, even though the league's lawyers thought they would win in court, the presidents decided it wasn't worth the time or the money. It was Ullrich who suggested Patriot League. It was also Ullrich who, after retiring as AD at Army in 1990, was chosen to succeed Childs as the league's executive director, in large part because he had the contacts to ensure that the new league would receive an automatic bid to the NCAA basketball tournament, an absolute must for a Division I league to survive. Without that carrot — "come here and have a chance to play in the tournament" — recruiting, especially in a nonscholarship league, would be impossible.

The league celebrated its tenth anniversary in 1999–2000 after an often rocky decade of change. Fordham withdrew as a basketball participant after the 1995 season under tremendous pressure from alumni who were outraged at what the lack of scholarships was doing to the quality of its team. "Their alumni think they should be competing with St. John's," Brooks said. "What they really should be doing is competing with Columbia."

Fordham would have stayed in the league if the presidents had allowed it to restore scholarships in basketball. The presidents said no, Fordham withdrew (remaining in football), and the league was down to seven teams. Brooks retired in 1994 and two years later, under similar pressure from alumni, Holy Cross announced to the rest of the league that it intended to restore basketball scholarships, beginning with the class entering in the fall of 1998. This time the presidents couldn't say no. If Holy Cross withdrew, the league would be down to six teams, and seven is the minimum number required to receive an automatic NCAA bid. No Holy Cross, no bid. The presidents acquiesced. A year later, Lehigh, which had started awarding wrestling scholarships in 1991 (wrestling is by far the number one sport at Lehigh, and, since the school is not a league member in wrestling, there was no objection), announced that it intended to begin awarding basketball scholarships on a limited basis (two per year) in 1999.

Which left the league in a unique and uncomfortable situation. Three schools — Bucknell, Colgate, and Lafayette — continued to cling to the founding principle of need-based scholarships. Two were providing government-sponsored scholarships and two were now awarding athletic scholarships.

"Not exactly a level playing field," Colgate athletic director Mark Murphy said.

Not even close. No one was more horrified by his school's decision to begin awarding scholarships again than Brooks. "They didn't exactly consult me," he said dryly. "I think it's a very dangerous path for the school and the league. I honestly believe that a majority of our alumni thought we did the right thing when we joined the league. But there's a substantial minority, a very vocal minority, that was against it.

"I made two decisions as president that were controversial: the first was admitting women. The second was joining the Patriot League. The second was far more controversial."

What brought about the change more than any question of principle was what almost always brings about changes in athletics: losing. Holy Cross had once been a very good eastern football school. When it joined the Patriot League and phased out scholarships, it began to drop like the proverbial stone. The same happened in basketball. The last scholarship class at the school — the seniors of 1993 — won the Patriot League championship. After that, things went south rapidly, bottoming with records of 8-19, 7-20, and 7-20. Even before those awful seasons, the alumni drumbeats were growing.

"I think it was tougher for Holy Cross because it had never recruited nonscholarship kids in the past," said Dick Regan, the current athletic director, Holy Cross, Class of '76. "The other league schools had been nonscholarship in the past so they knew how to identify the kind of kid that would be interested in the school and how to convince them this was a good route for them. Holy Cross didn't have that experience."

Both Regan and Joe Sterrett, the AD at Lehigh, make articulate cases for returning scholarships on a limited and very controlled basis.

"It all depends on how you handle it," said Sterrett, who was a star quarterback at Lehigh in the 1970s. "If you go out and say, 'We're just going to take the best possible athletes,' then sure, you change the dynamics and you head down that slippery slope that we've seen so many schools go down.

"But if you handle it correctly, you can actually increase the academic quality of your athletes because you may have a chance to get some kids by offering them a full scholarship who you otherwise wouldn't get."

Patriot League schools often recruit against Ivy League schools. In most cases, all things being equal, the Ivy League school is going to win a recruiting battle for the simple reason that it is the Ivy League. Alan Childs calls it "reputational endowment."

Sterrett makes the case that if Lehigh is recruiting a basketball player with a 3.7 GPA and 1400 on the boards against Princeton and both schools offer the player $15,000 in financial aid (Patriot League schools cost a student between $29,000 and $33,000 annually), the player is going to choose Princeton at least nine times out of ten. But if Lehigh offers the same player a full scholarship and his parents don't have to go through the hassle of supplying all their financial records to the school in order to qualify for aid, he may very well choose Lehigh.

"If we have a weakness academically among our athletes, it's that we've all but eliminated the middle-class kid with good grades," Sterrett said. "Some just can't afford to come here, some will go to a Division II school that offers them a full scholarship. That means we have a lot of kids who are very rich and a lot of kids who are very poor who we can offer a lot of aid to, but very few kids in between."

There isn't a president in the league, past or present, including Brooks, who does not have great respect for Sterrett. They don't argue with his hypothesis. But those who favor only financial aid return to the principle.

"I don't think any group of students should be singled out that way," Lafayette president Arthur Rothkopf said. "And, at least at the moment, we're proving you can do it this way and still compete."

That argument, which is completely valid at Lafayette right now, is what makes the three coaches in the league who do not have scholarships — O'Hanlon, Colgate's Emmett Davis, and Bucknell's Pat Flannery — groan. "It's a catch-22," Flannery said. "If we're doing okay without scholarships, we make the argument against them. But what happens when one of us goes six and twenty-two and gets fired and then someone decides the next guy needs scholarships. I think that's what worries us."

Flannery is the most outspoken coach on the topic, in large part because he is outspoken on any topic he addresses. O'Hanlon likes to joke that if he wants to get Flannery upset, he just sidles up to him and whispers "athletic scholarships." But he is just as concerned about the future as Flannery is. As much as he loves Lafayette and the players he has coached the last five years, he feels compelled to keep his eyes and ears open when coaching jobs become available because he knows he can't be sure what the future is at Lafayette. In the spring of 2000 he came close to taking the job at Siena. The only reason he even interviewed for the Siena job was his concern about Lafayette's future as a nonscholarship school in an increasingly scholarship-dominated league.

Most people in the league believe that returning to athletic scholarships is inevitable if the league is to survive. In the spring of 2000, the league was out recruiting new members — "grow or die" is the way Childs describes the philosophy of college conferences these days — telling each potential candidate (Richmond, William and Mary, and most notably American University) that it would not have to give up athletic scholarships if it joined the league. When American did agree to join the league (beginning in the fall of 2001) it did so only after being told it did not have to give up its scholarships. The reality of college athletics in the twenty-first century is that only the Ivy League, with its reputational endowment, is likely to endure long term on the Division I level without athletic scholarships. Even Brooks, as much as he would like to see the utopian vision of equal treatment for all students continue, understands.

"The sign at the entrance to this school does NOT say, 'Basketball team of Holy Cross,' or 'Football team of Holy Cross,'" he said. "It says, 'College of Holy Cross.' But I know the pressures all our schools are facing." He smiled. "You know, when we first started the league and the presidents would meet, we would tell one another, 'We're building a model that others will follow.' So far, no one has followed."

Perhaps not. But that doesn't mean that the model is a failure. The Patriot League is not the Ivy League and does not pretend to be. But it is a league made up of seven high-quality schools that, scholarships or no scholarships, have refused to sell their souls in the name of winning games and cashing in on the athletes they recruit.

Most schools that compete on the national level — certainly almost all of the top 150 of the 318 Division I basketball schools — make huge academic concessions for basketball players. The stories that pop up in the newspapers regularly about academic fraud, players being given money or other benefits by street agents or alumni or AAU coaches, are the result of a system that rewards winning at all costs. During the 1999–2000 academic year, several top players at big-name schools were suspended by the NCAA for rules violations. Coaches around the country screamed that the NCAA was running amok, picking on innocent kids. St. John's Coach Mike Jarvis, whose star point guard Erik Barkley was suspended by the NCAA on two occasions, likened the NCAA to Nazi Germany and accused the organization of Gestapo tactics. He said he felt as if someone had come into his house and raped him. (The last remark he later apologized for.)

The NCAA is a classic bureaucracy that makes so many mistakes it is impossible to keep count. But when all was said and done, Barkley and the other accused players had broken rules — serious rules. They were not innocent kids, they were role-players in a system that turns kids into spoiled takers, often before they are eighteen. It is a system that leaves most high-profile college basketball players with a sense of entitlement that borders on ridiculous.

In the wake of the Barkley suspension, Duke Coach Mike Krzyzewski, whose program is often held up as the shining star of big-time college basketball, made the comment that no college program, including his own, could withstand a thorough NCAA investigation without taking some kind of a fall. There is no doubting the fact that he is correct. He made the comment as an indictment of the NCAA. In truth, it is an indictment of what big-money college basketball has become.

Some players do go to class. Some graduate. A majority don't. And, even those who do go to class and do graduate chose their college because of what it offered to them as basketball players. Their first priority is basketball. That's why there are so many transfers — playing time matters more than anything else. These are pros-in-training.

There are sixteen schools playing Division I college basketball who can call their players "student-athletes" with a straight face: the eight Ivy League schools, the seven Patriot League schools, and the Air Force Academy. In 1999 the five nonmilitary academies in the Patriot League had overall graduation rates ranging from 82 percent to 91 percent, according to the official NCAA statistics. Since Army and Navy do not have "athletic" scholarships, they do not file their graduation rates with the NCAA. Historically, though, the attrition rate for athletes at the academies is lower than for the student body overall. In 1998, Navy had seven seniors on the basketball team. All seven graduated.

There are a number of reasons for these successes. First and foremost, the schools simply won't give in to the temptation to take gifted athletes who are poor students. The sharing of the AIs is one reason, the general approach of the schools to athletics is another.

"It doesn't do you any good to get high-risk kids into school, because they're either going to be miserable struggling with the academics or they're not going to make it at all," Flannery said. "Occasionally there's a kid who strikes you as someone whose numbers may not be good but will be able to do the work. Then you might take a chance. But you also need a track record with your admissions department. If you're bringing in kids who do well, they might go along with you on occasion. If not, forget it."

If not, you probably won't have a job for long anyway. Patriot League schools and Ivy League schools fire coaches for losing too often the same way schools in the big-time leagues do. Fran O'Hanlon was hired at Lafayette in 1995 because his predecessor, John Leone, had gone 2-25, even though Leone was highly thought of as a person by everyone on campus. Sal Mentesana succeeded Paul Duke as the coach at Lehigh in 1996 after a 4-23 season. Don DeVoe took over for Pete Herrmann at Navy in 1992 after four straight 20-plus-loss seasons. Ralph Willard was hired at Colgate in 1999 because Bill Raynor failed to win 10 games in a season three years in a row.

No one ever questioned the character of the fired coaches. And each probably lasted longer in a losing situation than they might have in the ACC, the Big East, or the Big Ten. (Witness Herrmann's record.)

The difference is this: in the big-time leagues, winning is just about all that matters. A coach is more likely to survive NCAA probation than three straight losing seasons. And graduation rates have become almost a moot point if you win enough games. When Michigan State won the national championship in April of 2000 it became the first national champion in seven years whose basketball team had a graduation rate higher than 50 percent during the 1990s since North Carolina (78 percent) in 1993. The Spartans graduated 63 percent of their basketball players during the decade. No one who won a national title from 1994 through 1999 was higher than 44 percent (Connecticut). The low was Arizona at 28 percent.

As low as those numbers are, graduation rates at big-time schools can be deceiving. Basketball players receive all the free tutoring they want, all the free summer school they can handle, and have academic advisors who guide them into classes with jock-friendly professors. Larger schools also have majors where weaker students can be "hidden." Check the media guides of some schools and you will find a lot of "general studies" majors. Not to mention physical education.

"There's no place to hide at Holy Cross," Father Brooks said. "If you can't do the work, that's going to be apparent very quickly."

That's true at all seven Patriot League schools. Even top academic schools like Duke and Georgetown that have respectable graduation rates (78 percent and 68 percent, respectively, in the 1990s) make huge concessions in the name of winning basketball games. At Duke, where the average SAT score is over 1400, it is not uncommon for basketball players with under 1000 on the SAT to be accepted. No matter how culturally biased the SAT may be, that is a huge gap. Georgetown goes even further. During the 1999–2000 season, according to a story in the *Washington Post*, four of Georgetown's basketball players had been admitted to school having met *none* of the NCAA minimums in the areas of SAT (820), GPA, or core courses.

Brooks, who is friends with a number of his fellow Jesuit priests at Georgetown, says he often discusses what has happened at Georgetown with his friends there. "Some defend it, some don't," he said. "Some will tell you that [former coach] John Thompson did great things for the school, put it on the map, made it a lot of money. My answer is always the same, 'At what cost?' I would say it was too high in terms of academic integrity."

Several years ago Brooks was asked by Holy Cross graduate Bob Cousy to appear on a panel that included Thompson and then–North Carolina Coach Dean Smith, another coaching legend. When the subject turned to the question of star players leaving college early to pursue big money in the NBA both Thompson and Smith argued that if the money was there, the player had to take it. Everyone looked to Brooks for rebuttal.

"I told them that I agreed with them a hundred percent," Brooks said. "They were all stunned. And then I said, 'Because what you people are doing has very little to do with education.'"

According to Brooks, both Smith and Thompson were furious. Smith, who would rather discuss the doctors and lawyers who have come through his program than the All-Americans, rambled on about post-graduate degrees and the emphasis on academics at North Carolina. Brooks wasn't buying. During his thirty-six years at North Carolina, Smith probably worked as hard as anyone coaching a national contender at maintaining some sense of academic integrity. Nonetheless, North Carolina routinely accepted basketball players whose academic numbers fell way below other students' at the school. In fact, it often accepted players who had not yet met NCAA academic minimums and once accepted a player who never enrolled at the school because he failed to graduate from high school.

Thompson went even further. He convinced his "bosses" (and the word belongs in quotes) at Georgetown that it was okay to accept any basketball player on the grounds that he would benefit just by being in college — even if he never graduated. One notable player, Michael Graham, who failed to graduate from his high school, was admitted to Georgetown after passing some kind of equivalency test. He stayed at

Georgetown long enough to help the Hoyas win a national championship in 1984 and then departed. Who exactly benefited from this arrangement?

In the Patriot League, such an arrangement could never have happened. The league isn't about winning national championships. The presidents and ADs aren't *opposed* to the idea — they just believe that if it takes the kind of academic shenanigans that produce a Michael Graham for Georgetown to win one, they'll do without.

When the panel was over, Thompson, all six-ten, 300 pounds of him, confronted Brooks, who was giving away at least a foot and about 150 pounds, angrily telling him that he couldn't "understand" what Thompson and his program were all about. "I think I understand exactly what you're about, Coach," Brooks remembers answering.

Brooks is right when he says that others have not followed the Patriot League model. Maybe they should have.

3

LOOKING TO THE FUTURE

AMONG the Patriot League's seven coaches, Don DeVoe and Ralph Willard were considered the deans, even though Willard was in his first year in the league. That was because of their experiences before landing in the league. DeVoe had spent most of his career in the so-called coaching big time, having been at Virginia Tech, Wyoming, Tennessee, and (briefly) Florida. Each school was in a multi-bid basketball conference where a 100-percent graduation rate and a losing record would earn you a gold-plated bus ticket out of town.

Willard's background was similar. He had been an assistant coach at Syracuse and Kentucky and the head coach at Western Kentucky and Pittsburgh. At Western Kentucky, he had been a hero, because he had taken the school to the Sweet Sixteen in 1993. That had made him a hot coach, and he subsequently landed at Pitt in 1994. Five seasons later, with a losing record, he resigned under pressure.

DeVoe and Willard had both seen what the big-time life and the pressures that went with it were like. Neither was uncomfortable being in the Patriot League. "I enjoyed coaching in Madison Square Garden and the other big arenas," Willard said one afternoon during a Holy Cross practice in the Hart Center. "But look around here. A gym is a gym. Coaching is coaching. These kids aren't as talented as the kids I was coaching the last few years. But they will work as hard or harder than anyone I've ever coached. In the end, that's what coaching is all about. I started out as a high school coach, sweeping the gym out myself. In some ways, those were my happiest days as a coach. This is getting back to those days a little bit."

Even so, although he understood intellectually that coaching at Holy Cross was a far cry from the places he had been in his prior life, the adjustment to coaching at his old school wasn't always easy. Willard had been at Syracuse in 1987 when the Orangemen lost the national championship game to Indiana at the buzzer. He had spent two years as an NBA assistant, working for the New York Knicks when his long-time friend Rick Pitino was the coach. He had followed Pitino to Kentucky for a year before getting his first head coaching shot at Western Kentucky.

The Sweet Sixteen team had been one of three straight that had won at least 20 games. Western Kentucky had lost to Florida State in overtime in that Sweet Sixteen game. If the Hilltoppers had won they would have faced Kentucky — and Pitino — for a chance to go to the Final Four.

"They would have murdered us," Willard said, smiling.

In the spring of 1994, Willard was a hot coach. Both Providence and Pittsburgh were wooing him. He was all but set to take the Providence job before a meeting with Pittsburgh chancellor Dennis O'Connor convinced him he should take the job there. "That," Willard said, able to laugh at the memory now, "turned out to be a big mistake."

Willard's one concern about Providence had been that the president of the school was retiring and he had no idea who the new president would be. O'Connor had been a basketball player (a backup on Loyola of Chicago's 1963 national championship team) and had worked at basketball schools — UCLA and North Carolina. Dean Smith spoke highly of him. "This," thought Willard, "is a man I'll be comfortable working for." He changed his mind about Providence and went to Pitt.

Six months later, O'Connor was fired. A new chancellor and athletic director came to town and, in 1999, after back-to-back losing seasons rife with off-court troubles, Willard resigned even though he had three years left on his contract, which had been extended a year earlier.

"We had a lot of bad luck, some things that were really out of our control," Willard said. "When I got there, a new building was on the drawing board. When I left, five years later, it was still on the drawing board. But in the end, the bottom line is I didn't get the job done. In this business, that's all that matters."

Willard announced his resignation at Pitt ten days before the end of the season. Most basketball people thought he would end up back with Pitino, who was going through some serious struggles of his own as The Designated Savior of the Boston Celtics. Willard didn't want that, though, especially since his son Keith was already working for Pitino. When Virginia athletic director Terry Holland began seriously negotiating to become the coach at Vanderbilt, he talked to Willard about going there with him as his top assistant.

That was when Willard's phone rang. It was an old Holy Cross classmate, who was on the school's board of trustees. The school was in the middle of a search for a successor to Bill Raynor, who, like Willard, had resigned prior to the end of the season after five difficult years, the last three producing a combined record of 22-59. Willard had been one of those alums who had disapproved of the school's move to the Patriot League and need-based scholarships, but he had been far too busy with his own life to pay much attention. The school was now giving scholarships again. Would Willard be interested in coming back to coach?

Yes. On April 1, Willard was introduced as Holy Cross's new coach. He was excited — to have a job. "After what happened at Pittsburgh, I considered myself lucky to get another head coaching job," he said. "To be honest, I really didn't expect it."

Willard might not have gotten the job if Drexel Coach Bill Herrion had been interested. Herrion's father had been an assistant at the school in the 1960s (and had coached Willard), so he had a connection to Holy Cross. But he ultimately decided to take the job at East Carolina, clearing the way for Willard.

Willard met with his new team several days after taking over. Their feelings about the arrival of a new coach were mixed. Every one of them liked Raynor, seeing him as a friend and mentor. But they all knew the last three seasons had been disastrous. They knew Willard's background, his pedigree. At that first meeting, it was clear from minute one that Holy Cross had hired someone 180 degrees different from Raynor.

"He was all business from the minute he walked in the room," said Jared Curry, who had been recruited by Raynor out of nearby Braintree, Massachusetts, and had battled injuries throughout his first two years at the school. "We knew things were going to be different."

Which was exactly what Willard wanted. He knew what the record had been for three years. He knew he was going to have to get out and recruit better talent. Holy Cross hadn't advanced beyond the first round of the Patriot League Tournament since 1996. But he also knew he owed it to the current players to get every ounce he could from their abilities. He told them that off-season workouts would begin the next morning. No one had a guaranteed spot on the team, including the four rising seniors. The players would work in groups of four and the first group would be expected on the floor, ready to go, at 7 A.M.

"And by the way," Willard said, "on the floor at seven ready to go means you're warmed up and ready to work with me. I would recommend you get here at least a half hour early."

The next morning, Willard walked into the Hart Center at 6:30 and found the four players assigned to the first group sitting on the floor in the hallway waiting for him. That wasn't a shock; after all, players usually want to make a good first impression on a new coach. The shock was what they were doing while they waited for him.

"They all had schoolbooks open on their laps," Willard said. "It brought me up short. I remembered where I was."

He wasn't in the Big East, the Southeastern Conference, the Sunbelt, the NBA — or Oz — anymore.

Josh Sankes was in the second workout group that morning. When Willard finished with the first group, he left the floor briefly to go to the bathroom and give Sankes and the other three players a couple of minutes to warm up. When he returned, Sankes was nowhere in sight.

"Where's Josh?" he asked Roger Breslin, the only holdover assistant coach from Raynor's staff.

Breslin pointed to a corner of the gym, behind the bleachers. Sankes, all seven-one, 270 pounds of him, was doubled over, throwing up.

"Is he sick?" Willard asked Breslin.

Breslin shook his head. "No," he answered. "Just terrified."

No one was more nervous about Willard's arrival than Sankes. He had been down this road before.

Growing up on Grand Island, New York — a suburb of Buffalo — Sankes was tall at an early age — his parents are six-six and five-eleven — and became a highly recruited player once he was in high school. He was an excellent student — 4.0 GPA and 1300 on the College Boards — and he fit into that old coaches' cliche: "You can't coach height." The first recruiting letter he got as a junior came from Mike Krzyzewski. "That was like a dream come true," Sankes said. "I had always been a Duke fan, especially since Christian Laettner [another Buffalo kid] had gone there."

All the big-name schools lined up early to get in on the Sankes sweepstakes. Of course getting a letter from a school, even calls from coaches, doesn't always lead to a scholarship offer. By the time Sankes was a senior, Duke was pursuing Jason Collier (who ended up at Indiana) and Sankes had to look elsewhere. There was still plenty of interest: Wake Forest, Penn State, Rutgers, William and Mary, and Delaware, among others.

Sankes had trouble making a decision. For a while he wanted to go to Delaware, but his father talked him out of it. "He thought I should shoot higher academically," Sankes said. "And he was a little bit nervous how long Coach [Mike] Brey would stay. We thought he would build the program and move to another job quickly." Brey did build the program quickly, but he didn't take another job until the summer of 2000, when Notre Dame called.

Sankes ended up choosing Rutgers. He liked Coach Bob Wenzel and the idea of playing in the Big East. He enjoyed his freshman year at Rutgers — perhaps too much. Life as a basketball player was good. Freshmen weren't allowed to have on-campus parking passes — unless you were a freshman basketball player. Freshmen basketball players were also guided into the right courses and were treated like heroes on most of the campus.

"I partied too much," Sankes said. "I started going to the racetrack with my friend [and teammate] Geoff Billet. One day I lost four hundred dollars betting on a sure thing."

The only sure thing was that the Rutgers lifestyle wasn't going to produce a 4.0 GPA. "Two B's and two C-pluses," Sankes said. Which wasn't all that bad compared to a lot of Division I basketball players.

The start of the season curtailed Sankes's partying. He played in eighteen games in a limited backup role, but the practice time and travel time forced him to cut back on his trips to the track. As it turned out, Sankes's fears about losing a coach proved correct — if misplaced. Two days after Rutgers' season ended in the first round of the Big East Tournament, Wenzel was fired. As is usually the case, the players weren't caught by surprise. They had played poorly and they had known Wenzel was in trouble.

The search for Wenzel's replacement was a lengthy one. At one stage it appeared that Tom Penders, then at Texas, would be the coach. Then it looked like Florida State's Pat Kennedy would take the job. Then it appeared certain that Bill Herrion, still at Drexel back then, was coming to Rutgers. None of them did. Finally, Kevin Bannon, who had been very successful at Rider, did take the job.

Sankes was delighted. He was familiar with Bannon because he had been one of his most eager suitors. In fact, Bannon had once sent Sankes a card that said "Rider and Kevin Bannon love Josh Sankes." A heart with an arrow through the middle of it indicated the ardor directed at Sankes by Rider and Bannon.

"I figured it would be great," Sankes said. "He knew me and he liked me. It sounded perfect."

Like any new coach, Bannon came in determined to change the direction of the program. Early morning runs became mandatory. "We ran so much I thought I was on the track team," Sankes said. Bannon wanted his players to be stronger. He felt Rutgers had been pushed around in Big East play and that was due to a lack of strength inside. A new weight training program was implemented and Sankes and the other big men were told to start taking creatine, a legal diet supplement designed to build muscle strength. Sankes was taking creatine that summer while working at a camp for big men on Long Island. Not being familiar with creatine, he didn't understand how important it was to drink a lot of water after taking it. He became dehydrated on a hot afternoon, collapsed, and ended up in the hospital for four days. That was frightening. What was discouraging was that no one from Rutgers came to see him while he was there.

Things got worse once school started. Sankes had hoped to become a starter as a sophomore, but he found himself buried on the bench. The harder he tried, the worse things got. Then, shortly after the team returned from Christmas break, things bottomed out. One day in practice, Bannon decided to hold a strip–free throw shooting contest. Each time a player missed a free throw, he had to remove a piece of clothing. By the time the contest was over, Sankes and another player, Earl Johnson, along with two managers, were running wind sprints naked while the rest of the team and the coaches watched.

Sankes was humiliated and miserable. Later, when Johnson filed a lawsuit against Bannon and Rutgers because of the incident, Bannon claimed that the drill had been "optional." The lawsuit was thrown out of court by a New Jersey judge, but Sankes still remembers the day vividly. "Optional?" he said. "How can he say it was optional? Who would do something like that if it was optional? Your coach tells you to do something, there's nothing optional about it."

After that practice, Sankes decided to transfer. He was hoping to enroll at William and Mary for the spring semester, but Rutgers refused to grant him a release. "They said they loved me, that I was going to be a player for them down the road," he said. "They said they were keeping me from making a mistake."

By March, their tune had changed. Sankes ended up playing less as a sophomore than he had as a freshman, getting into nine games for a total of thirty-two minutes. When the season was over, Bannon called him in and told him he had no future as a player at Rutgers. He wanted to use his scholarship on someone else.

It is an unfortunate fact of NCAA life that a coach has the right to do this. Athletic scholarships are a series of one-year contracts. The school has the right to not renew a scholarship at the end of any school year. An athlete can be an A student but if he is not producing in his chosen sport, the coach can simply take his scholarship. The only protection an athlete has — and it is marginal at best — is the bad publicity that can be engendered if a coach gets in the habit of running off too many players.

Most players are loath to admit they have been stripped of their scholarship, because it makes them appear to be damaged goods. In most cases, the school will simply announce that the player has decided to transfer to a school where he will have a chance at more playing time. The translation of that statement is "We ran him off."

Sankes wasn't even that upset about being run off. Bannon's constant threats to make the team run at six o'clock in the morning (or earlier) had turned him into an insomniac. "I would lie awake in bed waiting for the phone to ring, someone saying we had to go run because somebody had screwed something up," he said. "I hated basketball, everything about it." He had also developed an ulcer to go along with the insomnia.

Gary Sankes, Josh's dad, owns a construction business. He told his son that if he wanted to stay at Rutgers, he would gladly pay for him to go to school. Sankes was tempted. The minute he was no longer part of the basketball team, life had become better. He started sleeping again and found he enjoyed being a regular student, even without the perks that came with being a basketball player.

Then came a call from Holy Cross Coach Bill Raynor. Would Sankes be interested in coming up and taking a look at the school? Basketball scholarships were going to be available again beginning with the fall semester. Sankes decided to take a look for two reasons: first, he thought it was silly for his parents to pay for him to go to college if he could go someplace for free. Second, he couldn't say no to Chris Spitler.

Spitler and Sankes had been teammates at St. Joseph's High School. They were a textbook example of opposites attracting. Sankes was quiet, high-strung, nervous like a young colt getting ready for his first race. Spitler was a foot shorter than his friend, a motormouth, someone who exploded into a room with a one-liner or a quip loaded up and ready to go. Sankes had been recruited by everybody, Spitler by nobody — literally nobody.

"Actually the coach from [Division III] Rochester invited me down to a game once," he said. "Then I got down there and he said, 'I'm sorry I got you to drive down here, you really aren't good enough to play for us.'"

Spitler is the oldest of Kevin and Mary-Elaine Spitler's four sons. His father is six-four and two of his brothers are six-four. His youngest brother, who is in ninth grade, can dunk. Chris can dunk, too — off a ladder. "I got screwed genetically," he said.

Physically perhaps, but not intellectually. Kevin Spitler is a lawyer, Mary-Elaine Spitler is a social worker. Their oldest son had a 3.9 GPA in high school and 1400 on the College Boards. He chose Holy Cross after visiting both Harvard and Yale. "I know they're both great schools," he said. "In fact, I don't know if I could have gotten into either one of them, but when I was there, something told me they weren't right for me. What's the old line about a feeling that is both above and beneath intellect at the same time? That was the way I felt. When I walked on campus here, I knew it was right."

Holy Cross gave Spitler an academic scholarship and he chose to pay the rest of his tuition himself, meaning he held a work-study job throughout his four years in college and graduated with $27,000 in loans to pay off. As a senior, his work-study job was to sit at the security desk at the Hart Center. On some nights, he would play in the building for several hours and then guard it for several hours. "I'm a lot better guarding a building than basketball players," he said, deadpan.

Spitler played on the junior varsity as a freshman for no other reason than that he loved to play. At the end of the season he went to see Raynor to ask him if he could try out for the varsity the following season. "Sure you can," Raynor said. "But I've seen you play, Spit. You're not good enough to make the team."

"I know I'm not," Spitler said. "Can I try out anyway?"

Raynor said fine. Spitler went through tryouts in the fall and made the team. Raynor called him in to give him the news. "I'm keeping you," he said, "because I love your attitude and your work ethic. But you're going to be the last man on the bench. You won't play, but I need you to come to practice every day and work hard. Can you handle that?"

Spitler could. Midway through the season, with the Crusaders mired in last place in the Patriot League, he was reading a basketball magazine on a bus trip. The magazine ranked the thirty-one Division I conferences in America. At that moment, the Patriot League was ranked thirty-first. Spitler started thinking. "Let's see, if I've got this straight, I'm the worst player on the worst team in the worst conference in Division I. Wow! I'm the worst Division I player in the whole country!"

Spitler took this role quite seriously. At parties, he would often walk up to women and say, "Hey, do you know who I am?"

"The answer was usually something like, 'Yeah, you're a loser trying to hit on me,'" Spitler said. "And I would say, 'Aha! I'm not just *any* loser. I happen to be the worst Division I basketball player in the country. Now what do you think of me?'"

No doubt the routine worked every time.

Sadly, Spitler was stripped of his status before season's end. After a 27-point loss to Lafayette, Raynor called Spitler into his office and told him he was thinking about starting him at Bucknell. Did he think he could handle it? Of course he could, Spitler told his coach, heart pounding. He then ran to a phone and called his parents to tell them the news. The Spitlers had already gotten into the habit of making the six-and-a-half-hour drive from Buffalo to Worcester to watch Chris *not* play, so they would certainly make the trip to Lewisburg — a mere five hours — to see him actually get into a game.

As it turned out, virtually every person named Spitler made the trip to Lewisburg. On the first play of the game, Spitler coolly drilled a three. On the next trip down he threw a backdoor pass for a layup. "Nothing to this," Spitler thought. "I'm going to go for about eighty [points] and twenty [assists]." As he ran down the court, he could hear his uncle's voice quite clearly from behind the Holy Cross bench. "The trip was worth it just to see *that!*"

He didn't go for eighty and twenty, but he did play twenty-nine minutes. He shot 5-for-8 from the floor, had 11 points, five assists, four rebounds, and, of all things, a blocked shot. When he fouled out with a minute left diving on the floor for a loose ball, the entire crowd of 2,300 in Davis Gym gave him a standing ovation, knowing he was a walk-on who had played a grand total of twenty varsity minutes prior to that night.

He was a starter for the rest of the season. While his career was taking off (relatively speaking), his old pal Sankes was living through the nightmare that had become life at Rutgers. When Spitler heard from his parents what had happened to Sankes, he went to see the coaches. He explained to them that he had a friend at Rutgers who was seven-one, a good student, and needed a place to play. Holy Cross doesn't often pursue transfers, but they decided to consider making an exception in the case of Sankes. Which was why Raynor had placed the call to him.

Even with Spitler campaigning on both sides of the fence, it almost didn't happen. Sankes wasn't thrilled when he visited Holy Cross. The campus was small compared to Rutgers and he sensed the work would be a lot harder. The team had been bad and he didn't see any signs it would get better very soon. On the flip side, the Holy Cross people were shocked by Sankes's transcript. The grades weren't too bad, but most of the courses were in the general studies area. "I took everything easy I could find," Sankes admitted.

Spitler told Sankes to give Holy Cross a chance. Raynor, seeing that Sankes was as huge as advertised, convinced the admissions people to look at his high school record and recognize the potential. Sankes was admitted and transferred. He went through immediate culture shock. Classes were hard. No one arranged to get him a parking pass. He had to wait in line like any other student to register for classes. And if a class was closed, it was closed. No one pulled any strings to get him in.

"I thought I had made a mistake," he said. "Then I started to get used to it."

He had shoulder surgery during the summer for a rotator cuff problem and didn't practice until January. By then, Spitler, who had been forced to try out for the team *again* in the fall, was back in the starting lineup and the team was back at the bottom of the Patriot League. Raynor resigned in February. "Oh God," thought Sankes, "not again, not another new coach who is going to come in trying to prove how tough he is." He went to see Athletic Director Dick Regan, hoping to find out what kind of coach he was thinking of hiring. Regan told him not to worry, everything would be fine. This was the Patriot League, not the Big East.

Then, Regan hired Willard — out of the Big East. Sankes remembered one of the last things Bannon had said to him on the day he had been told he would never again play for Rutgers. "We're looking to become more athletic, Josh," he said. "We want to have a team that's more like Pittsburgh. You don't fit that mold."

And so it was that when Willard walked onto the floor for his first workout with his seven-one center, he found him in a corner, doubled over, literally sick at the thought of playing for this new coach.

"Josh," he told him when Sankes finally made it onto the court, "I'm not here to hurt you. I just want to make you better."

Sankes nodded tentatively. And then they went to work.

The gym in which Willard and Sankes began their work is different from most college gyms. These days, most college basketball arenas have almost as many banners as seats. There are banners for just about everything: NCAA participation, conference championships, fielding a team. There are banners for basketball and field hockey and volleyball and, in some places undoubtedly, chess. Everyone takes bows for anything and everything. Some schools retire numbers almost as frequently as they award varsity letters. He once made four straight 3-point shots? Retire his number.

There are exactly two banners hanging in the Hart Center. One says "NCAA Champions 1947." The other says "NIT Champions 1954." There are no retired numbers in the building, although Bob Cousy's number 17 will never be worn again because the NCAA banned the use of any number higher than 5 a few years ago to make it easier for referees to signal a player's number to the scorer's table.

Holy Cross has a basketball history that can be matched by few and cannot be touched by the other members of the Patriot League. That may explain why the school feels no need to hang banners honoring hat tricks by hockey players. But that does not mean the other six league schools lack history and heroes.

Army is the only league school that has never played in the NCAA Tournament. But it has been coached by two men who have gone on from West Point to win five national championships and participate in thirteen Final Fours. Bob Knight was coaching junior varsity basketball at a small high school in Ohio in 1963 when Fred Taylor, his coach at Ohio State, called him to say he might be able to get the job as assistant coach at West Point, if he was willing to enlist in the Army as a private. Knight enlisted, went to work for Tates Locke for two years, and ascended to the head coaching position in 1965, six months before his twenty-fifth birthday. He never rose above the rank of private in the Army, except in the eyes of the media, which labeled him "the General." The ex-private loved the nickname, espe-cially since his hero and role model was General George S. Patton. In six years at Army, Knight went 102-50, took the school to the NIT four times (finishing fourth twice and third once) and became a hot young coach — not to mention a hotheaded young coach — on the national scene.

As an assistant coach, Knight recruited a hawk-nosed, slick-haired guard with a funny-sounding name out of Chicago's South Side. Mike Krzyzewski didn't really want to be a cadet, but his parents talked him into it. He became Knight's team captain on the 1969 team that upset nationally ranked South Carolina en route to that third place NIT finish.

In 1971, Knight left Army to find fame, fortune, national champi-onships, and national notoriety at Indiana. He was succeeded for four years by Dan Dougherty. After a 3-22 record in 1975, Dougherty was succeeded by twenty-seven-year-old Mike Krzyzewski, a year out of the Army (he became a captain in five years and has never blinked when friends call him "Captain"), during which he had served an apprenticeship as a graduate assistant under Knight at Indiana. Dougherty, who went on to become a very successful high school coach, likes to introduce himself to people as a trivia question: who was the coach at Army in between the two Hall of Famers?

Krzyzewski was 73-59 in five years as coach at his alma mater. One of his first recruits was Pat Harris, an intense kid from the Bronx who reminded Krzyzewski a lot of himself coming out of Chicago ten years earlier. Today, Harris is the coach at his alma mater and he and his coaches meet during games in a room adjacent to the players' locker room whose walls are adorned with pictures of Knight and Krzyzewski, complete with their Army-coaching resumes underneath the pictures.

"Intimidating?" Harris will joke as he looks at the images of his coaching mentor and *his* coaching mentor. "I'm only, what, twelve hundred wins behind them?" The actual number beginning the 1999–2000 season was 1,267.

The most famous name in the history of Navy basketball is David Robinson, who, as with Knight and the Army, has been given a rank by media and fans — Admiral — which he never achieved. The future Navy ensign enrolled at the academy in 1983 as an awkward six-seven academic whiz kid who was far more interested in engineering than basketball. He graduated four years later as a seven-one All-American who had led the school to the Elite Eight of the NCAA Tournament, had been on the cover of *Sports Illustrated,* and would go on to be the number one pick in the NBA draft. After two years in the Navy, he was granted an honorable discharge and has gone on to a more than honorable (and lucrative) career with the San Antonio Spurs. The Hall of Fame no doubt awaits him when he retires.

Lafayette also has a storied history. Pete Carril, the legendary Princeton coach, grew up in the shadow of College Hill in Easton, Pennsylvania, and graduated from Lafayette in 1952. Butch Van Breda Kolff, who would go on to coach Bill Bradley at Princeton and Wilt Chamberlain with the Los Angeles Lakers, coached at Lafayette twice — in the early 1950s and then again in the 1980s. Dr. Tom Davis, who went on to Boston College, Stanford, and Iowa, also coached at Lafayette. His assistant in the early 1970s — in those days most schools had only one assistant coach — was Gary Williams, now in his twelfth season at Maryland.

Davis and Williams coached the Tripucka brothers, Tracy and Todd, the school's number one and number six all-time scorers. In a twist to the story, the youngest of the Tripucka brothers, Kelly, starred at Notre Dame and later played in the NBA. In 2000, the color commentator for Patriot League basketball telecasts was Kelly Tripucka — the non–Lafayette grad. Davis was also Lafayette's coach in 1972 when the Leopards achieved their first — and only — post-season victory, beating Virginia in the opening round of the NIT on a free throw by Jay Mottola. These days, Mottola runs the Metropolitan Golf Association in the New York area and still gets stopped by people who remember The Free Throw almost thirty years later.

Lehigh's most famous coach was Carril, who stayed one year (1966–67) before moving on to replace Van Breda Kolff at Princeton. He stayed at Princeton for only twenty-nine years. Brian Hill, who later coached the Orlando Magic and Shaquille O'Neal into the NBA Finals, coached at Lehigh for nine years in the 1970s and 1980s. His assistants were Pat Kennedy, now the coach at DePaul, and a young coach named Sal Mentesana. Like Carril, Mentesana grew up in the shadow of Lafayette's College Hill. But Mentesana grew up a Lehigh fan. Today, the old Lehigh fan is the Lehigh coach. And, like Carril and Hill and every Lehigh coach but one (Fran McCaffery) dating back to 1932, Mentesana has lost more games than he has won.

Bucknell also had a famous coach: the late Jim Valvano, who spent three seasons at the school from 1972 through 1974 before moving on to Iona and then North Carolina State, where he won the national championship in 1983. Shortly after Valvano left Bucknell for Iona, he attended a party in New Rochelle, where Iona is located. He was so excited about his new job that he circled the room, introducing himself to everyone: "Hi, I'm Jim Valvano, Iona College." Finally one woman looked at him skeptically and said, "Aren't you a little young to own your own college?"

Colgate may have less basketball history than any school in the league. It had never reached the NCAA Tournament prior to the formation of the Patriot League and was much better known for producing football players — including current AD Mark Murphy, a Pro Bowl safety for the Washington Redskins — than basketball players. But Jack Bruen and Adonal Foyle changed that in the 1990s. Bruen rebuilt the Colgate program and when the gifted and brilliant sixten Foyle decided to pass on Duke and Syracuse and instead attend Colgate — his legal guardians were both Colgate professors — the school ended up in back-to-back NCAA Tournaments in 1995 and 1996 and, arguably, played the two most competitive games in Patriot League postseason history, losing tough games to top seeds Kansas and Connecticut. In 1997, Foyle became the first — and only — Patriot League player to leave before his senior year to turn pro, becoming the eighth pick in the NBA draft. He is currently the only Patriot League player in the NBA (Robinson played at Navy when it was still in the CAA) and is also a Colgate graduate, having completed his degree requirements in 1999.

On a road trip last winter with the Golden State Warriors, Foyle showed up in a hotel lobby one day carrying a book entitled *Fooling Around with Words: The Life and Times of the Great Poets*. Not exactly your standard NBA reading fare.

In short, all seven schools have had their moments in basketball, although some have not been recent. More important, the schools are strikingly similar. The oldest, West Point, was founded in 1802. The youngest, Lehigh, in 1865. The smallest is Lafayette with slightly more than 2,200 undergraduates. The largest is Lehigh with 4,400. The total number of undergraduates in the league — about 23,500 — is almost 20,000 fewer than the number of undergraduates enrolled at Michigan State, the current national champion. All the coaches in the league moan about the restrictions placed on them by their schools' academic requirements, limited budgets, and lack of national exposure. In the next breath, they all talk about how much they enjoy coaching their players, knowing they aren't out with agents at night or flunking out of school by day.

"Now I lie awake in bed every night worrying about how to win basketball games," Ralph Willard said. "Before I lay awake in bed every night worrying about everything *but* winning basketball games."

Willard, Don DeVoe, and, thanks to his success the last two years, Fran O'Hanlon, are the only coaches in the league making six figures. Adding camp money and TV and radio money into the mix, Willard and DeVoe probably make close to $200,000 annually. O'Hanlon is probably closer to $125,000 — double what he was making when he took over a staggering program in 1995. By comparison, the minimum compensation package in the ACC these days is about $500,000.

Willard (Class of '67) is one of three league coaches working at his alma mater. The others are Harris (Army '79) and Pat Flannery (Bucknell '80). The best player among the coaches in the league was probably O'Hanlon, who was captain of a Villanova team that reached the Elite Eight in 1970. He then played for one year in the old ABA before playing overseas for many years. DeVoe played on a Final

Four team as a sophomore at Ohio State in 1963 and on teams ranked in the top ten the next two years. Harris was a three-year starter for Krzyzewski at Army from 1977 to 1979. Flannery was a two-year captain at Bucknell and Willard was Holy Cross's captain in 1967, though he averaged just 3.5 points per game that year. "Poor coaching," he says, laughing — sort of, because his senior year was marred by illness and lack of playing time. Mentesana never played basketball at Providence and Colgate's Emmett Davis was cut from his college team — by Paul Evans, who later helped get him involved in coaching.

At fifty-eight, DeVoe is the league's oldest coach, having been a head coach for twenty-seven years. The youngest is Davis, DeVoe's former assistant, who is forty-one — two years younger than Harris and Flannery.

They all share one thing: an absolute love of what they are doing. Each lives comfortably on the money he makes as a coach, but none got into the profession expecting to become wealthy. And none of them expects to be rich or famous anytime soon. But none of them would want to do anything other than what they are doing.

Like Willard, they all need three things to be happy: a gym, a ball, and kids who will work just as hard as they themselves are working. In the Patriot League, that's exactly what they get.

4

BEGINNINGS

BEING relatively young, the Patriot League does not have as many traditions as some of the more established leagues around the country. It is still working to make the conference tournament a must-attend event for fans of the seven schools the way some other conference tournaments are. The conference television package is still something the conference pays the TV people for rather than the other way around. And, because the league has never pulled a first-round NCAA Tournament upset, a majority of the country has no idea what the Patriot League is or who plays in it.

But among those in the league, there are traditions and there are very serious rivalries. Army-Navy and Lehigh-Lafayette are rivalries that date back to the nineteenth century. Even though Navy and Lafayette have been very good in recent years and Army and Lehigh have been very bad, their games are almost always competitive. Steve Aylsworth, Lehigh's point guard, had a career average of 4.3 points per game. As a freshman, he scored 29 points in a game against Lafayette. As a junior he had 31 in a game — against Lafayette. His career high in assists? Eight, against Lafayette as a sophomore.

"Every year he gets one vote for all-conference," Lafayette Coach Fran O'Hanlon said. "Me. In fact, I think I may have voted for him for All-American."

But the traditional rivalries aren't the only ones that spice the league. One might think that basketball players who have lives away from the basketball court might not be quite as intense about the sport as those who live it, breathe it, and hope to ultimately become rich because of it. Nothing could be further from the truth.

Just before his team took the floor to play its opening conference game of the 1999–2000 season, Colgate Coach Emmett Davis asked Pat Diamond, the only senior on the team, to explain to his younger teammates what they could expect from conference play. Diamond is a bright, warm young man who wants to be a lawyer. He had already given a good deal of thought to what the end of his basketball career was going to mean to him.

"It's pretty simple," he said quietly. "We know everything about all of them and they know everything about all of us. No surprises." He paused. "And we all hate each other."

Hate? Wasn't this the Patriot League, where sports are kept in perspective, where everyone shakes hands at the end of each game, where the athletes keep the whole thing in perspective? "It is," Diamond said later. "But when you're competing for something that's important to you, things get emotional sometimes. And you're always going to see the guys over and over again. Sometimes the hard feelings linger."

In fact, hard feelings may linger longer in the Patriot League than in the big-time leagues because the conference championship is the one and only goal of every school in the league. Winning the Patriot League Tournament is the Holy Grail because that is the only way to get into postseason play. In the glamour leagues, four, five, sometimes six teams will routinely get into the NCAA Tournament. Any team that finishes with an overall record of .500, no matter how awful their nonconference schedule may be, will get an NIT bid because the NIT would rather take a 15-15 team out of the Big East or the ACC than a 23-6 team out of the Patriot League or any of the other small conferences. In 1988 Connecticut won the NIT after finishing *last* in the Big East. Once, when Navy Coach Don DeVoe was asked how far he thought the league was from the day when it would receive a second postseason bid, he shook his head and said, "Light years."

As a result, winning within the league is far more crucial than in leagues where multiple teams receive bids. Because even though the NCAA bid is decided by the conference tournament, seeding for the tournament is critical. The championship game is always played on the home court of the highest-seeded team. This is done for ESPN, which pays the league the princely sum of $12,500 for the right to televise the final. In return, ESPN tells the league when to play the final and insists that it be played on a home court in order to guarantee a pumped up rah-rah atmosphere in the building. Even though everyone agrees that a game that makes or breaks the season should always be played on a neutral court, the league (among others) goes along with this to make ESPN happy. In the eight years of playing the championship game on a home court, the visiting team has won once (Holy Cross in 1993). That's why the regular season is so crucial.

There is also the matter of playing with a little bit of a chip on your shoulder. In order to make their budgets work, every Patriot League team plays a couple of "guarantee" games every year. These are games smaller schools schedule on the road strictly to make money. That's why Army played at Duke and Seton Hall; Lehigh and Bucknell played at Penn State; Lafayette played at Villanova and Georgia Tech; Colgate played at Syracuse and Siena; Holy Cross played at Providence and in Indiana's Christmas Tournament; and Navy played at Rice and SMU. This was one area where Navy had an advantage on the other league teams: DeVoe was able to get teams to give him return games in large part because a lot of coaches liked the idea of bringing their team to Annapolis.

In 1999, Wake Forest played its season opener at Navy and DeVoe walked a wide-eyed Wake Forest Coach Dave Odom and his staff through the King Hall dining area during lunch. "Next time, we'll bring the players to see this," Odom said, watching 4,000 midshipmen march in, eat, and march out in less than thirty minutes. DeVoe smiled. He liked the sound of the words "next time."

Generally speaking, a guarantee game pays $25,000, occasionally more. Pat Harris scheduled his guarantee games with Duke and Seton Hall because of his friendships with Mike Krzyzewski and Seton Hall Coach Tommy Amaker, like Harris a former Krzyzewski point guard. Holy Cross had been scheduled to go to Duke, but Ralph Willard, who had known Krzyzewski for years, called and pleaded with him to find another victim. "We've already got at Providence, Boston College, at Princeton, at Indiana and Alabama-Birmingham in the Indiana Tournament," Willard said. "We don't need to go down to Duke and get killed. Not this year."

Some of the guarantee games are traditional. Bucknell has always made the one-hour trip up Route 322 to Penn State. Colgate and Syracuse was once a great rivalry, dating back to 1901. Now, Syracuse has won the last thirty-four games between the two teams. Colgate's last win was in 1962 and the last time Syracuse played at Colgate was in 1977.

In 1999, Lafayette played at Villanova in a guarantee game that seemed to make sense. O'Hanlon grew up in Philadelphia, graduated from Villanova, and has a number of players on his team from Philadelphia. But the game came about only because Villanova Coach Steve Lappas had a hole in his schedule created when he decided to drop a game against Delaware. As predicted by Josh Sankes, Mike Brey had built the Delaware program to the point where Lappas saw the game as a no-win. If he beat the Blue Hens, well, he was supposed to beat Delaware. If he lost to them, he had lost to Delaware! The Big East can't lose to the America East. So, he called Brey to tell him he couldn't play the game.

"I'd like to give you a bunch of excuses, but I'm gonna tell you the truth," Lappas said. "I don't want to play you. In fact, lose my phone number."

Brey appreciated the honesty and was flattered. Lappas understood Brey's position because he had been in a similar situation at Manhattan before coming to Villanova. "When I first took the job at Manhattan I walked into the office and there were messages from every coach in the country wanting to play us," he said. "My first goal was to get that stack down to nothing. Four years later, no one would return my calls."

O'Hanlon was having a similar experience. Taking over a team that was 2-25, he was every coach's best friend. At 7-20, he was still quite popular. Now, after 19-9 and 22-8, a lot of guys couldn't remember Easton's area code. But Lappas wanted to play. He knew Lafayette was good, but they couldn't be *that* good.

Or could they? After his team had barely survived a down-to-the-wire 74-70 game, Lappas shook O'Hanlon's hand and said, "Don't you understand that when we guaranteed you $25,000, you were supposed to guarantee us a win?"

That's why they call them guarantee games: guaranteed money for the visitor, a guaranteed win for the home team. Most of the time, they worked out that way. Occasionally, the visitor forgot his role and threatened to win or actually won the game. Holy Cross opened the Ralph Willard era in 1999 with a stunning 53-41 victory at Providence. In December, Bucknell very nearly shocked Penn State.

The players didn't mind playing guarantee games. For them it was a thrill to play in Cameron Indoor Stadium or the Carrier Dome or Conseco Field House, the new arena in Indianapolis. All four Lehigh seniors listed their trip to Duke as freshmen among their greatest thrills as players. Lehigh had lost the game, 103-51. "And it could have been twice that," Coach Sal Mentesana said, "if Mike [Krzyzewski] had wanted it to be."

Those games could be thrilling and humiliating. The more difficult games to play were the ones against mid-major teams who looked at a Patriot League team as something they should beat every time out. As with football, the Patriot League played a lot of games against Ivy League teams. These were evenly matched, emotional games. So were games against teams like Manhattan and Towson State and Wagner. Except for the occasional game against a Division III team, there was no such thing as a walkover game for a Patriot League team. Almost every nonconference game was difficult to win. That's why teams tended to arrive at league play in January a little more emotionally beat up than the big-time teams who spent most of the preseason playing guarantee games at home or the occasional made-for-TV glamour game. No one from the Patriot League played in any of those games.

By the time January rolled around, players and coaches were edgy, wound up, perhaps a little bit angry. They wanted to get on the court against teams they knew they could compete with physically and prove some things. Emotions ran high and tempers flared easily. Even, on occasion, some hate.

If there was one team in the league everyone loved to hate it was Navy. To most players, coaches, even administrators, Navy was Darth Vader in blue and gold. The Midshipmen played physical basketball, too physical, according to some opponents. They were confident, maybe even cocky. They always had great depth because they could send players to the Navy prep school for a year, in effect redshirting them, something the five nonmilitary schools couldn't do. They had the largest, newest arena in the conference and could recruit in unlimited numbers since the government paid the freight.

Of course Army had similar advantages, especially when it came to finances and the prep school, but it had not been able to make those things work for them the way Navy had. Knowing the intensity of the rivalry between the two schools, other league coaches would often commiserate with Army Coach Pat Harris about Navy's depth. Harris would nod quietly and think, "Absolutely right. And if I have my way, we'll be just as deep for the exact same reasons in a couple of years."

Navy's success, combined with Army's failures throughout most of the 1990s, were a source of great anguish at Army. While the two schools had remained evenly matched in football — still far and away the most important sport at both schools — the gap in basketball seemed to widen and deepen with each passing year.

Army had won ten games in a season three times in the 1990s (10-19 in 1990, 12-16 in 1995, and 10-16 in 1997). After going 8-19 in his first season at Navy, DeVoe had won no fewer than fifteen games in any season and had won twenty on three different occasions, reaching the NCAA Tournament three times during that period.

What made all of that especially tough to take on the banks of the Hudson was that DeVoe could have been coaching at Army all that time. In 1990, he had interviewed for the Army job. Having been an assistant under Bob Knight at Army for five years in the 1960s he understood the academy and, he told the search committee, he understood what it took to win at an academy. Unlike many people he wouldn't get frustrated by all the rules and red tape that surround the school and, having coached at the big-time level for so many years, he would welcome the notion of coaching players he didn't have to worry about away from the court.

"At an academy, you almost always know where your players are at night," he liked to say. "Because if they aren't studying, the chances are they won't be your players for too much longer."

The search committee was impressed with DeVoe and his approach.

But David Palmer, the superintendent who had helped make the decision to join the Patriot League, had decided it was time to bring a grad back as coach. He was bolstered by the fact that there was a grad available who was a logical candidate: Tom Miller, who had played for Knight and had gone on to coach at Cornell and Colorado, the former with great success, the latter with mixed results.

Miller was hired amidst great fanfare. He was going to be Knight and Krzyzewski rolled into one, the hard-nosed teacher who would understand Army players and Army ways because he had lived through it. It should have worked. Miller is a bright, personable man who understands basketball as well as anyone. Only it didn't. Army won fourteen games total in Miller's three seasons and he was fired after a dispute with General Howard Graves, Palmer's successor.

DeVoe was forty-eight when he didn't get hired by Army, and he worried that his coaching career might be over. He had resigned under fire at Tennessee in 1989 — after making the NCAA Tournament that year — and had made the mistake of signing on as an interim coach the next season at Florida after Norm Sloan was forced to resign in the wake of an NCAA investigation.

"I thought at the time that staying out of coaching for a year might hurt me," he said. "And I guess I was like any coach with an ego, I thought I could be the guy who would get talented players who had attitude problems to straighten up. Boy, was I wrong."

He was wrong to the tune of 7-21, the most miserable season he had ever suffered through as a coach, not so much because of the losing but because he wasn't prepared to deal with players like Dwayne Schintzius, who was a lot more interested in his latest haircut than in basketball or — God forbid — going to class. "I would get on the guys about their academics and they would look at me like I was from Mars," DeVoe remembered. "It was not a fun year."

DeVoe sat out the next two seasons and was beginning to wonder if his phone was ever going to ring again, when Jack Lengyel called. The Navy athletic director needed a coach. He knew about DeVoe's Army background and he was friendly with Knight, who had urged him to contact DeVoe. Navy hadn't been close to a winning season since David Robinson's graduation in 1987. The pay would be decent, but nothing like what he had been making at Tennessee. Was DeVoe interested?

"When can I start?" was DeVoe's response.

He turned the program around in just two years. One of his first and most important moves was to retain both of Herrmann's assistants, Doug Wojcik and Emmett Davis. Wojcik had been the point guard on the Robinson teams and he knew exactly how to sell Navy to a basketball player. Davis had been at Navy for six years, had an understanding and feel for the place. Just as important, both were workaholics. Wojcik was single, Davis divorced. DeVoe put them on the road recruiting every single day that was allowable under NCAA rules that first season.

"We didn't see many games," Davis remembered. "Which, given our record that year, was probably a good thing."

Both Davis and Wojcik were on the road the night Navy basketball bottomed: December 8, 1992. Already 0-3, the Mids lost to Division III Gettysburg, 78-76, in overtime. After the game, both assistant coaches called in to the basketball office to update their boss on their recruiting efforts. Each asked, almost casually, how the game had gone that night. "We lost," DeVoe said. Each had the identical reaction: he's joking. Then they heard the silence on the other end of the phone and it occurred to them that DeVoe wasn't joking. "It was a sick feeling," Davis said. "A very sick feeling."

Later that winter, Wojcik went to see a guard from Anderson, Indiana, named Brian Walker. He came back to Annapolis telling DeVoe he had to see this kid play.

"How big is he?" Devoe asked.

"Five-eight," Wojcik answered.

"Forget it," DeVoe said. "Little guards can't play man-to-man defense. It won't work."

Wojcik pleaded with DeVoe to at least take a look at Walker. He was convinced Walker could play man-to-man defense and that he had the kind of toughness a player needs to be the point guard at Navy — on and off the court. DeVoe relented and, against his better judgment, went to see Walker play. It took him about five minutes to understand what Wojcik was talking about. A year later, Walker was inserted into the starting lineup in January with the Midshipmen reeling again at 5-10. From that moment on, the program was transformed. Navy won twelve of its last fifteen games, tied for first place in the Patriot League, and won the conference tournament to get into the NCAA Tournament.

DeVoe and his lieutenants built from there. The Midshipmen had not finished lower than second in the league since. That was a large part of the reason why they were so unpopular with their league brethren: they won a lot. But the 1998–99 season had ended on a major downer for DeVoe. After finishing the regular season with four straight victories, they had gone into the Patriot League Tournament as the second seed behind Lafayette.

In the first round, the Mids played Lehigh, which had just completed an 0-12 regular season in which almost every key player had been injured at one time or another. Navy had beaten the Mountain Hawks by 30 and by 33. The game was looked at by almost everyone as little more than a walkover, an early Saturday warm-up for what figured to be a tough semifinal the next day against Bucknell. When a friend mentioned to DeVoe that he was planning to attend the Sunday game, DeVoe said, "Well, if we're not there, you can look for me floating in the Chesapeake."

The bay can be very cold in early March. But not nearly as cold as DeVoe's team was against Lehigh. Desperate for something to give his team hope, Sal Mentesana had decided to abandon his aggressive man-to-man defense and play zone, forcing Navy to shoot the ball from outside. The Mids ended up 17-for-76 from the field — very patriotic — but not likely to win too many basketball games, even against an opponent that had lost eighteen straight games. Lehigh won 53-45 in what still must rank as the most shocking upset in the history of the league.

"During warm-ups, they were joking around and having a good time," Lehigh point guard Steve Aylsworth said. "Heck, who could blame them? They had killed us twice. Our best player [Brett Eppeheimer] hadn't played since December and they knew they were good. During the game, you could tell they just knew we were going away at any minute. But we didn't. I'll never forget the look that came onto their faces as the game went on. It was very empowering to see their frustration."

"They couldn't even look us in the eye when it was over," Jared Hess, the Lehigh captain, remembered. "They were in shock."

Shock might be an understatement. Losing to Lehigh had seemed as likely to the Midshipmen as winning the NBA title. Beyond that, there was no chance for redemption. They had won twenty games and their season was over. The two seniors, Josh Williams and Skip Victor, were inconsolable. They had never dreamed for an instant when they suited up that day it would be for the last time.

The Lehigh loss had been on the minds of the players throughout the summer. The team had made a trip to France and Italy in early August. They returned to Annapolis a few days before the the start of classes in late August. On the afternoon of August 26, DeVoe held a team meeting to remind the players that school was underway now, that they needed to get a good start to the year academically, and that they needed to be sure to keep themselves out of trouble. DeVoe was completely aware of how easy it is to run afoul of the myriad rules at the academy and he wanted to be sure the players understood how much it hurt the team if anyone got into trouble.

They all nodded attentively as he spoke. The upperclassmen had all heard the speech before and they knew why DeVoe was giving it. DeVoe is a no-nonsense coach, an Ohio farm boy who grew up in a tiny town, played at Ohio State, and always wanted to coach and teach. He followed in Bob Knight's footsteps after college — getting hired as Knight's assistant in 1965 after agreeing to enlist in the Army. He spent five years with Knight, went back to graduate school at Ohio State to get a master's degree and work as a graduate assistant under his old coach, Fred Taylor.

He became a head coach at twenty-nine when he was hired at Virginia Tech. He won the NIT in 1973 — winning four games by a total of 5 points, the last over Notre Dame in overtime — and took the Hokies into the NCAA Tournament with twenty-one victories in 1976.

All of which got him fired.

Throughout that season, DeVoe had been prominently mentioned as a candidate to replace Taylor at Ohio State. Naturally, he was interested in the job. Two days after losing in the opening round of the NCAA Tournament to Western Michigan, DeVoe flew to Columbus to interview. When he returned to Blacksburg the next day, an assistant athletic director met him at his office to tell him that he had been replaced as coach.

"I think they just figured I was going to Ohio State," DeVoe said, shaking his head at the memory years later. "They didn't like uncertainty around there. So, there I was, fired at Virginia Tech, not knowing what Ohio State would do."

Ohio State hired Eldon Miller. DeVoe ended up at Wyoming for two years and was a finalist for the UCLA job in 1977 when Gene Bartow stepped down after two years as John Wooden's successor. He didn't get that job either, but Athletic Director J. D. Morgan recommended him a year later to his friend Bob Woodruff, the AD at Tennessee.

DeVoe was truly a hot coach his first seven years at Tennessee. He won twenty games six times and made the NCAAs five times. But things began to slide a little bit as the Southeastern Conference became more basketball oriented and recruiting became, to use a polite term, a little more intense. Recruiting in the SEC in the 1980s may have been best summed up by a conversation then–North Carolina assistant coach Eddie Fogler had with a high school coach, who called him one summer day about a player he was coaching.

Fogler listened as the coach talked about his player and then asked one question: "Coach, what are the chances I'm going to be able to get him out of the state of Georgia for tuition and books [and nothing else]?" Fogler listened another few seconds, nodded his head and said, "That's what I thought. Thanks for calling, Coach."

DeVoe wasn't handing out anything other than tuition and books at Tennessee either and it hurt him. He had his first two losing seasons ever as a coach in 1986 and 1987, but then bounced back to make the NIT in 1988 and the NCAAs in 1989 with a 19-11 record.

Then he got fired again. Sort of. "I asked [Athletic Director] Doug Dickey if he believed enough in the direction we were going to give me a contract extension," DeVoe said. "He said he just couldn't do it. I said that was fine, but I couldn't recruit without that support, so I resigned before he could get around to firing me."

Which may make DeVoe the only coach in college basketball history to twice lose a job after taking his team to the NCAA Tournament.

After Tennessee came the Florida debacle and then the phone call from Jack Lengyel that jump-started his career. DeVoe was very happy in Annapolis. His first marriage had ended shortly after he got the job at Tennessee and he had remarried in 1983. He had a grown daughter from his first marriage and two teenagers, Elliott and Ana Lise, with his second wife, Ana. They enjoyed living in Annapolis and DeVoe was very comfortable coaching Navy kids. He had been given a ten-year contract in 1997, shortly after football coach Charlie Weatherbie had been given a ten-year contract.

He had both hopes and doubts about his team in the fall of 1999. Several players would have to play more important roles than they had in the past if Navy was to be successful. But he felt confident that they were capable of doing that. The trip to France and Italy had been a bonus. Now, he wanted to be sure all his players got off on the right foot, "on the hall," as life within the academy's thirty-two companies is called. So, even though he knew everyone but the plebes had heard it before, he gave them his annual send-off speech, the theme of which was always the same: get your work done, stay out of trouble on the hall, be ready to go when practice starts full blast in October.

Shortly after DeVoe finished his little talk, nine of the team's ten juniors and seniors headed into downtown Annapolis to help Chris Worthing celebrate his twenty-first birthday. Worthing was a junior from Inman, Kansas, who had been ardently recruited by Wojcik, now departed from his alma mater because he had taken a job the previous spring at Notre Dame. Wojcik loved Worthing's athletic ability. At six-one, he could dunk the ball with two hands and had the kind of quickness needed to play defense at Navy.

But Worthing had never been able to figure out DeVoe's man-to-man well enough to earn consistent playing time. Still, he was popular with his teammates, and it is an academy ritual to take a midshipman out on the day he turns twenty-one and help him celebrate his right to drink legally.

Unfortunately, the celebration got out of hand. By the time the nine basketball players made it back to Bancroft Hall, the huge dormitory that houses all 4,000 midshipmen, Worthing was a sick young man. "We thought he'd just get it all out and we'd put him to bed," Sitapha Savane, the senior co-captain, said later.

If that had happened there wouldn't have been any problem. Worthing would have been nothing more than another twenty-one-year-old mid with a hangover the next morning. But things kept getting worse. The officer-of-the-day on the hall was convinced that Worthing needed medical help. He told the basketball players to get Worthing to the hospital.

An ambulance was called and the team's two seniors, Savane and Jeremy Toton, went to the hospital with Worthing to make sure he was okay. As they were pulling out of Gate 3 of the academy, they encountered assistant coach Jimmy Allen, who was driving back to the basketball office to make some postmidnight calls to recruits in California who would be settling down to watch TV at that hour. When Savane and Toton spotted Allen, they stopped him and told him what had happened. Allen turned his car around and followed the ambulance to the hospital.

As it turned out, Worthing was never in serious danger. The doctors got his convulsing under control quickly and he was able to return to Bancroft within a couple of hours. At a normal school, that would have been the end of it except for some early-morning running as punishment from the coaching staff. But Navy isn't a normal school. The OD had to file a report on what had happened with his company officer. Word of the incident quickly moved up the chain of command. By the time it reached the school's commandant, Gary Roughhead, the story went that Worthing had needed to have his stomach pumped.

Early the next morning, DeVoe was awakened by a call from Roughhead. "Don," he said, "we almost lost Chris Worthing last night."

Then he told DeVoe what had happened.

DeVoe went through about six different emotions in ten minutes. He was stunned, then frightened, then concerned, and, finally, furious. He had just finished talking to the team about acting responsibly and his upperclassmen go out and pull a stunt like *this*? He couldn't believe it. He was angriest with Savane because Savane was supposed to be the team captain and leader and because Savane had been in trouble before and knew — *knew* — he couldn't afford to run afoul of the school's top guns again.

Once he had confirmed that Worthing was all right — and had learned that he hadn't needed to have his stomach pumped — DeVoe began calling the players in one by one. He would leave the discipline up to the academy because he knew it would be severe. For now, all he was going to do was demand that each player call his parents and tell them what had happened — he wanted them to do it because he knew it would be more painful for them that way — and he wanted to make it clear how disappointed he was in all of them. Savane could forget about being the captain at least for a while. The players all remember DeVoe repeating one phrase over and over: "What could you possibly have been thinking?"

No one felt worse about what had happened than Savane. He *was* the captain and he and Toton should have known better. They should have had Worthing out of the bar sooner. He understood that at another school, this would not be that big an issue. But he also understood that Navy was not another school. "We get a lot of benefits being midshipmen," he said. "But responsibility comes with that. You can't take the perks and blow off the responsibility. That's what we did."

That statement alone was evidence of how far Savane had come since arriving at the academy. He was not your typical midshipman in any way. To begin with, he was from Senegal, and the government of Senegal was paying for his education in return for Savane pledging four years to the military after graduation.

He was the son of political activists who had met in France during the 1960s while each was living there as an exchange student. They had both been Maoists during that period, and it was probably a fair bet that there weren't a lot of midshipmen wandering the Yard — as the campus is called — whose parents had been card-carrying Communists at some point in their lives.

His father, Landing Savane, had been a leader of the opposition party in Senegal for as long as Sitapha could remember. Although the country had stabilized politically in recent years, Sitapha had boy-hood memories of the military police coming to his house to arrest his father for "crimes against the government."

"I remember once they showed up during dinner," he said. "Dad just stood up, left with them, and was back a couple days later."

His mother had been a leader of the feminist movement in Senegal and in Europe. Eventually she had gone to work for the United Nations, and Sitapha and his older brother Lamine had moved to New York. There, as he grew to six-seven, Sitapha became a serious basketball player, playing at the U.N. School. He was very unpol-ished, since he was just learning the game, but a number of coaches saw both his potential and his transcript and thought he was worth the risk.

Initially, Savane's first choice was Colgate. He had eliminated Navy after he had been told by the government that he would have to serve ten years in the military after graduation. The thought of practicing against Adonal Foyle every day for two years (Foyle was entering his junior year) appealed to Savane. Then he got another call from the Senegalese government. On second thought, they would require only four years in the military. That put Navy back in the picture. When he saw Annapolis, Savane was sold.

His best friend almost from day one at Navy was Toton, whose background could not have been more different from Savane's. Savane had traveled the world, Toton had traveled Indiana. Toton knew everything there was to know about basketball, Savane knew almost nothing. Toton had grown up in Evansville hoping to play someday at Indiana for Bob Knight. Savane had never heard of Bob Knight.

As it turned out, Knight had played a crucial role in Toton's deci-sion to attend Navy. Indiana had never recruited Toton. At six-six, he was considered a solid inside-outside player who was one step down from the Big Ten level. But Knight's one-time assistant coach Jim Crews, the coach at Evansville, was very interested in him. So was Southern Indiana, a very good Division II program. And Navy.

Toton was torn. He loved Evansville basketball. Short of playing for Indiana, playing at Evansville would be exactly what he had always wanted. But Crews had backed off during Toton's senior year.

He still wanted him to come but had told him he couldn't guarantee him a scholarship until his sophomore year. Southern Indiana, which was also close to home, was offering a full ride. So, of course, was Navy.

March became April, April became May. Toton was thinking he would still go to Evansville, but Crews's uncertainty had made him uncertain. On a May night, he went to bed, struggling to sleep as he weighed his options. Finally, well after midnight, he slept. And dreamed. In the dream, Bob Knight showed up in his room, demanding to know what he had decided to do about college.

"I don't know what to do, Coach," Toton told Knight after explaining his options.

"Well, son, let me tell you something," the Knight apparition said. "If you have a chance to go to the United States Naval Academy, you can't afford to say no."

Toton awoke in the morning, went straight downstairs, and told his parents he was going to Navy. He never told them why. And people say Bob Knight can't recruit anymore.

Toton and Savane were both junior varsity players as freshmen. DeVoe had built a deep program by then and wasn't inclined to play freshmen unless he was certain they were ready. By the time he was a sophomore, Savane was playing regularly and improving rapidly. In the Patriot League championship game, he had 15 points and six rebounds and was voted to the All-Tournament team. Toton's role was far more limited. He scored 10 points coming off the bench in the team's third game of the season and then scored 17 more, total, the rest of the season.

But the year didn't end well for Savane.

Late in the semester, swamped with work, he did what midshipmen occasionally do when faced with a test they think they can't pass: he took a cheat sheet with him into an exam. "About two questions in, I said to myself, 'What are you doing? What are you thinking?'" he said. "I put it away and took the rest of the test without it."

He was too late. The professor had noticed the cheat sheet. When the test was over, he asked Savane if he had anything he wanted to tell him. Savane confessed immediately. He made no excuses, simply told the professor he had panicked and had made an awful mistake.

Because there have been academic cheating scandals at both Army and Navy in the past, there is very little tolerance at either place when someone is caught cheating. Savane was saved by two factors: the professor had seen him put the cheat sheet away almost as soon as he had taken it out, and he had confessed right away with no excuses and asked for no slack. He was placed on restriction for the fall semester and suspended from the basketball team for all of fall practice and the first four games of the season. Just for good measure, DeVoe kept him out of the starting lineup until the end of the fall semester.

"I was lucky," Savane said. "That's the single dumbest thing I've ever done in my life. I was just glad they let me come back."

He came back and had a solid junior season, averaging 12.7 points and 8.5 rebounds a game. He was one of the players DeVoe knew had to show improvement if Navy was going to be any good by March 2000. Now, because of the Worthing party, he and Toton and seven juniors were placed on restriction by the academy. The rest of the players got thirty to forty-five days. Savane got sixty since this was not his first appearance before a disciplinary board.

Restriction means just that: no weekend passes, no leaving the academy except in an emergency, and showing up three times a day — five on weekends — for restriction muster, where any defect in your uniform can lead to more trouble. In fact anything, including looking at the officer in charge of the muster in a way he doesn't like, can lead to trouble.

The players knew they had screwed up. They knew they had set themselves up for a difficult fall as midshipmen. And being basketball players for Don DeVoe wasn't going to be any picnic either.

5

SQUARE ONE . . . AGAIN

NO one in the league was likely to lose any sleep over the plight of the Restricted Nine at Navy. That probably went double for Pat Harris. It wasn't that Harris didn't like DeVoe or respect DeVoe. He did and he did. In fact, DeVoe's program was the role model for what Harris was trying to piece together at Army.

But Navy, after all, was Navy. And Harris was an Army graduate — U.S. Military Academy Class of 1979. His record as a player against Navy had been 3-1 and he was still annoyed about the one loss, 47-45, in his last game as a college basketball player. His college coach, Mike Krzyzewski, who had found that loss just as distressing as Harris had, was not above pointing out to him that Army had never lost to Navy during the four years he had played at the academy.

The feeling that exists between Army and Navy may be best explained by a pregame talk Krzyzewski gave in 1986 when his Duke team was about to face a David Robinson–led Navy team in the Eastern Regional Final with a Final Four spot at stake.

After he had finished going through the matchups and points of emphasis for the game, Krzyzewski told his players about playing Navy. "You need to understand something," he said. "Those kids in that other locker room are great kids — every one of them. For them to have reached this game is unbelievable. They will never quit, never give up, never talk trash, and never stop playing hard. I can't even begin to tell you how much I respect them because I *know* what they go through to play basketball at the academy."

He paused for a moment and looked around the room. "But I want you to know one thing: if you don't go out there and kick their butts from here to Annapolis and back, don't even bother coming back into the locker room. They're Navy. I'm Army. We *never* lose to Navy."

Duke won the game, 71-50, with the Duke students serenading the Midshipmen with chants of "Abandon Ship!" throughout much of the second half.

But the halcyon days of Knight and Krzyzewski, when Army beating Navy in basketball was virtually a given (the two men were a combined 10-1 against the Mids as Army coaches), were long gone. DeVoe's record against Army as the Navy coach was 17-1, and a majority of the games had been one-sided.

Harris was the fifth coach at Army in the post-Knight-Krzyzewski era. Army's record during those fifteen years, even including Dan Dougherty's 3-22 in his final season, had been 206-175. In the seventeen seasons prior to Harris taking over in April of 1997, the record under Pete Gaudet (two years), Les Wothke (eight years), Tom Miller (three years), and Dino Gaudio (four years) had been 154-316. One winning season. Five 20-loss seasons.

Harris was hired in 1997 for several reasons: first and perhaps foremost, he had Krzyzewski's endorsement. Second, he was a grad, although the Miller experience made that less of a factor than it might have been otherwise. Third, his approach to Army basketball was 180 degrees opposed to Gaudio's.

No one at Army had anything but respect for Gaudio's abilities as a coach. In fact, Army had played some decent basketball under him, most notably in his second season, when the record had been a 1990s best 12-16 that included a first-round upset of Bucknell in the Patriot League Tournament and a respectable semifinal loss to Navy.

But Gaudio had believed that the way to make Army basketball succeed was to battle the system. The players had to be different from the rest of the cadets because being the same hadn't worked in the past. He came up with different-looking road uniforms — something a lot of coaches do — but not something that was going to be looked upon kindly at Army unless the new uniforms seemed to produce more victories. They didn't. He even committed the cardinal sin of saying publicly that Navy was just another important Patriot League game, no more significant than the Bucknell game, the Lehigh game, the Lafayette game. He bridled at the red tape that comes with life at the academy and made it clear to most that his goal was to piece together a good enough record that he could move on to another job.

When Gaudio managed to squeeze ten wins out of his team in 1997, it opened a window for him and he jumped through it — to Loyola of Maryland. One could hardly blame him. The Army job had by then earned the reputation as a graveyard for ambitious young coaches.

Which was why Harris was a perfect choice to succeed Gaudio. He didn't look at the job as a stepping-stone, he looked at it as the ultimate. He knew you couldn't fight the academy; you had to figure out a way to get the academy to work with you. He hated losing to Navy. And he had Krzyzewski on his side.

"The day I got the job, Coach [Harris is ten years younger than Krzyzewski but still calls him Coach] called me and congratulated me, told me I would do a great job," Harris remembered. "Then he said, 'Now, the first thing you're going to do is get rid of those goddamn road uniforms that look like goddamn pajamas.' I said, 'Hang on a minute while I get a legal pad. I better start taking notes.'"

Some coaches might not have wanted input from their old boss or mentor, not to mention an alumnus who still remembered the good old days, but Harris wanted all the help he could get from Krzyzewski. For one thing, he needed every edge he could find. For another, he knew Krzyzewski knew what he was talking about when it came to Army and when it came to basketball.

Which is why he had listened during those early conversations when Krzyzewski had told him he should keep a close eye on a player named Chris Spatola, who was about to enter Army's prep school. Harris actually knew the name well because he had seen Spatola play at the same place Krzyzewski had: Duke's summer camp. Spatola and his younger brother JP had been campers at Duke throughout junior high school and high school.

Krzyzewski had taken an interest in Spatola because he liked his hard-nosed approach to the game and because Spatola had started dating his youngest daughter, Jamie (also a point guard), during the summer of 1996. When Krzyzewski asked Spatola, who was about to enter his senior year at Lawrence Academy in Massachusetts, what his plans for college were, Spatola told him he had been talking to a number of Division II schools.

"No, wrong," Krzyzewski said. "You are not a Division II player. You're a Division I player. Not ACC or Big East Division I, but mid-major Division I."

Encouraged by Krzyzewski, Spatola began writing letters to mid-majors with strong academics, since he was a good student with solid boards. Most of the interest he got came from the Patriot League. Army was the most aggressive.

Gaudio, still the coach then, wanted Spatola to consider a year at the prep school. His boards were reasonable (1080) but not great for an entering freshman at West Point. He was also small, five-eleven, 145 pounds, and Gaudio thought a year at the prep school would give Spatola's body a chance to mature.

Spatola wasn't sure. He was a good enough student to get in at a number of schools other than Army. He wasn't certain he wanted to go to a military academy in the first place. But when he visited, he liked the school and the other basketball players, and once he talked to Harris after he was hired, he decided to accept the offer to attend the prep school.

Like almost every athlete who has ever gone through the prep school at Army or Navy, Spatola hated the place when he first arrived. In some ways the prep school is a tougher adjustment for an eighteen-year-old than West Point or Annapolis because the prep-sters are trained by drill sergeants rather than upperclassmen. Picture the opening scene of *An Officer and a Gentleman,* and you have some idea of what the early days of a prep school summer are like.

Spatola survived, played well, got his grades and his SATs up, and arrived at West Point in the summer of 1998 figuring he would come off the bench for a year and then compete for a starting job as a sophomore. Army had two senior guards: Babe Kwasniak and Jamie Uptgraft, who figured to get the bulk of the playing time. But it quickly became apparent to Harris that Spatola needed to play. He was still undersized, but he had a feel for the game, an ability to get the ball to the right spots, and a soft shooting touch, something that was desperately needed once Joe Clark went down for the season.

Unwittingly, Clark had become the symbol of Army basketball. He had been recruited out of Corydon, Indiana, by Gaudio and had averaged 21.2 points and 5.6 rebounds during a season at the prep school. In Harris's first year, he and Seth Barrett were freshman starters, providing genuine hope for the future. Barrett averaged almost 8 points and five rebounds a game and Clark, starting in twenty-five games, averaged 8.4 points, just under five rebounds and two assists a game. At six-seven, Clark had a feathery jump shot, averaging almost 40 percent from outside the 3-point line.

But Clark broke a foot during the off-season and had to have a screw inserted in it. He was still working his way back into playing shape in December when he landed awkwardly in a game against Manhattan and broke the screw. That meant more surgery and the end of his season. By then, Barrett was a starter and the team's second-leading scorer behind senior George Tatum.

Harris was expecting Clark, Barrett, and Spatola to be the heart and soul of his team. There were no seniors, a reflection of a poor final recruiting year by Gaudio and his staff and the attrition that West Point often struggles with. Clark and Barrett were the team's only juniors and the team captains.

Barrett was from Santa Rosa, California. He had been a decathlete and run cross-country in addition to playing basketball in high school. He was from a military family. One of his grandfathers had been in the Air Force, the other had been in the Army. Unlike most athletes, he had come to West Point because he wanted to be an Army officer. The opportunity to play basketball was just a bonus.

Barrett's true passion was cars. He could take them apart and put them back together and knew everything there was to know about them. "If he loved basketball the way he loves cars he would be an All-American," Harris liked to say. Barrett was flaky. One day he would come to practice with a warrior's mentality, the next day it would be clear his mind was elsewhere. He had played in the low post for two years at six-four, 240, but had chosen to *lose* weight over the summer, making his task of playing inside against bigger players even more formidable.

Barrett might have been the smartest guy on the team. He did consistently well in school and was as quick-witted as anyone around. When he was asked whether he liked cross-country or basketball better in high school he shook his head and said, "Have you ever heard anyone say that they *enjoyed* cross-country? You don't see a lot of people smiling at a cross-country meet."

Harris was counting on the two juniors, Spatola, and another sophomore, Jonte Harrell, to provide the bulk of his team's points. He knew that scoring would be critical if the Cadets were to improve on the 8-19 records they had posted in Harris's first two seasons. Army always played good half-court defense because half-court defense is about work and attitude. But it always struggled to score because scoring is about athletic ability and having the quickness and strength to get good shots. Harris knew his team would do a good job stopping other teams. He just wasn't certain how they would do when they had the basketball.

Spatola and Clark could shoot. Harrell had pretty good quickness. Barrett, undersized as he was, could be hard to guard inside. Another sophomore, Charles Woodruff, had flashed some potential. He liked two of his freshmen, six-one guard Michael Canty and wide-bodied six-seven freshman Adam Glosier. If the seven of them could produce with some consistency and the other players could chip in here and there on offense, the chance to be better was there.

The question was how much better.

Army had won four Patriot League games in 1999, matching its highest victory total in nine years of league play. Two of those victories had come over Lehigh, which wasn't surprising since Lehigh had gone 0-12 in conference play. Army's overall record in the Patriot League was 29-129. The only school it didn't have a losing record against? Lehigh. The schools had split eighteen games.

Lehigh had played basketball for ninety-seven years. Twice, it had reached the NCAA Tournament, the first time in 1985 with a 12-19 record. The second time, in 1988, the team was 21-10 and was led by the school's two all-time leading scorers, Darren Queenan and Mike

Polaha. That was the only 20-victory season in school history. In fact, Lehigh has had seven winning seasons since 1940.

Basketball has never come close to being the number one sport at Lehigh. The school has been nationally ranked in wrestling for years. There is little doubt that Stabler Arena, which opened in 1979, is the only Division I basketball facility in America that has the word *advantage* on the scoreboard — advantage being a wrestling term.

Lehigh must also be one of the few — if not the only — Division I school in the country that actually acknowledges the struggles it has had in basketball in its media guide. Most media guides read as if the school has been to the Final Four on an almost annual basis. In the 1999–2000 Lehigh media guide is a letter from Athletic Director Joe Sterrett. The first paragraph of this letter states: "At various points in our long history, Lehigh basketball has seemed to struggle for full and proper recognition as a sport of significance and great tradition here on South Mountain. This struggle has been somewhat mysterious in light of the outstanding individuals and outstanding coaches who have shared the Lehigh experience."

The letter then goes on to explain a new commitment made by the university (read: scholarships) to Lehigh basketball. Even so, it is unusual to say the least.

Never had The Lehigh Struggle been more apparent than during the 1998–99 season. The Mountain Hawks — the school changed its nickname from Engineers in 1997 because it didn't want to be known as just a school for prospective engineers — seemed to be headed in the right direction as the season began.

Sal Mentesana was in his third year as coach, having come down the road from Division II East Stroudsburg in 1996 to replace Paul Duke. Lehigh had gone 4-23 in 1996 and Sterrett was looking for a coach who knew something about rebuilding and about Lehigh. Mentesana fit the bill. He had grown up in Easton as a Lehigh fan, had graduated from Providence in 1969, and had gotten his first head coaching job at Notre Dame High School in Easton in 1975. There, he had taken over a team that had won three games in two years. Four years later, he won the league championship. From there, he had moved on to Lehigh, where he worked for Brian Hill for four years. When Hill left for Penn State and later the NBA, Mentesana could have replaced him at Lehigh but decided to take a job at William and Mary as Bruce Parkhill's number one assistant. He stayed there until 1987 when East Stroudsburg, which had been averaging four victories a year, offered him a chance to be a college head coach. This time, he felt ready. After going 6-21 in his first season, Mentesana was 129-94 the next nine and took East Stroudsburg to its first NCAA Division II Tournament.

That resume was what Sterrett was looking at when he hired Mentesana. He had a track record of turning bad situations into good ones and that was what Sterrett thought — knew — Lehigh needed. Mentesana's first game as the Lehigh coach was at Duke. Welcome to the big time. "The good news," he said, looking back, "was that I figured we'd gotten the worst loss out of the way first."

Worst in terms of margin perhaps, but not the most frustrating. With no seniors and seven freshmen, Lehigh won one game that season, finishing 1-26. A year later, though, with the freshmen maturing and guard Brett Eppeheimer beginning to emerge as a star in the Patriot League, the record was 10-17. That might not sound like much but the nine-win jump was the largest in Division I that season. That was why Mentesana seemed to have legitimate hope when his third season, 1998–99, began.

Sure enough, the team got off to a 5-3 start, even though starting forward Fido Willybiro went down in the second game with a knee injury. That was damaging, but bearable. What wasn't bearable was Eppeheimer's knee injury, suffered in a rout of Division III Drew University. Eppeheimer was a legitimate player-of-the-year candidate in the league and was averaging 22.2 points per game when he got hurt. During the next two months, every Lehigh starter missed at least one game and during one six-game stretch three starters were out.

When you are Lehigh there is no margin of error. To compete, everything has to go right. Instead, nothing went right. The Mountain Hawks began losing games by huge margins — Army by 18; Columbia by 20; Bucknell by 17; Colgate by 15; not to mention the two Navy debacles. They did manage to get their act together for the home game against Lafayette, losing by just 73-70, as Aylsworth had another of his All-American vs. Lafayette nights with 31 points and seven rebounds.

They lost eighteen straight times before the miracle win over Navy in the league tournament salvaged something from a lost season. The next day against Bucknell, they appeared ready to pull off a second straight miracle, leading by 5 with eight minutes left. But seconds after draining a 3-pointer to put his team up by 5, Jared Hess, the team's best shooter, went down with a separated shoulder. Bucknell took over from there, winning 58-50.

The Navy win made the summer bearable. At least they had gotten something in return for their effort all winter. With four freshmen coming in — two of them, Matt Logie and Tanner Engel, the school's first scholarship players — and four experienced seniors returning, there was reason to believe the new season might be different.

Mentesana certainly hoped so. Even though his three-year record was 17-65, he knew he didn't have to worry about losing his job. Sterrett understood that the program was a work in progress, one that had suffered serious setbacks the previous year. "I just want to win for the sake of my sanity and the kids' sanity," Mentesana said one afternoon in October. "We've lost a lot of basketball games the last three years. It hasn't been a lot of fun. When you work this hard at something, you'd like to see some return. I'm not saying I expect to win twenty, but fifteen would be nice."

The fall had not been easy for Mentesana. His mother had been in and out of the hospital on several occasions and, since she lived alone, he had spent a lot of time at her house taking care of her when she wasn't in the hospital. It had been draining and exhausting but Mentesana thought it important that he do it rather than have his mother end up in a nursing home. "Her independence is important to her," he said. "And I don't blame her. I just have to help her any way I can."

Equally troubling in a completely different way was the illness of assistant coach Al Keglovitz. A year earlier, Keglovitz had been diagnosed with brain cancer. He had undergone chemotherapy and appeared to be in remission. But in the fall, the tumors had reappeared. Keglovitz was now undergoing experimental treatments, since standard therapy hadn't worked. He was forty-seven, had two teenage children, and was very popular with the players. Just talking about what Keglovitz was going through was difficult for Mentesana.

On most days, Mentesana is a hail-fellow-well-met, outgoing and funny. His one passion in life other than basketball is expensive clothes. Mentesana may not have the talent or the resume of Mike Krzyzewski or Tom Izzo or Bob Knight or Roy Williams. But none of them can touch him when it comes to clothes. "I'm an addict," he said. "I go into a store with nice clothes and I can't stop myself."

Other coaches in the Patriot League marveled at his wardrobe. "I feel completely outclassed every time we play them," Don DeVoe said. "I come out in my blue blazer and he comes out in Armani and he looks great. It's not even a contest."

Of course Mentesana would gladly trade his wardrobe for DeVoe's in return for some of DeVoe's players . . . maybe.

As practice began, he knew he had a new challenge ahead of him. There was talent on this team, but it was going to have to be blended. The four seniors might not be as talented as the four freshmen, but they had experience the freshmen didn't have. What's more, he owed it to the seniors to give them every chance to walk away from Lehigh on an up note after three years that had been filled with so many downers.

"We're running out of time," Hess said one day. "None of us wants to leave here feeling as if we never really got anything done. We have a chance to be good this year. But it's our last chance."

6

LET'S TALK MONEY

OTHER than Don DeVoe and his ten-year contract, the two most secure coaches in the Patriot League had to be Fran O'Hanlon and Pat Flannery. O'Hanlon had produced a near-miraculous turnaround at Lafayette, going from 7-20 in his first season to 22-8 and the NCAA Tournament in his fourth. Flannery hadn't been as spectacular at Bucknell, but he had been remarkably consistent: in five seasons, his teams had never finished lower than third in the league. His best record had been 18-11; his worst 13-15.

Lafayette and Bucknell had played in the 1999 Patriot League championship game. Lafayette had won a taut, tension-filled game, 67-63. Bucknell might very well have won the game if Tyson Whitfield hadn't tossed in a seventy-five-foot bomb at the halftime buzzer to cut a 7-point lead to 4, turning the momentum of the game around.

The matchup came at a critical time in the evolution of the league. Holy Cross had just finished its first season with scholarship players and was in the process of hiring Ralph Willard, causing rumors to fly that the school wasn't long for the Patriot League. Lehigh was about to bring in its first scholarship class in the fall. At Lafayette, Bucknell, and Colgate there was considerable tension over the scholarship issue.

"We're sort of all holding on to each other's hands and saying, 'You aren't going to crack, are you?'" Colgate athletic director Mark Murphy said. "There's a lot of looking over our shoulders going on."

Murphy believed that he had almost talked his president, Fred Dunlap, into going the scholarship route for basketball based on the Joe Sterrett–improve-academics-through-scholarships model. But Dunlap had retired and been replaced by Charles Karelis, who was virulently antischolarships. Bucknell was also in transition because president William Adams had resigned, effective at the end of the school year. Lafayette president Arthur Rothkopf was an ardent believer in the original Patriot League model: need-based scholarships only.

"I think last year's championship game proves that you can compete without scholarships," he said. "I know it isn't easy, but it is doable."

But for how long? That was the concern O'Hanlon and Flannery both had, although O'Hanlon was more low-key about it. "It's a catch-22 situation," Flannery said. "As long as we have winning seasons and finish in the top half of the league, people will say we don't need scholarships. But if the schools giving scholarships now jump ahead of us and we drop near the bottom of the league, what happens then? Do Fran and Emmett and I get fired and the next guy gets scholarships? Or do we just dig in our heels and say it's okay to lose as long as we're not giving scholarships?"

The difficulties of running a nonscholarship program had been driven home to O'Hanlon once again during the summer, when he had received a phone call from Lafayette's financial aid office. Brian Ehlers's older brother, Tom, had graduated from Princeton. Since his parents were now paying college tuition for one son instead of two, Ehlers's "package" for his senior year would be cut almost in half, from $17,000 to about $9,000. That meant that the Patriot League player of the year would be paying $23,000 to attend school.

Exactly how much Ehlers's play had been worth to Lafayette in dollars and cents was difficult to calculate. But he had been the key player on a team that had made the NCAA Tournament, given the school exposure on national television twice, taken attendance from close to nothing to regular sellouts at home, and had made Lafayette alumni around the country feel good about their school — a boon, no doubt, to fund-raising. None of that mattered. The formula said the

Ehlers family now had more money available so they had to pay higher fees.

As long as all five nonmilitary academies in the league weren't giving scholarships, everyone was playing on a level field. Now, that field had been tilted. Already the coaches at the three nonscholarship schools were noticing skepticism from recruits and their families when they started talking about "packages," the term used to describe financial aid. In the past, they could simply cite league policy as the reason they couldn't offer an athletic scholarship. Now it was more complicated than that.

For the moment at least, the three nonscholarship schools seemed to be on firm ground. They had finished 1-3-4 in the league standings in 1999 and had solid players in the program. But knowing that Holy Cross and Lehigh, who had taken turns sharing the bottom rungs in the league with Army in recent years, would certainly improve made everybody nervous. The subject of expansion also tended to send eyes darting around the room. The league had hired a new executive director that summer, Carolyn Schlie Femovich. She had walked into her new job with an immediate mandate to find an eighth school — at least. As Femovich began talking to presidents, one thing became readily apparent: no one had any interest in joining the league if it meant giving up their scholarships. All of which made the coaches at Bucknell, Lafayette, and Colgate just a little more uptight when they thought about the future.

Flannery had other things on his mind as practice began. The memory of his team's close call in the final against Lafayette was still fresh in his mind. Bucknell had five returning seniors — more than anyone in the league — four of whom would be starters. Flannery knew how good Lafayette was going to be and he assumed that Navy would also be good, but he had vowed to make the season memorable for the seniors. And he — and they — knew the only way to do that was to win the Patriot League championship.

"It doesn't seem fair that your whole season ends up being judged on what you do in three days," said Valter Karavanic, one of the senior starters. "But in this league, that's the way it is. We may know that we had a good season if we don't win, and we can get some satisfaction from that. But the way we'll be looked at is simple: Did you make the NCAA Tournament?"

Karavanic was one-third of a trio of senior starters who had consistently been honor students at Bucknell. Brian Muckle carried a GPA of 3.6, as did Dyrika Cameron. Karavanic, whose major was electrical engineering, had a 3.8. His teammates complained that he never had to work very hard to get his grades, either. "It's one of those things," Karavanic said. "If you understand engineering, you can get a lot of the work done in class. I've always done that. It's really not all that hard."

Sure. If you understand engineering.

The fourth senior starter was Dan Bowen, who had a 2.8 GPA and liked to refer to himself as the class dummy. Bowen was bright, funny, and articulate — and the best player in the group. At six-nine, with good hands and the ability to play facing the basket, Bowen was a good enough player to think about playing professionally overseas when he graduated. "I might do that for a couple of years," he said, smiling. "Unless, of course, I go in the first round of the NBA draft. Then I might have to give that a shot."

Karavanic also had a shot to play overseas if he so desired. Being Croatian he would have the advantage of not counting against a team's limit of American players (usually three in European leagues). But he wasn't counting on it. He had lived in the United States since his junior year of high school and had adjusted to the American lifestyle quite comfortably. Still, he wasn't sure if he wanted to live in the United States once he started a family.

"There's not as much time at home with your family here," he said. "There's so much more time spent commuting and working late. In Europe, the commute is shorter and you leave your office at five o'clock every day. There's more ritual to it. I'm used to being here now, but I could easily see being back there too."

Karavanic grew up in the southern part of Croatia, near the Italian border. As a high school sophomore, he went to a boarding school in Milan so he could play for an Italian club team there. He was spotted by Rob Meurs, one of the many men who scout in Europe and recommend young players to high schools and colleges in the United States. Meurs called Karavanic's house one night during the summer to ask him if he had any interest in playing ball and going to school overseas.

"At first I thought it was one of my friends playing a joke," Karavanic remembered. "I was telling him I'd love to go, when could he get me a plane ticket. After a while, I realized the guy was serious."

Karavanic's parents were delighted that their son might have the opportunity to leave home. This was 1994 and Croatia was being torn apart by the civil war that had split Yugoslavia. Before leaving for Milan, Karavanic and his schoolmates were often herded out of their classroom into nearby bomb shelters during the day when air raid sirens went off. "It was awful," he said. "We would just sit there and wait and wait, doing nothing. Then we'd go back to class."

The war seemed to be getting closer and closer to Pula, the town of about 70,000 where the Karavanic family lived. If he stayed home, Karavanic would be compelled to join the Croatian army when he graduated from high school. The United States was an escape from all that.

He landed eventually at St. Benedict's Prep in Newark, an inner-city boys' school that was about 90 percent African American. Karavanic had never met a black person. He spoke English, but he didn't speak American, especially street American. "The first couple weeks I was there, I would hear guys say, 'Hey, dog, what's up?' " he remembered. "I couldn't understand what they were talking about because there were no dogs around."

While he was adjusting to American life slowly, Karavanic had little trouble adjusting academically. Like most Europeans, he was shocked at how easy American schools were. "At home I took about fourteen or fifteen courses and I took them for a whole year," he said. "I got to St. Benedict's and they said I had to choose four courses. I said: 'Choose, I get to choose? And I only have to choose *four?*' Wow. I could handle that."

And so he had. Foreign players almost always do very well academically once they acclimate themselves to speaking and writing in English every day. Karavanic had only two problems when he first arrived at St. Benedict's: no girls and figuring out which neighborhoods not to frequent.

St. Benedict's is not a boarding school. Karavanic was one of two foreign students, so he was assigned a room in the administration building with the other foreign student — a soccer player. On his first night, Karavanic's roommate had gone off to soccer practice. Bored and alone, Karavanic decided to take a walk. He had no idea what he was doing, so he wandered into one of Newark's tougher neighborhoods looking for something to eat. He found a market, bought himself a sandwich and a Pepsi, and headed back to school. As he was leaving he was stopped by three men.

"Want to buy a watch or some jewelry, kid?" one of them asked.

"I don't know, maybe," Karavanic said, figuring this was the United States, so why shouldn't people sell watches on the street.

Hearing his accented English and thinking they had a real mark on their hands, the men produced a watch for Karavanic to examine. How much, they asked, would he pay for it.

"Well, actually, I just spent all my money," Karavanic said. "But I can give you a Pepsi for it."

He made it back to St. Benedict's without further incident. When Hank Cordeiro, his coach, found out where he had been, he told Karavanic in no uncertain terms that if he ever got hungry again to call him first.

The next day, Karavanic walked into an assembly for the entire school that began the first day of classes. Looking around, he noticed something was missing from the room. "Where," he asked someone sitting next to him, "are all the girls?"

"There are no girls," he was told.

"If they had told me that before I came, I might not have come over," he said, laughing at the memory.

He adjusted. He learned that not all dogs had four legs. There were places around town to meet girls. And, once basketball practice began, his life had structure and purpose. "I was still homesick," he said. "The toughest part was knowing that I couldn't go home. I was just *there*. It wasn't like Milan, where I could get home in a few hours anytime I really wanted to."

He began to learn about American basketball. In Pula, one TV station would show an hour a week of American sports highlights. Karavanic knew about two college teams: Duke and North Carolina. Like every Croatian, he had worshiped Drazen Petrovic, the Olympic star who had become a top NBA player only to die in an automobile acci-dent in 1993. Now, for the first time, he was exposed to a lot of basketball.

"I really liked Kentucky," he said, "because they shoot the ball all the time. Lots of threes."

Threes were Karavanic's specialty. At six-seven, he was the tallest player St. Benedict's had, so he had to play inside a lot. But what he liked doing best was wandering the perimeter and flicking his soft, lefty jumper from outside the 3-point line. It seemed close to him after growing up with the international 3-point line, which is almost a foot farther out than the U.S. line.

Colleges began to notice him. He had good grades, solid boards even though he "struggled" on the verbal, and a soft jump shot. Clemson was interested, which thrilled Karavanic because he knew by now they were in the same league with Duke and North Carolina. By his senior year, when things got serious, the schools pursuing him were smaller Division Is: nearby St. Peter's, Monmouth, and several Patriot League schools, most notably Bucknell.

He really liked Monmouth Coach Wayne Szoke but when he visited Bucknell — even though it rained all weekend — he was hooked. "It just felt so comfortable," he said. "It was almost like being home. Everyone was friendly and outgoing. I knew it was where I wanted."

Bucknell is one of those places that *looks* like a college. Once you turn in the gate off Route 15, in Lewisburg, Pennsylvania, there's no doubt that you are on a college campus. The buildings are set into a hill and the place oozes charm. It is small — 3,400 students — but there's plenty of room to walk around, to feel as if you have escaped from the real world outside the campus gates. Coming from the inner-city atmosphere of St. Benedict's, it is no wonder Karavanic fell in love with the place.

He was part of a key recruiting class for Flannery, who had just completed his first season at his alma mater. As obvious as the move had seemed when he made it, Flannery almost turned the job down. He had been coaching for five years at Division III Lebanon Valley — about an hour down the road from Bucknell — and had just gone 28-4, won the national championship, and been voted Division III national coach of the year.

Then his old college coach, Charlie Woollum, left Bucknell for the job at William and Mary. A lot of Bucknell alums thought it natural to bring Flannery back. He had two Bucknell degrees, his wife was a Bucknell grad, and he had proven he could get the job done in an academically oriented environment. Flannery wasn't so sure that Rick Hartzell, then the athletic director, saw things quite that way. Hartzell worked in the winters as an ACC referee and knew a lot of people in a lot of big-time programs. Flannery thought that Hartzell might want to hire an ACC assistant coach rather than a Division III head coach.

He went through the interview process at Bucknell, met with the search committee and with Hartzell. He actually found Hartzell to be more enthusiastic and warm than he expected. But as he drove back to Lebanon Valley something in his gut told him this wasn't the right move for him and his family. He pulled off the road, found a phone, called Hartzell, and asked him to withdraw his name from consideration. Hartzell was surprised.

When Flannery got home and told Patti, his wife, about his decision she didn't try to talk him out of it. But she did point out that it would be difficult to reach the same high at Lebanon Valley that had come with a national championship. And even though they had made a lot of friends at the school, they both had roots at Bucknell. Flannery called Hartzell one more time: could he un-withdraw? Again, Hartzell understood. A week later, Flannery had the job.

Woollum had left the program on solid footing. The junior and senior classes had talent. But Flannery needed to reload after his second season. Bowen, Muckle, Karavanic, Cameron, and Shaun Asbury had been that reload. They had been the guts of the team for most of four years. Now they had one chance left to play in the NCAAs.

"Back home in Manchester [New Hampshire] no one knows what the Patriot League is," Bowen said. "They ask me all the time: 'Is that Division I?' I understand. Until Bucknell started recruiting me, I would have asked the same question. But if we ever got into that NCAA bracket and they saw us in there against North Carolina or Duke or someone like that, it would be different. A lot different."

That was what made playing in the Patriot League tough at times. As the players gathered in the fall, playing their preseason pickup games, putting in hours and hours in the weight room, trying to figure out how to balance their class time with study time and basketball time, they knew that their fate would be decided by those three days in March.

"It may not be fair that we're judged that way," Bowen said. "But it's a fact."

No coach in the Patriot League had walked into a more difficult situation when he had taken his job than Emmett Davis. Succeeding a successful coach was never easy. Succeeding a successful and popular coach was very difficult. Succeeding a successful, popular coach who had died tragically of cancer was a monumental task.

Jack Bruen had been very much looking forward to the 1997–98 basketball season. On the face of it, he would be facing an uphill task, since Adonal Foyle, the greatest player in the history of Colgate, had decided to pass on his senior year to turn pro. Foyle had been a coach's dream come true. He was a superb, though raw, talent, a fabulous student — he was a two-time Academic All-American — and someone who brought national attention to a tiny school that spent most of the winter buried under snowdrifts in central New York.

But it hadn't been quite that simple. Bruen liked Foyle, loved coaching him, and was grateful for the back-to-back Patriot League titles and NCAA bids his presence had brought to Colgate. But by the time Foyle was a junior, Bruen's relationship with him and with his legal guardians, Jay and Joan Mandle, had started to sour.

The story of the Mandles and Foyle had been well chronicled. They were Colgate professors, who had "discovered" Foyle as a teenager on tiny St. Vincent's island. Foyle had been playing in a summer tournament in which the Mandles were working as referees. A friendship had started there that had led to Foyle's eventually moving in with the Mandles in Hamilton in order to pursue his education — both in basketball and the liberal arts. Foyle had become a top high school prospect while playing at Hamilton High School and was the subject of a fierce recruiting battle nationwide.

He chose Colgate over Duke and nearby Syracuse and received national attention for saying he had chosen Colgate because academics were more important to him than basketball. That comment didn't make Duke Coach Mike Krzyzewski terribly happy, especially given his school's academic reputation and graduation rate. "He chose Colgate because his guardians teach there," Krzyzewski said, "which I have no problem with. What I have a problem with is the notion that this was some kind of books-over-basketball decision. Colgate's a good school, but last time I looked it wasn't Harvard. And I think our library is still open down here."

Everything Krzyzewski said was true. And the Mandles' influence on Foyle has never been disputed by anyone who has come into contact with the troika. But Foyle makes an interesting point when he talks about his decision. "I know Duke is a very good school," he said. "I know how good a coach Coach K is. But when I visited there, every player I talked to had chosen Duke because they thought it was the best place for them to play basketball. Clearly, basketball came first for all of them. I knew I would graduate from there, but I just didn't feel I would fit in being in an environment where everyone around me thought of himself as a basketball player first and foremost. At Colgate, I knew basketball would be important, I knew we would work hard, but it wouldn't be *everything*."

For two years everything went as planned at Colgate. Bruen put together a brutal nonconference schedule so Foyle could test himself against top players. The Red Raiders did very well against Patriot League competition — 25-6 his first two seasons — in large part because Foyle was a man among boys. "I still remember the first time I saw him on the court," said Lehigh's Jared Hess. "He was huge. I mean, I've seen guys six-ten, but not built like this, not this strong. On one play, he went up to dunk and I just got out of the way. But he dunked the ball so hard it bounced straight off the floor and hit me in the face."

By Foyle's junior year, the tension between the troika and Bruen was evident. Foyle and the Mandles believed he needed to play facing the basket in order to prepare himself for the NBA. Bruen needed a low-post player in order to win basketball games, which he saw as his primary responsibility. Foyle now says there had been an understanding between the Mandles and Bruen when Foyle chose

Colgate that he would do whatever needed to be done to help Foyle get ready for the next level. Bruen isn't around to respond.

Agreement or no agreement, no one at Colgate was very happy that winter. With Foyle and Bruen at odds, the team played poorly, finishing a disappointing third in the Patriot League. Then they got bounced from the conference tournament by Bucknell in the semifinals, losing 71-58, to finish the season 12-16. That proved to be Foyle's last game at Colgate. He announced a few weeks later that he would pass up his senior season to put his name into the NBA draft.

"It had gotten to the point where there was no sense in any of us going through another year like that one," Foyle said. "I was unhappy, Jay and Joan were unhappy, Jack was unhappy. I thought I was ready."

Whether he was ready or not, he was the eighth player chosen in the draft, the first pick of the Golden State Warriors. His departure meant that Colgate would go from a preseason number one pick in the league to someplace in the middle of the pack. That was okay with Bruen. The pressure was finally off. No more arguing with Adonal and the Mandles; he could just coach. Colgate had been 18-10 and 17-12 in the two years before Foyle arrived, so Bruen was confident he could have success after his departure.

The pain started during the summer. At first he thought it was nothing more than the kind of back and shoulder miseries that come with being forty-eight and trying to play as much golf as possible while the weather is warm. By September, when Bruen traveled to Boston with Mark Murphy for the annual Colgate golf outing, Bruen couldn't take a full swing with a golf club. All he could do was putt. "When I saw that," Murphy said. "I began to get worried. For Jack not to play golf, something had to be seriously wrong."

By the end of October, everyone knew just how seriously wrong: it was pancreatic cancer and it had spread. Needless to say, the prognosis was awful. A lot of people thought that Bruen would resign and use whatever time he had left to travel with his wife, Joan, or to spend more time with his eight-year-old-son, Danny. That wasn't what Bruen wanted. He fully intended to spend as much time with Joan and Danny as he could, but the one thing he wanted to do most was coach.

Bruen coached his last game five days before he died. The players knew what was going on and they played inspired basketball in the early days of the season, opening with victories over Dartmouth and Cornell, then giving Syracuse the kind of scare that had become a thing of the past in the rivalry. Syracuse finally won the game, 78-74. On December 13, Colgate beat Marist 80-69 at home.

That was Bruen's last game. He had said he would stay with the team as long as he felt healthy enough to coach. He had now gone past that point. "Deep down we all knew," said Pat Diamond, who was a sophomore on that team. "He wasn't even getting on us anymore. That wasn't Coach."

Bruen was famous for his tirades and his sense of humor. Longtime Colgate sports information director Bob Cornell remembers the night he called time-out to yell at a wayward guard who had just thrown a crosscourt pass setting up a layup at the other end. "If I ever put you back into a game," Bruen ranted, "I want you to take the ball the first time you touch it and throw it into the tenth row!"

"Why, Coach?"

"Because that's a better place to throw it than where you threw it just now!"

When the tirades stopped, the players knew the end was near. On the night of December 18, Diamond showed up at Bruen's house. To this day, he's not sure what made him go that night, he just remembers thinking it was the right thing to do. Joan Bruen answered the door, let Diamond in, and went upstairs to see if Jack could handle a visitor. In reality, she said later, he probably couldn't. But it was one of his boys. She led Diamond up the stairs. Diamond sat on the bed with his coach for a few minutes and they talked about the past, even a little about the future. Bruen didn't make any Win-one-for-the-Gipper pleas, but he asked Diamond to tell his teammates how much he was going to miss coaching them. Diamond could see that Bruen was tired and weak, so he said good night softly and walked back into the frigid night feeling as sad as he could ever remember feeling.

Jack Bruen died a few hours later. Every nook and cranny of the Colgate chapel was filled for the funeral, three days before Christmas. Coaching friends and ex-players had flown in from all over the country. It was as cold a day in Hamilton as anyone could remember — which is saying a lot — the wind whipping down from the top of the campus, knocking the mourners backward as they slowly made their way up the hill to the Colgate cemetery. Bruen was buried at the very top of the cemetery, his headstone looking straight down at the campus and the town he had come to love so much.

Bruen's top assistant, Paul Aiello, took over the team for the rest of the season. It was an impossible situation for everyone. The players were drained by what they had been through, as were the coaches, who had no idea what the future held for them. Ideally, Murphy would have promoted Aiello, but the team was 7-15 the rest of the way under him and Murphy wondered if a fresh start wasn't the best thing for everyone — including the coaches. Memories of Bruen always made people smile, but this soon after his death, they also made people cry.

When the season was over, Murphy put together a couple of search committees, one made up of four players, to interview coaching candidates. Aiello was one of the coaches interviewed, an awkward forty-five minutes for both the players and the coach. Diamond still remembers when Davis came to meet with the players.

"We had mixed emotions about it," he said. "On the one hand, he was from Navy and we hate Navy. On the other hand, we knew they weren't good by coincidence and if this guy had worked with Coach DeVoe he must know what he's doing. So, we tried to keep an open mind."

They liked what they saw and heard. Diamond laughs, remembering that his impression of Davis was "relaxed, laid back." Davis sat back in his chair while he talked to the players, an arm draped over the seat next to him, appearing to enjoy the give-and-take.

Little did the players know that Davis was anything but relaxed. He was thirty-eight and had been at Navy for twelve years, first under Pete Herrmann, then under DeVoe. He had interviewed in the recent past for the Lafayette job and for the Army job. Eve Atkinson, Lafayette's athletic director, was ready to hire him if Fran O'Hanlon had said no. "I remember Franny kind of wavering just before he took it," Atkinson said. "I finally told him, 'I need an answer now because I've got a guy who is very good, and ready to take it if you don't.'" O'Hanlon said yes. Davis might very well have gotten the

Army job if not for Mike Krzyzewski pushing for Pat Harris. Having been burned once by saying no to Don DeVoe, the Army search committee was very serious about Davis, whose approach to his interview was: "This is how you win at a military academy. We did it at Navy, I can do it at Army." Again, he made a great impression but came away without the job.

By the time he interviewed for the Colgate job, Davis was tired of making good impressions. He also felt it was time for him to move on. He had done about all he could at Navy, helping DeVoe turn the Midshipmen into the scourge of the Patriot League. What's more, he had grown up not far from Colgate in Gloversville and had gone to college at not-so-far-away St. Lawrence University. The cold winters in Hamilton wouldn't bother him.

Murphy liked everything about him. And so, on April 24, 1998, a little more than four months after Bruen's death, Davis was named to succeed him as Colgate's coach. He knew one thing for sure as soon as he took the job: he couldn't be Jack Bruen. As laid back as he might have come off to the players in his interview, Davis is anything but. He's more like DeVoe: intense, driven, always searching for a way to better his team. Away from the basketball court he has a lively sense of humor, but he is absolutely all business when it comes to basketball. The players quickly discovered that when he met with them after his hiring.

"It was pretty clear that things were going to be different than they were with Coach Bruen," Diamond said. "We liked him, but there was no doubt he was different."

Across the country the word reached Adonal Foyle that a Navy assistant coach had been hired to replace Bruen. "A Navy guy?" Foyle said in disbelief. "They hired a Navy guy? Wow. He better be good."

Emmett Davis understood.

7

THE CHAMPS

ALTHOUGH Fran O'Hanlon may have had some serious concerns about the long-term future of basketball at Lafayette, he had to admit — quietly of course — that the immediate future was worthy of some equally serious optimism.

Lafayette was in a unique position. It was the first team in the history of college basketball to field a team that had two returning conference players of the year. In 1998, Stefan Ciosici had been the Patriot League player of the year. When he had been forced to sit out 1999 after knee surgery, Brian Ehlers had stepped into his starring role and had succeeded him as player of the year.

Now they were both back as seniors, along with a solid, experienced core of players. Naturally, the Leopards were the unanimous pick to win the league title again. Naturally, that made O'Hanlon nervous. "You still have to play the games on the court," he said in his best coach-speak.

In truth, O'Hanlon had reasons for concern. Before his injury, Ciosici (pronounced Cho-sich) had become a dominating low-post presence, using his six-eleven, 260-pound body to clog the lane at both ends of the floor. Once he caught the ball near the basket, there were very few players in the Patriot League who could do much to stop him. Everything Lafayette did on offense revolved around Ciosici. There were very few possessions when he didn't touch the ball, either to shoot or to dish the ball back outside when he was double- or triple-teamed.

His absence had brought about a change in the offense. His replacements inside, Ted Cole and Frank Barr, didn't take up the space and were not the offensive players he had been. They didn't have to occupy the low post. That opened up the middle for Ehlers, who was good enough that defenses had to respect his outside shot but was most effective slashing to the basket.

Now, with Ciosici back, there might not be as much room for Ehlers and the others as there had been the year before. At the very least, there would be a period of adjustment for everybody. O'Hanlon wasn't going to lose much sleep over a problem like that. He was thrilled to have Ciosici back, in part because he believed Lafayette would ultimately be a better team with him but also because he knew what Ciosici had gone through to get back on the basketball court.

Ciosici is one of those people whose personality completely belies his appearance. Because he is huge and wears his hair in a buzz cut, he is an intimidating presence anytime he walks into a room. Add the Romanian accent and you might think he was invented by a mad scientist rather than born, an only child, to Doru and Maria Ciosici in 1976.

Doru and Maria Ciosici were both physical education teachers in Timisoara, a city of about 400,000 people. Stefan was always a big kid, and like most Europeans, he started out playing soccer. When the local basketball coaches spotted him, they dragged him to the basketball court since he was taller than anyone else in the schoolyard. "At first I hated it," he said. "I was terrible. I had no idea what I was doing. But after a while I started getting better and didn't want to stop playing."

He kept playing as he kept growing, reaching six-eleven by the time he was a sophomore in high school. By then he was playing for one of the top club teams in Romania and also making close to straight As at the local high school. "There wasn't any choice about the schoolwork, since my parents were teachers," Ciosici said. "They made it very clear to me that if my work or my grades ever slipped there wouldn't be any more sports."

Being six-eleven and playing on a good team, Ciosici was spotted by a number of scouts, who in turn informed a number of American college coaches. One of those coaches was Fran O'Hanlon, who was then an assistant coach at Pennsylvania. O'Hanlon had played and coached in Europe for fourteen years after graduating from Villanova and had a lot of contacts there. When one of them told him about a six-eleven Romanian kid who was an A student, he went into action.

"The first thing I had to find out was if our financial aid department would offer aid to a foreign student," he said. "They said they would if he qualified, which he did. Then I got in touch with Stefan."

Ciosici and his parents were intrigued by the idea of an American college. Romania was still dealing with the massive changes that had come about in the wake of the overthrow of the Communist dictatorship in 1990. Ciosici was thirteen at the time and can still remember watching the execution of Nicolae Ceauşescu on television. "It was very graphic and very frightening," he said. "But we all knew what it meant."

Romania had changed greatly since then and had become a good deal more Americanized. Ciosici was being recruited very aggressively by both Penn and Davidson, another strong academic school. But he also had an offer to play for a club team in Germany. The team would pay for his education while he continued to develop as a player. It was much closer to home, he had relatives in Germany, and he would be surrounded by people with similar backgrounds to his. So he decided to play in Germany for at least a year and then decide if he still wanted to go to the United States.

The German team finished its season with a flourish and earned a promotion from the second division of the German league to the first division. Team management felt it needed to bring in more experienced players to compete in the first division rather than players who might need more time to develop. The offer to Ciosici was withdrawn. This was in late June. Desperate, he called Davidson. No scholarships left. Perhaps he could go to junior college for a year and reapply. That didn't work. He called Penn, looking for O'Hanlon, and was told O'Hanlon had left to become the head coach at some place called Lafayette. All of a sudden Ciosici had gone from multiple options to no options. The summer began to slip away. June became July, July became August.

Then his phone rang. It was O'Hanlon, calling from Lafayette. The Penn coaches had called to tell him that Ciosici might be looking for a place to play. Taking over a team that had just gone 2-25, O'Hanlon had plenty of spots. He sent Ciosici some brochures describing the school. Ciosici looked on a map and saw it was near New York City. O'Hanlon called a few days later to say the school had approved a full financial aid package if he wanted to come. Three weeks later, Ciosici was on a plane en route to the college he had never seen and the coach he had only talked to on the phone.

He was a couple of days late arriving and walked into his first class — turning every head in the room since no one at Lafayette had ever seen someone his size in a classroom — the day after he arrived. Soon after that, he reported to O'Hanlon with a quizzical look on his face.

"Coach, I'm confused," he said. "I went to my first class today and there were a couple of kids sitting there with hats on, turned backward."

"Uh-huh," O'Hanlon said.

"And there was another kid drinking a Coke."

"Yes."

"That's allowed?"

"Allowed? What do you mean allowed?"

Ciosici shrugged. "In my country you do that they'll probably shoot you."

Every day was a learning experience for Ciosici. Like Karavanic and other Europeans he was shocked by the light workload. His biggest problem was adapting his book English to American. On the first day of practice, O'Hanlon told the players to line up for wind sprints. Ciosici was baffled. How could you run wind sprints indoors with no wind? A couple of days later things got worse when O'Hanlon got exasperated and told everyone to line up for suicides. "Suicides?" Ciosici thought. "I left Romania to get away from violence."

He got the hang of things soon enough, although some of his European ways never changed. Midway through his senior season, O'Hanlon was driving through campus one day when he saw Ciosici walking on the other side of the quad. He slowed down and yelled hello to Ciosici, waving a hand at him as he did. Suddenly, Ciosici began sprinting across the quad at him. O'Hanlon wondered what could be wrong.

"Stef, what's wrong?" he asked when Ciosici pulled up to the car.

Ciosici looked baffled. "Nothing, Coach," he said. "Didn't you wave for me to come over here?"

The toughest adjustment for Ciosici was on the basketball court. The speed of the American game was completely different from anything he had seen in Europe, and he felt — his words — completely clueless on the court as a freshman. Still, he averaged better than 11 points and seven rebounds a game and was the Patriot League rookie of the year. Not too bad for being clueless.

He continued to improve and feel more at home as a sophomore and the team also improved, going from seven wins in O'Hanlon's first season to eleven his second. But it was the next year that both the team and Ciosici began to blossom. Ciosici became a dominant force inside, averaging 17 points a game, hitting better than 58 percent of his shots, and opening things up on the outside for teammates because he now had to be double-teamed (at least) every time he touched the ball.

The only downer that season was a 93-85 loss at Navy in the conference tournament final. Lafayette had won its last nine league games in a row — including a win at Navy — to tie for first with the Midshipmen at 10-2. Deciding who would be the top seed for the tournament was crucial, since the top seed would get to play the championship game at home if it got that far. The teams had split head-to-head and each had one loss to Bucknell. The last tiebreaker was a coin flip. Navy won the flip, got to host the final, and won a down-to-the-wire game. Ciosici was heartbroken. Everyone at Lafayette was frustrated, because all of them believed that a coin flip had ultimately determined the championship. It hardly seemed fair.

The consolation for Ciosici was that there was another chance. He had been voted Patriot League player of the year, and he and three other solid juniors would return along with Ehlers and Tim Bieg, who had taken over the point guard position early in his freshman season and had run the team like a four-year starter.

That summer, Ciosici, Ross Harms, and Tyson Whitfield went to work at Seton Hall's summer camp as counselors. Every night, after

the last session of camp, the counselors would play, the games beginning after ten and usually going on until about midnight. Late one
night, Ciosici came out to defend on someone as they went up for a
jump shot. To this day he can't — or won't — remember the name of
the player. As the shooter came down from his shot, he and Ciosici
got tangled and fell to the floor. Basketball players fall down thousands of times in their career. They almost always get right back up.

This time, Ciosici didn't. He had somehow landed badly, twisting
his knee into an awkward position. The pain shot right through him.
"I knew as soon as it happened that it was pretty bad," he said. "I just
didn't know how bad."

Briefly, he tried to get up. There was no way. Eventually he was
helped off the court and the Seton Hall trainers did what they could
to alleviate the pain. There was no way for them to know how serious
the injury might be. They suggested he go home, get into bed, and
hope that staying off it might get the swelling down. Ciosici was in
agony all night and couldn't get out of bed in the morning. When
Whitfield and Harms reported this to the Seton Hall people, they put
in a call to O'Hanlon.

As soon as he heard what had happened, O'Hanlon jumped into
his car and made the seventy-five-minute drive to Seton Hall. He
found Ciosici crumpled up in bed, his face pale with pain, his knee
looking like it had a basketball inside it. Ciosici managed to make it to
the car. O'Hanlon stretched him out as comfortably as possible in the
back seat of his Jeep. Ciosici had tears running down his face from
pain and frustration on the whole trip back to campus.

"He kept saying, 'Coach, I'm sorry, I'm really sorry,' as if he had
done something wrong," O'Hanlon said. "I tried to tell him that
unless he had hurt himself on purpose, there was nothing to be sorry
for."

The doctors at Lafayette told him the knee needed to be drained.
That would help with the pain and would also tell them how seriously
he was injured. "They said if the liquid in the knee was clear, it wasn't
a big deal," Ciosici remembered. "But if there was blood in it, we had
a problem."

The knee was drained. The doctors showed the results to Ciosici.
"Pure red," he said.

It was a torn anterior cruciate ligament, the worst kind of knee injury there is. It is an especially difficult injury for a big man because any loss of mobility can leave you virtually immobile. Ciosici would certainly be out for the 1998–99 season. The question was whether he would play again, and if so, could he be effective?

The other question was whether he could play for Lafayette even if the knee allowed him to play. Technically, there is no such thing in the Patriot League as a redshirt year, medical or otherwise. What's more, since Lafayette has no graduate programs, the school has a strict policy of eight semesters of financial aid and out. But there was a loophole. A student could apply for an extra year of financial aid if he or she decided on a double major. And, if an athlete sits out a year for medical reasons, he can apply to the league for a fifth year of eligibility. Ciosici cleared both hurdles. He added German to his original major, biology. Then he set about rehabbing the knee after surgery. In the meantime, basketball went on without him at Lafayette.

Everyone was shocked when they heard about what had happened to Ciosici. And yet, there was a sense that the team could still succeed without him. O'Hanlon felt almost as bad for the other three seniors, Ted Cole, Ross Harms, and Dave Klaus, as he did for Ciosici. They had all come out of the loss to Navy in March vowing to make 1999 their year. Now, the key to that year had been lost.

It was a measure of the respect Lafayette had gained throughout the league that even without Ciosici the Leopards were the preseason pick to finish first. "Easy for them to say," O'Hanlon joked.

But "they" knew what they were talking about. With Cole and rapidly improving seven-foot sophomore Frank Barr taking up the slack for Ciosici inside, with Ehlers emerging as a star (his teammates started calling him "Supe" halfway through the season — short for superstar), with Bieg and others playing important roles, Lafayette was the best team in the league. Once again they went 10-2 in conference play, this time earning the top seed outright — no coin tosses needed.

The team also had perhaps the two tallest managers in the history of college basketball: six-foot-eight-inch backup forward Nate Klinkhammer, who had hurt an elbow and was out for the season, and Ciosici. This was a long way from O'Hanlon's first season, when the team had been so bad that there had been no managers at all. By the second season, there were two managers, a great relief to assistant coach Pat Brogan, who no longer had to spend twenty minutes before practice each afternoon pulling the curtain that separated the basketball area of Kirby Field House from the track area into place.

Ciosici was sitting on the bench in street clothes when Lafayette beat Bucknell for the championship. At the end of the game, as everyone swarmed the floor to celebrate, the trainers told him to stay off the court because they didn't want him to risk reinjuring the knee in the postgame melee. And so, Ciosici had to watch the celebration, the same way he had watched the season.

"It was bittersweet," he said. "I was happy for my teammates, especially the three guys I had come into school with. But I didn't really feel as if I was part of it. I hadn't really contributed, except as a cheerleader. I wanted a chance to be a part of it."

That day, watching the nets come down, Ciosici made a promise to himself: he would get his own cut of the net before his college career was over.

The pundits were all predicting that Ciosici would get his net as practice got underway in the fall. If O'Hanlon rolled his eyes at the notion that his team would dominate the league, Ciosici had more serious concerns. Put simply, his knee still hurt.

It had taken him six months after the surgery to get back on the court, and then he had built back up carefully under the watchful eye of the Lafayette doctors and trainers. The rehab had been torturous, dull work, but he had kept at it because he knew it was the only way to get back to where he wanted to be. He had also realized during his time away how much he had come to love basketball. In the past it had been something he did because he was big and because he was good.

Now Ciosici wanted a chance to play professionally. But he knew he wasn't going to get that chance if the knee didn't improve. He didn't mind wearing the bulky brace the doctors had given him. What he did mind was walking down the hill to the gym in the afternoon and feeling so sore that he wasn't sure he'd be able to get into his practice uniform, much less run up and down the court.

The start of practice made the problem even more clear to him. One of O'Hanlon's favorite defensive drills involves wing denial — a big man coming out to the wing to deny a pass, then being able to peel back if the offensive player makes a backdoor cut. Before the injury, Ciosici had been able to consistently get to the wing to deny the initial pass, plant, and get back to cut off the backdoor. Now he could get to the wing, but when he had to plant and reverse direction, he simply couldn't do it. Time and again, he was beaten back-door. The coaches didn't get on him about it because they knew he was trying. But they noticed. Everyone noticed.

"It was hard to watch sometimes," Bieg said. "Because we all knew how hard he was trying and how far he had come just to get back on the court. But it was obvious he was still hurting."

Ciosici didn't mind some pain. What he minded was not being able to do the things on the basketball court that had come easily before the injury. After a while, he came to understand that the most difficult part of his rehab wasn't going to be the physical pain. It was going to be staying patient — over and over again.

O'Hanlon sat him down early in the fall to explain to him that the offense had changed in his absence and that it might take time for the team to readjust to his presence, that everyone would have to adjust to a different role as the team evolved.

Ciosici nodded and said he understood. "If I'm not starting, Coach, it's okay," he said. "I understand."

O'Hanlon burst out laughing. "Not starting?" he said. "You think I'm nuts? You were the player of the year in this league, Stefan. Don't forget that."

Ciosici was trying not to forget that. But every time the knee throbbed, it was a little bit harder to remember.

There were three other seniors at Lafayette, each a character in his own way. Klinkhammer looked like a big tough guy at six-eight, with his shock of red hair and a beard to match, but was the most soft-spoken member of the team, the one player O'Hanlon could count on to remember the "thought for the day" that he made a part of each day's practice plan. He was a vegetarian who read Milton and quoted

Einstein — among others — and had a complete understanding of his role on the team: back up the big guys, give up his body when necessary.

Mike Homer had been considered the star of O'Hanlon's first full recruiting class four years earlier. He had started eighteen games as a freshman, averaged 11.6 per game and had scored 22 points in a game at Maryland. Gary Williams, the Maryland coach, had predicted full-blooded stardom for Homer after the game when someone told him that the kid who had done all the scoring for Lafayette was just a freshman.

But Homer's playing time had slipped each season. He had gone from twenty-eight minutes a game to fourteen minutes a game to eleven minutes a game. He hadn't gotten worse, but the players around him had gotten better. "I remember an exhibition game Mike's freshman year in which he took twenty-three shots," O'Hanlon said. "We were fine with that because we didn't have anyone else willing to shoot the ball."

Like any competitior, Homer wasn't thrilled to see his playing time dwindle. But after going through periods of self-pity, anger, and frustration, he had made his peace with it. He was an art major with a decidedly artistic approach to life that allowed him to enjoy being part of the team even if his role wasn't as large as he wanted it to be.

Homer almost never said anything that was predictable. During his freshman season, the Leopards had made a post-Christmas trip to New Orleans to play in the Sugar Bowl basketball tournament. Since there was a day off between games, O'Hanlon had given the players a late curfew after their opening-round game against Tulane. Naturally, many of the players headed straight for Bourbon Street. Just as naturally a number of them had too much to drink. One of them, starting point guard Sam Gilbert, walked out of a bar with Homer right behind him and found himself staring straight at the backside of a mounted policeman. Perhaps inspired by *Blazing Saddles,* no doubt emboldened by alcohol, Gilbert hauled off and slugged the horse.

He didn't hurt the animal, but the mounted policeman saw no humor in the act. He leaped off the horse, grabbed Gilbert, pinned him against a wall, and began to put handcuffs on him as Homer watched in horror. Hearing the policeman tell Gilbert that he was under arrest, Homer ran up to the cop, pleading with him not to take Gilbert to jail.

"You can't arrest him, Officer," Homer pleaded. "You just can't."

"Why can't I?" the cop asked. "He assaulted my horse."

"Well, because, because . . . he's our starting point guard!"

Sadly, the policeman was not that concerned with who started at the point for Lafayette. It was several hours later before O'Hanlon could get Gilbert released. He was not happy with anyone involved in the incident. When he asked Homer how he could possibly allow his teammate to be led off to jail, Homer told him he had tried everything he could think of to prevent the arrest. "I felt as if I had failed the whole team," he said. "I should have told the cop that Sam was our leading scorer."

Homer's approach to basketball was probably best summed up by his answer on a questionnaire for the Lafayette media guide. In response to the question "What would you entitle your autobiography?" Homer's answer was "A Legend in My Own Mind."

Brian Ehlers didn't answer that question for the media guide. If he had, it might have been "The Sounds of Silence." To Ehlers, answering true or false was the essay portion of a test. Some athletes are quiet around the media and chatterboxes with their teammates. Not Ehlers. His teammates called him "The Silent Assassin," because he was a killer on the court but said very little before, during, or after a game.

It wasn't that Ehlers wasn't friendly. He was. He had an easy smile and was polite to a fault. He was so polite that he never corrected anyone when they mispronounced his name, including his own coaches. O'Hanlon had called him "El-lers" when he first arrived at Lafayette until someone had told him that the correct pronunciation was "A-lers." He asked Ehlers which he preferred and Ehlers shrugged and said, "Doesn't matter to me." O'Hanlon then asked his mom and dad. They said it didn't matter. So, he had continued calling him El-lers. Don DeVoe called him Ee-lers. Pat Flannery called him I-lers. Ralph Willard called him "What's-his-name-the-scorer."

Ehlers didn't care. They could call him anything they liked as long as he could play basketball every day and make as few speeches as possible. That had been the hard part of winning all the awards the previous year. He always had to make a speech.

The other funny thing about Ehlers was that when he first got to Lafayette, recruited out of Bay Shore High School on Long Island, O'Hanlon and Brogan had spent most of his first semester convinced they had recruited a dud. Ehlers was completely out of shape. He tired so quickly in practice that he could barely run up and down the court. Everything they had heard about what a hard worker he was in practice was quickly proven to be false.

They decided he had too much potential not to get his work habits turned around. They kept him late after practice; they made him run until he dropped; they screamed and yelled and called him names. The weird thing was, the kid never complained. He was willing to try to work, but no matter what they did, they couldn't seem to get him in better shape. Finally, completely desperate, O'Hanlon sent him to a doctor. Maybe something was wrong with him.

Something was wrong. Ehlers was iron deficient. That was why he couldn't run up and down the court. The coaches felt awful. They had been convinced the kid was a dog when, in fact, he was sick. Ehlers was put on medication and everything changed. He worked harder and longer than anyone on the team. By the end of the season he was starting and averaging in double figures. He kept getting better and better after that.

For a while O'Hanlon wondered why Ehlers hadn't said anything through all the screaming and yelling, hadn't told them that he *was* trying as hard as he could. "Of course then I realized, knowing Brian as I did by then, that he would never complain about anything. That's just not his way."

No, it wasn't. But asking Ehlers to explain why wasn't all that revealing. "Doesn't usually do much good to complain," he said with a shrug. "Never really changes anything except that people think you're a complainer."

No one would ever call Ehlers a complainer. Of course if they did, he wouldn't complain about it.

8

STARTING FROM THE BOTTOM

ONE of the suggestions Mike Krzyzewski had made to Pat Harris after Harris had been hired by Army had been that he start an annual series with Duke. Krzyzewski even volunteered to bring his team to West Point to inaugurate the Harris era.

If Harris had thought the idea terrible, he probably wouldn't have told his old coach. But he thought it was a good idea, especially since bringing Duke to the Holleder Center could do something that only the presence of Navy or orders that the Corps of Cadets show up (handed down by the West Point brass) could usually do: fill the place.

The Holleder Center sits directly across the street from Michie Stadium, one of the most hallowed places in college football. It is generally considered one of *the* places in the country to watch a college football game; in part, because Blanchard and Davis once played there. When *Sports Illustrated* put together a millennial list of the twenty best places in the world to watch a sporting event, Michie Stadium finished *third*, behind Yankee Stadium and the Augusta National Golf Club. That put it ahead of Wimbledon, Fenway Park, and any other college football venue on the planet — among others. Michie is almost always sold out or close to it, regardless of Army's record, because of its tradition, history, and aesthetics. The Holleder Center has no such aura.

Opened in 1985, it houses both the basketball and hockey teams in side-by-side arenas. Christl Arena, like Michie Stadium and the

Holleder Center, is named for a West Point graduate killed in battle. It seats 5,043. It has been sold out five times in fifteen years. Most nights, the crowd is less than 1,000, which means Army rarely has much of a home court advantage.

Harris had played in the old field house back in the days when the place was regularly packed to see Krzyzewski's teams play. He knows that part of the reason for the sparse crowds is the team's lack of success. But he also thinks location is a factor. The field house was located within easy walking distance of the cadet barracks. Holleder is on the other side of the post. "There was something cool about going down to the field house," Harris said. "There doesn't seem to be the same feeling about going *up* to the Holleder Center."

For Duke, though, the cadets would come. So would a lot of people. And so it was that Harris's first game as coach at his alma mater was played in front of a loud, sellout crowd of 5,055 — 12 more than capacity. Duke dominated the game, leading 35-9 at halftime and coasting to a 78-45 win, but that hardly seemed to matter. The Army players loved the charged atmosphere and there were moments for each of them to savor. Joe Clark, playing in his first college game, swished a 3-pointer. Seth Barrett, also in his first game, blocked a dunk attempt by Duke's Mike Chappell, sending the crowd into paroxysms of joy.

"It was one of those deals where you're playing harder than you've ever played in your life, you get beat by thirty-three, and you don't mind," Barrett said. "It was great, absolutely great."

In short, it was everything Krzyzewski and Harris had hoped it would be when they decided to play. Krzyzewski enjoyed being back at his alma mater and walking onto the court as the visiting coach to a standing ovation. Harris loved the enthusiasm of the entire day.

Now it was two years later. Scheduling problems had caused the schools to skip a year, so it was Army's turn to go to Duke. Bringing Duke to Christl to play was one thing, taking a team with no seniors and only two juniors to Cameron Indoor Stadium to open the season was another. "I'd feel a lot better about it if I was starting five seniors instead of two freshman, two sophomores, and a junior," Harris said.

The reason he was only starting one junior (Barrett) was that Joe Clark's foot was hurt *again*. After breaking his foot during the spring of his freshman year and then breaking the *screw* in his foot ten games into his sophomore season, he was having trouble with his foot again during preseason of his junior year. Team doctor Dean Taylor decided to put a new screw into the foot two weeks before the Duke game. Clark was finally starting to feel better, but wasn't going to be ready to play against Duke.

"I'm available for a game-winning shot," he told Harris during the team's game-day shootaround.

"I'm kind of hoping to be up eight in the last minute," Harris answered.

He knew an 8-point lead at any stage of the game was about as likely as Michael Jordan showing up that morning pleading for a try-out. This was actually an awful time to play Duke. The Blue Devils — and Krzyzewski — had been through a difficult off-season, during which three underclassmen had left for the NBA and a fourth had transferred. Krzyzewski had undergone surgery to replace his hip and Duke was starting the season with six freshmen among its ten scholarship players. The Blue Devils had opened the season in New York by losing to Stanford and Connecticut, both top-ten teams. Nonetheless, a team that had finished 37-2 a year ago was now 0-2 and coming back to Cameron for its home opener in a bad mood.

"They need to win and they need to play well," Harris said. "Their freshmen will be all pumped up playing their first game in here. Plus, I don't know how my guys will react to the atmosphere in this place."

The atmosphere in Cameron cannot really be described. It must be experienced. The building is sixty years old and allegedly seats 9,314. No one really knows the capacity because the students, who surround the court on all four sides, never sit on the bleacher seating provided them. The roof is low, meaning the noise has no place to go, and on a warm November day in which the temperature outside would hit 70 degrees, the place would be an oven at game time with so many people packed into it.

Even so, the Cadets were thrilled to be there. They all knew that someday they would tell their kids and grandkids about the day they played in Cameron Indoor Stadium against Coach K's team. Spatola, who had been in Cameron when it was empty dozens of times as a camper, was the unofficial tour guide during shootaround. He pointed out the national championship banners, all lit up at the far end of the court, and told stories from camp days. "Right here," he said, pointing to a spot opposite the Duke bench just outside the key, "is where JP fell and cut himself. He was bleeding all over the floor."

JP was Spatola's younger brother, a point guard at the Army Prep School whom the coaches were counting on for the following season. But that would be then, this was now, and Spatola would start along with Barrett, fellow sophomore Jonte Harrell, and freshmen Adam Glosier and Michael Canty.

Glosier was a six-seven wide-body whose potential the coaches loved. He had been projected as a starter all fall. Canty was starting in Clark's place but he had already been a pleasant surprise. Canty was a reed-thin six-one, 170, with a baby face that belied the kind of hard-nosed personality that fit right in at West Point in general and on the basketball team in specific. He was an excellent defender, especially for someone still learning the basic concepts of Army's man-to-man, and didn't seem intimidated by much of anything, including playing in Cameron.

His background may have had something to do with that. Canty was the third of five brothers and had been just five when his parents divorced. Ken Canty was a lawyer, a defense litigator, and he continued to live nearby, coming to see all the boys play in their games, even on the weekends when he didn't have visitation. Lucille Canty was a registered nurse. Just prior to Michael's junior year in high school, she joined the Air Force to further her career and was sent to San Antonio, Texas.

Dave, the oldest of the boys, was already in college by then. The other four boys went with their mother to San Antonio. Michael had a good year playing basketball at Central Catholic High School. He made all-state and was the league's co-MVP. But, like any sixteen-year-old, he missed his friends. So did his brothers. After one year it was decided that the boys would go back to Massachusetts and live with their father.

By now, Michael was thinking about college. His grades and board scores were good, but not great. He was smart enough to know that none of the big-time schools were going to recruit him, but he thought he had a chance to get into an Ivy League school or a Patriot

League school as a basketball player — if he could improve his academic standing. And so when Worcester Academy accepted him on the condition that he repeat his junior year, he didn't balk. "They wouldn't take you for less than two years," Canty said. "At first I thought, 'Hey, I don't want to go to high school for an extra year.' But then I realized that long term I would benefit."

He had a good repeat–junior year, in both basketball and the classroom. His board scores went up to almost 1200, his grades to close to 3.5. As he had hoped, those numbers, along with his outside shooting ability and hard-nosed approach to basketball, brought schools from the Ivy and Patriot Leagues to Worcester to see him play. By the time summer ball was over, Dartmouth, Columbia, Yale, Lafayette, Lehigh, Army, and Navy had all shown interest in him. Holy Cross, right on his doorstep, didn't.

That was okay with Canty, though, he had plenty of choices. Then, on a warm summer day just before everyone was supposed to go back to school, his older brother Matt, who had just finished his freshman year at St. Anselm College and was preparing to transfer to Old Dominion, took a curve too fast while en route to see his grandparents. His Acura swerved across a lane and was crushed by an oncoming Jeep.

Amidst all the moving around and with the tension that had existed for so many years between their parents, the Canty boys had become very close, especially Matt and Michael, who were a little more than a year apart. Matt's death was almost impossible for Michael to deal with. He couldn't concentrate on basketball or his schoolwork for long stretches. When he did find himself refocusing he would start to feel guilty about being able to do that. It was a bad year in every way.

College basketball coaches are pragmatists. They are looking for players who can help them, not players who need help. Canty wasn't the same player he had been as a junior. He was still good, averaging 13.5 points and 8.5 assists a game, but he wasn't dominating games at both ends the way he had before. The recruiters began to melt away. By springtime only one Division I school was still involved: Army.

"At first I wasn't so sure about the military commitment or if I wanted to go there," Canty said. "I knew they had struggled for a long time in basketball. But then when I met Coach Harris, he convinced me that there were advantages to graduating from a place like this and that we were going to get better. I already knew a little about the military because of my mother, so I thought I would try it."

He almost didn't make it out of "Beast Barracks." From the first day, he was in trouble with his chain of command. Never anything serious, but enough to make life difficult. Once, he called a sergeant sir. Sergeants aren't sirs. Another time he walked into the hallway after a shower in the wrong shorts and T-shirt. More trouble. By the end of the first week he had been assigned a table in the mess hall with only upperclassmen. That meant he was constantly being rated and given assignments. These days, plebes are supposed to be allowed to eat a full meal, even during Beast. "At best I got in three bites a meal," Canty said. Already thin at 170, he lost fifteen pounds before Beast was over.

But he kept going, he said, in large part because he never had time to think about doing anything but continuing. Once school and basketball started, things began to improve. He was hanging in academically and he had been the surprise of preseason on the basketball court. Harris had thought before the year began that a plebe named Justin Fuller, a shooting guard out of California, might be able to contribute early. But Fuller had been in trouble from day one and would be gone from the academy before the end of first semester. The freshman surprise was Canty.

That was why he was Harris's choice to start in Clark's place. He didn't want to give him too much time to think about the notion of starting his first college basketball game at Duke, so he waited until the team had come back into the locker room after pregame warmups to tell him he was starting. A few minutes later, as the Cadets took the court with the screams of the Duke students ringing in their ears, Canty took a moment to drink it all in.

"It was like a dream come true," he said. "Me, starting my first college basketball game at Duke. I had to catch myself and think about what I had to do. That was the toughest part of it all."

Late in the first half, Spatola swung the ball on the right wing to Canty, who spotted up for a 3-point shot. He let fly without hesitation and the ball hit the bottom of the net an instant later. It was the first basket of Canty's college career. "I'll watch the tape of that forever," he said, unable to stop smiling at the memory.

Duke would start a lineup almost as young as Army's — two freshmen, two juniors, and a senior, with one sophomore and four freshmen on the bench — but it was a lineup filled with kids who had been on the McDonald's High School All-American team. The closest any of the Army players had come to that team was seeing the names of the players who made the team listed on the wall of the McDonald's that was just outside Thayer Gate at West Point.

The pregame atmosphere was almost collegial. Krzyzewski, who had coached both Harris and his top assistant, Marty Coyne, at Army, stopped by the shootaround to chat for a few minutes. When the Army players went out to shoot early, the Duke students, all in their seats two hours before the 5 P.M. tip-off, gave them a nice round of applause. Then they helpfully kept count for backup center Matt Rutledge while he was doing a tip drill against the backboard. When Rutledge was finished, he waved at the students to say thank you. Everyone was having fun.

The differences between a program like Army's and a program like Duke's were evident during warm-ups. As each Duke player came onto the floor, he was greeted with warm, respectful applause. The students even sang "Happy Birthday" to freshman center Carlos Boozer since, naturally, they all knew it was his birthday. Boozer didn't even smile in response to the serenade. He was a high school All-American who had been recruited by every school in the country. He was used to adulation, expected it. Of course the Duke student body knew it was his birthday, he was Carlos Boozer.

Back downstairs in the visitor's locker room, Harris had put the matchups on the blackboard. The chatter that had buzzed around the room earlier quieted. Harris had written several keys on the blackboard. Nothing earth-shattering: intensity, rebounding, value the basketball. The basics of basketball.

He knew his players were about to walk into a cauldron of noise and heat and pressure that was completely different from anything they had ever experienced. He also knew what Duke's talent level was like compared to his team's. But he had to do everything he could to convince his players that they could compete in this game. So he went back to the theme that he had built the program around from his first day on the job: forty minutes of Army basketball. Outside the basketball office at West Point was a poster explaining forty minutes of Army basketball. The recruiting brochure the coaches handed out said on the front cover: "40 minutes of Army basketball." The poster handed out to all the local businesses said: "40 minutes of Army basketball."

To Harris it was symbolic of playing as hard as you possibly could in every game for the entire forty minutes, of being willing to do anything to win the game. He knew he had to do two things to make the theory work: get the players to believe in it (not difficult) and get players good enough to win when they executed it (very difficult). He looked around the room and knew the players believed in it. He also knew that was no better than half the battle.

"We came down here for one goddamn reason, fellas," he said finally. "To kick their ass. It's right there for you. This is a great atmosphere for college basketball. *Enjoy it.* Let's go win the game."

They charged up the steps, thrilled to be there, believing in miracles, knowing they were ready to play this team in this gym. They ran onto the floor into a sea of noise that made Harris's final instructions in the huddle almost impossible to hear. They walked onto the court for the opening tip-off, each one of them thinking the same thing: "This is what college basketball is about; a game like this; a crowd like this; the chance to show people who had no idea who you were just how good you were." The adrenaline was almost bursting through their veins.

Boozer scored inside for Duke, but Barrett answered right back with a short jumper. One minute played, 2-2. So far, so good.

Then Duke scored the next 11 points. Every time one of the Cadets tried to throw a pass, someone was in the passing lane. Jason Williams, the freshman point guard, made a spinning move on Spatola that turned him inside out. Mike Dunleavy, a six-nine freshman who was taller than all the Cadets but played *guard* for Duke, grabbed a rebound, weaved through everyone in black, and tossed in an easy layup. The gym got louder and louder. Four minutes in, Harris called time. They came to the bench looking not so much like deer-in-a-headlight as deer-already-run-over.

"Calm down!" Harris screamed over the din. "Calm down! Stop shooting with twenty-seven seconds left on the shot clock. Do the things you've done every day in practice."

They tried. Spatola and freshman Ray Fredrick hit jumpers to cut the lead to 13-6. But that was the last spasm of competitiveness. Duke went on a 29-2 run the next eight minutes and they found themselves staring at a scoreboard that said it was 42-8. No miracles in this place. An ass-kicking, yes, but not the kind Harris had talked about. Standing on the edge of the huddle during a time-out, Joe Clark had a tortured looked on his face. He turned to Colonel William Held, the officer-rep who traveled with the team, and said, "This is killing me."

"Next year," Held said.

"That's what they said last year," Clark said mournfully.

The only Clark who could have helped Army in this game was Clark Kent — and even he might not have been enough. It was 52-15 at halftime. Their heads were down, way down, in the locker room. Harris tried to pick them up. "Now we'll find out how we deal with adversity," he said. "We should all be angry right now because we could not have been more tentative out there. You can't play in a game like this and be tentative! Every day in practice you play like maniacs and then you come in here and you're tentative. Don't be afraid to make mistakes. Play!"

They tried. But they were outmatched at every position. Duke scored the first 15 points of the second half. The score got worse and worse until Krzyzewski finally began putting his walk-ons in with eight minutes to play. By then it was 82-18. The final was 100-42, the Cadets having to endure a chant of "Navy's better" during the last few minutes, courtesy of their friends, the Duke students.

The postgame handshakes were brief. The Army players wanted to get off the floor as quickly as possible. The Duke players knew there was nothing to say. "Nice game" when the final is 100-42 sounds awfully hollow. Krzyzewski and Harris shook hands quickly. They would see each other later, but at that moment it was hard for either to look the other in the eye. Krzyzewski had been through awful losses, too. Inflicting one on a friend gave him no pleasure.

The Army coaches gathered outside the locker room before going inside. Harris always asks his four assistants — Coyne, Andy Johnston, Chris Beal, and Denny Carroll — for input before he talks to the team. They were searching for positives.

"The defense was better the second half," Johnston said. "At least we got back and didn't give them layups every time."

Everyone nodded. Silence. Coyne, who could speak to Harris as a friend and a peer in a way the others couldn't, shrugged. "We have to put this behind us right now. All that matters is Cornell on Tuesday. It isn't even worth going over what went wrong. I say look straight ahead."

Harris was looking straight ahead. "The bottom line," he said, "was that we sucked."

No one argued.

Harris made it short, if not sweet, with the players. He took Coyne's advice and focused on Cornell. But he made it clear he wasn't happy. Across the way, Krzyzewski was concerned about the final score. "I couldn't just play the walk-ons in the first half," he said. "That would have been even more humiliating. And you can't tell your kids not to try."

He sent one of his assistants, Steve Wojciechowski, through a back door, so he would be unseen by the media, to the Army locker room to find Coyne and bring him through that door to the Duke coaches' locker room. "Is Pat all right?" Krzyzewski asked.

"Coach, he understands," Coyne said. "We know you weren't trying to rub it in." He smiled. "The bottom line is simple. We just have to get better."

Sal Mentesana knew that the bottom line at Lehigh was exactly the same as at Army. His season, however, would start with a more reasonable opener than Army's: Yale — at home.

Of course no game was a gimme for Lehigh. Mentesana's three-year record — 16-65 — was evidence of that. But there was a feeling around Lehigh that a corner was about to be turned. The win over

Navy in March had provided the program with a level of hope that hadn't existed in a long time.

"It's amazing the way one game can make you feel so completely different about yourself," Mentesana said. "I mean, we had gone through about as miserable a winter as any basketball team can go through and we walked away from the season actually feeling pretty good about ourselves."

There were four seniors left from Mentesana's initial recruiting class of seven players. One, Pete DeLea, had recurring back problems that would make playing impossible. But he wasn't ready to put basketball behind him, so he remained with the team as an unofficial manager/assistant coach and occasional color commentator on the radio during road games.

The other three seniors were about as different as three people who had become good friends could be. Fido Willybiro had lived all over the world and spoke five languages. He and Bobby Mbom, a sophomore backup forward, often spoke to each other in French in the locker room because it was the language they had both grown up with. Willybiro's parents were originally from the Central African Republic. In fact, his grandfather, who had been a very powerful general in the Central African Army, was so upset when Greg Willybiro began to get serious about his daughter that he had him jailed for five days to try to discourage him. It didn't work.

"My grandfather didn't come to the wedding, because he was still upset," Fido said. "It was only after I was born that he decided my dad was okay. He liked the part about grandchildren."

Willybiro lived in Romania, France, and Belgium growing up, moving with his father, who was a diplomat. His parents divorced when he was eight, and he and his sister remained with their father. Eventually, both went to high school in the United States. Fido ended up at the Newport School, in Kensington, Washington. That was where he began to blossom as a basketball player, growing to six-six by his junior year.

Jared Hess was an inch shorter than Willybiro, but a decidedly different kind of player from a very different sort of background. Where Willybiro was second in the league as a junior in blocked shots and a low-post player, Hess was second in 3-point shooting, a perimeter player with a soft touch from outside. Where Willybiro was the grandson of an army general and the son of a career diplomat, Hess was the son of a teacher, a Mennonite who was — literally — a choirboy.

Hal Hess was a gifted musician who had grown up singing in the Mennonite church. He had met Christine Schumacher in college, and after they were married they had moved to Atlanta to be a part of the pacifist movement during the Vietnam War. They later moved to Cincinnati, where Jared and his sister, Alison, were born and grew up. Jared never did much musically as a kid because he was intimidated by his father's talent. But when he got to Lehigh he began going to one of the local Mennonite churches, in large part because of the music. He began singing in the choir there and soon after began singing in the Lehigh choir, even though basketball practice sometimes interfered with choir practice.

"They put up with it my freshman year because they were going to Europe that summer and they needed a bass," he said. "But after that, they said I was missing too much time for basketball."

And thus Hess probably became the first Division I basketball player ever cut from his school choir. He still sang in church and was part of a barbershop quartet with his father and two of his uncles.

Steve Aylsworth wasn't likely to be caught singing in any church choirs or speaking to anyone in the locker room in French. He was a California jock who had grown up on the beach in Malibu, someone who looked as if he had stepped straight off the set of *Beverly Hills 90210*. In fact, the previous summer, Aylsworth and his girlfriend had appeared on one of those funky teen shows, called *Change of Heart*, in which two couples trade with one another for a date and then return to the show to decide whether to stay together or make the trade permanent. Aylsworth and his girlfriend had stayed together.

Steve was the third Aylsworth to attend Lehigh. His father and older brother had played football for the school and Steve had arrived in 1996 planning to play both football and basketball. Even though he had some success at both sports, he decided to stick to basketball after his freshman year because trying to play two sports and go to school was just too much.

Aylsworth was five-ten and claimed to weigh 170. That may have been with his various knee wraps on. He looked more like a gymnast than a basketball player and had the face of a choirboy. He was not, by any stretch of the imagination, a naturally gifted basketball player. He seemed to shoot off-balance about 90 percent of the time and watching him work the ball upcourt against a pressure defense could be painful.

But he lived to compete. He would do anything to win. He was probably the best listener on the team. He would try anything Mentesana asked him to try. If the coaches had told him they needed him to guard Stefan Ciosici, he would undoubtedly have sprinted onto the court, thrown his body into Ciosici's path, and tried to take a charge.

"If we could put Steve's mentality into some of these freshmen we might have something," Mentesana said on the eve of the season opener. "That's the trouble we've got right now. We've got these seniors who have been to hell and back and will do anything to turn this thing around but who all have limitations on the basketball floor. Then we've got these young kids who have talent, but have no idea how to play, no idea how to compete, and no idea how much it hurts to lose. We've got to find a way to combine those groups and figure out what works."

It would not be easy. This was Lehigh's first freshman class with scholarship players. Unlike Holy Cross, which would eventually have a full-scholarship team again, Lehigh was taking a partial approach — two scholarships a year, eventually reaching a total of eight. The two scholarship freshmen were Matt Logie, a six-five shooter from Mercer Island, Washington, and Tanner Engel, another good shooter, from Kearney, Nebraska. The other two freshmen, Zlatko Savovic and Matt Crawford, were on financial aid packages.

Savovic had taken perhaps the most fascinating route of anyone in the league to reach college. He had been born in Bosnia and had escaped with his family during the war. This was no small matter, since his father was Serbian and his mother was Muslim, which meant that wherever they were, someone wanted them dead. Savovic was twelve at the time and still has memories of being stopped at various checkpoints, thinking each time that this was it, this was the time when their forged papers weren't going to get them through. Somehow, they made it to Zagreb, where they were reunited with a number of other family members.

The family then sought asylum in the United States, thinking that was the place for all of them to begin anew. Savovic's uncle went to the U.S. Embassy seeking a visa for the family to enter the country. An American diplomat asked him if he had any idea where he wanted to go with his family to settle. Thinking that the capital city of any country is a good place to be, Savovic's uncle said, "Washington." The diplomat nodded, wrote it down, and asked, "Any particular area of Washington?" apparently wanting to know if the Savovics preferred city, suburbs, or out in the country.

"All I care about," Savovic's uncle said, thinking about his war-torn country, "is that we go someplace where it's quiet."

Their wish was granted. The Savovic family was sent to Everett, Washington — three thousand miles and a lifetime away from what they had envisioned.

It turned out fine, though. Zlatko was a talented basketball player and his skills developed quickly playing against American competition. Mentesana was convinced he could become one of the better point guards in the Patriot League, someone whose minutes, playing behind Aylsworth and junior Tiwan Hawkins, would increase as the season moved along. The same, he hoped, would be true for all four freshmen.

The opener was encouraging. In an atmosphere slightly different from the one Army would face at Duke, Lehigh defeated Yale 69-56 in front of a less-than-raucous throng of 699 in Stabler Arena. Stabler seated 5,600 and, in the late 1980s and early '90s, occasional sellouts and consistent crowds of three to four thousand were the norm. But the last winning season had been 1991 and fans were taking a wait-and-see approach as another season began.

Mentesana and his players weren't concerned about the crowd at the Yale game. All they knew was that they were 1-0. That was a long way from 1-26.

9

NO MORAL VICTORIES

PATRIOT LEAGUE teams are almost never in a position to take winning for granted. Certainly not when they play other Division I teams. But the mood at Lafayette as the season began was different from the mood at the other six schools; different, in fact, from what it had ever been.

The team's success in the winter of 1999 had brought a new level of basketball mania to the normally quiet little campus tucked up on College Hill overlooking Easton, Pennsylvania. Yes, Lafayette had basketball tradition. But that tradition was little more than a dim memory to most of the people at the school near the end of the millennium. Prior to the '99 season, Lafayette had appeared in the NCAA Tournament once — in 1957. It had last appeared in the NIT in 1975. No one on the team had been born in 1975 and, in all likelihood, neither had anyone among the 2,244 students on the all-undergraduate campus.

That meant it was all new. Which meant it was all quite thrilling. The Leopards began playing to capacity crowds in Kirby Field House, led by a group that dubbed itself "The Zoo Crew." They wore yellow "Zoo Crew" T-shirts to each home game, marching in just after tip-off to a reserved section of the stands waving a giant yellow Zoo Crew flag. At staid, laid-back Lafayette, 150 students acting crazy passed for wildness.

The atmosphere was so charged and so electric on game nights that Scott Morse, the assistant athletic director who ran the sports publicity department, walked into the gym one night, blinked his eyes in disbelief, then walked out again so he could reenter and drink the whole thing in with proper appreciation.

Players in the Patriot League grow used to playing in front of small, quiet crowds. Navy's players jokingly called Alumni Hall "the Mausoleum," and the truth was the crowds there were — generally speaking — larger and louder than those at Army, Lehigh, Holy Cross, and Colgate. Davis Gym at Bucknell, which seats only 2,300, was almost always full or close to full because the school had both tradition and a consistent level of success working in its favor.

The crowds at Kirby were at a different level. The gym could seat about 4,000 if extra bleacher seating was added for a big game, and throughout the winter of 1999 the place was at or close to capacity for most games and filled to overflowing for the conference championship game against Bucknell.

"The whole thing was a joy ride for all of us," Lafayette president Arthur Rothkopf remembered. "Going into that gym was tremendous fun for everyone. It was a very positive thing for the entire school."

It helped that the team was not only good but eminently likeable. Ciosici took to sitting with the Zoo Crew at times during games and his presence was representative of the genuine link between the team and the students. At a lot of schools where the basketball team is successful, there is a very real gap between the players and the rest of the student body. Even though the NCAA finally got around to outlawing the ludicrous concept of athletic dorms in the 1990s, athletes at the elite ball-playing schools tended to live together on or off campus. They ate together, partied together, and, in many cases, were put on such pedestals that other students were almost afraid to speak to them. Often, they made it clear that they had no desire to be spoken to.

That wasn't going to happen at Lafayette — or any Patriot League school. For one thing, the schools were too small for athletes to be segregated in any way. For another, they rarely missed classes, they spent time in the library, and they studied, not with private tutors, but with other students. For another, most of them were regular guys. None were besieged by agents in the locker room after games. In fact, the Lafayette players regularly attended a postgame reception held in Kirby for fans, families, and friends for two reasons: they liked the company and the pizza was good.

The feeling on campus as the weather began to turn cold in November was different from what it had been the previous winter. Nothing feels the same the second time as the first. There was almost an assumption around the quad that the basketball team would win the Patriot League again and be back in the NCAAs. Never mind the fact that three key leaders — Ted Cole, Ross Harms, and Dave Klaus — had graduated. Never mind the questions about Ciosici's knee. Never mind all the returning seniors at Bucknell or the talent at Navy. Everyone had read all the preseason magazines. Everyone now knew — because Morse and basketball sports information director Phil LaBella had researched it and let it be known anywhere and everywhere — that Lafayette was the first school in NCAA history to return two conference players of the year to the same team.

The players were not immune to this. They knew they were good, they all figured that hard work during the off-season would make them better individually. They had been the best team in the league a year ago and they saw no reason why that would change.

"I think the feeling around here is that people are excited about the games early against the bigger teams," Tim Bieg said. "That's an opportunity for us to make a mark that hasn't been made at Lafayette. We think we're good enough to beat some of these teams."

The nonconference schedule was ambitious — games at Villanova, Georgia Tech, Princeton, and Penn in addition to a trip to New Mexico's tournament that would begin with a game against St. Joseph's. None of the glamour games were at home because no name team had any interest in making the trip to Easton to play in Kirby. So O'Hanlon and company had to go on the road to try to make a name for themselves.

The first of the name games was at Villanova. It concerned O'Hanlon that his players looked less than wired in the three games leading up to Villanova, a pair of exhibition games at home and the season opener at Columbia. During the second exhibition game, against an AAU team from Pennsylvania, he really got after the team at halftime. This was rare for O'Hanlon. He could be sarcastic when he wasn't happy, but more often than not he was clinical. This time, he was angry, even though the Leopards were leading the game, 38-27.

"At what point do we start to play as if we care about what we're doing?" he said, walking between the players, who sat squeezed together in front of their lockers in the tiny, walk-single-file-at-all-times locker room. "If you don't play hard now, you aren't going to play hard Saturday [at Columbia]. You can't just turn it on like a faucet. You can't just sit back and say when we get to Villanova we'll come to play. That's not how it works, guys. You know that."

He paused, looking around the room. All eyes were on him. "How many of you were on the floor after a loose ball that half? How many? I'll tell you how many — one. Spencer Williams is the only guy on the floor after a ball. He's the newest guy on the team and he has to be the one to set the example on how to play hard? Come on, guys, let's get this going."

O'Hanlon had brought up Williams to make a point about consistent work ethic, especially to the older players, who had been central to the team's success a year earlier. Williams had only been on the team for a couple of weeks, having been brought up from the JV team by O'Hanlon because he had impressed him playing noontime hoops in the gym.

Noontime hoops is a tradition on most college campuses, a mixture of faculty and students showing up and choosing sides, then playing for an hour. Even though his fifty-one-year-old knees were so creaky that he winced going up and down stairs, O'Hanlon still played any day he had the time. The jump shot that had earned him the nickname "Rainbow" as a kid was still there, but the first step took a little longer now than it had thirty years earlier.

Williams, who had come to Lafayette from nearby Lakeville, had hoped to make the team as a walk-on. But there was so much talent that he had played JV as a freshman and was figuring to do so again as a sophomore. Then he began showing up for noontime hoops. "I figured if he could go by me, he must be good enough to play on the team," O'Hanlon joked.

What was amazing about Williams's elevation to the varsity through noontime ball was that he was not the first member of his family to achieve the feat. Thirty-five years earlier, when his father was a Duke sophomore, he had played noontime hoops. One of the players most days was Bucky Waters, then an assistant coach under Vic Bubas. Waters was impressed enough with Ed Williams that he offered him a chance to walk on the Duke team — which he did, successfully. Now, a generation later, history had repeated itself.

O'Hanlon's anger may have had more to do with concern about his team's health — physical and mental — than about effort. Brian Ehlers was taking the night off because of shin splints. The doctors said he would be fine for the weekend, but the last thing O'Hanlon wanted was Ehlers gimping on shin splints a week before the Villanova game. Ciosici was still having trouble with his knee. There was scar tissue and his mobility was extremely limited.

Everyone seemed to be in a preseason funk. The coaches sensed it, the players did too. "We play that same team late February, we beat them by sixty," Brian Burke said later. "But we weren't at that level. We weren't ready to play that well yet. Maybe we all were expecting too much."

Maybe. Expectations don't just affect fans and the media. Lafayette was now the Patriot League's showcase program. It was playing a schedule that would put it in the spotlight one way or the other. Everyone was aware of that. Pressure comes in different forms. None of the players were worrying about their draft position in the spring or whether or not they would get a shoe deal when they turned pro. Their worries were different. They had been good a year ago and it had been fun. They wanted to be good again. They wanted to feel the way they had last March.

Whether it was O'Hanlon's anger or Williams's example, Lafayette played much harder and better in the second half against the Pennsylvania all-star team. This was hardly serious opposition. The only player who had had a noteworthy college career was Gary Massey, who had played at Villanova and briefly in the NBA. Massey could still shoot but it was unlikely that *he* could have gotten around O'Hanlon in noontime hoops at this stage of his life. The Leopards ended up winning, 89-56.

Four nights later, they went to Columbia and played well enough to win, finally pulling away late for a 59-52 victory. Only later, when Columbia played very competitively in the Ivy League for the first time in a number of years would O'Hanlon realize that the win at Columbia was probably more impressive than he had thought at the time.

Either way, Columbia was just the prelude for the trip three nights later to Villanova. There were four players from the Philadelphia area on the team: Tim Bieg, Brian Burke, Frank Barr, and Greg McCleary. The head coach was also from Philadelphia: Villanova, Class of 1970. This would be a homecoming. That, naturally, was the last thing O'Hanlon wanted anyone thinking about or talking about. It was, just as naturally, on everyone's mind.

The minute the Leopards walked in the back door of the DuPont Pavilion, it was apparent that this wasn't going to be just another guarantee game in the life of a Patriot League team.

Several TV crews were there awaiting their arrival. Almost everyone O'Hanlon had ever known in the Philadelphia sports media was also there. O'Hanlon had known there would be a certain amount of attention. He had lots of friends in Philadelphia, not just from growing up in West Philly, not just from his years on the Main Line at Villanova, but also from his six years as Fran Dunphy's top assistant during a very successful run at Penn.

His rise at Lafayette happened to coincide with some difficult times for two of the coaches in Philadelphia's famed Big Five. Speedy Morris, the longtime coach at LaSalle, had known great success in the late 1980s and early '90s, but the program had fallen on hard times in recent years. There had been rumors throughout the 1998–99 season that Morris was going to be fired and that O'Hanlon was the number one candidate to replace him. But, at the end of a 13-15 season, Morris had been given a three-year contract extension with the understanding — or so it seemed — that the losing seasons needed to stop soon.

Steve Lappas had never had a losing season in seven years at Villanova. He had been to five NCAA Tournaments, including in 1999 when the Wildcats had won twenty-one games. But he hadn't quite connected with the demanding Villanova fans and alumni. Even though Rollie Massimino had been considerably less popular when he left town in 1992 than he had been after winning the national championship in 1985, his record still spoke for itself: a national championship and four other trips to the Elite Eight. Lappas hadn't yet been out of the second round of the NCAA Tournament, and every March, when the Wildcats lost, everyone in town seemed to notice his New York accent just a little bit more.

No one thought Lappas's job was in trouble, but there was just enough insecurity floating around the Main Line to make the notion of O'Hanlon bringing his Little Patriot League Team That Could into DuPont to take on the big boys from the Big East an intriguing story. That, and the fact that everyone genuinely liked O'Hanlon, brought the media out in droves, even on a miserable, rainy November night.

They were all waiting patiently when the Lafayette bus finally showed up. The bad weather had tied up traffic all over Philadelphia, and the Blue Route, which connected with the northeast extension of the Pennsylvania Turnpike north of the city, was at a standstill. "If our driver hadn't gone up on the shoulder, we'd still be sitting there," Tim Bieg said, shaking the rain out of his hair in the locker room. O'Hanlon was out on the floor trying to give everyone who had asked for five minutes the ten to fifteen minutes they actually wanted.

The four Philly-area players on the team were doubly excited about the game. Not only would they be playing in front of a sellout crowd of 6,500 including friends and family, they would be sleeping in their own beds that night. Since there were no classes on the Wednesday before Thanksgiving, O'Hanlon had told the local players they didn't have to make the bus trip back to Easton after the game.

Once he had finished with the Philadelphia media, O'Hanlon came back to the visitors' locker room. Lafayette's pregame ritual is as short and simple as any in the college game. Many coaches will go through an entire scouting report, including looking at tape one more time, in the locker room before a game. Some will go on at length about what the game means, about why this game is different from all other games. O'Hanlon does essentially the same thing before every game, whether it is a November exhibition, an NCAA Tournament game, or a guarantee game at his alma mater. He writes his keys to the game on the blackboard, offense on one side, defense on the other. They are almost always the same. On defense: transition, identify shooters, get around screens, rebound. For Villanova he had singled out point guard Bobby Smith as a point of emphasis: "Play #3 for the drive." On offense, it was just as predictable: be strong with the ball; move the ball; set hard screens. And, always, poise and confidence.

The only thing different was the last thought O'Hanlon would write on the board after the team went out to warm up. On this night it was "Respect your opponent." He didn't draw a giant period at the end of the sentence but that was what he meant: respect them — period. Don't be in awe, don't be overwhelmed. This was a good team, a talented team, but not one to be afraid of or nervous about playing. Everyone was nervous, but not about the opponent. They were nervous because they knew the opportunity to win the game would be there if they played the way they were capable.

The applause for O'Hanlon was warm when he walked on the court, warmer when the public address announcer asked the fans to "Please welcome back Fran O'Hanlon." A moment later, the ball went up, O'Hanlon's jacket came off (as it always did right after tip-off), and old home week was forgotten.

As one would expect from a Big East team, Villanova had size and quickness. Its depth was young, but it was talented. Rebounding and the inside strength of six-ten senior center Malik Allen were major concerns.

The first half went about as well as Lafayette could have hoped. At one point, the Leopards led 21-14 after Ehlers reversed the ball to a wide-open Bieg, who calmly drained a 3-pointer. Villanova responded with an 11-0 run, helped by 7 straight Allen points inside that came just after Ciosici came to the bench with his second foul. At seven feet, 215, Frank Barr just didn't have the strength to keep Allen from dominating him in the low post. Barr did respond with the last 4 points of the half, though, the final 2 coming just before the buzzer when he rebounded a Tyson Whitfield miss and put the shot back to tie the game at 32. Ciosici had only played nine minutes because of foul trouble, and the score was tied.

The second half also started well. A Whitfield 3 almost three minutes in put the Leopards up 37-36. Then, after Brian Lynch had answered that with a 3 for Villanova, things began to go wrong for Lafayette. Jostling for rebounding position on the next possession, Ciosici suddenly pitched over and let out a loud scream. He went down on his back, clearly in pain. Everyone on the Lafayette bench froze. Ciosici had been given a cortisone shot to ease the pain from the scar tissue on his knee before the Columbia game and had said the knee felt better than it had in months. But now, no one had seen what had happened and everyone's first thought was about the knee. O'Hanlon and trainer Dawn Schleiden were out in an instant, while the building went quiet.

It turned out that Ciosici had caught an elbow flush in the stomach from Lynch during the scramble for the ball. Ciosici thought it was intentional and wanted no part of any apologies from Lynch. On tape later, it appeared the elbow was inadvertent, but at that moment the Lafayette bench was hot. O'Hanlon and assistant coach Pat Brogan were all over referee Jody Sylvester for missing the elbow — intentional or not. Brogan is Lafayette's designated ref cop. He sits at the end of the bench and keeps up a running commentary with the officials on how they are controlling the game. Brogan never misses a foul, a walk, a double dribble perpetrated by the other team. He is also a great anticipator: "Watch the illegal screens," he will warn helpfully at numerous junctures throughout a game. He also has a keen eye for any dragging pivot foot or anyone stepping in the lane an instant too soon on a free throw. He is smart enough to always address the officials by name, just to keep things friendly — "Jody, watch out for Ten, he always has his elbows up"— and almost never raises his voice. Unlike a lot of assistant coaches, Brogan almost never stands up to get on an official. In the unofficial officiating handbook, rule 1A says "Never — ever — let an assistant coach show you up." Brogan, a true workaholic who always carries a pen that says "Recruit Every Day," never does. He knows how to play the game.

Now though, Ciosici had to come to the bench and no amount of pleading (O'Hanlon) or cajoling (Brogan) was going to get a foul called on Lynch. To make matters worse, he promptly hit a 3 at the other end and, with Ciosici on the bench, Villanova went on a 17-3 tear. When Lynch hit two foul shots shortly after that to make it 59-44 with 8:18 left, it looked as if the Wildcats would coast home.

During a TV time-out, O'Hanlon was as calm as ever. "There's a lot of time," he said. "Let's just keep our poise. They're tired, we're not. Let's get a stop and a shot each time."

They followed instructions, whittling away. Villanova had forgotten about getting the ball to Allen, even though Ciosici had four fouls. A Frank Barr dunk and a Whitfield 3 cut the margin to 59-56 with more than five minutes left. For the rest of the night, Lafayette was the little dog wrapped around Villanova's leg that refused to go away. The Wildcats punched the lead back up to 69-63 with less than two minutes to go. Then Mick Kuberka, the quiet six-nine sophomore from Buffalo, buried a 3. Lynch missed and Brian Ehlers made two free throws with forty-eight seconds to go. Now it was 69-68 and Villanova couldn't afford one more lost possession. The Lafayette kids were convinced they were going to win the game.

Lappas ordered the ball inside to Allen. He knew Barr, in the game to protect Ciosici, had four fouls. Allen caught the ball on the post. Rob Worthington dropped down to try to help, an instant too late. Allen hit a tough ten-footer from the baseline as Worthington fouled him with twenty-six seconds to go. He made the free throw. Ciosici scored 11 seconds later to cut the lead to 72-70, and Lafayette fouled point guard Bobby Smith on the inbounds.

If Smith missed both shots or made one, Lafayette would at the very least have a chance to tie. He made the first. Then he made the second. Lappas and the Villanova fans started breathing again. Whitfield missed just before the buzzer and Villanova had escaped, 74-70.

An hour later, as the Lafayette bus pulled out of the parking lot, Lappas stood watching it leave. He shook his head. "Boy, they're a good team," he said. "Patriot League teams aren't supposed to be that good. I mean nonscholarship, are you kidding me? No one in the building tonight understands how good a win that was for us. I mean, we played *well* and it's all down to one possession. If Malik doesn't make that tough shot there. . . ." His voice trailed off. He didn't want to consider the alternative to Allen's making the shot.

The Lafayette players heard all the kind words. O'Hanlon laughed when Lappas joked with him about a guarantee game being a game where the home team is supposed to be guaranteed a victory. They read all the things that were said about their grit and toughness and how close they had come.

And they felt lousy about the whole thing.

"We're tired of close," Tim Bieg said. "When we were starting to get good, Coach always told us there was no such thing as a moral victory. Now we understand what he meant. Moral victories are still losses. We aren't in this for moral victories."

10

NOT SO SWEET REDEMPTION

NO one was happier to see the season get underway than the basketball players at Navy. The tone for the entire fall had been set on August 26 by Chris Worthing's twenty-first birthday party and the restrictions and embarrassment for the entire team that followed.

Don DeVoe had two basic themes throughout preseason practice: no one on this team has ever really been part of a championship team at Navy and your first act as the leaders of this team was to get yourselves put on restriction.

"Every time something went wrong in practice, it was one of those two things — or both," said Chris Williams, one of the Restricted Nine. "We had it pretty much committed to memory by the time the season started."

Navy had won the Patriot League title in 1998 but the only member of the current team who had played a major role that year was Sitapha Savane. Even then, he had been a key player off the bench, not the key player on the team as he was expected to be in his senior season. Jeremy Toton, the other senior, had barely played as a sophomore and the only current junior who had played any minutes at all was Williams. The others had either been spot players or members of the JV team.

It wasn't as if Navy had been awful in 1999. After all, the Mids had won twenty games in the regular season. But the bitter taste of the loss to Lehigh, combined with starting the new season with

Worthing-gate, had left everyone feeling tense and troubled. And while the players were struggling through restriction muster each day, moaning about cruel fate, they had no idea that their coach was going through a real-life nightmare far worse than having to stand at attention in a spotless uniform several times a day.

DeVoe had become a grandfather for the first time on September 7. His daughter Donna had given birth to a girl, Mary Kate, but the birth had not been marked by unbridled joy. As early as May, doctors had told Donna and her husband, Chris Roberts, that the baby was going to be born with heart problems. Long before Mary Kate was born, the doctors had planned two procedures to strengthen her heart before open-heart surgery. Even so, the doctors were optimistic, saying that many children have this same problem and grow up to live perfectly normal lives.

The first procedure, performed the day after Mary Kate was born, went fine. So did the second one. The surgery was scheduled for the last Monday in September. Two days prior to the surgery, DeVoe flew to Houston to meet his granddaughter and spend some time with Donna and Chris. Knowing the problems the baby was going to have at birth, Donna and Chris had chosen Texas Children's Hospital as the place where they wanted her to be. DeVoe spent several hours with Mary Kate and, as grandparents tend to do, fell completely in love with her. "It's amazing," he said, "how quickly you bond with them."

On Sunday morning DeVoe returned to the hospital with Donna and Chris. When they went to the infants' nursery, the pod where Mary Kate was supposed to be was empty. "We knew right away," DeVoe said, "that something had to be very wrong."

As it turned out, Mary Kate's heart had started to give out while Donna, Chris, and DeVoe were en route from the hotel where they were staying. "We got there probably about seven minutes after it happened," DeVoe said.

Chris and Donna went in to talk to the doctors while DeVoe waited anxiously. A few minutes later, when they came out, both were crying. Mary Kate was in surgery, which had been originally scheduled for the next day. A doctor walked over and told DeVoe, "This is very, very serious."

The doctors worked on Mary Kate's tiny heart all day. But nothing could be done. At 6:30 that night, she died.

DeVoe flew home the next morning and then on to the funeral in Knoxville later that week. He felt all the things one feels at a time like that: crushed, devastated, and, most of all, helpless and powerless to do anything for his daughter. There was nothing for him to do but throw himself into his work. In that sense, he was fortunate because practice was underway and there was plenty for him to do. But it was a sad, difficult fall for DeVoe and the doubts he had about his team only added to his troubled mood.

The players could tell that DeVoe was not terribly happy, but they assumed it had to do with concerns over the coming season. DeVoe told his coaches what had happened. Mary Kate's death was reported in the Knoxville papers but not in any of the Annapolis-area papers. What's more, like all college kids, they had enough on their minds that they didn't give all that much thought to what might be bothering their coach.

The season began with a disappointing loss at Rice, disappointing because the Mids led most of the game before poor free-throw shooting down the stretch allowed Rice to rally and win in overtime. This was not a good way to start, even though Rice was a decent team and winning on the road was never easy. DeVoe knew that this was a team that needed to create an identity, to build some confidence in itself. The endgame had never been a strength of Navy's, in part because DeVoe tended to recruit with defense in mind. In this case, not being able to close the deal at the foul line had hurt his team.

They came home facing a difficult week. On Monday they would play Wake Forest, the toughest team on their schedule. On Wednesday, the night before Thanksgiving, they would play Richmond, which always had a solid team. And on Saturday they would play Air Force, one of those rivalry games that are never easy. The good news was that all three games were at home. The bad news was that the Wednesday and Saturday games would take place with the Yard virtually empty for Thanksgiving break, meaning that Alumni Hall would really feel like a mausoleum.

DeVoe was as upbeat as he had been in a long time on the morning of the Wake Forest game. He and Wake Coach Dave Odom were longtime friends and he was looking forward to having lunch with Odom and his staff and to seeing just where his team was when faced with a quality opponent.

Shortly before Wake Forest showed up for its morning shoot-around, Jeremy Toton came to see DeVoe. Toton was about as unhappy as he had ever been at Navy. His career simply hadn't turned out the way he had planned. For as long as Toton could remember, basketball had been the dominant force in his life. His father, Gary, had been a good athlete growing up in Evansville but had been forced to give up organized sports at a young age because his family needed him to work. Being from Indiana, he never lost his passion for basketball, and when his first son was born he began raising him to be a player almost from day one.

"We were the only ones on our block who had a hoop in the driveway," Toton remembered. "I can remember my dad dragging me out of bed at five in the morning to do some shooting before school. I played all sports growing up, but basketball was always what I did. Playing on the college level was what I wanted to do and what we all knew I was going to do."

Gary and Marilyn Toton never missed one of their son's basketball games, winter, summer, or fall. "No matter where they sat, no matter how loud the gym might be, I could always hear my dad's voice," Jeremy said. "Sometimes I couldn't even hear my coach telling me what to do, but I could always hear my dad."

Gary Toton was a believer that no matter how well you played, there was always room for improvement. He drove Jeremy, pushed him, never let up on him. Naturally, that led to father and son clashes. "One night I scored forty-two points and we lost the game at the buzzer," Jeremy said. "I thought I had done everything possible to try and win that game. But when I came home he was all over me, shots I missed, plays on defense I could have made. It just wasn't good enough."

Fortunately Gary's drive never caused a real split in the family. Jeremy came to understand why his father wanted so much to see him play well. He had worked in a General Foods factory for a number of years and then became a teamster, driving construction dump trucks after the factory closed down. No one on his side of the family had ever been to college. Gary Toton was absolutely determined to see his son get the chance to go to college and basketball was the route.

Jeremy grew to six-six in high school and began attracting a lot of attention from midsize schools. His ultimate ambition was to play at Indiana for Bob Knight but he knew that was unlikely. Dream 1A was Evansville. Everyone in Evansville was a fan of the Aces, and the Totons had season tickets. Coach Jim Crews and his staff had shown a lot of interest in Jeremy during his junior year and right into his senior year. But as the year went on it became apparent that the school was recruiting three players with only two scholarships to offer.

Still hoping things would work out with Evansville, Toton began to look for alternatives. The first recruiting letter he had ever gotten had been from Navy. "I just tossed it," he said. "No way was I going there."

But DeVoe had seen Toton playing summer ball and had been impressed. Assistant coach Doug Wojcik had made the trip to Evansville on several occasions to see him play. He was not exactly greeted with open arms, most notably by Toton's high school coach Bill Wilgus, who thought Toton should stay home and play at Evansville. Gary Toton felt the same way. He had never missed seeing his son play a game and wanted to keep that streak alive when he went to college. The one person in the family who was intrigued by Navy was Marilyn Toton. She liked the idea of a degree from a place like the Naval Academy and thought Jeremy should give it serious thought.

It never would have happened if Crews had offered him a full scholarship. But he didn't. Instead, he offered him a financial aid package with a promise that he would try to get him a full scholarship as a sophomore. It would cost Toton $8,000 to go to Evansville as a freshman. Gary Toton was willing to pay that much, even though it would be a drain on the family's finances. Other schools had gotten involved at this point and Jeremy was truly torn.

Then came the dream in which Bob Knight told him he had to go to Navy. Toton awoke the next morning and, following the instructions of the nocturnal Knight, told his mother he was going to Navy. She was delighted, even though she didn't know why. When he told

Wilgus to tell the other schools about his decision, Wilgus tried one more time to convince him to stay home and go to Evansville.

"Basically he kept saying I was a local hero in Evansville and that I should stick around and build on that," Toton said. "But I remembered a couple of months earlier I had been in the grocery store and I recognized the guy bagging my stuff — he had been the local high school hero in Evansville about ten years earlier and had stayed home to go to school. I knew going to Navy was the right thing."

He couldn't go straight to Annapolis, though, because even though his grades were good his boards were not, just under 1000. There was no way to get him admitted directly to the academy. Instead, he went to the prep school for a year, improved his board scores considerably, and arrived in Annapolis figuring he was ready to play and play often.

Then he spent his freshman year on the JV team. That was okay because his pal Savane was on the JVs and DeVoe had made it clear that he preferred playing experienced players while the freshmen learned the system. By sophomore year he was in the playing rotation and in the third game of the season against Towson State, he came into the game in the first half and promptly drilled three 3-point shots. He had arrived. But that 10-point game proved to be the high point of the season. His playing time fluctuated. Junior year was more of the same. He had worked hard throughout the summer knowing he had one more chance to be a major factor on his college team. The Chris Worthing affair hadn't helped matters because DeVoe had held Toton and Savane, the two seniors, primarily responsible. The difference was that DeVoe might get mad at Savane, might holler at him, but he wasn't going to stop playing him. Toton's role was more tenuous.

As the season approached, Toton's playing time in practice dwindled. He was getting less and less time with the second team. DeVoe always plays a lot of people in practice, in fact the JVs often work out with the varsity. But Toton had been around long enough to know that the playing patterns in practice were not pointing toward a lot of game minutes for him.

Desperate and unhappy, he went to see assistant coach Tom Marryott. He told Marryott he didn't want to be a spectator during his senior season, that he thought he deserved to play more and could help the team. Marryott tried to be soothing but he wasn't going to lie to him. "Jeremy, you may have to accept the fact that this team needs you as a vocal leader," he said finally.

Translation: You're a cheerleader in a uniform.

Toton then went to Jimmy Allen, the number one assistant, to plead his case. Allen was just as soothing and just as honest. But he did say, "Give it some time, Jeremy. Things do change around here."

That part was true. DeVoe is almost never wedded to a lineup or a rotation. A player might play twenty minutes one night and zero the next. Someone buried on the bench in December could be starting in January. Or the other way around. Toton decided to wait and see what happened when the season actually began. At Rice, he was a vocal leader. The game lasted forty-five minutes and Toton was a vocal leader for forty-five minutes. On the bench.

Over the weekend, he decided to take his case directly to DeVoe. And so, there he was on Monday morning in the coach's office telling him what he had told Marryott and Allen, telling him how much it had hurt not getting into the game at Rice. DeVoe listened. He understood. He had never been a great player in college either and had worked his way up from almost no playing time as a sophomore to starting as a senior. He knew Toton was a good kid and a hard worker. But he couldn't make him any promises. He told him he would do the best he could and that he wanted him to be an on-floor contributor. Toton understood. He wasn't thrilled with what DeVoe had said but he felt better. At least DeVoe was now aware of his distress.

"I felt terrible for Jeremy that day," DeVoe said. "There's never been a kid here that worked harder, tried to help in any way he could. Whenever we needed someone to take a recruit around the Yard, he was always the first to volunteer. But finding a role for him just wasn't that easy."

DeVoe took Odom and his assistants to lunch at Riordan's, the popular restaurant on the Annapolis docks run by Mike Riordan, the former pro basketball player. At fifty-six, Odom was two years younger than DeVoe. "I don't know about you, Dave, but it gets a little tougher for me physically every year," DeVoe said. "I tire more easily and sometimes I worry that I get more impatient with the players because of it."

He then filled Odom in on the Restricted Nine and how it had affected the fall. Odom's eyes went wide. Like most coaches at civilian schools it never occurred to him that anything short of an arrest could get a basketball player into serious trouble. "It's a different world, isn't it?" he said. DeVoe laughed at that one. Odom didn't even know the half of it.

The crowd in Alumni Hall that night was a very respectable 4,218. The quality of the opponent, DeVoe's rousing speech to the Mids at lunchtime, and the fact that it was the last game before Thanksgiving break all created a solid turnout.

They came hoping to at least see a close game. Realistically, Navy wasn't going to beat an ACC team, especially an ACC team picked in preseason polls to finish in the top four in the league, perhaps as high as second. "This is the most talented team we'll face this season," DeVoe told the players before the game. "That doesn't mean if we go out there and play smart and play hard for forty minutes that we can't beat them."

Before every game, DeVoe fills the locker room board with offensive and defensive keys after the assistant coach in charge of scouting the opponent has gone through the personnel. In the upper-right-hand corner of the board, DeVoe always writes a goal for projected points for and against. This is an optimum figure. Most nights he will write something like "Navy — 80s," and then below that for the opponent the team name and "50s." For someone like Lafayette he might put Navy in the 80s, Lafayette in the 60s. For a Division III team it will probably be Navy 90s and the opponent 40s. On this night, DeVoe wrote: "Navy — 70s, Wake — 60s." That was a sign of how tough he thought the Deacons were going to be. In his mind, best-case scenario, the final score might be Navy 70, Wake 69. The players understood. It wasn't a lack of confidence in them, but an acknowledgment that tonight the Mids would need to be just about perfect to have any chance.

For most of the first half, they did have a chance. After falling behind 8-0, they rallied to within 26-22 with under six minutes to play. It was still 34-27 with 3:30 left before the game fell apart for them. Most of the damage was done by All-ACC guard Robert O'Kelly, who kept getting into the lane and setting his teammates up for easy baskets. Then, in the final minute, he made three straight plays to break the game open: stealing the ball and feeding Nicky Arinze for a layup; blocking a Jehiel Lewis jumper and converting on the other end; finally, the backbreaker, a 3-point shot just before the buzzer. Suddenly, a competitive game was a rout: 46-29. Navy wasn't going to come back from that kind of deficit against a quality opponent.

The only good news in the second half was that Jeremy Toton got a chance to play. Midway through, with the margin at 20, DeVoe called his name. As Toton headed to the scorer's table to report in, DeVoe stopped him and looked him in the eye. "Okay, Jeremy," he said, "this is your chance to show me something."

Toton nodded. And then he did just that. In nine minutes he didn't score, but he had three rebounds and four steals, proof that he could play the kind of defense DeVoe is always looking for. "Jeremy asked for a chance that day and when I gave it to him, he really did show me something," DeVoe said. "What was most important was what he did on the defensive end. The score didn't matter at that point, but the way he kept his head up and looked to make things happen did."

The final margin was a discouraging 90-55. No one in the Navy locker room had any doubt that Wake Forest was good, but no one had envisioned that wide a gap — especially at home. As the players waited for DeVoe to finish his postgame radio show, Mark Alarie, who had left a good job working for a Wall Street firm to try his hand at coaching, tried to put a positive spin on what had just taken place. "The way to look at it, fellas, is that's the kind of team you'll be facing in the first round of the NCAA Tournament," he said. "That's where we have to get to if we're going to compete in a first-round NCAA game. It gives us something to work toward."

The players all knew that Alarie knew about NCAA quality teams, having played on three of them at Duke in the 1980s. But at that moment, their thoughts were a long way from March and the NCAAs. So were DeVoe's.

"Hey, guys, we need to put this behind us," he said when he reached the locker room. "The one thought we need to have right now is that forty-eight hours from now we *must* be right here celebrating a win over Richmond. That is an absolute must for us right now."

Before he could worry about getting that win over Richmond, Sitapha Savane had to worry about getting off restriction. He had finally made it to his fifty-ninth day, and Wednesday would be his last day. When someone has been on restriction for a lengthy period of time, the second to last day is his "slide day." On slide day, once the final muster is completed, a restrictee is rolled (or slid) by his friends across the floor of the rotunda inside Bancroft Hall, where the restriction musters take place. The symbolism in the slide comes from the notion that the end of restriction means the end of the need for a perfect uniform. Once the restrictee has done his slide across the rotunda floor, he jumps to his feet, throws his cover (hat) to his friends, and usually gives a short speech that, broken down, goes something like "Free at last, I'm free at last."

Even after sliding, Savane still had to get through Wednesday, which would be no small task. On the last day before Thanksgiving break, the mids all wake up at 5 A.M. so they can get through an accelerated class schedule that gives everyone a chance to get home as early as possible for the holiday.

That's everyone except the basketball team. They remained on the rapidly emptying Yard preparing to play Richmond. This was a typical early season Patriot League nonconference game. Richmond was a solid Colonial Athletic Association team, once a major rival of Navy's when the Mids played in that league. In 1998, the Spiders had reached the NCAAs and pulled a major first-round upset, going in as a number fourteen seed and beating number three seed South Carolina.

This Richmond team was not as good as that one, but it had quickness and shooters and a fine coach in John Beilien. In short, a winnable game, but also a losable game. DeVoe knew his team was going to walk into a dead building for this game, especially compared to Monday's raucous crowd. The mids had all gone home. There was no pep band. A crowd announced at 1,124 that looked and sounded like even fewer roamed the many empty seats.

"Hey, guys, we bring our own enthusiasm tonight," DeVoe said before the game. "I know there will be a lot of blue [seats] in that arena but it doesn't matter. What matters is making sure Richmond is glad when this game's over and they can get on the bus and go home because we've worn them out."

DeVoe got part of his wish. Richmond was certainly glad when the game was over, but that was because the Spiders had escaped with an ugly 58-52 victory. For twelve minutes, Navy looked superb, building a 25-11 lead. The rest of the night was a struggle. Richmond took the lead on the first possession of the second half and never trailed again. Navy did get even, at 52-52 on a pretty steal and dunk by Chris Williams with 2:42 left, but didn't score again. In fact, on their last nine possessions, with the game hanging in the balance, the Mids only got two shots off. They ended up with twenty-eight turnovers for the game, a pathetic number against a relatively soft defense.

They all stood staring straight into space, every face blank during the playing of "Blue and Gold," a scratchy recording replacing the pep band's normal postgame rendition. This was a new low for everyone. DeVoe had never once been 0-3 as a head coach. They had played horribly and they knew it. And now Air Force, which had beaten them two years in a row, was coming to town Saturday.

DeVoe paced around the locker room for several minutes as if trying to decide what to say. He talked about wanting them all to enjoy Thanksgiving either with their families if they were in town or with their sponsor families. He told them to get some rest and be ready to work hard on Friday. Then he stopped, looked around, and shook his head.

"You know what this is, guys," he said. "This is God's sweet redemption for all our screwups this fall. That's what it is. You guys acted immaturely and irresponsibly, you got yourselves in trouble, and it affected us all fall. It affected all of you. And now this is redemption for that. We deserve this. We all do."

He went on for a while longer before leaving them with one final encouraging thought: "There is only one Division I basketball team in the country right now that can say it has lost two straight games to Air Force. That is one goddamn statistic that better change on Saturday."

Savane and Toton, who lockered next to each other, both stared at the ground thinking the same thing: Is this what our senior year is going to be like? Is that August night going to haunt us straight through the winter? Is our season going to go down the tubes before we even get to conference play?

"It was a truly awful moment," Savane said. "I think we were all in shock. We were upset by losing, upset by what Coach DeVoe said, upset by everything that was going on. It was like, where does this all end?"

Thinking about the end, Savane glanced at his watch. It was 10:15. He bolted upright and began pulling his coat on. He had fifteen minutes to get back to Bancroft, get into uniform, and report to his final restriction muster. If he was late, the day — his sixtieth — wouldn't count and he would have to spend Thanksgiving Day on the Yard reporting to muster.

"That," he said, "would have been the end."

Savane made muster. Everyone enjoyed the day off. It was a relief to not think about the academy or basketball for twenty-four hours. Toton's family had made the drive to Annapolis for the holiday and he enjoyed seeing them, even though he couldn't help but express dismay over what DeVoe had said to the team after the game. At least he was getting a chance to play.

On Saturday morning, before the rest of the team arrived for the three o'clock game, Savane and Toton sat down and talked. Technically, the team had no captains at that point. In the media guide, there was no mention of captains. In fact, the players were listed in alphabetical order, rather than by class starting with seniors, as was normal. Savane would not have his stripes restored until his upperclass privileges (car, civilian clothes, the ability to come and go on the Yard without checking in and out) were returned to him at semester's end. But they were the team's seniors. They needed to provide some leadership.

And so, for the second time in a week, Savane asked DeVoe if the players could have a brief, players-only meeting before the game. He had done the same thing before the Wake Forest game but that had been more to remind the other players that DeVoe was right when he said that they all had something to prove in their new roles. This was different. This was a meeting about sticking together and not letting anything get them down. The only way to get DeVoe to quit talking about August was to play the way he wanted them to play and, more important, the way they all wanted to play. They had to quit worrying about getting yanked from games and play aggressively. They hadn't done that the first three games.

"I don't care if we're playing the Little Sisters of the Poor," Savane said. "We need a win today and we can't let Air Force come in here and think they can beat us."

DeVoe didn't give any fire and brimstone pregame speeches. Instead, he just wrote on the board: Air Force — 97, Navy — 88. That had been the score at Air Force the previous December. He reminded them once more about the two-game losing streak to the Falcons. That was enough.

The gym was just as empty and quiet as it had been Wednesday night, but that didn't seem to matter to Navy. From the beginning, Savane and Chris Williams dominated the game. The Falcons couldn't guard either one of them. At halftime it was 45-25. The lead grew to 25 before a brief Air Force spurt cut it to 13. From there, the Mids cruised home to win, 93-78. Savane had 25, Williams 17, and freshman Scott Long 14; Jehiel Lewis (13) and Robert Reeder (11) were in double figures. Reeder, who had been zero-for-eight from the free-throw line the first three games, even managed to go three-for-five from there.

"I had faith, Robert," DeVoe said when it was over. "I had faith that you were going to make one before the end of the millennium."

The sound coming out of the Navy locker room that afternoon was one that hadn't been heard in a long time: laughter. Winning makes the world look like an entirely different place. On a warm, sunny November afternoon, even an empty Naval Academy suddenly looked a lot nicer to the Navy basketball players than it had looked in a long time.

Savane had a huge smile on his face as he left the locker room. There was no muster to go to. And, for the first time in what seemed like forever, there was a victory to celebrate.

The Lehigh curse was finally behind them.

So too, they hoped, was the night of August 26.

11

BUILDING BLOCKS

IF there was one thing Emmett Davis had been determined to change from his first season at Colgate to his second it was the name of his season-opening opponent. He knew his team had to go to the Carrier Dome to play Syracuse because of the tradition and, more important, because of the money. But he had no desire to begin the season there.

He had done that in year one. The final score had been 93-40. "I had coached one game and I felt like I was oh-and-four," Davis joked.

Perhaps the only person who had a worse night in the Carrier Dome than Davis was Devin Tuohey. The game at Syracuse was his first game as a college player. Tuohey was a slender, dark-haired nineteen-year-old from Washington, D.C., who was generously listed in the Colgate media guide as six-oh, 170 pounds. Like Chris Spitler at Holy Cross, he had been screwed genetically: his two older brothers, both basketball players, were six-four. "I keep saying, where are my last four inches?" he said. "I'm still waiting for them to show up."

Like his older brothers, Brendan and Sean, Tuohey had gone to Gonzaga High School in downtown Washington. Brendan had been a four-year letterman at Colgate, playing on the two NCAA teams with Adonal Foyle. Sean had gone to Lehigh for a year and a half and had been the starting point guard. But the coaching change that brought Sal Mentesana to the school had not gone over well with him and he had transferred back home to play Division III ball at Catholic University.

Devin, though not blessed with his brothers' size, loved to play. He was the typical little brother, following the big kids to the school yard and playing "up" with older kids for as long as he could remember. His father, Mark, a partner in a big-time D.C. law firm, and his mother, Marty, a psychotherapist, had always chosen to live in Washington rather than in the suburbs. Most of the kids the Tuohey brothers grew up playing with in their neighborhood were black, something Devin has always been thankful to his parents for.

"We lived in a truly diverse neighborhood," he said. "I played basketball every day growing up with four kids, three of them black, one of them Jewish. I think it gave me a different view of the world than a lot of kids who grow up going to Catholic school or private school." He smiled. "It also probably helped make me into a decent player."

Devin followed his brothers to Gonzaga but did not have the sort of immediate success they had. In fact, his sophomore year was extremely difficult: Sean was the captain of the varsity, while Devin wasn't even starting for the JV. "It got so bad that quitting actually entered my mind," he said. "But basketball had always been part of my life and I wasn't ready to give it up."

He made the varsity as a junior and was the seventh man. As a senior he became a starter and had a good season on a good team, making honorable mention All-Met on a 30-4 team. Jack Bruen, having coached Brendan for four years, was interested in having him at Colgate. Dartmouth also expressed interest, which thrilled Devin. "If I could have gotten into Dartmouth as a senior, I think I would have gone there," he said.

But his 1100 board scores weren't high enough to get him into Dartmouth. Several people recommended he go to prep school for a year. That would give him a chance to improve his boards, mature physically, and improve his late-blooming game. Thinking that the road to Dartmouth might lead through prep school, Devin enrolled at Lawrenceville in New Jersey.

Overall, the decision proved to be a good one. His grades, always solid, got better. His boards went up to 1250. The one time Bruen came down to see him play, he played well, confirming Bruen's notion that he could succeed at Colgate. But Dartmouth lost interest and the Ivy League dream never panned out. Tuohey visited Colgate's upstate New York campus in November, loved the place, and committed to play there. Only after the visit did he learn that the reason for Bruen's thinness was that he had pancreatic cancer.

"We had known him for a long time and when I saw him I was amazed at how much weight he had lost," Tuohey remembered. "But I was naive. I thought he had just been working very hard on losing weight."

If Brendan had been in the country, Devin no doubt would have heard about Bruen's illness earlier. But he was playing basketball in Ireland. So Devin learned how sick Bruen was only a few weeks before his death. He was devastated, but it didn't change his feelings about Colgate. He had liked the school and the players and the idea that even though it wasn't the Ivy League it was a top-drawer school academically. "Coach Bruen was almost like a member of our family because we had known him for so long. He had played for my high school coach [Dick Myers] so we went way back with him. But I had chosen Colgate as a college, not because of a coach."

Very rarely does this occur in Division I basketball. Most players choose a coach. Often, when a player commits to a school or signs with a school and the coach leaves, he will try to get out of that commitment. Sometimes he will even go with the coach to his new job if he can get a release from the original school. That tends not to happen in the Patriot League. After Pete Herrmann was fired at Navy in 1992, Doug Wojcik and Emmett Davis spent a month on the road recruiting, having no idea who the next coach would be. "Most of the kids we were talking to were interested in the academy regardless of who the coach was," Davis said. "I'm not sure that would be the case at a lot of places."

It was the case with Tuohey and Colgate. He didn't meet his new coach face-to-face until his first day on campus. It was quickly apparent to him that Davis was a lot different from Bruen. "Coach Davis knows there's a time to have fun and a time to work," he said. "Coach

Bruen worked hard at his job, but his approach was more laid back. Coach Davis is pretty intense."

All the intensity in the world couldn't save Davis or Tuohey or the Red Raiders on that November 1998 night in the Carrier Dome. Syracuse Coach Jim Boeheim hadn't been happy with the way his team had played against Colgate the previous year, trailing by 11 at halftime before winning by 4. Even the mitigating circumstance of Bruen's illness wasn't enough of an excuse as far as Boeheim was concerned.

"They started pressing us when we got off the bus," Davis remembered. "Here it was my first game as a head coach and I'm not only playing at Syracuse but I'm playing against them when they're mad."

Late in the first half of the blowout, Davis looked down the bench and decided to give Tuohey a shot at running the team for a couple of possessions. A true baptism by fire. Tuohey entered the game with a little less than a minute to play. After Syracuse had scored, he took the inbounds pass, looked up, and saw six-nine Etan Thomas on his left and six-seven Ryan Blackwell on his right.

Houston, we've got a problem.

"I tried to fling the ball over Thomas's head," he said. "He just reached up, caught the ball with one hand, took one step, and dunked."

The second possession of his college career went better. This time Tuohey got the ball across half-court. He was trying to hold the ball out near the jump circle to run the clock down for a last shot. Jason Hart, the All-American guard, was on him. "I remember thinking to myself don't cross over [dribble] because if you do, he'll steal it," Tuohey said. "The message didn't get from my brain to my hands, because I tried to cross over."

Hart swiped the ball and took off the other way, fully intending to slam the ball through the hoop. "I just couldn't get dunked on twice in the first thirty seconds of my college career," Tuohey said. "I took off after him. Just as I started to reach out and foul him, I tripped and went flying right into him."

Hart and Tuohey landed in a pile under the basket. Hart was furious, thinking Tuohey had tried to hurt him. "I kept saying, 'Jason, I'm sorry, I tripped, I didn't mean to tackle you,'" Tuohey said, able to laugh about the whole thing a year later. "He just kept screaming, 'Get off me, get off me.'"

By the time Tuohey and Hart got untangled, 20,000 people — or so it seemed — were screaming at Tuohey. Hart made the two free throws and the half mercifully came to an end with Syracuse leading 47-23. As Tuohey walked off the court he heard the crowd. "All I heard again and again was 'You suck, Twelve, we're going to *kill* you when this game is over.'"

Davis didn't dare play Tuohey in the second half. His stats line for his first college game (unofficially) read: one minute played, two turnovers, one foul, and six death threats.

Of course he had the unfailing support of his teammates. When he came out of the game after the Hart play, his roommate Jim Detmer looked at him and said, "Devin, I'm really sorry. But that's the funniest thing I've ever seen."

Tuohey, whose parents pay full tuition for him at Colgate, shook his head. "My parents are paying $32,000 a year," he thought, "for *this?*"

A year later, everyone could look back on the Syracuse debacle and joke about it. Nonetheless, with a still-young team (one senior, three sophomores, and a freshman starting) Davis was very happy not to begin the season at Syracuse again. Instead, the Red Raiders would play three games prior to the Syracuse trip: two in Connecticut as part of the Mohegan Sun (a casino on an Indian reservation) Classic and then a home game against Canisius.

Davis was hoping to establish some confidence before the Syracuse game, rather than have his players all hopped up about playing at Syracuse and then have that confidence crushed — the way Pat Harris had watched his team start at Duke.

The plan almost worked perfectly. With Devin Tuohey in the starting lineup against the school that didn't want him, the Red Raiders lost a tough 68-65 game to Dartmouth in the opener, but then bounced back the next night to beat Albany easily. That was followed by an encouraging 76-59 victory over Canisius. In that game, sophomore forward Jordan Harris was superb, with 33 points and 11 rebounds.

There was a good deal of talk around the Patriot League about Colgate's two sophomore forwards, Harris and Pat Campolieta. Campolieta had been the league's rookie of the year in 1999, and Harris seemed to be growing as a player with every game. When Delaware Coach Mike Brey looked at Colgate on tape to prepare for his team's game against it, his first comment was, "Jordan Harris is not the kind of athlete you expect to see on a Patriot League team."

Harris had been an absolute steal for Davis, the first real victory he and his staff had come up with after getting hired. In an era where there is no such thing as a sleeper because all players get seen sooner or later, Harris was a sleeper. He had grown up in New Jersey, but had moved to the Phoenix area with his mother in junior high school. He had played at Brophy Prep there and was a good player and a good student. He had been recruited for a while by Davidson but for some reason no one had really gone after him during his senior year. He had graduated from Brophy and, with no scholarship offers, was planning to walk on at Arizona State in the fall.

In the meantime, Davis and his staff, having been hired the last week in April when recruiting was all but over, were scouring the country hoping to find someone to add to their team in the fall. They did have one important commitment — Campolieta — who had decided on Colgate before Bruen's death and, like Tuohey, decided to stick with the school even though he didn't know who the new coach would be. But, hoping to find someone to add to the team, Davis and his assistants began calling coaches they knew at academic-minded schools to find out if anyone they had been recruiting but had decided not to sign might still be out there. The Davidson coaches mentioned a kid named Harris from a small private school in Arizona with good grades and boards over 1200.

"We figured it was worth a phone call to see if he had anything going on," Davis said.

Harris had nothing going on. So, when Davis offered him the chance to visit the campus in July, he flew out, liked what he saw (most of the snow in Hamilton has melted by mid-July), and, when the school said it could offer him almost a full scholarship based on his mother's finances, he decided to take a chance. "Of course," he said, "they didn't tell me that it snows a hundred inches every winter."

Harris was raw, but talented. In a sense, he was the perfect match for Campolieta, who played the game with a kind of instinct that can't be taught. Not all that quick, Campolieta had thirty-seven steals as a freshman and would lead the league in steals as a sophomore. He was as consistent as Harris was inconsistent. Harris had averaged only 7.5 points per game as a freshman and Davis wanted to see him be more aggressive about shooting the ball as a sophomore. The 33 points against Canisius was a true breakout game for him — almost doubling his previous career high of 17 points.

Davis knew that the second full week of the season would not be easy. On Monday, the team would make the trip to Syracuse. On Wednesday, they would board another bus and travel five hours (assuming the weather was decent) to Newark, Delaware, to play a Delaware team that was coming off back-to-back NCAA bids and played every home game in front of a full house. In the Patriot League, when an itinerary mentions what time a charter leaves it is a reference to a bus, not a plane.

The Syracuse trip turned out about as expected: it snowed the night before, it snowed the day of the game. Syracuse pressed the entire forty minutes. Devin Tuohey improved his line from a year ago — sort of. After making six of ten shots from the floor in the first three games (doubling his field goal output from freshman year) he was zero-for-six when faced with the specter of Thomas (who blocked nine Colgate shots), Blackwell, Hart, and the Carrier Dome crowd. But he did have a steal and two assists and, at least as far as he could hear, no death threats. The final was 93-49, not pretty but an improvement. Davis's main concern was that his team come out of the game healthy and without suffering a loss of confidence, since he believed an upset of Delaware was possible.

He knew that two of Delware's senior starters, John Gordon and Darryl Presley, both key players, were hurt. He had also looked at enough tape to know that Delaware was a very good offensive team, but hardly an overwhelming defensive team. "I'm not at all impressed with their defense," he told the players. "We can score on them."

That analysis would come as no surprise to Brey, who had been telling friends even before Gordon and Presley got hurt that he was concerned about his team's defense because his two best defensive players had graduated. "We'll have to outscore people," he said. "Because we aren't going to stop them."

Delaware was, in many ways, the role model for what a mid-major Division I program should aspire to be. Its arena, the Bob Carpenter Center, which seats 5,200, was sold out for the season. Every corporation in Delaware — or so it seemed — was a sponsor of the Fightin' Blue Hens. In fact, Brey's concern about his fans was malaise. His team had won so often the previous two years — forty-six games — that winning at home against a team like Colgate was seen as a given, even with two senior starters in street clothes.

"We've become a little bit of a wine-and-cheese crowd," Brey said, referencing a famous comment made by ex–Florida State guard Sam Cassell about the sometimes somnambulant crowd at North Carolina's Dean Dome. "Our people don't understand that Colgate's pretty good."

The first half seemed to prove the crowd right. After Colgate had jumped to an early 16-12 lead, Delaware took control, consistently beating the defense down the court for open shots. The Hens went on a 24-10 run to close the half and were up 36-26 at the half. Davis was very unhappy at the break because, like all coaches, he believes that transition defense is about effort. If Delaware shot the ball well from outside, he understood. If his team shot poorly from outside — and it had, zero-for-five from the 3-point line — he knew that was part of the game. But not getting back on defense was unacceptable.

Things didn't get any better at the start of the second half. When the lead got to 43-30, Davis yanked all five starters. With the game going on behind him, he turned to the bench and said to them, "If you can't play hard, you can't play. Sit here and watch until you're ready to play hard again."

The benching lasted a little less than a minute. After each team had failed to score in a trip downcourt, Davis turned to the starters again and asked, "Are you ready?"

"Yes!" they shot back in unison.

Quickly, he called a thirty-second time-out to get the starters back in. Almost as quickly, Campolieta found Pat Diamond with a pretty backdoor pass to cut the lead to 43-32. A moment later, a TV time-out intervened (as they always do). Davis thought he had his players' attention — finally. "Listen to me, guys," he said during the time-out. "I believe in every single one of you. This is a chance for us to get noticed around the country by beating this team on this court. Let's make something happen."

They did. In the next four minutes they scored 7 straight points and shut Delaware out. They were getting back on defense and Delaware's 3s weren't falling. When Diamond hit a 3 to make it 43-39 with 11:25 to go, the Delaware wine-and-cheese crowd suddenly realized it had a game on its hands. So did the Blue Hens. They pushed the margin back to 10, but as Brey had predicted, they didn't have enough defense to shut down Campolieta or Diamond. The only thing keeping Colgate from gaining control of the game was Harris having a cold (three-of-thirteen) shooting night. Still, they kept creeping back. It was 51-47 with 4:33 left after a Diamond follow shot. Playing the odds, Colgate fouled center Ndongo Ndiaye, a 30 percent foul shooter. In the scouting report, assistant coach Rod Balanis had instructed Colgate's inside players to foul Ndiaye anytime he had a layup. Following orders, Campolieta hammered him before he could go up and dunk a miss by shooting guard Billy Wells.

Ndiaye had been brilliant all night on defense. He would finish with nine blocks and eight rebounds and he had hit four of five shots from the floor. But now he was on the foul line, normally a terrifying experience for him. He missed both shots. Colgate had a chance to cut the margin to 2. But Ndiaye made up for the missed free throws by deflecting a Campolieta shot and grabbing the loose ball. The Raiders never got that close again. Down the stretch they twice fouled Ndiaye after getting to within 6. This time he ruined the strategy by sinking all four foul shots. The final was 65-56, Ndiaye blocking one last shot by Campolieta — who had been superb, with 22 points and ten rebounds — as the buzzer sounded.

Davis wasn't sure how to feel. On the one hand, he knew a chance had been missed to beat a good team on a night when it was vulnerable. On the other hand, his team had come from 13 down to 4 down with the ball on the road in front of a packed house. Davis opted to go the positive route in talking to his team.

"I'm damn proud of you," he said. "You fought your hearts out. That's an NCAA Tournament team and so are you — *if* we keep improving. We're a young team and a young program and we need to learn from nights like this." He paused and smiled wanly. "One thing, guys. We've got to stop letting players break school records for blocked shots against us."

Ndiaye's nine blocks had been a school record, just as Thomas's nine at Syracuse three nights earlier had been a school record there.

Again and again, Davis returned to the same theme: we must improve to be an NCAA Tournament team. In every locker room around the Patriot League, from Lafayette and Navy to Lehigh and Army, coaches kept repeating that theme: we can be an NCAA Tournament team if . . .

Only one of them could be right.

12

ONE MORE CHANCE

NO one in the Patriot League had gotten off to a better start than Bucknell. Like Colgate, the Bison had opened their season in a pre-Thanksgiving tournament on the road. They were playing in Pough-keepsie, New York, in the Pepsi-Marist Classic. As if opening on Marist's home court wasn't bad enough, there wasn't a single Coke in sight all weekend.

Bucknell began the tournament with a victory over Maine, which was no small thing. The Black Bears had been the last team to win at Delaware the previous season and would go on to win twenty-four games by season's end (including two more wins over Delaware), before a devastating injury to their point guard in the opening round of the America East Tournament ended their hopes of reaching post-season. The America East is a rung up from the Patriot League in the Division I pecking order. Most of the time it will get two postseason bids: one to the NCAA and one to the NIT. In March of 2000, Hofs-tra would be the league's NCAA rep; Delaware would go to the NIT; and Maine, even with twenty-four victories, would sit at home.

The next night, playing in the championship game of the tourna-ment, the Bison beat Marist, 54-48. They then came home and beat Robert Morris before losing on the road to a good Rider team. But they won their next two over St. Francis of Pennsylvania and Mount St. Mary, where they trailed by 17 with fifteen minutes to go before rallying to win.

What made the 5-1 start so impressive was that it had not been an easy fall. Pat Flannery had started preseason practice with one major concern: replacing point guard Willie Callahan, who had graduated in the spring. As it turned out, the point guard spot was the least of his troubles.

The previous spring, Pete Santos, then a freshman, had been horsing around in his dorm with some friends, jumped off several steps, and broken his right femur. The doctors inserted a rod in the leg and told him he should be able to play in the fall. They were right, but it was apparent when practice began that he was favoring the leg and had almost no push-off from the right side. By early November, Flannery was certain that Santos wasn't going to be able to play.

That cost the team some depth. The next injury was far more significant. Ten days before the start of the season, the Bison hosted Drexel in a preseason scrimmage. Three minutes into the scrimmage, Jake Ramage, who had been the team's second-leading scorer as a sophomore, went up for one of his trademark 3-point shots, came down wrong, and crumpled in agony. He had torn the ACL in his knee. His season ended that day.

Ramage's injury left the Bison without one of their two consistent outside threats — Valter Karavanic was the other — and with the need to establish another perimeter scorer to balance the inside threats of Dan Bowen and Dyrika Cameron.

The good news was that the point guard position was not going to be a headache. Flannery had gone into the fall with four candidates to replace Callahan: sophomore Bryan Bailey, junior Nyambi Nyambi, and a pair of freshmen, Dan Blankenship and Chris Zimmerman. By the time Ramage went down, there was no doubt that Bailey was going to be the starter. From day one, it had been clear to everyone that this was his team to run.

That fact was remarkable considering that Bailey had walked on the team a year earlier as a freshman. He grew up on Long Island, in Hempstead, and played both football and basketball at South Side High School. The only Division I school that recruited him at all was SUNY–Stony Brook — and that was for football.

In the spring of his senior year he visited Bucknell, not as a basketball player, but as a regular student. He did, however, come prepared.

During the visit, he showed up at the basketball office unannounced and handed a tape of himself to assistant coach Don Friday. It is not that unusual for unrecruited players to present themselves to college coaching staffs claiming they can play if only given a chance. More often than not, the coaches will take a cursory look at the tape and then write a polite note explaining to the player that they don't think he will fit in with their team. In fact, Bailey had delivered an identical tape to the coaches at Boston University when he visited there and never heard back from them.

This was a little bit different. Friday was impressed enough with what he saw on Bailey's tape to tell Pat Flannery about him. They checked on Bailey with admissions and found that he had been admitted to school on an academic scholarship that would pay about 50 percent of his tuition and fees. Friday called Bailey and told him he was welcome to work out with the team when he got to school and to be a part of the JV team from day one. Bailey went to the first JV meeting in September. But he never had any intention of playing for the JVs.

"My attitude was that I didn't want to play Division III ball or Division II ball and I didn't want to play JV ball for a Division I school either," he said. "If I wasn't good enough to play varsity, then fine, I'd just concentrate on school."

When the varsity players began playing pickup games in the afternoon, Bailey showed up, hoping to play. For three days, he was a spectator. Finally, his fellow freshman Pete Santos picked him for a game.

"If not for Pete, I might still be sitting there," Bailey said, smiling.

Once he got into a game, though, continuing to play was not a problem. "It took about two possessions," Dan Bowen said, "to see that this guy could play. He was the quickest guy on the court, hands down."

Bailey comes by his speed and quickness honestly. His mother was a track star as a kid, running both the 100 and the 200. "I can beat her," Bailey said. "Now." His younger brother Maurice, also a Division I walk-on (at Rider) is, according to Bailey, quicker than he is.

Bailey became a member of the team and his minutes increased as the season went on. He didn't play at all in the first three games and, when Flannery finally put him in at Florida International, he turned the ball over the first time he touched it. "I thought to myself, 'Uh-oh, this isn't the way to build the coach's confidence,'" he said.

He had three more box score DNPs (Did Not Plays) in the next five games, but by Christmas break, he started getting more minutes and began to build some confidence. By the time Patriot League play began, he was getting a solid twelve minutes a game behind Callahan at the point guard spot and he kept improving as his confidence grew. When the players began their pickup games in the fall of 1999, Bailey didn't have any trouble getting chosen for games. In fact, some of the time he did the choosing. He had scored a career-high 14 points in the comeback against Mount St. Mary and was the only nonsenior in the starting lineup, which also included Karavanic, Bowen, Brian Muckle, and Cameron. The sixth man was another senior, Shaun Asbury. The rest of the rotation consisted of three freshmen: Blankenship, Zimmerman, and six-ten Brian Werner. The injuries to Ramage and Santos had left the team with a strange chemistry: five seniors, one sophomore, three freshmen. For six games, it had worked.

The win over Mount St. Mary left Bucknell with one game to play before their break for exams: at home, against Princeton.

The case could be made that this would be Bucknell's most important nonconference game of the year — for several reasons. First and foremost was the humiliating loss the Bison had suffered at Princeton a year earlier, losing 68-27. The players and coaches all felt they had come a long way in the twelve months since that game, and this was a way to prove it.

It was true that games later in the month at Penn State and at Arizona State would be against teams that had more talent than Princeton. But those were guarantee games. The players would go into them believing they could win and, as they would prove at Penn State, would be capable of winning them. But Bucknell wasn't supposed to compete with a Big Ten team or a Pac-10 team on a regular basis. The Ivy League was another story, especially when the Ivy League team was Princeton.

In a very real sense, Princeton was the role model for everyone in the Patriot League — and, for that matter, the Ivy League. It was not a putdown of Pennsylvania, the Ivy League's other dominant team, to make this statement; although Penn people might not see it quite that way. Fairly or unfairly, Princeton had become the poster child for "smart" basketball. In 1965, Princeton had made the Final Four led by future Rhodes Scholar, U.S. Senator, and presidential candidate Bill Bradley. That team had been immortalized for fans of basketball and literature by John McPhee, who had taught Bradley, in his book *Breaks of the Game.*

Bradley graduated in 1965. His coach, Butch Van Breda Kolff, left two years later to coach the Los Angeles Lakers. Van Breda Kolff was succeeded by Pete Carril, who made patient offense and the back-door pass his trademark and stayed twenty-nine years, consistently winning with kids who were capable of explaining the way they ran their offense based on geometric angles. Carril retired in 1996, but only after his team's upset of defending national champion UCLA had given him a final moment in the spotlight.

More talented teams hated playing against the Tigers because of their patience and their ability to squeeze the game into the 40s or 50s. The final score against UCLA had been 43-41. For a team with UCLA's talent to play a game like that had to be like having water dripped on the players' heads for forty minutes. Carril's most famous game had been a loss. Seeded 64th in the 1989 NCAA Tournament, the Tigers took on the top seed in the field, Georgetown. The Hoyas won the game 50-49, but only after almost being backdoored right back to Northwest Washington and only because a cowardly official swallowed his whistle on the game's final play and didn't call a clear hack by Alonzo Mourning as Princeton center Kit Mueller released what could have been a game-winning shot. Even though Princeton didn't win, that game became the rallying cry for every team given no chance in an NCAA Tournament opening-round game.

It wasn't that Penn wasn't as successful as Princeton. The Quakers had also been to the Final Four, in 1979, with a center who was a con-cert pianist. Their players also spoke in complete sentences and grad-uated, and they had dominated the Ivy League in the mid-1990s under Fran Dunphy. It was just that Princeton was ranked with Harvard and Yale among the nation's great universities. Penn was a fabulous school, but it wasn't Princeton. And so, when a coach like Pat Flannery looked at Princeton and what Bill Carmody had been able to achieve in the four years since he had succeeded the legendary Pete Carril, he could only shake his head and think, "Boy would I love to be that good every year."

Princeton had actually been better under Carmody — who had been Carril's assistant for twelve years — than under Carril. It had gone undefeated in the Ivy League during Carmody's first two seasons and had been 27-2 in 1998, the only losses coming at North Carolina in December and in the NCAA Tournament against Michigan State. That Princeton team ranked right up there with the Bradley team when it came to sending intellectuals into paroxysms of joy.

That was why beating Princeton would mean so much. The Tigers, even with a relatively young team, were good — they were always good. Some years they were better than good. Like Bucknell, they had players who were smart and good kids. You couldn't lose to Princeton and walk off the court thinking, "Yeah, but our guys will get better jobs when they graduate." Princeton's guys would get very good jobs when they graduated. And, like the Bucknell players, they would graduate.

The good news about playing Princeton in the last game before exams was that Flannery wouldn't have to worry about having his players' attention. The name of the opponent would take care of that. Davis Gym would be packed, it would be hot (even on a cold December night), and it would be loud.

Bucknell has played basketball in Davis Gym for sixty-two years. For almost that long, there has been talk about building a new gym to replace it. Davis is a throwback, a tiny 2,300-seat gem, that looks and feels a lot more like a high school gym than a place where a team that is eligible to win the NCAA championship plays. Flannery lovingly calls it "the steam bath."

Opponents hate the place. They complain about the heat and the proximity of the front-row seats to their bench. They complain about the fact that the bathroom in the visitors' locker room is open to the public before the game and that they have to fight their way through a mobbed hallway to get from the locker room to the gym. It doesn't soothe them at all to know that the home team has to walk through the school's weight room, which serves as a snack lobby during games, to get to and from its locker room.

If you are anyone but the opponent or someone who doesn't like being in an overheated gym on a winter night, Davis is a wonderful place to watch a basketball game. A core group of Bucknell students — their version of the Zoo Crew — sit in the end zone nearest to the Bucknell bench and do everything they can to taunt or distract the opponent. One of their favorite chants whenever Bucknell is in trouble is "Safety school." That might not have been accurate in Princeton's case, but it didn't stop them from chanting it anyway.

Bucknell wasn't in very much trouble in the first half. The Bison were primed and ready to play this game. Flannery is a detail-a-holic when it comes to preparation. The players are not only given a four-page scouting report, they are given a fifth page that includes a question sheet. The purpose of the question sheet is to be certain they are paying attention to the scouting report. But it also gives some insight to player personalities. Dyrika Cameron answered every question in great detail and complete sentences. Fellow senior Dan Bowen rarely gave an answer longer than three or four words.

Example: Question — In Princeton's matchup defense, by screening their wings, where can we attack them?

Cameron: We can attack them on the baseline. We can attack their back line because they like to keep their big guys inside.

Bowen: Corner.

Both answers were correct. In fact, Bowen used a total of fifteen words to answer the five questions on the Princeton scouting report. Cameron used fifteen to answer the first question.

Flannery didn't much care how many words anyone used as long as they understood the points the scouting report was trying to make. Throughout the first half, it appeared that everyone had studied the scouting report perfectly. Leading 9-8 six minutes in, Bucknell went on a 16-3 run, holding Princeton to one bucket, a 3-pointer by Nate Walton (son of legendary UCLA center Bill Walton) during a stretch of almost thirteen minutes. Princeton, normally a superb 3-point shooting team, was awful from beyond the arc — making only one of its first twelve shots from there. The spell was finally broken when Mike Bechtold, a 3-point shooting specialist, hit the only shot he would take all night. Bowen answered from inside before halftime, and the margin was 27-14 at the break. Davis was shaking with noise.

No one in the Bucknell locker room felt cocky at halftime. Everyone knew Princeton would not continue to shoot the ball so poorly. There was also a sense that the lead could have been — should have been — even bigger than it was. Every coach with a big lead at halftime says the exact same thing to his players: "It's zero-zero when we go back. First five minutes, guys. That's the key. First five minutes."

Flannery told his players exactly that and he was exactly right. The game turned completely around in the first five minutes of the second half. Princeton came out about as hot as it had been cold in the first half. Sophomore center Chris Young, who had been zero-for-four in the first half, started it by drilling a 3 on the Tigers' first possession. All of a sudden, it was Bucknell that looked shell-shocked. Karavanic missed two wide-open shots from in close and Princeton, six-for-twenty-one at halftime, hit the first seven shots it took in the second half. After six and a half minutes, the Tigers had the lead, 33-31. Any hopes for a blowout were gone. The game settled down into one of those every-possession-is-life-and-death deals. Princeton tends to thrive in such an atmosphere because that's the way it plays almost every night.

"Hey, guys, we fell asleep for a while," Flannery said during a timeout with the score tied at 35. "It's okay though. We're tied zero-zero and we have to make sure we play good defense."

Both teams played good defense down the stretch. Princeton went up 47-43 when Mason Rocca, the team's only senior starter, ducked his shoulder and got past Bowen for a layup with 3:36 left. Bailey promptly answered that with a drive of his own. Young hit one free throw but Karavanic, colder than the outside temperature all night, finally nailed a 3, falling down as he did, to tie the score at 48 with 56 seconds left.

Brian Muckle then made a great defensive play, blocking a layup attempt by freshman Spencer Gloger (who had turned down a scholarship at UCLA to play at Princeton) and getting the ball back for Bucknell with the shot clock turned off and a chance to play for the winning basket.

Flannery wanted Bailey to run the clock down and then try to penetrate and react to the defense. He had been Bucknell's best offensive player, doing just that all night, scoring 19 points. But as the clock rolled under thirty seconds, Bailey and Bowen miscommunicated. Bowen gave the ball to Bailey and then headed for the low post. Bailey thought Bowen was going to stay outside as a passing outlet for him while they killed the clock. He turned to pass the ball sideways to Bowen and realized a split second too late that Bowen wasn't there. The ball went out of bounds, right into the stunned Bucknell bench.

Now Princeton had the ball, with the chance to play for the last shot. The Tigers let the clock slip to five seconds before Eugene Baah tried a jumper from the right side. It hit the back rim, but before anyone from Bucknell could make a move toward the rebound, Rocca swooped in from the left side, yanked the ball down, and in one motion flipped it right-handed back at the basket. In his scouting report, assistant coach Don Friday had written as his final words about Rocca: "MUST BOX OUT!" At halftime, Flannery had brought the subject up again. "Rocca is their toughest guy," he said. "He's not a choirboy. He'll go through you to get to the ball. Get a body on him every time."

Rocca hadn't had an offensive rebound in the entire second half — until the last five seconds. He was going across the lane, falling away from the basket, when he got to the rebound. His shot hit the rim twice, went high in the air, and — with one second left — dropped in.

That was the winning basket. Final: Princeton 50, Bucknell 48.

All losses hurt, but some really sting. This had been a chance for redemption and they had failed to convert, even with a big lead. The game had been decided by a mental mistake and a missed box-out. That really hurt. What's more, they had to wait thirteen days — and survive exams — before they would get a chance to play again.

As he always did before he spoke to the team after a game, Flannery met briefly with his assistants: Friday, Terry Conrad, and Carl Danzig. Conrad and Danzig had actually been at Bucknell longer than Flannery, having been part of Charlie Woollum's staff. Friday had been with Flannery at Lebanon Valley and had come to Bucknell with him. The four of them had meshed into a close staff in six years. Now they looked at each other blankly.

"No sense beating them up," Conrad finally said. "They've got a lot to deal with the next few days."

Everyone nodded. They knew the players would beat themselves up regardless of what was said at this point, and exams lay just ahead.

"Put this out of your minds as quickly as possible," Flannery told them in the silent locker room. "You've got an important job to do the next few days. When that's done, we'll worry about what happened tonight, we'll look at our mistakes and we'll figure out how to get better. I promise you, guys, we *will* get better."

He paused as if deciding whether to stop there or go on. He wasn't quite ready to let go. "We told you first five minutes, guys, didn't we? That's where we lost the ball game. The turnover, Danny and Bryan, that's on me. That was miscommunication. I take the hit on that one. The box-out — a mistake, sure. But that's not where we lost the game. We let them back in the game emotionally the first five minutes, and you know what? We let the refs back in the game, too. They're Princeton so they get the calls when the game's close. That's *our* fault because we let it happen. No one to blame but ourselves."

He felt himself starting to get angry, so he stopped there. The only moment when he got snappish came when a couple of players were a little slow moving into the huddle. "No self-pity," he said. "No heads hanging. This season has just begun. The only thing I guarantee you, guys, is that the sun's gonna come up tomorrow morning. And when it does, you'll have exams to take. So put this behind you as soon as you can."

Flannery's wife, Patti, was waiting for him on the floor. Friends and family linger after games at Bucknell because, as at Lafayette, there is always a postgame reception, win or lose. Patti Flannery is a Bucknell graduate, and most nights she will bring Ryan, five, and Jesse, three, to home games. But the boys need to get home right after the game is over. Patti Flannery tries to stick around long enough to gauge her husband's mood and to find out how late he thinks he needs to stay — either at the reception or in the office with his assistant coaches.

"When do you think you'll be home?" she asked.

"Just as soon as it stops hurting," Flannery answered, forcing a smile. He shook his head. "Actually, I'll be home a long time before that happens."

Bucknell was 5-2, with several impressive victories. At that moment no one in Davis Gym remembered very much about those wins.

Bucknell's preseason might have been a bit bumpy because of the injury to Ramage and Santos's inability to return. But it was an absolute cakewalk compared to what was going on at Holy Cross.

Especially for the four seniors.

Ralph Willard had made it clear in the spring that none of them was going to be guaranteed a spot on his first Holy Cross team. There would be two classes of scholarship players in place in the fall and Josh Sankes would be eligible, having sat out Bill Raynor's final season following his transfer from Rutgers.

From the beginning, it was evident to everyone on the team that Willard's style was entirely different from Raynor's. Willard was all business on the basketball court, a complete no-nonsense guy. He had a dry, self-deprecating sense of humor off the court, but the players didn't get to see it that often. Raynor had been everyone's friend, someone the players joked and kidded with. There weren't a lot of yucks around Willard.

"From day one, it was clear this guy was 180 degrees different from Coach Raynor," said Tony Gutierrez. "I don't remember ever getting tired in practice or a workout with Coach Raynor. With Coach Willard, I was sucking wind after ten minutes every day."

The four seniors were Gutierrez, James Stowers, Malik Waters, and Chris Spitler. Early on, the senior most likely to make the team seemed to be Stowers. The senior least likely to make the team was Spitler.

Stowers was the most established of the four. He had averaged 10.4 points per game in Patriot League play and had been the team's leading scorer down the stretch, averaging almost 20 points a game in Holy Cross's last six games. He was the third-leading 3-point shooter in the league, a deadly standing-still shooter. Anyone who could shoot the ball that well was bound to find a spot on the team.

Only it wasn't that simple. Stowers's relationship with basketball was a complicated one. He had grown up in Orange Park, Florida, a suburb of Tampa, and had been an excellent tennis player before the finances of tennis and his jump shot drew him in the direction of basketball. This pleased his father, Bill, because he had gone to Colorado on a basketball scholarship but had ended up transferring to a small Christian college during his sophomore year, giving up basketball.

"I can remember one summer-league game when I was in high school where I really didn't play well," James said. "My dad was all over me. He told me to either play or not play, but not to do it halfway. He kept telling me he had lost his chance to be a player and he didn't want me to lose mine."

Stowers grew from a five-seven high school freshman to a six-four sophomore. That was when his game began to come together and the notion of basketball being a route to college began to become real to him. But, after an excellent junior year that drew little attention from college recruiters, he decided to transfer from St. John's Country Day School, a small private school, to Orange Park High School, because he and his father were convinced he needed to play on a bigger stage to get noticed by college coaches. Additionally, Darryl Lauderdale, the coach at Orange Park, had coached at Chaminade, the tiny school in Hawaii that had become forever famous in basketball circles in 1982 when it had upset top-ranked Virginia and Ralph Sampson in what is generally considered the most shocking regular-season upset in college basketball history.

Lauderdale had come to Chaminade years after The Upset, but his time there had left him with numerous contacts with college coaches. Stowers had a good senior year and solid board scores (1200) and grades (3.2 GPA), and Lauderdale was certain someone would offer him a scholarship. For a while, Davidson was interested, but that fell through. Then Stowers got a dream phone call. It was Pete Carril. The Princeton coaches had seen him on a tape when they were watching another player. Carril really liked the way he played, not just the way he shot, but his feel for the game. The Stowers's sent in their financial information and were told James could receive a $29,000 financial aid package — almost a full ride. Stowers applied to Princeton early decision. "It never occurred to me that they would tell me they could get me that kind of financial aid package if they weren't convinced I would get in," he said.

The number of schools in the country that would ever turn down a basketball prospect — especially a basketball prospect who was wanted by their legendary coach — with a 3.2 GPA and 1200 on the boards can easily be counted on one hand. Unfortunately for Stowers, Princeton is one of that tiny group. Princeton turned him down.

"I was devastated," he said. "Worst of all, I hadn't been talking to anyone else. I had almost no other options." A couple of Division II and Division III schools were after him, but that wasn't what he was looking for.

"The dream had always been Division I basketball," he said. "I thought I was good enough if someone gave me a chance."

No one seemed willing to give him a chance. In late April, Lauderdale drove Stowers to the district tennis championships. During the trip, Stowers told Lauderdale how disappointed he was that he hadn't been offered a chance to play basketball at a Division I school. He didn't blame Lauderdale, he just wished it had turned out differently.

Lauderdale felt he had let Stowers down. The next day he put together a highlight tape of Stowers and sent it to several coaches. One responded — Bill Raynor in Worcester, Massachusetts. He liked what he saw and was willing to put together a financial aid package for Stowers at Holy Cross even though he had never seen him play in person. Stowers accepted. It was a good school, it would save his parents some money, and it was his chance to prove he could play on the Division I level.

His career at Holy Cross had seesawed. He had played very little as a freshman on a veteran team. As a sophomore he had been a starter early in the season and seen his playing time slip as the season went on. He had put hours and hours into basketball that year and had watched his grades slip badly in the process. Midway through his junior season, still struggling, he decided it was time to turn his priorities around.

"It occurred to me that all the work I had been doing in basketball still hadn't made me into a player who was a star or even playing regularly on a bad team," he said. "That was a pretty strong indication that basketball wasn't meant to be the thing I built my life around. I decided I wanted to go to law school. But I knew it was going to be an uphill battle."

Stowers's GPA midway through his junior year at Holy Cross was 2.5. Second semester junior year he pulled a 3.6. He also played the best basketball of his life. "It seemed as if when it mattered less, I played better," he said.

This isn't surprising. Stowers is a deadly serious young man who clearly puts tremendous pressure on himself to succeed. He has a James Dean–like quality about him except there's no cigarette dangling from his mouth. He often looks as if the future of the world may ride on his next test or jump shot.

Like the other players, Stowers was immediately impressed with Willard. He could feel himself improving as a basketball player during the off-season drills. But Willard's system is built on defense. Stowers was a shooter. As preseason progressed, he began to worry about his status on the team. He was also worried about his grades. He was working day and night, knowing he had to continue to get high grades if he wanted a realistic shot at law school. Shortly after midterms, he got sick and missed a week of class and practice.

When he felt better, he went to see Willard about his future with the team. Willard had been holding off on cutting players because he was truly torn about it. His own senior year had been a struggle. His coach, Jack Donahue, ran an inside-oriented offense and Willard first saw his scoring go down and then his minutes, even though he was the team's captain. He had gone through a coaching change (as a junior) just as these seniors were now going through a coaching change.

Stowers told Willard he just wasn't sure he could handle the stress of basketball and trying to maintain high grades. He didn't know if he was going to make the team or not and he thought maybe the best thing was just to try to keep his head above water academically. Willard let Stowers do the talking in the meeting. He felt the decision should be his. He wasn't going to push him either way. Stowers finally told Willard he was going to give up basketball.

That night he called his father and told him what had happened. "Did you get cut?" his father asked.

"I'm not sure if I would have been cut or not," Stowers said. "We never even got to that part of the discussion."

Bill Stowers had to know. He called Willard the next day and asked him the question directly: Was James going to get cut? No, Willard told him, James was not going to be cut.

"I need to talk him out of this, then," Bill Stowers told Willard. "I owe it to him to not let him make the same mistake I did."

Willard didn't think Stowers was making a mistake. He told Bill Stowers that he thought he should be proud of James, that he had made a difficult decision with his future in mind. "He's showing a lot of maturity the way he's handling this," Willard said. "I think he can help our team. But basketball isn't his future; law school is. And he should play basketball only if he wants to, not because you think he should."

Bill Stowers hung up the phone and decided to stand by his son's decision without any further discussion.

Willard did cut a couple of walk-ons and he cut Malik Waters, who had come back the previous season from major knee surgery but simply didn't have the quickness Willard thought imperative to contribute in his system. Stowers was so busy with his schoolwork that he didn't really have a chance to brood about not being a basketball player anymore. Waters did. He sat around the dorm in his practice gear for days, clearly adrift and devastated.

"It was tough to see," Chris Spitler said. "I don't think anyone envisions their basketball career ending that way." He smiled. "Except maybe me."

Spitler had figured his chances of making the team to be fifty-fifty at best. When Willard first met him in the spring he had figured Spitler's chances were slightly less than that: like zero. "I thought he was Eddie Haskell," Willard said. "I mean, every day he would show up with all this enthusiasm and rah-rah. Every day it was, 'Coach, how are you today? How are things? How are you settling in? Anything I can do to help, Coach?' I didn't think it could be real. In fact, I knew it couldn't be real. No one is *that* enthusiastic."

When Willard expressed this sentiment to Roger Breslin, the one holdover coach, Breslin was sorely tempted to tell him how wrong he was. But he didn't. "I thought he would just think I was trying to defend the kid because he was going to be a senior," Breslin said. "Plus, I figured if he gave it long enough he would figure out that he was wrong about Spit."

Willard figured it out. At some point during the fall, it occurred to him that the Eddie Haskell act, if it was an act, would have to break down at some point. But it never did. Spitler was always in the gym, always willing to do anything the coaches asked, always there to help a teammate in any way he could. "I realized that after a lot of years in coaching, I'd gotten a little jaded," Willard said. "I hadn't coached anybody like Spit for a while. My only regret was that he didn't have the ability of some of the guys I'd coached who didn't have an attitude anywhere close to his."

Spitler made the team, continuing the annual ritual that Holy Cross sports information director Frank Mastrandrea had taken to calling "The Three Phases of Spitler."

Phase One: You can't possibly play on this team.

Phase Two: You're on the team, but you will never see the floor during a game.

Phase Three: You're starting.

Mastrandrea had seen Raynor go through all three phases with Spitler during his sophomore and junior years and was convinced Willard would go through all three before the end of Spitler's senior year.

The other senior to make the team was Tony Gutierrez. While Stowers dreamed of law school, Gutierrez wanted medical school. He had grown up in San Diego, the son of Mexican parents who moved to San Diego from Tijuana so he could attend an American high school. Gutierrez played on very good teams at the University of San Diego High School, with, among others, Nate Walton, who was now a starter at Princeton. He had a 4.2 GPA as a senior on a 4.0 scale (he took AP courses) and close to 1300 on his boards. Both Stanford and Harvard offered him academic scholarships.

Gutierrez knew he wasn't good enough to play ball at Stanford, but he was surprised when Harvard told him he could walk on the team if he wanted but that the coaches weren't all that interested in him.

Army Coach Dino Gaudio was very interested in him, and unlike at Harvard and Stanford, where his parents would have had to pay some tuition, Army would cost nothing. Gutierrez's father is a civil engineer but, working in Mexico, his annual income was about $13,000 a year. Thus, a full ride meant a lot to him. He decided on Army.

And was miserable. "I hated it the first day I was there, the last day I was there, and every day in between," he said. "It just wasn't for me, the whole military thing."

He left before the start of second semester plebe year, sat out all spring, and enrolled at Holy Cross — which had also recruited him — the following fall. For two years his playing time fluctuated between starting and playing not at all and, if not for the fact that he had to stay on the team to keep his financial aid package intact, he might have quit. He was thrilled with Willard from day one and thought Willard's system would make him a better player.

But schoolwork was closing in on him. He knew his GPA — 3.0 — wasn't good enough to get him into medical school. He was struggling with chemistry. At midterms, he was up all night drinking coffee and popping caffeine pills. "I was a complete wreck," he said.

He made the team. But seeing Waters and Stowers go hurt him. He and Spitler were the only seniors left, and the locker room didn't feel the same without the other two seniors. Waters had been one of his closest friends on campus and Stowers had been his roommate. He woke up one Saturday morning wishing he could sleep a little longer, and then hit the books instead of going to practice. He walked up the hill to the Hart Center and made a decision.

"I saw Coach in the hallway when I walked in and I asked him if he had a minute," Gutierrez said. "We went into his office and I told him I just didn't want to play anymore, that I just didn't feel the passion was there."

Willard understood. He gave Gutierrez a couple of minutes alone in the locker room to tell his teammates. At first they didn't believe him. Come on, Tony, quit fooling around and get your gear on for practice. Gutierrez shook his head. He was serious. He was done.

The only person in the locker room who knew Gutierrez wasn't kidding was Spitler. "You could see the look on his face," Spitler said. "I think if not for missing his teammates, he would have quit sooner."

Gutierrez nodded at that thought. "Exactly right," he said. "Once I had proved to myself that I could make the team, I could make a clean break. It was *my* decision. I've never looked back."

On the same night that Princeton was beating Bucknell, Gutierrez, Stowers, and Waters went into downtown Worcester to an arena called the Centrum to watch their former teammates play Boston College. Once upon a time, this had been a heated rivalry. In fact, Holy Cross still led the series, which dated back to 1906, 46–35. But the two schools had traveled very different roads since 1979, when Boston College had said yes when invited to join the Big East and Holy Cross had said no.

Father Brooks, who had made that decision on behalf of Holy Cross and then had taken the school into the Patriot League, had no regrets. He was quick to point out that although BC had known some success in basketball (reaching the Elite Eight in 1994) it had been rocked by gambling scandals in both football and basketball and had lost Coach Jim O'Brien a couple of years earlier after O'Brien and the admissions department had a very public and ugly falling out over who did and who did not belong in school.

Now, BC was struggling to stay out of the Big East cellar, and Willard — who had split ten games with the Eagles during his time in Pittsburgh — was trying to make Holy Cross a factor in the Patriot League. BC had won eight straight times, dating back to December 1990, the first year of the Patriot League's existence.

The season had started well — unbelievably well — for Holy Cross. The Crusaders had gone to Providence for a guarantee game and won, beating the Friars, 54–43. Like BC, Providence was a struggling Big East team. Nonetheless, a win for a Patriot League team over a Big East team — any Big East team — was monumental. Chris Spitler, who had always supported the Brooks position that athletic scholarships were more trouble than they were worth to an academically oriented school, admitted to some second thoughts on the topic while walking the campus on Monday.

"Everyone just had these big grins on their faces," he said. "The whole school was psyched because of what we did at Providence. I have to admit seeing that made me think again about the value of scholarships. I could care less if the school makes money on basketball. I do think it is good for the collective psyche of the place when we do well."

The collective psyche of the place went in the other direction after the Providence game, however. Harvard, Fordham, and Dartmouth all beat the Crusaders by double digits.

The Boston College game was the best the team had played since Providence. Although they shot the ball horribly all night (seventeen-for-forty-five) and Josh Sankes turned the ball over nine times and scored just 5 points in twenty-seven minutes, the Crusaders stayed in the game by playing the kind of defense Willard insisted they play. They trailed just 21-18 at halftime, hung close almost until the end, and lost, 50-43.

Watching was difficult for the three ex-players. Gutierrez, who was most at peace with what had happened, was the most enthusiastic, cheering his buddies on, hoping they could figure a way to win. Waters was at the other end of the spectrum. He was still hurt by what had happened. He sat and watched quietly. Gutierrez sensed that he wasn't even certain who he wanted to win the game. Stowers was torn. Part of him said he was doing the right thing, that he couldn't put in the time that was needed to still be playing basketball. Another part of him hadn't let go yet. And, watching the team struggle to score, he knew — *knew* — that he could have helped.

The worst news of the night wasn't the final score. It was Ryan Serravalle's knee injury. Serravalle, the sophomore point guard, had become the first freshman in twenty years to lead Holy Cross in scoring the previous year and was leading the team in both scoring and assists. Initially, it was thought that he had just twisted the knee and might be able to play two nights later against Yale. A further look revealed a torn meniscus. Serravalle joined Jared Curry, who had pulled up with back spasms in the Harvard game, in street clothes.

It wasn't as if Holy Cross was deep. The five starters in the Providence game — Serravalle, sophomore Patrick Whearty, and juniors Curry, Sankes, and Juan Pegues — all had some college basketball experience. Among the seven players on the bench, only Spitler had ever played in a college game prior to the season. Now, with Curry and Serravalle both out, a pair of freshmen, Brian Wilson and Mark Jerz, would start against Yale. The bench would consist primarily of sophomore Guillermo Sanchez, a walk-on who had played on the JV a year earlier, freshman Tim Szatko, who had been prepared to walk on at Notre Dame before getting a last-minute phone call from Willard offering a scholarship, and, of course, Spitler.

Phase three loomed.

On the day after the Boston College game, Spitler wasn't even at practice. He had been excused because he had to take an oral final exam in a seminar taught by Father Brooks called "Modern Christology." Spitler had been studying several great theologians throughout the semester with Brooks, and in his final he had to explain to a panel of experts put together by Brooks what the writings of the nineteenth-century philosopher Pierre Teilhard de Chardin meant as they related to Jesus Christ.

The day before the exam, Spitler had joked to Brooks that he might make his presentation in French. "Your accent better be good," Brooks told him. Spitler backed off quickly. He would stick to English.

He arrived from the exam and the post-exam dinner Brooks took his students to each semester looking like anything but a senior basketball player. He wore a jacket and tie, was carrying books under his arm, and was preparing for an evening of studying while working on the security desk of the Hart Center.

"My friends all keep telling me I don't have to work hard anymore because I've got a job," he said. "Force of habit."

Spitler had learned earlier in the week that he had won a much coveted two-year internship with Goldman-Sachs in New York. This came as something of a shock to him, since he had applied for the internship more for the experience of going through the interviews than anything else. He was an English major with a 3.5 GPA and high enough law boards that he was applying to Ivy League law schools. Many of his friends who were economics majors would have killed for a Wall Street internship. Spitler had gotten one. He had decided to accept it, because by working for two years he would be able to pay off the $27,000 in student loans he would have when he graduated. Then he would go to law school.

He knew he wanted to be a lawyer, not only because his father was a lawyer but because he had worked as a paralegal in a Buffalo law firm over the summer and had been fascinated by the work. He had spent a good deal of the summer working on a case involving a nineteen-year-old woman who had been accused of murdering her infant child. After she had been convicted of involuntary manslaughter, he contributed to the presentencing brief, hoping to convince the judge to give her a suspended sentence. The judge had sentenced her to two years in prison. Spitler had been so stunned and upset by the decision that he had written an emotional, five-page paper for one of his classes. He had yet to make a phone call to find out how the young woman was doing.

"I'm afraid to," he said. "I'm not sure I want to know."

On the face of it, a trip to Yale was just what Holy Cross needed. Yale was — like every Ivy League school not named Princeton or Penn — a basketball gulag. Its last coach to leave with a winning record had been Howard Hobson (120-118), who had retired in 1956. In forty-three years of Ivy League play Yale had finished first once — in 1957, the league's first basketball season. Dick Kuchen, the school's most recent coach, had finished second in back-to-back years (1990 and 1991) and had actually pieced together three straight winning seasons, including a 19-7 record in 1990. But more typical times had followed: seven straight losing seasons, including 4-22 in 1999.

It was not surprising, then, that Yale's most distinguished basketball player was Chris Dudley (Class of '87), who had played in the NBA for thirteen years, making his mark as a solid backup center who was best known as perhaps the worst free-throw shooter in league history. It was also not surprising that on the page in the Yale media guide that listed ninety-seven of Yale's "famous alumni"— among them presidents, Nobel Prize winners, Supreme Court justices, senators, congressmen, cabinet members, Pulitzer Prize winners, Tony Award winners, and men like Dr. Benjamin Spock and former baseball commissioner Fay Vincent — Dudley was the only basketball player included. Chances were good that in any publication that was *not* the basketball media guide, Dudley wouldn't make the list. Certainly, swimmer Don Schollander and football players like Calvin Hill and Brian Dowling would seem likely to rate mention over Dudley in most places.

Kuchen had been fired after the '99 season, his place taken by thirty-five-year-old James Jones, once an assistant under Kuchen. Like Holy Cross, Yale was starting from square one. Yale was 2-5, coming off a win at home three nights earlier against Army, a game the Cadets had led at one point 21-8 before falling apart en route to a gruesome 48-42 loss.

Willard was concerned about Yale. They had a lot of experience up front, starting two seniors and a junior. On tape, they were playing very hard on defense for their new coach and they had a dangerous freshman guard named Chris Leanza, who could shoot the ball. With Serravalle out, that matchup became even more dangerous.

Taking a team to play in the John J. Lee Amphitheater would be a slightly different experience for Willard than Madison Square Garden had been. The floor of the John J. Lee is on the basement level of sixty-eight-year-old Payne-Whitney Gym. There is no gym, arena, or field house in America that looks like Payne-Whitney. It is nine stories high and from the outside it looks like a twelfth-century European cathedral. Walking in, Jared Curry immediately pulled the hood of his jacket over his head and began singing out in as deep a bass voice as he could find, "Aah-main, Aah-main." The halls were dark enough that one almost expected to see silent monks coming in at any moment.

Chris Spitler walked across the court before the team had even found the locker room and sat down on the last seat of the visitors' bench. "I'm just testing it for comfort," he said.

Willard laughed when he heard that line but that was going to be his last light moment for a few hours.

The announced attendance in the building was 610. But the Yale pep band made plenty of noise and a road game was a road game. Holy Cross fell behind 17-9 early on a Leanza 3, but with Sankes and Patrick Whearty playing well inside managed to lead 29-24 at the break. Spitler got into the game long enough to take a charge — his specialty — but earned Willard's enmity when he tossed up a 3 with the shot clock off and Holy Cross playing for the last shot.

"I thought," Willard said as they walked off the court, "that being smart was your strength."

"Absolutely untrue, Coach," Spitler said.

Willard almost smiled.

Holy Cross led throughout the second half, but it wasn't easy. Only a foolish play by another smart kid (one would assume all Yale kids are smart) kept the Crusaders in control. With the score 54-50 and the amphitheater almost loud, Yale freshman Ime Archibong stole the ball and went in for an uncontested dunk that would cut the margin to 2 and, in all likelihood, force Willard to call a time-out. Somehow, Archibong missed the dunk and, in the process, grabbed the rim and hung on to it. If you hang on to the rim — unless you've been fouled — that's an automatic two-shot technical foul. James Jones hated the call, but that didn't matter. Whearty made one-of-two, Holy Cross got possession because of the tech, and Juan Pegues hit two more free throws. When Whearty drained a 3 thirty seconds later, it was 60-50, and it was Yale that had to call time.

Yale didn't go away. In fact, after Leanza hit two straight 3s when the defense somehow left him open, Yale had the ball with a chance to tie. But center Neil Yanke missed inside and Brian Wilson, hit a ten-footer with 1:06 left to finally put the game away. The final was 72-65, and everyone was exhausted.

"I can't tell you how proud I am of you guys," Willard said. "We're banged up, we're on the road, I know you've all got exams to worry about. That's a great win."

Whearty had been excellent, with 19 points; Sankes had come up with 15 points and fourteen rebounds; Pegues 11 and ten. But the revelation had been Guillermo Sanchez, the walk-on sophomore guard. He had come off the bench to play thirty-two minutes and had produced 13 points and four rebounds.

"G-O," Willard said, calling him by his nickname. "Son, that was great."

As the players dressed for the two-hour bus ride back to Worcester, Willard slumped on a chair staring at the statistics. "When I first took the job I thought I knew two things for sure," he said. "One was that it would take us a while to be a good team. Two was that I'd be coaching good kids." He smiled. "Turns out I was right about the first part, wrong about the second. It will take us a while to be good. But these aren't good kids, they're great kids."

He was drained, but happy. He was in the John J. Lee Amphitheater, struggling to beat Yale. Twelve months earlier he had been coaching a team that had beaten UCLA. And yet he seemed to be exactly where he wanted to be.

13

THAT LIGHT IS A TRAIN

DURING the first nine years of its existence, five of the eight teams that played basketball in the Patriot League (Fordham having departed after the 1995 season) had represented the league in the NCAA Tournament. A sixth, Bucknell, had twice played in the championship game and had won the regular-season title once. The Bison, in fact, had been the league's most consistent team. They had finished under .500 in league play just once and had the best winning percentage of anyone in regular season play.

Which left two teams out in the cold: Army and Lehigh. Lehigh had entered the league in 1990–91 at a time when the program was going well under Paul Duke. The Mountain Hawks were 10-2 in conference play that first season, finishing second to Fordham, and were 8-6 and fourth the next year. Since then, they had not been higher than fifth and their seven-year record in conference play was actually worse than Army's: 20-70, compared to the Cadets' 22-68.

All of that made getting off to a good start of paramount importance at both schools. Pat Harris had known Army was going to be in for a long night opening at Duke, but he believed the next three games were winnable: at Cornell, followed by a pair of games at home against Division III teams. Sal Mentesana had scheduled Lehigh's Division III games a little bit later. But he believed his team could win three of its first four games — Yale, Harvard, and Wagner — all at home. A trip to Penn State for a guarantee game after opening against Yale had to be thrown in for the sake of the budget.

The win over Yale was a big deal for the simple reason that it was a win. When a team finishes a season by losing nineteen of its final twenty games, beginning the next season with a win is a huge confidence booster. "It's as if they think to themselves, 'Hey, maybe the worm has turned,'" Mentesana said. "Is Yale a great team? No. Are they an awful team? No. Are we a great team? No. But after that game we had a right to think that at least we were getting better."

The 69-56 loss at Penn State wasn't discouraging either. Lehigh hung in the game — down 2 — until the last eight minutes and never felt overwhelmed. The only disappointment came in the final minute when Zlatko Savovic, who was beginning to look like a point guard who could do things on offense that Lehigh point guards hadn't done for a while, sprained an ankle, meaning he would be out at least two weeks.

Losing to Harvard hurt because the game felt winnable. The Mountain Hawks led 31-22 at halftime before crashing and burning in the second half, losing by 10. Mentesana was convinced that the difference in the game was confidence: Harvard had it, his team didn't. The Crimson had gone 13-13 in 1999 and finished fourth in the Ivy League. When they got behind, there was no panic. "They trusted their stuff," Mentesana told his players. "They were behind, but they knew it would work and they stuck with it. When we got behind, because of what happened to us last year, we didn't have that kind of confidence. That was the difference."

The loss was difficult, but not backbreaking. Three nights later, Wagner came to Stabler Arena for what Mentesana considered a key game in his team's development. Wagner had been the first game Lehigh had played the previous December after losing Brett Eppeheimer. The 73-45 loss had proven to be a sad harbinger of what Life Without Brett was going to be like. Now the Seahawks were coming to Lehigh with a rookie coach — Dereck Whittenburg — and a young team, one with far less experience than Lehigh.

Winter was already closing in on northeast Pennsylvania on the last day of November. There was snow in the forecast and a cold wind was whipping through South Mountain, which separates Lehigh's two main campuses. Stabler Arena, which opened in 1979, is on the Goodman campus, which is five miles across the mountain from the main campus. The location of the arena is not exactly a boon to student attendance, nor does it make life simple for the players who have to make the trek back and forth on a daily basis — as do the coaches, since the basketball offices are located on the main campus, too.

That, however, is the least of the building's design flaws. In many ways, Stabler is a model for a midsize arena. It seats 5,600, most in chairbacks. It is well lit and has plenty of parking around it, since Lehigh's football stadium is directly across the street.

Then there are the locker rooms. Apparently the architect who built Stabler didn't give much thought to the fact that it would be used by men's and women's teams. That may have been because wrestling, not basketball, is the dominant sport at Lehigh. Or perhaps he just had a strange sense of humor.

The locker rooms sit at each end of a long hallway underneath the south stands of the building. There are two for the home teams, two for the visitors. The door to the Lehigh men's locker room is approximately three feet from the door to the women's locker room. The players come and go through the same tiny entranceway. And there is only one bathroom and shower facility for the two teams.

In the politically correct Patriot League, the men's and women's teams always play doubleheaders during conference play. They do not do this for financial reasons: the teams travel separately. They do not do this for academic reasons; in fact, men's games often start after eight o'clock, either because the women's games run long or because — at Lafayette — they are scheduled that way. This means that the men's teams, who always travel home by bus after games, often get home at two, three, or four o'clock in the morning — depending on the length of their trip — on days when the players are expected to be up and in attendance at morning classes.

Pairing the men's and women's teams in doubleheaders is supposed to increase the number of people watching the women play. This thinking is also flawed. People who want to watch the men play aren't going to show up early to watch the women. And those who want to watch the women will show up whether there's a men's game to follow or not. And in one case, Holy Cross, the women's basketball team outdraws the men. While the men's program has struggled in recent years, the women, under Bill Gibbons, have flourished. The only sellout in the Hart Center during the 1999–2000 season was for a women's game against national champion Connecticut.

For years now, the men's coaches have complained about the setup. They don't like playing so late, especially on the road, especially on school nights, and they hate the notion that they often don't know the exact starting time of their game. When Lehigh and Bucknell met late in the season, the women's game went into double overtime, meaning the men's coaches had to tell their players to turn back at the locker room door and cool their heels for another ten to fifteen minutes twice. The scheduled 7:30 game tipped off at 8:20.

Every men's coach in the league has suggested at one point or another that if the doubleheaders are to continue the men should play first, if not all the time, then at least half the time. That suggestion is always turned down, because even though political correctness says all things must be equal, box office numbers and logic make it clear the men must be the feature game.

The doubleheaders make life particularly awkward at Lehigh. Mentesana likes to have his team in the arena two hours before tipoff to go over the scouting report. He will usually arrive close to three hours before game time to go through his scouting report and decide what he wants to put on the board to go over with the team. That means he's in his locker room while the women are in theirs getting ready to start their game. "Every time I open the door, I yell, 'Coming out!'" Mentesana said. "It makes for some silly and occasionally embarrassing moments. But I guess you get used to it after a while."

The visiting teams don't have the luxury of familiarity with the situation. When the women's game is finished, the men's teams take the floor to warm up. When they come back into the locker room for their final pregame instructions, the women are usually smack in the middle of their postgame showers. A lot of head-ducking and smirking usually ensues. On the Lehigh side, the men have grown accustomed to having to give up their locker stools during Mentesana's early chalk talk because the women need them on their side of the hall during halftime and there are only enough stools for one team.

On the afternoon of the Wagner game, Mentesana arrived at Stabler shortly after four o'clock, trying very hard to keep his mind on basketball. He had been dealing with his mother's poor health all fall, but he had just received a piece of news that had knocked him for a serious loop. The previous spring, Al Keglovitz, who had been an assistant coach at Lehigh for fifteen years, had been diagnosed with cancer of the esophagus at forty-six. He had undergone treatment and had been told during the summer that the cancer was in remission. He had returned to the team as a volunteer coach in the fall. But shortly after practice began, he started to feel sick again. One day in practice, he said to Mentesana, "I think I need a day or two off, if that's okay?"

Mentesana laughed because the *volunteer* was asking whether a day off was okay. Of course it was. Then Keglovitz had looked at Mentesana and said, "Sal, I couldn't remember the names of a couple of our players today when we were having our coaches' meeting."

That scared Mentesana. Keglovitz is quick-witted and clever. "I wasn't thinking cancer again or anything like that," he said. "But it sounded like something was very wrong."

Something was: Keglovitz had learned he had four tumors growing on his brain. The doctors had told him they were inoperable, and Keglovitz was about to start radiation and chemotherapy treatments. He told Mentesana he was also thinking of going to Mexico for experimental treatments involving cell growth.

"Two teenage kids," Mentesana said softly, sitting in sweats, waiting for his players to arrive. "I'm going to have to tell the players about it, but I'll wait until after the game. I'm just not up to dealing with those kinds of emotions beforehand."

On game day, there are two Mentesanas. The first one sits around in comfortable sweats, talking softly about how much he enjoys coaching the kids at Lehigh, telling funny stories about his life in coaching and the people he's met. The second one surfaces shortly after the players go on the floor to warm up. The sweats come off and a very expensive suit goes on. Clothes are Mentesana's addiction. He dresses so well that in the spring of 2000 when an Internet site staged a sixty-four-coach dress-off (complete with a full bracket, just like the NCAA Tournament), the national dressing champion was Mentesana. He beat Jay Wright of Hofstra in the Fashionable Eight (Wright had been the number one seed in the region but Mentesana knocked him off) and then beat Fang Mitchell of Coppin State in the semis and Willis Wilson at Rice in the title match. It was not a knockdown, drag-out affair. Couldn't be with so much expensive clothing involved.

The Armani-Mentesana is very different from the sweats-Mentesana. The game face is set in place as soon as the knot on the tie is tightened. During a game, Mentesana is loud, often angry, frequently funny, and wound so tight that his friends worry that he is going to make himself sick. Mentesana has had some minor heart problems in the past because of a rapid heartbeat. During the 1999 game at Bucknell, he got thrown out of the game before halftime, then felt sick in the locker room and had to be taken to the hospital.

"The funny thing about that is I was getting up to leave before I got thrown out," he said, laughing at the memory. "I didn't feel very good before the game and I was quieter on the bench than normal because of that. Then, with about a minute to go in the half, I yelled at one of the refs about an illegal screen and he gave me a T. I turned to [assistant coach] Jeff [Wilson] and told him I was leaving because I didn't feel very good. I stood up to walk to the locker room and couldn't resist one last swipe at the ref. I told him he was either a cheat or an incompetent. For some reason, he thought that merited a second tech. I can't imagine why."

Once in the locker room, Mentesana talked to the trainers from both Lehigh and Bucknell. He knew what was happening because he had experienced it before. But this was the second time in a week that it had made him feel really ill. They suggested he go to the hospital. There he was told that his heartbeat was rapid and a little irregular but there was nothing wrong with his heart. He had not had an episode since then.

"Fortunately, it's more related to fatigue than stress," he said. "Because if it was stress related, I'd probably have an episode every game."

Mentesana's message before the Wagner game was direct. After he had gone through the Wagner personnel and all their offensive and defensive sets, he stood right in front of the board and pointed at the words and numbers and drawings scribbled all over it.

"If you've paid attention to all this and understand what we expect them to do, that's great," he said. "But in the end, this game has nothing to do with any of that. It has to do with us, with what kind of basketball team we are. Are we a better basketball team than last year? I think we are. But I'm not so sure *you* think you are, and that's why we need to win a game like this. If we come out and play the way we played against Yale, against Penn State, and for a half against Harvard, we will win the game. We're better than they are — *if* we play."

The *if* was the problem. Lehigh started the game — in front of a crowd announced at 793 — as if it was in a trance. The first five possessions produced five turnovers. Mentesana was so upset with center Sah Brown that he yanked him forty seconds into the game. Less than ninety seconds in, he called a time-out — down 2-0 — and pulled point guard Steve Aylsworth. He continued mixing and matching players throughout the half, seeking solace and consistency.

Seven minutes in, trailing 13-7, Mentesana looked at his assistant coaches and said, "We should be down twenty." That was the good news; Wagner was young and struggling, too. Lehigh actually took the lead briefly before halftime before a 3-point shot by Wagner's Jeff Klauder with thirty-seven seconds left put the Seahawks up, 27-26. Lehigh held for a last shot and — naturally — didn't get one, committing a fifteenth turnover instead.

The half was best summed up by one Lehigh possession in which Brown missed an open dunk; Jared Hess missed a five-foot putback of the Brown dunk; Brown rebounded that miss, got fouled, and missed two free throws; and Tanner Engel missed a follow to the second free throw.

While the players sat in their locker room, Mentesana huddled in the now-empty women's locker room with his assistants: Wilson, Glenn Noak, and Chris McNesby. Normally, Mentesana is full of ideas, adjustments, comments. Now he looked at his three assistants and said, "I have absolutely no idea what to say to them after a half like that."

They were equally baffled. Sensing that tightness was the problem, Mentesana decided to try some humor. "Fellas, congratulations," he said, walking in. "You have just been part of a half that probably set basketball back a hundred years. The most amazing thing is, when you played just a little you got the lead. Relax. Don't play so tight. There's no reason to be so tight. It's important to win but it's still just a basketball game."

Walking back to the floor, Wilson, who had been with Mentesana all four years at Lehigh, put his finger on the problem. "They're not used to playing games they're supposed to win," he said. "They feel like they have something to lose now."

The second half was not a lot better than the first. Mentesana threatened to quit at one point: "If I can't coach them to play any better than this I need to get a job selling insurance," he said to his assistants. Later, he became the Wizard of Oz: "You have no heart, you have no courage, and you have no brains," he said during a time-out. He said several other things during that time-out that caused radio play-by-play man Jeff Fisher, sitting close enough to the bench to hear what was being said, to muse on the air, "Thank God the pep band is here to muffle the sounds coming out of the Lehigh huddle."

Mentesana was not whistling a happy tune at that moment.

Through it all, it actually appeared they would survive for a while. Bobby Mbom, the center from Cameroon whose nickname was "The Beast," because he is six-five, 260, and plays like the proverbial bull in the china shop, made back-to-back plays inside with the score tied at 41 to put the Mountain Hawks up 45-41. Then Engel and Aylsworth each buried a 3 to up the lead to 51-44, and it appeared all was going to be okay on South Mountain.

But they couldn't stand prosperity. The turnovers continued to mount, Wagner went on a 10-0 run to retake the lead, and even though Lehigh came back to tie the game (after being down 5) three times in the last two minutes, the game ended with Klauder coolly drilling a 3 with 1.6 seconds left, to win it, 71-68. The Wagner kids ran off the court celebrating while the Lehigh players stood staring at one another in disbelief.

It was the bad old days all over again. They had turned the ball over twenty-five times, had blown a 7-point lead in the second half against a team that should not have been able to rally, and had been done in by their worst enemy: themselves.

"I know exactly what they're thinking in there," Mentesana said to the coaches before he spoke to the players. "Here we go again. You know how I know they're thinking that? Because I'm thinking the same damn thing."

One person who was absolutely determined not to think that way was point guard Steve Aylsworth. Like fellow seniors Jared Hess and Fido Willybiro, he had never dreamed when he arrived at Lehigh that he would play on a team that would be 17-65 after his first three years. Like Hess and Willybiro, he had known — just known — after the Navy game the previous March, that his last year of basketball was going to be his best year.

"All summer long I worked with the thought in mind that if there was a reason for all those injuries, it had to be that we all were going to get so much experience that it would make a big difference this year," he said. "It kept me going every day. We all want something good before we walk out of here, for ourselves and for the school."

Aylsworth was probably more connected to the school than anyone else on the team. His father, John, had played football at Lehigh, graduating in 1972. His older brother Bob had been a quarterback at Lehigh, graduating in 1996. He came from a true jock family. His mother, Karen, had been a lacrosse and field hockey star for two years at Westchester College before she and John had gotten married and started having children. Steve was the youngest of four: John, Bob, and Colleen preceeding him.

John Aylsworth Sr. was a successful businessman who had worked for oil baron Marvin Davis for years before going off on his own, eventually becoming CEO of a company that managed riverboat casinos. He was very involved in the careers of his sons, holding all three of them back a year in junior high school to give them a chance to mature physically.

"You can see it made a big difference for me," Aylsworth said, laughing. At five-ten, 170, he looks like someone who belongs on a balance beam more than on a basketball court.

What the Aylsworth brothers lacked in size, they made up for in quickness, smarts, and toughness. John walked on the football team at UCLA for a year before transferring to Colorado and playing there.

Bob began his career at Tulane before transferring to Lehigh. Having seen what his brothers had gone through in big-time programs, Steve was homed in on Lehigh throughout his high school senior year, although he did take a visit to Penn.

"I was actually recruited by a lot of different schools because some wanted me for football and some wanted me for basketball," he said. "I finally decided on Lehigh because of all the family connections but also because they said I could play both sports."

He did — for a year. By the end of his freshman year, having gone from a 3.9 GPA as a high school senior to a 2.4 GPA as a college freshman, he knew he had to choose one sport or the other. "I never felt completely a part of either team that year," he said. "The football players looked at me as a basketball player and the basketball players as a football player. I was way behind in basketball because I missed so much practice in the fall, then I was way behind in spring practice because of basketball. Plus, I was struggling academically."

He chose basketball because it had always been his first love and because he liked the idea of playing twenty-seven games rather than eleven. The fact that he hit Lafayette for 29 points in his very first Patriot League game might also have helped him decide.

Like everyone else, Aylsworth was convinced the jump from one win in 1997 to ten wins in 1998 was just a beginning. Then everything had crashed in 1999. "It just didn't seem fair," he said. "Everything seemed set up for us to really be a factor in the Patriot League. Then everyone got hurt and we couldn't win a game for two months. It was a long, long winter."

Unlike some seniors in the league who harbored hopes of playing overseas for a couple of years after graduation, Aylsworth knew that his last game in a Lehigh uniform would be his last game as a basketball player. He was majoring in corporate finance and had been interviewing with Wall Street firms all fall. After his shaky freshman year, he had pulled his GPA up to 3.25 and, with his outgoing personality, figured to find work in the business world quickly.

"I have to admit, though, there are times when I think I'd like to give broadcasting some kind of shot," he said. "The hardest thing about being an athlete at a school like this is knowing realistically that college is the end of the road for you, that you're here training to do something completely different, and yet you've been an athlete all your life and the thought of life without sports is a little bit scary."

Aylsworth was comforted by the fact that his two older brothers had both gone through the end-of-sports routine and managed to survive. But he didn't want his final memories to be of nights when he and his team played the way they had against Wagner. "You need to believe there's a reason for all the work and all the frustration and all the setbacks," he said. "Navy last year gave us something to keep us going. But we can't live off that the rest of our lives. We need to do something this year that's better than that."

They were 1-3 after Wagner. With a lot of teams better than Wagner looming down the road.

The Army players were looking for the same sort of sign that the Lehigh players had been searching for when they walked single file into the historic Palestra in Philadelphia late on the afternoon of December 3. The town was abuzz with talk about Army, but that was because the football team was going through final preparations for the 100th Army-Navy game the next afternoon at Veterans Stadium.

The basketball players would have loved the chance to see that game, to march onto the field with the rest of the Corps of Cadets and stand in the stands in their gray dress uniforms and watch the football teams from the two academies play. "To march on for the Army-Navy game would be fun," Chris Spatola said. "Marching back at West Point is a bore, but for Army-Navy in that big stadium, we would enjoy that."

But they wouldn't get that chance. Pat Harris had thought long and hard about whether he should let his players go to the game. As a graduate, he wanted his players to be there, to share in the Army-Navy experience with the other cadets. Four years at West Point are filled with many long, dreary days and nights. The day of the Army-Navy football game is about as close to Christmas and New Year's rolled into one as the cadets (and the midshipmen) are likely to experience. Harris hated the idea that his players might never go through that day as cadets.

But allowing them to do it wasn't as easy as saying, "Go march on and have fun." Army had to play Pennsylvania on Friday night and then travel to Yale on Monday night. Harris knew that winning in the Palestra was a long shot. He also knew that winning in the John J. Lee Amphitheater was entirely possible. He wanted to do everything he could to ensure that he had a rested, prepared team at Yale.

"There's a lot you have to consider," he said. "What if it rains, or the weather is freezing and they're standing out there for four or five hours [the march-ons are a couple of hours before kickoff] and they get sick? What if they just get worn out standing all that time? If we stay for the game, we can't practice Saturday; that leaves one day to prepare for Yale. And most of the fun for the cadets at Army-Navy comes after the game, being turned loose in Philadelphia. How will they feel having to get on a bus and come back to West Point after the game while everyone else goes out?"

Harris had balanced all the factors and decided it was best to go back to West Point, watch the game on television together, and practice when it was over. "If we didn't have a game Monday, it would be different," he said. "But we do."

Army had played three games since the Debacle at Duke and Harris had been pleased with the effort in all three. The Cadets had gone to Cornell three days after the Duke game and had almost won, losing 67-66 in overtime after having a chance to take the last shot in regulation but failing to convert. They then played their annual pair of games against Division III teams, first against Bethany, then against Western Maryland. Winning those two games was expected — but not always a given — but the fact that they were won with relative ease (63-48 and 70-49) was encouraging. "I thought we played better and harder on defense in those two games than I've seen an Army team play in the last six years," Harris said. "Now, if we can just find some consistency on offense. . . ."

Harris was hoping two players would do that: sophomore Jonte Harrell and junior captain Joe Clark. He knew that Spatola would be a threat to score every night but he also knew that if he was the only threat, defenses would be geared to stop him, and an offense with a five-ten point guard as its centerpiece is going to be extremely vulnerable.

The question with Clark was health. He had missed the Duke and

Cornell games but had come back to play limited minutes in the two D-III games. Now was the time for him to assert himself, especially on offense, where his 3-point shooting range could be a weapon that would not only provide outside points but could open things up for Army's inside players.

Harrell was still adjusting to playing small forward. At a slender six-seven, that was the position that should suit him best, but he had played most of his minutes as a freshman inside. No one on the team had more scoring potential than Harrell, because he had the physical ability to do what most Patriot League players have trouble doing: creating his own shot. He was quick enough to beat players off the dribble, but needed to learn better what to do once he got into the lane with the basketball.

Harris was convinced he would make that adjustment as the season wore on. His larger concern was about Harrell's personality. He was shy and quiet by nature, not the kind of assertive player who is going to demand the ball. Harris had asked him in preseason to take charge of the team's pregame locker room prayer, wanting to give him a leadership role of some kind. Joe Clark and Seth Barrett, the juniors, were the captains. Spatola ran the team on the floor as the point guard. This was Harris's way of telling Harrell he was one of the team's leaders, too.

Harrell had grown up in Charlotte, North Carolina. His father, John, was an ex–Harlem Globetrotter who had starred at Charlotte Latin High School. Throughout his years at Latin, Jonte had felt pressure to live up to his father's famous name. He had come to Army thinking he would get a chance to play right away — and had, starting twenty-four games as a plebe. Now, as a sophomore, he had to become one of the team's major offensive producers if the Cadets were going to enjoy any success.

Their night in the Palestra started out as if it might be a stunning success. There is no building in college basketball that has the aura of the Palestra. Cameron Indoor Stadium may be more raucous and Allen Field House at Kansas can trace its roots all the way back to the man who invented the game, Dr. James Naismith. Pauley Pavilion at UCLA has more NCAA championship banners than anyplace else, and Cole Field House at Maryland has both history and atmosphere.

But none of them is the Palestra. Only the Palestra has a small plaque in its front lobby that, in a few words, sums up what amateur athletics ought to be about:

To play the game is great . . .
To win the game is greater . . .
But to love the game is the greatest of all . . .

No one is sure who spoke or wrote those three simple sentences, but the plaque has been in the building for as long as anyone can remember. The Palestra first opened in 1926, and although it has been painted and refurbished through the years, it doesn't look all that different than it looked in pictures taken in that era. Even though the Palestra is on the Penn campus, it was home to all the Big Five schools — Penn, Villanova, Temple, LaSalle, and St. Joseph's — until the politics of college basketball almost killed the Big Five in the 1980s and sent the other four schools scurrying to their own campus facilities. Until then, LaSalle's 1954 national championship banner and Villanova's 1985 title banner hung in the Palestra along with all of Penn's Ivy League championship banners.

The place seats 8,722 but the acoustics make it sound like more. It also has one of the great PA announcers in the world, John McAdams, who has been on the mike there since 1981. McAdams is eloquent without being fancy, enthusiastic without being screechy. He gets it just right.

The game was only the second of the season for Penn. The Quakers had played in the preseason NIT and, being an Ivy League team, had of course been sent on the road. Just as predictably, they had been fed to Kentucky in Rupp Arena. The game had been close until the last five minutes when Kentucky had broken away for a 67-50 victory. Since the possibility (however slender) had existed that Penn could have played four NIT games, Coach Fran Dunphy hadn't scheduled any other games until this one. That meant Penn would be excited about playing, but it also meant the players might be a little rusty, having not played a game for sixteen days.

For a little more than eleven minutes, Harris got a chance to see what his idea of Forty Minutes of Army Basketball might someday look like. The Cadets were dug in on defense, making each possession difficult for Penn. And they were getting offense from everyone on the floor. Barrett posted up for an early bucket. Then Michael Canty and Harrell buried 3s. Spatola fed Canty for one basket, then hit a spinning fifteen-footer himself. Barrett even hit a baseline jumper from seventeen feet. Ray Fredrick, the tiny freshman guard, came off the bench and got to the basket for a layup. When Spatola and Clark hit back-to-back 3s, Army led 22-17 and the Penn fans were looking at each other as if to say, "I thought we were playing Army."

They were. During the last 8:36 of the half, the Cadets got one basket — a Spatola 3 — while Penn began to take over the inside with its size and quickness. The Quakers closed the half on a 22-3 run that Harris was completely convinced was aided by the officials. Every call seemed to go against his team. So did every break. With the score 34-25, Clark spotted up for an open three and watched it go all the way down and then spin out.

Harris nearly picked up a technical in the final seconds of the half, screaming for a foul call to no avail. "Calm down, Pat, just calm down," referee Richard San Fillipo told Harris as the half ended with Penn up 39-25.

"I don't want to calm down, goddammit!" Harris screamed. "Why should I calm down! You guys aren't giving my players a fair chance. You think because we're Army we can't play, don't you? That's just a bunch of crap and you know it!"

"Pat, go to your locker room," San Fillipo said, walking away.

Harris took one step after him, then Marty Coyne grabbed his arm. By then Harris was turning in the direction of the locker room. But he was still steamed.

"No one is going to give you guys anything," he told the players. "Do you understand that! Until we show people that Army can play, that we're as good as anyone else, they're going to treat you like that. It's unfair bullshit but that's the way it is."

He started to write something on the blackboard, then hurled the chalk at the wall in disgust. After that he calmed down and went through the adjustments they needed to make. Before he sent them out for the second half, he reminded them not to get into any arguments with the officials. "You play, let me worry about the refs," he said.

They did, because Army players rarely argue with authority figures, which is what officials are. Penn's margin got as big as 60-33, but Army never did go away. The final was a respectable 71-56, and Fran Dunphy shook his head afterward and said, "They aren't kidding when they say those kids don't know what quit means, are they?"

Harris was proud of the way his team had competed. Canty was so exhausted afterward that he spent several minutes in the bathroom getting sick. "Play that hard every night, fellas, and we'll win games," he said. "We still have a lot to learn, but that's a good team. And for a lot of this game, we competed with them play for play."

Unfortunately, playing well in spurts is rarely good enough to win games. Three nights later, rested and ready, Army went to Yale. In front of a roaring crowd of 575 in the John J. Lee, the Cadets again came out of the gate looking like a good basketball team and led 21-8 after nine minutes. They were still up 28-22 at the half. But in the second half they shot four-for-twenty-six from the field, scored 14 points, and let the game get away, 48-42.

As if losing to Yale with an awful second half wasn't enough, Seth Barrett caught an elbow in the head early in the second half and had to be taken to the hospital for stitches. There was no way for Barrett to get home except on the team bus, so the bus had to wait for him to finish at the hospital. Then, to top off a perfect night, there was an accident on I-95 that had traffic stopped in its tracks. What should have been a midnight return became a 2:30 A.M. return.

Harris was convinced his team should be 4-2. Instead, it was 2-4. Exams were a few days away. And the football team had lost to Navy. At Army, they call the winter months "the gray days." On the morning after the Yale game — the fifty-eighth anniversary of the bombing of Pearl Harbor — the gray days were well underway at West Point.

14

NO REST FOR THE WEARY

EVERYONE in the Patriot League takes a mid-December break for exams, ranging, in 1999, from ten days (Lafayette and Holy Cross) to seventeen days (Navy and Lehigh). Unlike the big name schools, the Patriot League teams don't have to worry about CBS or ABC or ESPN tempting them with an extra game around exam time. Some schools in the TV leagues will play games right through exams, especially if there's a national television date available.

Going into the break, both Bucknell (5-2) and Lafayette (4-2) were off to good starts, although the Leopards had blown a 17-point lead at home in a baffling loss to Towson State. Navy had bounced back from its 0-3 beginning with three straight victories. Those three were supposed to be the class of the league and already they were looking like it. Everyone else was scuffling. Lehigh was 3-4, having won back-to-back games against Division III opponents. Colgate was 3-5, having somehow figured a way to lose at home to Long Island University. It had then bounced back six days later to crush Harvard at Harvard. Already the Red Raiders were proving to be the league's most mercurial team. Holy Cross was 2-4 after the win over Yale, and Army, adding a loss to Marist after the Yale defeat, was 2-5.

In short, as was always the case, nothing was easy for the Patriot League teams. There wasn't a single guarantee game against a Division I opponent in which the Patriot League team was the one guaranteed to win the game.

Once the exam break was over, everyone in the league took to the road to play guarantee games. Big-name teams love to host games during the Christmas break because their students have gone home and they can sell their seats to people eager to see the team play who normally can't get in when the students are on campus. Many teams host tournaments, usually looking to bring in at least two teams — if not three — that will take guaranteed money in return for guaranteed wins.

Holy Cross would play in the Hoosier Classic, hosted by Indiana. The Hoosier Classic had been held for twenty years. Indiana's record in the tournament was, you guessed it, 40-0. Ranked teams need not apply. Lafayette went to New Mexico for the Lobo Classic and Lehigh went west, not for a tournament, but to play games at Pepperdine and San Diego. "It's all really an excuse to go see Steve's [Aylsworth] house," Mentesana said. Aylsworth and his family lived in a mansion on the beach in Malibu, not far from Pepperdine.

Colgate wasn't traveling any farther than New York City to play Manhattan — the Syracuse game along with an $8,000 guarantee from the Mohegan Sun Classic meant another big guarantee game wasn't needed. Navy was playing a game at SMU as part of a home-and-home, and two games in the Mausoleum. Army was playing in a new tournament at SUNY–Stony Brook, hoping the competition there — Long Island University, Maine, and the hosts — would provide at least one win.

Bucknell was doing double guarantee duty, first making the annual pre-Christmas trip to Penn State, then, after a few days off for the holiday, heading west to play in Arizona State's tournament. "At least it will be warm out there," Pat Flannery said, thinking about how to guard ASU guard Eddie House, the country's leading scorer.

Flannery would worry about House after Christmas. First came the trip to Happy Valley to play the Nittany Lions. This was a guarantee game for Bucknell, but one the coaches and players believed was winnable. It was their last game before their Christmas break, and, with the luxury of a $25,000 payday, Flannery was able to get his players out of the empty dorms on campus and make the bus ride to State College the night before the game and put the team into a nice hotel.

"We get to live a little," he said.

Penn State was a middle-of-the-pack Big Ten team, meaning it should be more than a Patriot League team could handle, especially playing at home. It had one truly outstanding player in senior Jarrett Stephens and a pair of brothers, Joe and Jon Crispin, who were both hard-nosed, good-shooting guards. The Lions were 5-1, their only loss coming eight days earlier at Villanova. They had won at Penn and had beaten Boston College and Clemson, lower-rung teams in the Big East and the ACC, respectively.

Penn State was not an easy place to be successful in basketball — especially in the Big Ten. The school had joined the league in the early 1990s because football coach Joe Paterno wanted to join a league and the Big Ten was looking to expand. The basketball team, which had been very competitive in the Atlantic 10 under Bruce Parkhill, suddenly found itself buried underneath Michigan, Indiana, Illinois, and the like. There was no one resembling Duquesne on the new schedule.

Parkhill decided he had had enough in 1995, even though he had a team that appeared ready to be competitive in the Big Ten. Jerry Dunn took over for him and went 21-7 and made the NCAA Tournament. Since then, the team had been up and down. It had gone 19-13 and reached the NIT final in 1998 before slipping to 13-14 the following season.

One thing Penn State did have going for it was the Bryce Jordan Center, a four-year-old facility that gleamed from top to bottom. The locker rooms were huge, the weight facilities excellent, the coaches' offices spacious and comfortable. It sat directly across the street from the massive football stadium, which seats close to 100,000 people and may be the most impossible place to get in and out of in America on days when Paterno's team is playing. For a Sunday afternoon basketball game on the Sunday before Christmas, there would be no traffic problems. Route 322 was wide open on a cold, sunny day.

Being only an hour apart, the Bucknell and Penn State coaching staffs were familiar with one another. Chuck Swenson and Mike Boyd, Dunn's top assistants, had both been to the Final Four at other schools as assistants — Swenson at Duke and Boyd at Michigan. Both had been head coaches, too — Swenson at William and Mary,

Boyd at Cleveland State. Flannery's staff, Don Friday, Carl Danzig, and Terry Conrad, had spent most of its collective career at Bucknell.

While the teams warmed up, the five assistants stood near mid-court exchanging pleasantries. Head coaches don't kibitz during warm-ups, it's against the code. The assistants do.

"Whenever I go to a summer camp, I check to see who these guys are watching," Swenson said with a nod at the Bucknell staff. "I figure if the guy can play at all he's worth checking on because I know he's a good student. Otherwise, these guys wouldn't be wasting their time with him."

Conrad laughed. "Send me a check will you, Chuck?" he said.

When the staffs returned to their benches, Friday shook his head. "It always cracks me up the way we stand around and talk to coaches before a game," he said. "I like a lot of them. But ten minutes before tip-off? It's sort of like talking to your ex-girlfriend's new boyfriend. You ask how everything's going, you laugh, tell a joke, and all the time you're thinking, 'All I want to do is kill this guy.'"

The Bison did very little killing during the first half. Even though the crowd of 8,985 was library quiet, Bucknell couldn't seem to get started. It didn't help that Valter Karavanic picked up two fouls in the first five minutes. Or that Bryan Bailey, Brian Muckle, and Karavanic missed layups early. Or that Flannery and the officials were jawing from the opening minute. It was 15-6 when Flannery called his first time-out. "Hey, fellas, I got news for you," he said. "That's not the blue [second] team out there. That's a Big Ten team. Get your legs under you and let's go play."

It got worse before it got better. The lead was 25-8 after twelve minutes before Shaun Asbury came off the bench to hit a 3 and start to turn things around a little. Still, things didn't look good when Bryan Bailey had to come out with three fouls. Chris Zimmerman, the little five-nine freshman from just down the road in Shamokin, came off the bench hacking and coughing after a bout with the flu. He promptly nailed a 3 and led a 15-8 Bucknell run that closed the gap to 41-31 at the break.

"You're back in it," Flannery told them. "You were a little rusty from the break, now we're right into the game. You've got that team nervous right now, believe me. If we rebound better in this half [the margin was 27-14], we'll win the game. I promise you that."

It took them less than four minutes to get the margin to one at 44-43. Then Stephens and Joe Crispin went to work, building the margin back to 11 with a 10-0 run. Enter Zimmerman again. He should not have been ready for a game like this, but, somehow, he was. If there was one thing Zimmerman knew about, it was winning. In six years of junior high school and high school ball his teams had lost a total of thirteen games. Just being at Bucknell was a big deal for him and for his family. His father was a welder, his mother worked with mentally challenged adults. Shamokin was a town of about 8,000 whose hangout choices were either the Burger King or the McDonald's.

"There used to be a movie theater," Zimmerman said. "But it closed down. Now, we drive twenty minutes down the road to go to a movie."

Hacking and coughing, Zimmerman fed Bowen for a three. He then hit a 3 himself. The margin dwindled again. Finally, with 4:13 left, Zimmerman hit a fifteen-foot jumper to tie the game at 61. A moment later, he got into the lane, and when the defense came to him, he slid a perfect pass to Bowen, whose layup put Bucknell up for the first time in the game, 63-61.

Dunn called time and did a smart thing: he ordered his team to get the ball to Stephens in the low post. Bucknell couldn't guard him there. His layup tied the game at 63. The next two possessions decided the game. Bucknell ran the shot clock down and, with time running out, Zimmerman had to force a 3. But Jon Crispin, running out at him since he had made every other shot he had taken, fouled him.

No call. Flannery screamed in vain. Penn State came down and Titus Ivory, who was one-for-nine on the day from the field, made a baseline move on Karavanic. There was contact. Joe DeMayo, the official under the basket, right on the play, saw no advantage gained by either player and didn't blow his whistle. Zelton Steed, the trail official, who was out at the 3-point line, decided that he *did* see a foul.

In a sense, these two possessions are a microcosm of what Patriot League teams have to overcome in a game like this. Steed is a veteran ACC official, someone who advances to the round of sixteen in the NCAA Tournament just about every year. He wasn't biased against Bucknell or trying to help Penn State. But he didn't know the Bucknell players or the coaches. He probably would have laughed if Frosty Francis, the Patriot League supervisor of officials, called to offer him a game. And why not? If he could work Duke–North Carolina on national TV for $600, why would he want to work Bucknell-Lafayette for $450? Steed, DeMayo, and Jim Burr, the third official, were accomplished veterans. Burr would work the national championship game in April.

To them, this was just another Sunday basketball game in December. On one play, they saw contact as Zimmerman shot and, somewhere in the recesses of their mind, figured, "He's not making that shot anyway." No call. A moment later, Steed saw contact as Ivory went baseline and blew his whistle. No big deal.

Except to the Bucknell people, fighting and scratching to try to pull what would be, for them, a monumental upset, it was a huge deal. If the whistle had blown at both ends, fine. If it hadn't blown either time, fine. But this wasn't fine. It was deadly.

Ivory made both foul shots. Bucknell had two chances to tie in the final minute and got good shots each time: first for Bowen, then for Muckle. Both went in-and-out. Maybe the officials weren't the only ones who figured Penn State ought to win. The final was 67-63.

For the five seniors, this was a tough one to take. They had played at Penn State all four years they had been at Bucknell. The first two years they had been hammered. The third year they had a chance to win and didn't. The fourth, they felt they deserved to win and didn't. It all added up to 0-4.

Don Friday had been absolutely convinced Muckle's last shot was going in. Three years earlier Bucknell had played its final game before Christmas break on the same court. As it turned out, that was the last time Brian Muckle's dad saw him play. Shortly after the team got to New Mexico for their post-Christmas trip, the coaches got a call. Ross Muckle had collapsed and died of a heart attack that morning, at the age of forty-eight. Muckle still remembers Friday getting on the team bus just before it left for practice to tell him that Flannery wanted to see him in his room.

"I couldn't imagine what it was," Muckle said. "I thought maybe he was going to tell me I was going to play more or something."

He knew as soon as he walked in the door it wasn't anything that simple. Flannery was on the phone and his face was ashen. "He handed me the phone and said, 'It's your mom.' " There was no gentle way for Jean Muckle to deliver the news. Brian flew home and stayed with his family for ten days. Returning to school and the team was both a relief and a headache.

"I needed to get away from home," he said. "It just reached a point where there was nothing more to say or do. But when I got back everyone wanted to tell me how sorry they were and ask if there was anything they could do. It was like going through the whole thing all over again. I know everyone meant well, but it just made it tougher."

The only relief came one day when Gordon Mboya came by to pick him up for his first practice. "Gordon looked at me and said, 'We're in the middle of a five-game losing streak and you've been gone for ten days! What were you thinking?' It cracked me up."

Three years later, it was impossible for Muckle or anyone who knew him to walk into the Jordan Center without thinking about Ross Muckle.

"I just thought, in this place, the shot would go in," Friday said.

So did Muckle. He was a small-town kid, raised in Southington, Ohio, a town of 7,000 whose most famous resident was Mike Tyson. It was there that Tyson retreated after he got out of jail in 1995. Often, members of his entourage — bodyguards, friends, hangers-on — would show up at the Chalker Southington gym and play ball with members of the basketball team. Knowing that Tyson had a full court in his backyard, Muckle and his teammates kept agitating to move the game there. Finally, one day, the invitation came: come to Mike's to play that afternoon. They did. Midway through the game, Tyson walked out of the house dressed in Georgetown sweats (his wife graduated from law school there), introduced himself to everyone — "Hi, I'm Mike" — and joined the game.

"He wasn't very good," Muckle said. "But when he wanted the ball, you got him the ball."

Everyone stayed after the game for a barbecue, and the team often went back to Tyson's to play. Everyone at Bucknell knew that Muckle knew Tyson and liked him. Every time Tyson got into trouble, it came up in conversation. "Coach [Flannery] always says something like, 'So, what's your boy up to now?' " Muckle said. "It wasn't good for me around here after the [Evander] Holyfield fight."

Muckle went to the same school from kindergarten to twelfth grade and was in a graduating class of fifty-two. As a six-four sophomore, he was the tallest player on the basketball team, but played on the perimeter offensively because his coach, Charles Black, thought he had the potential to play at the next level if he developed outside skills.

"Naturally that caused some concern among a lot of the parents," Muckle said, shaking his head. "Small towns are like that. Everyone knows everyone. Some of them thought I should be inside all the time."

There wasn't a lot of complaining when Chalker Southington went 22-3 Muckle's senior year. By then Muckle was six-six, but most of the attention he was getting from colleges was from the Division II and Division III levels. Wagner was interested for a while and so was Kent State. Both dropped out. Then Bucknell and Lafayette invited him to visit. Muckle was the class salutatorian and had solid (1160) boards, so he was attractive to both schools.

He was supposed to visit Bucknell and then make the two-hour drive to Lafayette. But after seeing Bucknell, he canceled the rest of the trip. "It just looked like a college to me," he said. "It felt right. Everyone had told me I would know the right school when I got there. I knew I was going to pay full tuition regardless (Ross and Jean Muckle owned a construction company), so I figured I'd go where I would be happy and where I'd be closer to home."

His father's death stunned the whole team. After Muckle returned from the funeral and rejoined the team, everyone seemed to be walking on eggshells around him. "All I wanted was to have Coach Flannery scream at me during practice," he said. "That would get things back to normal."

Jean Muckle continued to run the family's construction business. But she had not missed a single game Brian had played in four years, making the five-hour drive from Southington to Lewisburg routinely. She was sitting in the stands — as always — when Brian's late shot spun out of the basket. Being back at Penn State wasn't easy for her or Brian. A shot to send the game into overtime and a victory would have been a nice way to exit the place for the last time.

Flannery had to kick something when he got into the locker room, so he did: a chair. It had been so close. "We had them on their heels," he said to the coaches. "How can he [Steed] make that call with ninety seconds left and the score tied? How does he do that?"

There was no answer to the question. Flannery was faced with telling his players one more time how proud he was of the effort, how well they had done coming back. He singled out Zimmerman, who sat doubled over, coughing nonstop. He talked about better starts and shot selection and rebounding and all the things coaches talk about after a difficult loss. Then he stopped. They were all going home that night for Christmas break. They would meet a week later in Arizona for the tournament out there.

"Listen to me, guys," he said, his tone changing. "When you're home, I know you want to see your friends and hang out. Do that. Enjoy yourselves. But please, please spend some time with your families. You can't know how much they miss you. And they only get you for a week, not a month like all the other kids in school. Spend a couple nights at home. Let them enjoy you. They deserve it. Believe me, you won't regret it."

Clearly, Don Friday wasn't the only one thinking about Ross Muckle that afternoon.

Flannery left the locker room to go talk to the media. He didn't bring up the officials at all. There was no point. In the Patriot League, it was all part of the job.

For all college basketball players, the Christmas holidays are a difficult time. While 99 percent of the world's college students take their last exam and immediately head home for a month, basketball players have to stick around campus until the last pre-Christmas game is played. Then they have a few days off and return right after Christmas — sometimes as early as Christmas night — to begin preparing for holiday tournaments.

"The worst day is the last day of exams," Lafayette point guard Tim Bieg said. "Everyone else is clearing out, excited and happy, and you have to go back to the empty dorm and get ready for practice. It can really be depressing."

Even worse for many is the post-Christmas return to school. Nowhere was this more difficult than at the military academies. For midshipmen and cadets, leaving on Christmas break isn't just leaving classes and tests behind, it is leaving the whole military regimen behind. It is a chance to wear dirty clothes, to sleep in past 6:30 in the morning, to not have an upperclassman screaming in your face all the time, to not have to call everyone in the world sir, to not have to worry that a missed salute walking to class might cost you weekend liberty.

"You forget what normal life is like," said Army freshman Michael Canty. "Then you go back to it and you think, 'Why in the world do I want to go back to all *that?*'"

Army's players were given five days off for Christmas. They were due back on the post on December 26 to start preparing for the SUNY–Stony Brook tournament three days later. As he drove back onto the grounds of West Point, Canty was almost overcome by an overwhelming desire to turn back and go home. It was a cold, wet day and there was absolutely no one in sight. All he could see was gray: the sky, the buildings, his outlook.

Pat Harris understood. He had gone through the same thing every Christmas he had played at West Point. He knew that it was particularly tough the first time, so he sat down with all his freshmen to explain to them that it would get better. At Army, the Corps of Cadets must report back right after New Year's for military intersession. While that meant spending four hours every morning in a classroom, it wasn't as grueling as regular classes and it meant that the barracks wouldn't be deserted every night when the players came back from practice.

Harris was hoping that the post-Christmas tournament would produce at least one victory. Although the team had shown some signs of life, the offense was still horribly inconsistent. Joe Clark had not yet found his shooting touch and Seth Barrett was having trouble scoring out of the low post. Barrett was only six-four, meaning he was giving away a lot of inches to most players inside, but he had been able to use his strength and quickness inside in the past. Now he wasn't as strong, because his weight had dropped under 220. He thought losing weight would make him a better officer. Harris didn't dispute that. But he knew that losing weight would not make him a better basketball player.

The trip to Stony Brook was a complete disaster. Canty and the other freshmen all looked as if they wished they were anyplace but where they were. The Cadets managed to lose to Stony Brook, which was in its first year as a Division I team, 49-45, in the opener. Then they got bombed, 72-56, by LIU in the consolation game. The coaches could see that their problem was fairly simple: they couldn't score. Spatola was the only consistent threat, and he couldn't bring the ball up, run the offense, and throw the ball to himself to shoot.

Much as he hated to do it, Harris thought it imperative that he change the team's offense. He simply didn't have players who were good enough going one-on-one against people to run the same kind of offense that Duke ran. They needed more set plays, more chances to have someone feed Spatola in a place where he could catch the ball and shoot. There were only two days between the LIU game and a January 2 game at home against Manhattan. Harris put the new offense in on New Year's Eve. It took four hours. By the time practice was over, most of the players were probably hoping the Y2K bug would prove to be the real deal.

"It feels like we've been back here forever," Spatola said, a hollow-eyed look on his face on the morning of the Manhattan game. "I can't remember ever being so frustrated. We work and we work and we work and we have nothing to show for it. The problem is not that we aren't trying. Everyone is. Every coach, every player, is trying as hard as they can. We just can't get over the hump no matter what we do."

The Manhattan game was no different. The new offense got Spatola more shots — twelve — and he scored 18 points. Harrell chipped in with 15. But Barrett and Clark shot a combined two-for-seven and Canty, still in his post-Christmas funk, didn't score and had six turnovers before fouling out in eighteen minutes. That wasn't going to be nearly enough. The final was 69-49. The attendance was 588. The only real highlight of the day was assistant coach Marty Coyne's twelve-year-old daughter, Audrey, singing the national anthem so beautifully it almost made you cry.

Everyone was smiling when Audrey's final notes died away. It was Army's last chance to smile for some time.

15

DAYS OF IVY

CONFERENCE play in the Patriot League starts a week later than in most leagues because there are only seven teams, meaning a twelve-game conference schedule. Most leagues play at least fourteen games, some play sixteen.

By the time New Year's had come and gone — without any sign of Y2K to rescue Army — there was some clarity to how the league would shape up. Army and Lehigh were struggling. Army hadn't beaten a Division I team and Lehigh had beaten only one — Yale, in the opener. Colgate had been a yo-yo: a near win at Delaware; an embarrassing home loss to LIU; a crushing of Harvard followed by a superb win at Manhattan; an overtime loss to Cornell. Bucknell was playing like a solid, veteran team. Navy was improving steadily, playing loads of home games over the holidays.

Holy Cross was so beaten up it was hard to judge how the team would play. Dekker McKeever, who had been part of the first scholarship class, in 1998, had broken a foot and missed his entire freshman season. He had then rebroken the foot during the summer, but was back in time for practice. He played three games at the start of the season, then broke the foot again, ending his sophomore season.

Patrick Whearty, the six-ten sophomore forward who had played so well in the Yale game, felt a twinge in his elbow near the end of that game. By the time the team came back to practice after exam break, the elbow felt worse rather than better. It turned out he had developed a blood clot in his arm and would not play again the rest of the season.

That meant three starters were down: Whearty, point guard Ryan Serravalle, and Jared Curry. Not for long. Curry came back to practice to see how his back felt on December 16, the first full workout after exams. Twenty minutes into practice, he went up for a rebound, caught Juan Pegues in the eye with an elbow, and fell to the ground writhing in pain.

This was a rare two-for-one: the orbital bone around Pegues's eye had been fractured. He would need surgery and be out for seven weeks. Curry's back was hurt again. He tried to play three days later against Vermont but came out after a few minutes and didn't play again for four weeks. That meant Holy Cross came out of the Vermont game (another loss) with one player who had started in the opener against Providence still standing: Josh Sankes.

Ralph Willard was beginning to wonder what kind of evil star was stalking the team. He was now down to nine able-bodied players, three of them unrecruited walk-ons. Assistant coach Roger Breslin was practicing with the team in order to give Willard ten players when he wanted to scrimmage. Chris Spitler was, of course, 100 percent healthy and ready and willing to play forty minutes; more if necessary. Willard decided he needed help before the team headed to Indiana after Christmas. He called James Stowers, who was home in Florida on Christmas break, having finished off the semester with a flourish academically. He told Stowers about the latest injuries and asked him if he might be willing to come back. There was no school to worry about at the moment, he had done well academically the first semester, and — unlike most of the team — he was healthy.

Stowers was seriously tempted. Even though his health and grades had both improved once he stopped playing basketball, he had missed it, especially during the games, knowing he could have helped the team. But he was concerned about getting into the same rut second semester that he had gotten into during the first. The law school dream was now close enough he could almost touch it. He didn't want to jeopardize that chance. He was also afraid that if things started to go awry and he left the team again, he would be viewed as a quitter.

Willard understood. "James, if it gets to be too much, you come and tell me," he said. "I will make certain that people understand that you came back to help us because of all the injuries and that by no means are you a quitter. Because you're not."

Stowers could feel his stomach twisting into the old familiar knot. He hadn't really reconciled himself to not being a basketball player anymore. This was a chance to go back and bring closure about in a proper way. "I'll meet you in Indianapolis," he told Willard.

His return was something straight out of a movie script. He had practiced with the team once, and even though he was knocked woozy by a flying elbow early ("He wouldn't be a true Crusader if he wasn't hurt in some way," Willard cracked), he scored fourteen points in the tournament opener against Alabama-Birmingham, including 11 in one three-minute burst when Holy Cross took control of the game. In what had to rank as one of the more amazing upsets of the basketball season, the Crusaders stunned UAB, 69-60.

That was the good news. The bad news was twofold: first, and foremost, Holy Cross would now have to play Indiana in the final, in a true Christians vs. Lions scenario. Second, by winning, the Crusaders didn't get to play Canisius in the consolation game. That meant that the Spitler brothers, Chris and Mark, would not be reunited. "We were planning some serious glaring from the ends of each bench," said Chris. Mark was a sophomore walk-on at Canisius who rarely played.

The Indiana game was every bit as awful as might have been expected. Holy Cross was spent from the UAB victory; Indiana was not exactly worn out from its win the previous night over Canisius. The final was 79-44. "Could have been worse," Willard said.

It certainly could have been. After all, no one in purple and white was injured. That was almost as big an upset as beating UAB had been.

The one coach in the league who was fairly certain about the quality of his team was Lafayette's Fran O'Hanlon. There had been one hiccup — the blown lead against Towson State — but other than that, the Leopards had played good basketball throughout their preseason schedule.

That didn't mean there had not been disappointments, most notably the non-upset at Villanova. The trip to New Mexico had started with a second game against a Big Five team and another agonizing loss, this one in double overtime to St. Joseph's. After an easy win in the consolation game over Alabama State, the team had gone straight to Atlanta to play a guarantee game on January 2 against Georgia Tech. Down 17, they had rallied to within 6, with the ball, before losing by 11. Still close, still no big win to prove that they were better than they had been a year ago.

The most frustrated member of the team was Stefan Ciosici. The cortisone shot in his knee in November had helped and the pain had lessened considerably in his knee. But he still didn't feel as if he was anywhere close to being where he had been — or where he wanted to be — as a player. He felt slow on defense, slow around the basket. O'Hanlon was constantly telling him not to rush with the ball because he kept thinking he had to start his moves sooner to compensate for his lack of quickness.

"Stefan, you're trying to shoot the ball before you've caught it," he said during a time-out one night. "Let the game come to you."

Ciosici was trying. He was smart enough to understand that he couldn't expect to be where he had been the last time he had played in a real game — March 1998. Emotionally, though, it was tough to take. Every game seemed to be the same: two quick fouls and he was on the bench cheerleading for Frank Barr. At six-eleven, 260, Ciosici was an easy target for referees. If he bumped someone, they moved. Foul. When someone bumped him, he rarely moved. And if he did, the officials often thought he was acting. After all, how could a guy that big be moved?

Prior to the season Ciosici had talked about wanting to continue playing after he graduated. "The injury really made me realize how much I love to play. I missed playing a lot more than I thought I would. When I was a kid, I played because I was tall. When I first got to Lafayette, it was hard for me. I didn't really know how to play or how to work at improving. Then I started to learn. I became a better player and just when I did, I got hurt. Now I know I want to keep playing for a while."

By the time the team came back from Christmas break, Ciosici didn't sound as certain about the future. "Right now I have no idea

Effort rewarded: Stefan Ciosici with the tournament MVP trophy.

Leopards huddle: Ciosici (facing camera), Tyson Whitfield, Tim Bieg, Brian Ehlers (32), and Mick Kuberka.

Brian Ehlers on the move — as always.

Don DeVoe pleads helplessly with ref John McDonell during the championship game.

Chris Williams — never still, never silent.

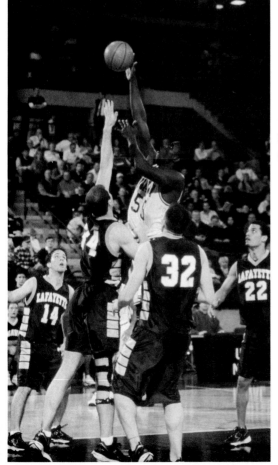

Sitapha Savane — always draws a crowd.

Dan Bowen fights to the bitter end against Fido Willybiro.

Pat Flannery counsels Bryan Bailey (left) and Valter Karavanic.

Pat Diamond guards Juan Pegues backed up by Pat Campolieta.

Campolieta fights for a position with Robert Reeder.

Chris Spitler —
always reaching.

Josh Sankes is counseled — again — by Ralph Willard (right) while
Roger Breslin listens.

Steve Aylsworth gets by the Lafayette defense — as usual.

Jared Hess — silky shooter with a sweet singing voice.

Chris Spatola directs Army's offense.

Jonte Harrell with a rare open shot.

about next year," he said. "Maybe I'll just stay here and work." He shrugged. "The way I'm playing, I may not have any choice."

Everyone on the team felt for Ciosici. They knew how hard he had worked to come back and how frustrated he was. Before his injury, he had averaged 17 points and 8 rebounds a game. Going into the final stretch prior to the start of league play, he was averaging 10.5 points and 5.4 rebounds. A lot of that had to do with the minutes he was averaging — 22 a game. Ideally, O'Hanlon wanted him to play twenty-eight to thirty minutes a game. Foul trouble had made that impossible most nights.

Lafayette's last two nonleague games were perfect tests for a team that hoped to dominate the Patriot League: at Princeton, at Penn. The cream of the Ivy League on the road. Chances were that no place in the Patriot League would be any tougher to play in than Princeton's Jadwin Gym or the Palestra. How tough were the two places for Lafayette? It had been forty-six years since the Leopards had won a game at Princeton, a losing streak of fourteen games. Overall, Lafayette was 12-39 against Princeton, although it had beaten the Tigers a year earlier at home. The same could not be said of Penn, which had come to Easton a few weeks after Princeton and beaten the Leopards. That upped Penn's overall record against Lafayette to 30-3.

In short, the chances of going to Princeton and Penn and winning back-to-back were very long. At least the Leopards had a couple of days off after the Princeton game before going to Penn. In the Ivy League, where teams play Friday and Saturday, teams play one of the powers on Friday, the other on Saturday, since Princeton and Penn are travel partners. In forty-three years of Ivy League play, 258 teams had attempted to win back-to-back at Princeton and Penn. Three had succeeded.

Jadwin Gym seats close to 6,500 but looks bigger because it has a high ceiling and all sorts of floor space behind the baskets. It was once home to a sneaker company–run summer camp that was one of the first true meat-market camps, athletes on display for college coaches to come and watch. Given Princeton's history, the presence of the camp was a true anomaly. It is now long gone.

Princeton Coach Bill Carmody had done what many thought impossible: successfully followed the legendary Pete Carril. There were even those at Princeton who, after looking around very carefully to make sure the coast was clear, would whisper: "He's better than Carril."

At the very least, he was damn good. Princeton still played Carril-style, holding the ball on offense, running the shot clock down, looking for backdoors and open three pointers. Princeton was one of a handful of teams that opposing coaches had to remind their teams to remain patient against — on defense. You couldn't rush into anything defensively against Princeton. If you did, a backdoor layup was almost always the result.

"You have to remember to play defense for thirty-five seconds on every possession, guys," O'Hanlon told his team. "Not twenty-five seconds or even thirty. Thirty-five. Stay in your stance and always be aware of the cutters."

This was Princeton's last game before it broke for finals. Princeton and Harvard both schedule their exams for after Christmas break, unlike almost every other school in the country. Jadwin was a sellout, with 6,432 people in the building, traffic snaking down the tiny back roads that lead to the parking lots right up until game time.

The game was worth the wait. Each team respected the other and each understood what had to be done to stop the other. "You know I'm not trying to set you up," Carmody said during the pregame handshake with O'Hanlon, "but I can honestly say your team is one of the few I actually enjoy watching on tape because you run your stuff so well."

The admiration was mutual. To O'Hanlon, Princeton was the model of what he wanted his team to be: smart, respected, able to play against big-name teams without being intimidated, able to recruit top players even without an athletic scholarship to offer.

Princeton had at least three starters who could have gone to big-name schools: Spencer Gloger, the freshman shooting guard; Nate Walton, the small forward; and six-eleven sophomore center Chris Young, who was a good enough baseball player that he would be drafted in the summer by a major league baseball team.

Young was going to be a handful for Ciosici and Barr to guard all night. Although he could score from the low post, he could also step outside and hit a jumper. The game started with Young running a classic Princeton back-cut and taking a pass from Walton for a layup. Then, as if to prove his versatility, Young stepped out and hit a 3.

But Ciosici was doing his part at the other end, starting the game with a left-handed hook, then putting back an Ehlers miss to give Lafayette an early 10-7 lead. Naturally, he picked up two first-half fouls — both on offense trying to jostle with Young for position. "Oh, was that awful," O'Hanlon screamed after the second foul was called. "You have to *see* the call, don't call what you *think* you see."

They seesawed to halftime. Gloger had 16 for Princeton and Young 13. But Lafayette was bombing from outside. Tyson Whitfield hit four 3-pointers and the team made a total of eight. Halftime score: Princeton 38, Lafayette 36. The second half was no different from the first. They traded the lead and momentum swings. The level of play was as high as you could ask for in a college game. Both teams made plays at both ends of the floor. Gloger tied it at 63 with 2:16 to go, with his fifth 3 of the game. Then both teams went cold, and they went to overtime still stuck on 63.

The overtime was filled with tension. Ehlers hit twice for Lafayette, but then missed two free throws with a 2-point lead. Ehlers missing two free throws in a row was about as likely as him giving up basketball to become a stand-up comic. For once his poker face broke. "Damn!" he yelled, coming to the huddle for a time-out.

"Forget it!" Ciosici barked. "It's okay!"

A moment later Young blocked an inside shot by Ciosici, who ran down the court screaming for a foul call. With 1:37 left, a 3-pointer by backup guard C. J. Chapman put Princeton up 68-67. O'Hanlon called time. He was hoping to get the ball in the post to Ciosici or on the wing to Ehlers. Naturally, Carmody was expecting just that and his defense set up to deny the two seniors a shot. The ball swung around the perimeter. Tyson Whitfield got into the lane, was double-teamed, and tossed it back to Brian Burke at the head of the key.

Once, Burke had dreamed of playing for Princeton. He had held Lafayette off throughout his senior high school season waiting to find out if he would get into Princeton. Only when he didn't get into Princeton did he seriously consider Lafayette. Now, in the gym where he had hoped to wear white, Burke was wearing visiting maroon. He coolly caught the pass from Whitfield and stepped into his picture-perfect 3-point stroke. Swish.

It was the twenty-fifth time the game had either been tied or had a lead change. Lafayette led, 70-68. Princeton went right back to Young, and Ciosici fouled him as he rolled to the basket, his fifth. Frank Barr had already fouled out. That meant six-eight Nate Klinkhammer — who was six-eight only when he stood up very straight — would have to try to guard Young down the stretch. Young made just one free throw and Lafayette still led, 70-69. There were fifty seconds left, so Lafayette couldn't run out the clock. Whitfield missed a floater and Princeton called time, to set up a final shot.

"Don't foul him, Nate," O'Hanlon told Klinkhammer, his tone almost pleading. "Try to push him off the block if you can."

Princeton inbounded. The ball went to Young. Klinkhammer pushed, Bieg dropped down to double-team. Young found Chapman, the open man, on the perimeter. His 3 bounded high off the rim. Nate Walton came down with the ball — Princeton's only offensive rebound of the night — turned, and tossed up a desperate push from the baseline. It was long. The buzzer sounded. It was over: Lafayette 70, Princeton 69.

Finally, they hadn't come close. Finally, they had gotten the bounce at the end. Klinkhammer was mobbed by everyone who knew what he had done keeping Young from getting the ball where he wanted it in the low post. O'Hanlon shook hands with Carmody, shrugged, and said, "Nothing to this game," as he picked up his jacket.

He was drained but buoyant. Beating Princeton was always going to be a big deal for Lafayette, especially at Princeton, even more so in a truly superb basketball game. Carmody was despondent over the loss, especially the final play. "You have to be able to get open against a six-five guy," he said, referring to Klinkhammer's defense on Young. "C. J. had a good shot, but right there, we didn't want a three."

He paused for a moment. "I'll tell you what," he added unsolicited. "I don't see Lafayette losing to anyone in the Patriot League."

There was one more game before Lafayette could start its march through the Patriot League, and it would be another difficult one emotionally for O'Hanlon. He had worked for Penn Coach Fran Dunphy for six years and had known him for thirty years. "Dunph was the one who gave me a chance at the college level," he said. "If not for him, I'd still be a high school coach. And he gave me a lot of responsibility. It's hard for me to be in a game where I want him to lose."

The Penn game was almost a carbon copy of the Princeton game: close throughout, played at a very high level with a lot of emotion. Again, Ciosici picked up two fouls in the first half, this time less than five minutes into the game. Again O'Hanlon was unhappy. "Two good box outs," he said to referee George Watts, "and I've got one of the best players in my league sitting next to me. That's not right."

The good news for Lafayette was that Frank Barr had progressed so far that the team's play really didn't drop off much with him in the lineup. The other players had grown accustomed to playing long stretches with Barr the previous year, so it didn't flip them out to see him trotting into the game.

Barr had come a long way since his days at Pennwood High School. He and Ciosici were about the same height but that was where their similarities ended. Ciosici looked like a supersized Arnold Schwarzenegger; Barr looked more like a seven-foot-tall jockey, having "bulked up" from the 185 he weighed as a high school senior to 210 as a fourth-year college junior. Ciosici's game was muscle; Barr's, finesse. Ciosici was more than happy to play rough and tumble; Barr was happier running the floor and using his speed.

Barr had come to basketball about as late as anyone his size ever did — as a sophomore in high school. He had been raised just outside Philadelphia by his mother and two sisters and there had never been any doubt that school came before sports. Arlene Barr had been on welfare at times, and when she did work she worked at night so she could be home to make sure Frank got his schoolwork done and didn't get into any trouble. His sisters, Diane and Debbie, both had postgraduate degrees: one in law, one an MBA.

But it was only a matter of time until a basketball coach noticed him. It happened one day late in his sophomore year when he was on his way to class. Coach Roy Bosco stopped him in the hall and said, "Son, you need to be playing basketball." Barr shook his head and said no thanks. Bosco responded by adding his name to the JV roster.

Barr then spent most of the year on the JV, wondering what in the world he was doing. But he blossomed as a senior, particularly as a shot blocker. His size, his lack of experience, and his grades brought college coaches running. Temple was interested; so was St. Joseph's. Lafayette recruited him, too. He finally decided on Hofstra, thinking he would have a chance to play there soonest.

But he played little as a freshman and clashed with Coach Jay Wright. He decided to transfer to Lafayette and had never looked back. "To be fair to Coach Wright, I was very immature," Barr said. "If I was the person I am now back then, I wouldn't have transferred. I just couldn't deal with getting yelled at *and* not playing much. I'm glad I'm at Lafayette but Hofstra didn't really do anything wrong."

Lafayette was an adjustment — especially academically. But he had grown as a player and as a student and he was an honor student second semester sophomore year. Ciosici's injury had given him the chance to play extended minutes, sharing the center position with Ted Cole, and his game had grown immeasurably.

Barr was a multifaceted youngster. He kept a daily journal — it was called "wuz.up" — and tended to punctuate all his sentences by saying, "That's cool." But he was also deeply religious, something he had come to in high school. He talked about religion only when asked, and when he did he was quite eloquent on the topic. "I'm not an evangelist," he said. "I just try to do what's right every day of my life."

O'Hanlon was comfortable with Barr in the game, although the team's style was very different when he was in the middle. Barr was a better shot blocker than Ciosici but not nearly as strong guarding the low post. He had trouble guarding big, strong centers like Penn's Geoff Owens and, like Ciosici, had a penchant for getting in foul trouble. O'Hanlon spent most of the first half trying to shuttle Ciosici and Barr, hoping Ciosici wouldn't pick up his third foul. He didn't, but only because he let Penn freshman Ugonna Onyekwe go around him on the final play of the half for a layup that gave the Quakers a 40-33 lead. Ciosici had no choice on the play. Picking up his third foul with three seconds to go would have been disastrous.

Being down 7 at halftime wasn't going to panic Lafayette. The Leopards started the second half with a 12-1 run. With Penn keying its defense to stop Ehlers and Ciosici, Tim Bieg had shooting room and he took advantage of it, drilling three 3-pointers. When the defense stepped up to guard him, Bieg put the ball on the floor, went to the basket, and got fouled. He scored 12 points in less than six minutes.

The momentum went back and forth. Lafayette went up 5, then Penn went up 6 when Michael Jordan (no, not *that* Michael Jordan) hit a 3, to make it 70-64 with a little more than five minutes to play. Lafayette came back with Ciosici dominating the inside to get to within 74-73. Then, with forty-four seconds left, Brian Burke reprised his Princeton heroics with another 3 off a pretty dish from Ehlers, and the Leopards led, 76-74. It appeared they might pull off the impossible double.

But Michael Jordan, although he wasn't Michael Jordan, was still a pretty good player. He tied the game with a baseline jumper. Then, after Burke was called for a questionable traveling violation, Jordan made a move worthy of the other Jordan: running the clock down to less than a second, creating space between himself and Tyson Whitfield, and draining the game winner with less than a second left. Rob Worthington instinctively called time out after Jordan made the shot, and since Lafayette had none left, a technical was called. The two meaningless free throws made the final 80-76.

It was a difficult loss to swallow because they had honestly thought they were going to win, especially after Burke's 3. It just seemed so right. First Burke beats the school that rejected him on Saturday, then he hits the game winner in his hometown in front of all his friends and family on Tuesday. But Jordan had other ideas.

"Hey, guys, we almost made history in here tonight," O'Hanlon said in the small locker room under the stands. "We played well, just not quite well enough. The important thing to remember is this: Our season didn't end out there tonight. In fact, it's just now beginning. We're a better team now than we were when we started playing, and we're going to keep getting better.

"The games we care about the most start Sunday. We're zero-and-zero."

So was everyone else in the Patriot League. It was just that Lafayette's zero-and-zero felt a whole lot more solid than everyone else's.

16

STARTING ALL OVER AGAIN

COLLEGE basketball seasons are divided into four distinct segments: preconference games; conference games; conference tournaments; postseason tournaments. The preconference games rarely have any real bearing on how a team's season is ultimately judged. They may provide some insight into where a team is going, and occasionally a serious injury may change a team's direction, but for the most part, they are warm-ups, a chance for a coach and players to find out where they stand before conference play begins.

This was especially true in the Patriot League, because all seven teams knew that their preconference record would have absolutely no bearing on their postseason aspirations. If Lafayette had been 11-2 in preconference instead of 8-5, it was still going to have to win the Patriot League Tournament if it wanted to make postseason play. Navy had recovered from its abysmal start to be 9-4, but the same held true for the Midshipmen. Conversely, Army at 2-10 and Lehigh at 3-9 both knew that a respectable record in conference play or one late spurt could easily rescue what appeared at that moment to be long, difficult winters.

League play began January 12. Because there were an odd number of teams, one league team always had to be playing a nonconference game. Lafayette had drawn the first bye and had played Penn the previous night. The Leopards would open conference play on Sunday, January 16, at home against Navy.

That meant Navy faced a difficult first week, since it was opening at Bucknell on Wednesday before the trip to Lafayette. Playing the other two top teams in the league on the road early could be a boon or a bust, depending on the outcomes. On the flip side of that ledger, Army opened conference play at Lehigh. Both teams had the exact same thought about the game: We have to beat *these* guys.

The third opening game was between the league's two question-mark teams. While Lafayette, Navy, and Bucknell seemed clearly established at the top and Lehigh and Army appeared likely to again do battle at the bottom, Colgate and Holy Cross were tougher to figure.

There was no questioning the fact that Ralph Willard had injected new life into the Holy Cross program. Even with the remarkable spate of injuries that had hit the team, the Crusaders had been competitive in every game they had played — except for the predictable rout by Indiana. The players looked forward to practice every day and they had bought into the notion that their only job was to get better. Whatever results that brought would be dealt with later.

The Colgate players firmly believed they could compete with the top-echelon teams in the league. After all, they had been the only league team that had beaten Lafayette the previous year, and they had done it twice. The third game, in the conference tournament, had been a 73-71 Lafayette win, the game being decided by a Brian Ehlers basket in the final seconds. The Red Raiders had lost twice to Navy, but both games had been close.

"Our season starts tonight," Emmett Davis told his players during their morning shootaround. "What we've done these first twelve games is prepare ourselves for tonight and what comes after tonight. You need to be prepared for an extra level of intensity from here on in, because every coach in the league is saying the exact same thing to his players that I'm saying to you guys. We're at home tonight. Guys, we don't lose at home. We let Holy Cross know right away where they are and that we're in charge of this game."

Coaches always preach to their players about defending their home court. But home court in the Patriot League is different from in the ACC or the Big Ten or the Southeast Conference. Colgate's Cotterell Court seats 5,000 when full, but it hasn't been close to full since Adonal Foyle left in 1997. Very few Patriot League games are sellouts. Since it started winning, Lafayette has come close to selling out 3,500-seat Kirby Field House (known as the Kirby Sports Center since its renovation in 1999) for most games. Bucknell often sells out 2,300-seat Davis Gym. But that's about it, except occasionally at Army or Navy when the school's leadership requires the cadets or the midshipmen to attend a game.

Pat Harris has a picture in his office in the Holleder Center taken during the Army-Navy game in his first year as coach. The shot looks down on a packed Christl Arena, the cadets all in their dress gray. "Look more closely," Harris will say to a visitor looking at the picture. "Almost all the cadets have books open on their laps. They're studying."

At Colgate, no one requires that the students go to basketball games and most don't. "The football players come," Davis said. "And actually, they make a lot of noise. They're good. But they're about it."

The football players would not be at the Holy Cross game, because school wasn't back in session yet. On a snowy night in Hamilton, the crowd would be well under 1,000 (555 announced). Actually, the snow wasn't really a factor. Most nights in Hamilton during basketball season are snowy. Basketball in the post-Foyle era at Colgate just wasn't a priority. Football and hockey were the two big sports.

Colgate is the league's most far-flung outpost (although Colgate people will tell you that Bucknell is more off the beaten track than they are). The school itself is very pretty, built on a hillside, the proto-type for a small, idyllic college campus. In the fall and the spring it is a very pleasant place to be. What's more, the people are friendly and warm as you might expect — or hope — in a small town.

But there is no easy way to get to Hamilton. The last sixty miles of the trip from just about any direction is two-lane road, and when the weather gets bad (always) it makes for some seriously unpleasant driving.

"Sometimes I don't know how our bus driver does it," Colgate center Pat Diamond said. "There have been nights coming home from games when we thought there was no way we were going to make it through."

That's pretty much the feeling visiting teams have when they come to Colgate. Getting there is hard. Getting out is often harder. There is only one hotel in town — the Colgate Inn — and if it is full there is no place anywhere close to town to stay. And it is always snowing. Except perhaps when it is sleeting. Loren Shipley, Navy's longtime basketball trainer, summed up the experience of visiting Hamilton this way: "Every time we pull in there I expect to see Jimmy Stewart running down the middle of Main Street hollering, 'Hello, movie theater! Hello, emporium!'"

Mr. Potter doesn't live in Hamilton, though. In fact, during his years there, Jack Bruen became the town's unofficial mayor, known and liked by one and all. As the teams came out of their locker rooms to warm up, with people trickling into the gym, Bruen's widow, Joan, sat ten rows up in the bleachers across from the Colgate bench and chatted with friends. Her mood was light and she was clearly happy to see everyone. She had brought her ten-year-old son, Danny, to the game. Naturally, everyone in town knew Danny Bruen.

"To say that people have been wonderful doesn't really explain it," Joan Bruen said. "There is a lot of warmth and generosity of spirit in all of these people."

But even though she sat with a smile on her face and rooted hard for Colgate, being back at Cotterell Court was difficult for Joan Bruen. She couldn't help but look at the bench and feel Jack's presence in the building. "So many memories," she said softly. "When we first came up here, I don't think people knew what to make of Jack. He's just one of those people who you think can't be that friendly and that funny and that self-deprecating until you spend time with him and find out that he is that way. This place really did become home for us."

But as much as she loved Hamilton and the people, she wasn't planning to stay. As soon as Danny finished fifth grade she was planning to move to Long Island, where her family lived. Part of it was the need to be closer to her family, part of it was the memories that followed her everywhere she went in Hamilton.

"Coming to the games is very hard," she said. "But I feel as if I owe it to the players, especially the ones who played for Jack. They lived

through the nightmare just like I did. But once Pat [Diamond] graduates, the ones he was close to will all be gone."

Talking about Diamond was difficult. Not only had he been at the
house a few hours before her husband died, he still stopped over
periodically just to check up on her and Danny. "He never makes a
big deal of it," Joan Bruen said. "He just shows up, comes in, spends
some time with me, spends some time with Danny. It means so much
because they [the players] were all Jack's kids, too. You don't realize
it, but you do fall in love with them. If Danny grows up to be like Pat
Diamond, I'll be thrilled."

As Joan Bruen talked, things were not going very well for her husband's former team. Holy Cross was still playing its patchwork lineup,
since Serravalle, Curry, Whearty, and Pegues were all still hurt.
Willard had given his players an impassioned pregame speech about a
new beginning. "We want to send a message to the entire Patriot
League tonight," he said. "And the message is: Holy Cross isn't going
to be pushed around anymore. Whatever we do out there tonight,
let's make that absolutely clear."

They had played with that kind of passion from the beginning,
most notably Josh Sankes. He had come a long way from that April
morning when he had been so terrified of Willard that it made him
sick. He was using his size (Diamond was seven inches shorter than
he was) and strength to get position inside and the Crusaders were
getting him the ball in places where he could score.

Foul shooting was still a problem. Davis had told his players to foul
him rather than let him dunk and they were doing just that. Willard
had tried just about everything to get Sankes over his free throw
shooting woes. "The worst thing is that when he stands next to me in
practice, I make eighty percent," Sankes said. "But he can't stand
next to me during games."

Willard had suggested that Sankes try to shoot the ball with one
hand, taking his left hand off the ball completely when he released it.
That was difficult for Sankes, though, because he had a slight tremor
in his hand, the result of a mild case of cerebral palsy. "When I was
born, I got stuck in the passage for a little while," he said. "They had

to do an emergency C-section to get me out, but my oxygen was cut off briefly. It's not a big thing, but when I get nervous, the tremor gets worse."

Shooting free throws made Sankes nervous. It wasn't as bad as his final year at Rutgers when he had literally prayed for officials to not call fouls when he had the ball. But it was still a struggle.

A late Colgate rally turned a 9-point Holy Cross lead into a 1-point margin at halftime. Davis and his assistants, Rod Balanis, Dennis Csensits, and Kevin Curley, were upbeat during the break. Davis has the youngest staff in the Patriot League. Balanis, who played as a walk-on at Georgia Tech, is thirty, the son of longtime coach George Balanis, who was head coach at William and Mary in the mid-1970s. He was the lone holdover from the Bruen/Aiello staff. Csensits is thirty-two, Curley, twenty-eight.

They are, though, a very serious-minded group, taking their cue from Davis, who oozes intensity during games. No one felt the need to make any major changes or adjustments. "What we need to do," Balanis said, "is shoot the basketball a little better. Everything else is okay."

Colgate took a brief lead on the first play of the half when Pat Campolieta, perhaps the league's most versatile player, posted up and scored. But then the shooting woes started again. When Tim Szatko drained a 3 and Brian Wilson hit a baseline jumper, Holy Cross had jumped back ahead, 44-37.

Remarkably, Colgate never got even again. The margin was 53-48 with 7:02 left after a Tim Sullivan steal and layup. Holy Cross kept going to Sankes and Colgate kept fouling. He missed two in a row. Then he missed three in a row — the first one didn't count because of a lane violation — so he missed two more. Then, shooting a one-and-one, he fired an air ball. Four different times the Red Raiders came down with a chance to cut the lead. Four different times they came away empty.

Guillermo Sanchez, the former walk-on who had been so heroic in the Yale game, finally broke the two-team drought with a drive in the lane on which he was fouled. His free throw made it 56-48. As it turned out, Sullivan's steal was the last field goal of the night for Colgate. Their entire offensive output the last seven minutes consisted of three free throws — the last two by Mark Akers in the final minute. The final was a stunning 68-51. The Holy Cross players were thrilled and, to some degree, amazed. The Colgate players were in complete shock. They had shot an appalling two-of-twenty-four from outside the 3-point line, compared to Holy Cross's thirteen-of-twenty-six.

"Guys, I told you about the intensity of league games," Davis said. "You can't just show up and think because you're home, the other team is going to roll over for you. That is not a great basketball team we just lost to. But you made them feel very good about themselves tonight."

The last part was true. They celebrated in the Holy Cross locker room with great gusto. "You played with heart, you played with energy, you played with emotion," Willard told them. "If you do that every night, you will always have a chance to win."

One statistic told Willard a lot about his team's approach to the game: deflections. Willard had known Hubie Brown, the ex–New York Knicks coach for many years. Brown had always maintained that in any basketball game, if a team deflected the ball — got a hand on it — on defense at least thirty-five times and shot at least 39 percent, it would win 95 percent of the time. Willard always tracked deflections as a measure of his team's defensive effort. There had been fifty-one deflections by the Crusaders. And they had shot 45 percent.

They had a five-hour bus trip back to Worcester ahead of them. It was snowing even harder now than it had been before the game. As head manager Patrick Maloney — whose father had been the head manager when Willard played at Holy Cross thirty-five years earlier — handed the players their postgame sandwiches to eat on the bus ride, no one even noticed it was snowing.

Except the Colgate players. They were staying in Hamilton. And they would have to face their coach the next morning.

As soon as Davis finished his postgame talk and told the players the schedule for the following day — no school, two practices — Pat Campolieta got up and stormed from the team's meeting area into the dressing area, slamming a towel angrily to the ground as he walked through the door.

On the surface, Campolieta was as mild-mannered as anyone playing Division I college basketball. He was unfailingly polite and soft-
spoken. Mark Murphy, Colgate's athletic director, often referred to
him as "Jack Bruen's last gift to Colgate."

Campolieta had grown up in nearby Syracuse and Bruen had convinced him to commit to Colgate in the fall of 1997, just before his
death. "We found out what kind of kid he really was," Murphy said,
"when he and his mom showed up at Jack's funeral."

Campolieta, Pat Diamond, and Jordan Harris, the team's three
starters up front, were the heart and soul of the team. They had a lot
in common. Each was a younger brother. Each had seen his parents
split, Harris in middle school, Campolieta and Diamond in their
sophomore year of high school. None of the three had really expected
to play Division I basketball until the latter part of their high school
careers.

"I used to tell my parents that if I got a full scholarship, they had to
buy me a car," Diamond said.

Diamond could have cashed in on that deal, because Army was
willing to accept him. Since his older brother, Robert, was at the
Naval Academy, Diamond had no trouble accepting the notion of
attending an academy. Since he had grown up on Staten Island, he
was very familiar with West Point, and when he visited there on a gor-
geous fall weekend in September of 1995, he was seriously tempted.
"I went to a football game and before the game the basketball team
had a tailgate party," he said. "Mike Krzyzewski was there because
they had honored him at a dinner the night before. I thought the
whole thing was pretty cool."

But he also knew that the academies weren't like other colleges,
that the social life was different and so were the responsibilities. "You
couldn't go to an academy with the idea that you were choosing it
because it was the best basketball situation," he said. "Because there's
a lot more to it than that. The more I thought about that, the more I
thought it might not be right for me."

He was convinced that Yale was right for him. Coach Dick Kuchen
recruited him very aggressively and he liked the players on the team.
He applied for early admission, convinced that a 3.6 GPA and 1220
on the SATs would easily qualify at a school hungry for basketball

talent. Apparently Yale wasn't that hungry. He was turned down. It was then that Colgate seriously entered the picture. Diamond visited, liked the school, the campus, and the coaches, and committed to go.

"Basketball was very hot here at the time," he said. "Adonal [Foyle] was finishing his sophomore year. They had won the Patriot League two years in a row and every home game was packed."

The crowds were still good his freshman year, but Diamond didn't play very much. "Mostly I got the hell beat out of me by Adonal every day in practice," he said. "I guess it was a learning experience, but I came home very sore at night a lot." One of Bruen's favorite plays for Foyle was called "St. John's." On the play, Foyle would start on one side of the lane and move to the other side while the two forwards both screened for him. Diamond felt a little bit like a pinball bouncing off those screens trying to chase Foyle.

Like everyone else he was disappointed when Foyle decided to leave at the end of the year, but he saw it coming. He and Foyle had become friends during the year and Foyle often told him that he, his guardians, Jay and Joan Mandle, and Bruen were at odds about where Foyle was supposed to be in the Colgate offense. "I remember coming into the gym a lot and seeing him working out alone with them [the Mandles]," Diamond said. "At first, I didn't think much about it. I was a freshman, what did I know? But then I noticed Adonal peeling off at halftime of games to go talk to them. That I thought was a little odd."

It was a little odd, and it had a lot to do with Foyle's departure to the NBA a year early. When he returned as a sophomore, Diamond was a starter. That was the good news. The bad news was Bruen's illness. "When we first got back to school, he looked a lot thinner," Diamond remembered. "But all I thought was that he was trying to get into better shape. I mean, he had been overweight. But when practice started, it was pretty clear he wasn't feeling very good."

On the afternoon of October 30, before practice started, Bruen sat the team down on the bleachers in the gym. He told them he had cancer. He would be getting treated for it and hoped not to miss much practice time. In typical Bruen fashion, he tried to make light of the whole thing.

"You know, when you get bad news about your health, there's two ways to look at it," he told the players. "On the one hand, if you die there's the possibility that you'll get to go to heaven. On the other hand, if you don't get to heaven, it means you'll get to spend a lot of time with your friends."

The players got a laugh from that, but there weren't a lot of laughs the next seven weeks as Bruen's health deteriorated. He began calling players over during practice for lengthy chats about their future, clearly knowing his time was limited. "In a strange way, it was a great time," Diamond said. "He was just as intense about coaching, in fact we worried about that sometimes. When we lost that Syracuse game that we could have won, he was angry about it. But most of the time, he was really involved with what we were all doing and thinking. We actually played very well during that period."

It was during that period that Campolieta visited campus. Bruen had seen him playing summer ball and had come down to visit him. Campolieta had been six-two as a high school sophomore and got a chance to start that year only because his brother Chris, who was a senior, tore up his knee and had to sit out the year. The injury turned out to be a blessing: Chris got a redshirt year and he and Pat got to play together the following year as starters, which would not have happened during Pat's sophomore year. What's more, Pat played on the perimeter that year and developed outside skills. A year later, when he grew to six-six, he was moved inside more. "I never would have had outside skills the way I do now if Chris hadn't gotten hurt," he said. "Strange how that happens sometimes."

Campolieta's recruitment advanced in stages. As a junior, most of the letters were from Division III schools. That summer, Division II schools started showing interest. By the start of his senior year schools like Colgate, Lafayette, Lehigh, Canisius, and SUNY-Albany were all interested. He liked Bruen, he liked the school when he visited. Colgate made a lot of sense.

Then he began hearing how sick Bruen was. When Bruen died, Campolieta wasn't certain if Colgate was still the right place for him. "I just wasn't sure I wanted to commit to a school when I didn't even know who the coach would be my freshman year," he said.

He waited to see if any other schools came into the picture late. Surprisingly, none did, because by now Campolieta was six-six, with a terrific feel for the game at both ends of the floor. Late in his senior season, his coach, Pat Donnelly, sat him down. There was nothing new on the recruiting front, he said. Rod Balanis had stayed in close touch throughout the season even though he, like everyone on the Colgate coaching staff, was in limbo. The offer to go to Colgate was still there. The financial package was very good: he would only have to pay about $2,000 a year. Since his father was a teacher and his mother was an eight-term elected Democratic county legislator, neither made a lot of money, and there were four children in the now-split family. The ride would be close to full. And it was a chance to go to a great school.

New coach unseen, Campolieta decided to commit to Colgate. A month later, Emmett Davis was named to succeed Paul Aiello, who had taken over the team after Bruen's death. Campolieta was delighted. The previous summer, Davis had tried to recruit him to Navy. "I had told him the military just wasn't for me," Campolieta said. "But I liked him. And I liked the idea that I was going to have a coach who had seen my game and liked it enough to recruit me."

Campolieta had a superb freshman season, averaging 13.7 points and 5.4 rebounds a game. He was a runaway choice for Patriot League rookie of the year. He and Harris were clearly the cornerstones of the program for the future, both sophomores who had started almost since day one as freshmen. They had been the only two players in double figures against Holy Cross: Jordan with 15 points, Campolieta with 13. They had combined to shoot eleven-for-twenty-one. The rest of the team had been eight-for-thirty-three. That was going to have to improve if the team's dreams of playing with the league's big boys were going to come true.

They had two days to prepare for the trip to Army. Everyone knew it would be a long two days.

As it turned out, the only home team to win on the first night of league play was Lehigh. The Mountain Hawks, in front of an overjoyed (but not overcrowded) crowd of 801, pounded Army, 81-64. Chris Spatola single-handedly kept the Cadets in the game for a half, scoring 23 of the team's 41 points. The game was tied at the break, but Lehigh put the clamps on Spatola in the second half, double-teaming him from the instant he left the locker room.

"If you want to stop a five-ten guard from getting the ball you can do it," Pat Harris said. "But it should open something up for your other guys. The problem is, our other guys are open and can't do anything about it."

It was Army's tenth straight loss. It was Lehigh's second straight victory. The Mountain Hawks had gone to California for two games and lost them both — to Pepperdine and the University of San Diego — but Sal Mentesana had been pleased with what he had seen in the San Diego game. The guards had played better and the freshmen seemed to be getting more and more comfortable. Center Sah Brown was finally showing some signs of consistency. They had come home to play SUNY-Albany, a first-year Division I school. This was another game — like the Wagner game — where it was not unreasonable to expect a win.

They got it — barely. The game swung back and forth for forty minutes; Lehigh was up 10 at the half, then fell behind by 9 in the second half before rallying. The game came down to the last two possessions. Trailing by 1, Lehigh brought the ball down and opted not to call time out. Steve Aylsworth was double-teamed at the top of the key and for a moment looked like he was going to turn the ball over. But he squirmed free and spotted Brown wide open under the basket. Just to make it suspenseful, Brown dropped the ball — while the bench groaned in agony — before picking it up and dunking.

There were still six seconds left. Albany Coach Scott Hicks also opted against a time-out. The ball was pushed downcourt, and as the Lehigh players scrambled to get back, Joe Vukovich came wide open on the left wing for a ten-foot jumper. He had made all five shots he had taken up until that moment. As everyone prepared for another brutal last-second loss, Vukovich went up, shot, and watched in dismay as the ball hit the front rim and bounced in the air and away from the basket. The buzzer sounded. Lehigh had — somehow — won the game, 75-74.

"We finally got lucky," Mentesana said. "I guess the kid was so shocked to be that open he didn't know what to do." He told the players he was proud of the way they had fought back, but added, "It's a start, guys. But it won't mean anything if we don't beat Army in here on Wednesday."

They had beaten Army. That made them 5-9, one victory shy of their total a year ago; one ahead of the number they had won in the Patriot League regular season. It put them in a three-way tie for first at 1-0 with Holy Cross and Navy. The Midshipmen had gone to Bucknell, a bugaboo place for them throughout the years — they hadn't won there since 1994 — and had beaten the Bison, 77-70. Everyone from Navy was pleased with the win, but understood that it was sullied by the fact that Dan Bowen hadn't played. Bowen had started ninety-six straight games dating to his freshman year, but a blister on the small toe of his right foot had turned into an infection, and Pat Flannery found out four hours before the game that he would be unable to play. He had surgery the next day to remove the infection and was able to play three days later against Holy Cross, but only after a hole had been cut in his sneaker to lessen the pressure on the infected toe.

This created another problem for Flannery. "If we send the sneaker back [to Reebok] and ask for a new one, they may say no on the grounds that we damaged the sneaker," he said. He was serious. Life in the Patriot League is different from in the TV leagues.

In the TV leagues, coaches routinely make well into six figures from shoe companies. Recently, shoe companies have taken to making deals with entire schools to outfit *all* teams in return for the publicity they gain from getting the basketball team to wear their stuff. That was how Nike had gotten Dean Smith at North Carolina and Mike Krzyzewski from Duke to start wearing the swoosh. Krzyzewski not only had a huge contract, he had stock options in the company.

To the big-time schools, unlimited equipment was a given. If a basketball team asked for one thousand pairs of basketball shoes during the course of a season, one thousand pairs would be delivered. At the Patriot League level, the coaches weren't paid at all. Getting a shoe company to provide free equipment was a bonus, and it was almost always an exact number. If you asked for extra sneakers or an extra warm-up outfit, there had better be a good reason.

Dan Bowen would get new sneakers. At least this time.

17

OPENING SALVOS

IT was shortly after nine o'clock on Sunday morning, January 16, and Navy was finishing its morning shootaround in Kirby Sports Center. In seven hours, when the Midshipmen tipped off their game against Lafayette, the place would be packed. The only people inside now were the members of the Navy traveling party.

Jimmy Allen, Don DeVoe's top assistant coach, looked around the empty building and smiled. "I love days like this," he said. "You play for days like this, you coach for days like this. There's nothing like the feel of a big game."

There was no question that Navy-Lafayette would have the feel of a big game. Lafayette had ascended to Navy's throne in 1999, winning the Patriot League title in both the regular season and the tournament. Navy didn't like what had happened at all. It didn't like the two losses in the regular season and it certainly didn't like being upset by Lehigh in the first round of the tournament and never getting a third crack at Lafayette. On the flip side, some of the Lafayette players admitted that, as thrilling as it was to win the tournament, there was a small feeling of incompleteness because they had not gone through Navy to win.

Navy-Lafayette had started to grow as a rivalry during the 1997 season, when Lafayette, still a young and upcoming team, twice pushed Navy for forty minutes before losing close games. The following year, the teams split during the regular season and finished tied for first place with 10-2 conference records. Since they had split head-to-head and had also split with Bucknell, the third-place team, a coin toss had to be used to decide who would be the top seed in the tournament. Navy had won the flip and, given a choice between a first-round bye or home court for the final — if it got that far — it had opted for home court. Both teams made it to the final, and Navy won a tension-filled game, 93-85, to win its third championship in five years.

The Lafayette players still had bitter memories of that game. Some of those ill feelings had been wiped out by winning the tournament in 1999, but not all of them. They still wanted the chance to beat Navy in the tournament. They had never completely gotten over the sight of the Navy players celebrating.

On the other hand, Navy didn't like Lafayette's newfound status as kings of the Patriot League. One preseason poll had actually picked Navy *third* behind Lafayette and Bucknell. DeVoe and Sitapha Savane had often reminded the younger players that, with the exception of Chris Williams, none of them had been a factor in a Navy championship. They were all a little tired of hearing that.

Now it was 2000 and both teams were starting again. Navy already had the victory at Bucknell in the bank, and even without Dan Bowen, it was still a head start for the Midshipmen to have beaten the league's other known quality team on the road. If the Mids were to come in to Lafayette on a cold, clear Sunday afternoon and win, they would be in command of the league race just one week into the season.

DeVoe was feeling good about his team. The Mids had won ten of eleven games since the disastrous 0-3 start. Savane was emerging as a true force at center. Chris Williams, the talented but mercurial small forward, was playing with considerably more consistency. Reggie Skipworth had made tremendous strides at the point guard spot. And two freshmen, Jason Jeanpierre and Scott Long, were disproving DeVoe's notion that plebes couldn't handle the pressures of the academy *and* Division I college basketball.

The decision to give the freshmen some serious minutes was one of two out-of-character decisions DeVoe had made early in the season.

The other was to try to play a full-court game. For the first time in memory, Navy was pressing all over the court, jumping into a pressure defense after they made baskets and free throws. DeVoe called this new defensive scheme "Dynamite." Also, the players had the freedom to push the ball whenever they got their hands on it, rather than walk it up and set up a half-court offense. DeVoe's sideline mantra had become "Push the ball, push the ball," which in his Ohio farm-boy accent came out "Poosh the ball, poosh the ball." The Mids had been pooshing quite successfully.

The Lafayette coaches had noted the change in style and had prepared their team accordingly. They had preached all week to their guards to stay away from the sidelines against the Navy pressure. And when the double-teams did come, to make sure they always knew where to find Brian Ehlers.

As important as it was for Stefan Ciosici to be healthy, for Tim Bieg to run the offense effectively, for Tyson Whitfield and Brian Burke to hit from outside, Ehlers was the heart and soul of Lafayette's team. He wasn't just the go-to guy at the end of games, he was the guy who kept everyone calm and controlled at all times, because he was always calm and controlled. There was absolutely no way to tell what kind of a game Ehlers was having by looking at his face. If he made ten straight shots, his expression never changed. If he missed ten straight, the deadpan stayed in place. He never pouted, never complained, never trash-talked, never celebrated.

Chris Williams, his Navy counterpart, called him "the silent assassin. He never says a word. He just kills you."

Ehlers was the classic gym rat. He loved to play, whether it was in a game on national television or in an empty gym by himself. He had grown up in Bay Shore, Long Island, following in his brother Tom's footsteps all through high school. His dad, John Ehlers, had been a good player in high school and captain of the team at Springfield College, a longtime Division II power. When he graduated from college and went to work as a high school PE teacher and coach, John Ehlers kept playing in teachers' leagues and rec leagues. Brian's earliest memories are of watching his dad play in those games. "He would take Tom and me to the games, set us up on the sideline with a couple of basketballs to work on dribbling and passing, and play," Brian said. "I guess you could say I'm the son of a gym rat."

Shortly after that, John, Tom, and Brian began playing on the back-yard hoop John had set up. As the boys grew (all three Ehlerses are now six-four) the games became more intense. By the time he was in seventh grade, Brian's passion was for basketball. He had been good at both soccer and baseball, but basketball was what he loved. "I was always happiest playing basketball," he said. "For as long as I can remember I've been that way. I still am."

Tom graduated from Bay Shore High School and turned down the chance to play at smaller schools in order to go to Princeton. He played on the JV team there for two years but never made it to the varsity. Brian was recruited by Princeton, but eventually decided he didn't want to go there because he didn't think he would enjoy their slowdown style of play. At the end of his junior year, he was highly recruited by both Patriot and Ivy League schools and some other mid–Division I schools. When he averaged 31.4 points per game as a senior to lead the entire state in scoring, he thought he might draw some interest from some bigger schools. But it never happened.

"Boston College, one letter, that was it," he said. "The rest of it was Patriots, Ivies, and smaller schools." He smiled. "Maybe it was the traffic."

With a 3.6 GPA and 1270 on the SATs he was a dream recruit for schools at that level. He considered Cornell and Colgate for a while but never took official visits there because he decided to commit to Lafayette after visiting. Rob Jackson, then an assistant to O'Hanlon, had recruited him right from the start.

He settled on Lafayette because he liked O'Hanlon and the campus and because he saw the developing program as a place where he could play right away. O'Hanlon thought Ehlers had the potential to play right away, too — until practice began, and Ehlers, because of his undiscovered iron deficiency, appeared to be so out of shape.

"It was completely baffling," assistant coach Pat Brogan remembered. "Fran and I would sit there every night and try to figure out what could be wrong with the kid. We knew he loved to play. We tried giving him extra work to get him in shape, we tried screaming at him, cajoling him. Nothing worked."

Finally, after Ehlers had run up and down the court twice one day in practice before collapsing in an exhausted heap, they decided to find out if something was wrong that went beyond simple conditioning. That was when his iron deficiency, known as "sports-induced anemia," was discovered. Walking around, Ehlers had no problem. But as soon as he exerted himself in practice, the lack of iron in his system made him weak as a kitten.

Ehlers began taking an iron supplement several times a day. Slowly, his strength returned. It was well after Christmas before he began to feel 100 percent, but at least he was making progress. By the middle of the Patriot League season he was starting, and he ended up making the all-rookie team even though Lafayette didn't nominate him. "We weren't playing well enough to nominate people for awards," O'Hanlon said. "Then we won our last three games."

By his sophomore year, Ehlers was becoming a star. He averaged 16.3 points and 5.4 rebounds a game, finishing behind Ciosici in both those categories. He was second-team all-league. Then Ciosici got hurt during the summer and it fell to Ehlers to be the team's best player.

Ehlers would have been just as happy without the attention. He is polite and friendly but a lengthy answer to a question for him rarely breaks a word count in double figures. The coaches liked to joke about the fact that he had "come out of his shell" from freshman year to senior year but he wasn't really in a shell. He was just quiet.

No one's name got mangled in as many ways or by as many people as Ehlers's. His response was a shrug and a buried 3 or a quick-step drive to the basket. What set Ehlers apart from most Patriot League players was his versatility. He was a very good 3-point shooter, but if a defender came up on him to deny the 3, he was quick enough to put the ball on the floor and go by him. He also had what coaches call a "middle game," the ability to stop a drive ten or twelve feet from the basket and shoot off the dribble. Very few college players can score from all three areas: outside, inside, middle.

Navy had one player with the ability to match Ehlers: Chris Williams, who was a decent 3-point shooter, had a solid middle game, and had a great move to the basket off the dribble. Ehlers was a better shooter; Williams was a little better on the drive — both were good in the middle.

The two players had become friendly during their three years as court rivals. They could not have been more different as people. To Ehlers, back-to-back sentences represented a lengthy speech. Williams could talk for twenty minutes and just be clearing his throat. Ehlers was from Long Island, a Knicks fan from the cradle; Williams was from Savannah, Georgia, and thought of Manhattan as a foreign country. Ehlers had been recruited early on by the military academies and had firmly told them no thanks. Williams was the son of a career naval officer who had settled in Savannah after retiring to teach math at Savannah State College.

It was in Savannah that Chris had blossomed as an athlete. His brother Claben, five years his senior, always took him along when he went to play basketball, and Chris spent a lot of time either watching or getting into games and getting beaten up by the big kids. "Now I go back and walk in the gym and everything stops," he said, a wide grin on his face. "When I was a kid, no one would choose me. Now, I do the choosing."

He can remember hours and hours on hot schoolyards with Claben and another friend, taking turns playing one-on-one while the guy who was out of the game went and stood next to a fan to cool down. As he grew and matured, he began to play football, too. By high school he was a six-foot-three-inch, 215-pound wide receiver who could run a 4.6 forty and outjump almost any defensive back for the football. Recruiters began showing up in droves: Florida, UCLA, Florida State. By his junior year just about the entire Southeast Conference had been there at one point or another.

The basketball recruiters weren't quite as enthusiastic. Although there were not a lot of minority kids from Georgia running around who could run a 4.6 forty and dunk with either hand, his jump shot was a question mark and some of the basketball schools were convinced he was going to play football. Still, there was national interest, and because of his grades — Williams had a 3.9 GPA and 1440 on his SATs — tremendous interest from both the Ivy League and the Patriot League.

"The first thing I had to do was decide which sport I was going to play in college," he said. "There were some schools that came in and said I could play both, but I knew how tough it was trying to play both in high school. During the summer, when I needed to be playing summer basketball, I was getting in shape for football. Then I would start basketball practice late and feel out of it for the first few weeks. I knew in college I would miss most of spring football for basketball. I figured I would end up not doing either one as well as I could."

His decision was made during a state football playoff game. He was playing safety, trying to shut down a sweep, when his knee got twisted by a blocker cracking back on him. He kept playing, but learned the next day that he had a torn meniscus in the knee. It wasn't serious, but it did give him pause to think about his future.

"I knew the guys I'd be playing against in college, especially if I went to a big-time school, would be a lot bigger, stronger, and faster than the high school guys," he said. "I might have played offense or I might have played defense. I didn't know. I just decided basketball was a lot less risky."

It was a mature decision, since he was being given far more big-time treatment at that point by the football recruiters. Georgia was still interested in him for basketball, but then-coach Tubby Smith told him that while he would offer him a scholarship, he couldn't guarantee early playing time. Then Williams heard that Smith was recruiting Dion Glover. He had played with Glover in AAU ball and he knew that Glover was at a different level than he was. "I felt like going to the SEC or the ACC would probably be tough, certainly in the beginning," he said. "Tubby didn't get Dion [Georgia Tech did — for one year] but that's the kind of player he was looking for. I felt the same way about [Georgia] Tech even though I knew it was a good school, since Claben had gone there."

The decision eventually came down to Navy or the Ivy League. Williams certainly would have received financial aid from an Ivy League school, but Navy wouldn't cost a cent. Being the son of a naval officer and having attended a military academy in high school, he had no qualms about being in the military. "Great education, guaranteed job," he said. "I wasn't figuring I was an NBA player, so this seemed the right fit."

Until he arrived. Like a lot of people who think they're ready for Plebe Summer, Williams was caught off guard. "I'd been there four days and I felt like I'd been screamed at for four straight months," he said. "I still remember thinking on the Fourth of July, 'I gotta get out of here.' But I never quite got around to it."

He was a role player coming off the bench as a freshman, getting a steady fifteen to twenty minutes a game on a team dominated by seven seniors. He became a starter as a sophomore, averaging close to 14 points a game. There was no doubt starting the season that he and Savane were going to be looked to by DeVoe as the team's main men.

And yet it hadn't been easy for Williams. His outspoken nature didn't always play well at the academy. He was smart, funny, and friendly. But he always spoke his mind. He dreamed of being a politician some day and he had the kind of personality that would make that possible. He was extremely up-to-date on what was going on in the political world, and he and Savane, the one-time Communist, often had lengthy debates about the merits of Communism vs. Capitalism.

"Sitapha says all the time that the idea of Communism is right, that it's about sharing and everyone being equal," Williams said. "I don't disagree with that. But then I ask him, 'When has it ever worked? Why do Communist countries always end up as dictatorships? Why did Eastern Europe collapse?' I mean, utopia is a nice idea, but it doesn't exist."

Even within the team, Williams was seen as something of an iconoclast. Most of the players liked to listen to loud rap music — usually supplied by Savane — in the locker room before the game. Williams liked country music and said so, usually not loud enough to be heard over the rap.

"Sitapha thinks that stuff is some kind of Senegalese war dance," he joked. "I can't stand it."

The coaches occasionally accused him of being selfish because he had a penchant for going one-on-one, which was, generally speaking, not a part of the Navy offense. When he made a spectacular move and it worked, there were no problems. When it didn't, he often found himself with a not-so-comfortable seat on the bench and a not-too-happy DeVoe in his face. Being the son of a math professor, Williams was into numbers and always knew what his were — good and bad — down to the decimal point. Trainer Loren Shipley called him "Stats Man."

There was no debating that Navy needed his production to be a good team. As good as Savane had been in the weeks leading up to the Lafayette game, Williams remained the one Navy player consistently able to create a shot for himself. DeVoe understood that and tried not to lose it when he occasionally created wild shots. The only thing that made him crazy was when Williams — and others — started jacking 3s without running offense. DeVoe had turned fifty-eight on New Year's Eve and he was trying not to be a stick-in-the-mud coach. That's why Navy was playing up-tempo and pressing. But a missed 3 still sent his blood pressure soaring, especially if it came early in the shot clock.

"That's *not* what we do," he would scream at the trigger-happy shooter, especially if it was Williams.

On the board before the Lafayette game, DeVoe had written his usual list of offensive and defensive keys. As the number one priority on offense he had written simply: *"Get the ball to 55!"* (meaning Savane). What wasn't there but was visible to everyone in the room were the words "That means *you,* Chris Williams."

As much as O'Hanlon and DeVoe liked and respected each other, the simmering nature of the rivalry was never very far from the surface.

Lafayette had undertaken major renovations to the Kirby Field House, adding a sparkling new annex for football and redoing the main lobby and the basketball offices. The basketball locker rooms had also been renovated, but they had not increased in size. In fact, Lafayette's locker room was actually *smaller* than the old one had been. "They're trying to bring us closer together as a team," Tim Bieg joked.

Needless to say the visiting locker rooms were no bigger than the home locker room. When Navy arrived on Sunday morning and

DeVoe got his first look at the new and improved locker room, his first comment was, "So this is what they spent twenty-six million bucks on, huh?"

Since Navy travels a full complement of fifteen players, there was not enough room for everyone to sit down in the tiny room while DeVoe talked to the team. Several players had to stand in the doorway leading to the bathroom, while others sat on the floor.

"I guarantee you they've got a lot more room than this down the hallway," DeVoe said to his coaches.

In truth, they didn't. But that wasn't really the point.

Navy's presence in town normally would have guaranteed a sellout, but the students weren't back for another week so there were scattered empty seats in the building. The attendance was 2,882 — about 600 under capacity. "No Zoo Crew," Pat Brogan noted as the teams were warming up.

The Zoo Crew had become a phenomenon unto itself the previous year, a band of rabid students who showed up at home games in yellow "Zoo Crew" T-shirts, waving a giant Zoo Crew flag. They sat together in a corner of the bleachers, thought up different chants to aim at visiting players, and kept things raucous through most of the game. They had received — and clearly enjoyed — a good deal of attention.

In truth, the Zoo Crew had been far less evident early in the new season. Their numbers had swelled to close to two hundred during the 1999 season but at many of the preconference games the number had been closer to fifty. Some attributed the drop-off to a lack of leadership. Gerrit Nieuwenhuizen, who had been the leader and organizer of the group a year earlier, had graduated, and it appeared that the void had not been filled. Others saw it as a sign of malaise in the student body. Winning was no longer that new or that special at Lafayette. Everyone would wait for the big games later in the season to get wound up the way they had been the previous winter.

"We would beat someone by ten," Tim Bieg said, "and the next day in class people would be saying, 'So what's wrong, you guys only won by ten last night?' It wasn't that long ago that we didn't beat anyone, much less take beating someone by ten for granted. But that's the way it is now."

Even without the Zoo Crew and with very few students in attendance, Kirby was jumping with noise before game time. This had
become the league's best rivalry since O'Hanlon's revival of the
Lafayette program, and the Patriot League had chosen the game to
be the opener of its TV package. The Patriot League TV package is a
little different from, for example, the ACC's TV package.

In 2000, the ACC was in the fourth year of a five-year deal with
Raycom that guaranteed the league $21 million. It was in the process
of negotiating a new ten-year deal with Raycom that would be worth
more than $80 million. In other words, each ACC school would
receive just about $1 million a year from the TV package.

The Patriot League schools would receive exactly $1 million a year
less than that from their TV package. In fact, the league *paid* to have
its games televised. The ten-game TV package was a time buy, a syn-
dicator putting the package together and selling it to various TV out-
lets in return for a fee paid by the league.

In short, it was a way of buying publicity for the schools. Each
school's media guide prominently mentioned the TV appearances
the team would make during the season. Lafayette and Navy
would appear the most, because a number of their nonconference
games were part of other packages. The other schools also picked
up occasional appearances in nonconference games, although that
was a mixed blessing. For Army, being on regional TV against
Duke was nice to talk about beforehand, not so great after the
fact.

The league package existed to guarantee each school at least two
TV shots each year. There had been some talk among the ADs about
revamping the package to include more of the so-called glamour
games in the conference schedule, but actually doing that would no
doubt send the teams in the lower half of the conference running
from the room screaming.

This game, though, was one of the big ones. And Navy came out
flying. Their press didn't surprise Lafayette, because the coaches had
seen it on tape and had worked on it in practice. But knowing something is coming and actually responding to it are often two very different things. Less than seven minutes in, trailing 12-6, Mike Homer
was trapped with the ball and had to call a time-out.

O'Hanlon rarely laces into his players during time-outs. He is the most soft-spoken coach in the league, someone who focuses strictly on Xs and Os during 95 percent of play stoppages. Now he was in his team's collective face. "It amazes me," he said, "that we tell you that they're going to play this way and you guys still come out and get sucker-punched! Now come on! Play ball! Talk to each other, help each other, stay away from the sidelines against the press!"

They nodded. Then they went out, turned the ball over again, and watched Chris Williams drain a 3 to make it 15-6. But then they caught a break: trying to stop an Ehlers drive, Williams picked up his second foul and had to come out. Navy is the deepest team in the league, and freshman Jason Jeanpierre came in and promptly nailed a 3 to continue the carnage, but Williams's absence was going to be felt. Down 22-10, the Leopards finally began to right themselves. With Savane taking a breather, Ciosici took advantage of backup Michael Cunningham, posting him up twice in a row, once for a 3-point play. Then Brian Burke came off the bench and hit a driving layup and a 3.

They lurched back and forth until halftime, Ehlers finding Ciosici inside as the half ended for a layup that cut the margin to 40-34. By now everyone was uptight. Savane was absolutely convinced that Ciosici was intentionally backing into him with his bulky knee brace. He had cuts on both knees and DeVoe was unhappy about it. O'Hanlon wasn't at all happy with the officiating and spent a few seconds barking at the refs before leaving the court. DeVoe stood a few feet away, wanting to be sure he wasn't making any points that might affect his team.

Both coaches spent some of halftime talking about technical matters and some of it telling their players that this game was a test of their manhood. "You have to play through the tough spots," DeVoe said. "Forget the crowd, forget all the other stuff, and play. Sitapha, you let me worry about the referees and Ciosici, okay?"

O'Hanlon told his players they had to take the inside away from Navy, that if Navy couldn't dominate the boards, it couldn't win the game. "You cannot let them come in here and make you back down," he said. "We have to be aggressors. We didn't do it the first twenty minutes, let's see if we can do it the second twenty."

They did. It took a little more than three minutes to get the game tied. Ehlers started it with a drive, then Rob Worthington, playing power forward at six-six, did exactly what O'Hanlon insisted his players had to do: he fought between three Navy players to tip in a Tyson Whitfield miss. Whitfield hit a 3. So did Ehlers. It was 44-44. Now the crowd was very much alive. DeVoe called time, to settle his players and tell them, "Let's hit a shot and get the crowd out of it again."

It was too late. The crowd was now committed. So was the team. The Leopards led most of the second half. Ciosici, who was having his best game of the season, hit back-to-back shots over Savane and made it 63-60. Then Skipworth scored and Chris Williams was fouled inside. Navy had a chance to lead again, but Savane mind-blocked and stepped into the lane early. That wiped out the one-and-one and gave Lafayette the ball.

They seesawed. Navy led 68-63 with 5:15 left before a 6-0 Lafayette run. The lead changed hands twice more, then Ehlers hit two free throws and it was 74-72 with 2:16 left. Skipworth missed a jumper and Ehlers hit a fifteen-footer to make it 76-72. Chris Williams finally hit a jumper to cut the margin to two with twenty-three seconds left. The Mids fouled Bieg on the inbounds. He made the first, missed the second. The lead was 77-74. Williams rebounded the miss and blew down the right side of the court. DeVoe was screaming for a 3, but Williams thought he would score quickly to cut the margin to one, then they would foul again.

He got into the lane and flew over everyone to shoot. But the shot rimmed out with under ten seconds left. Bieg rebounded. It was over. The final was 80-74.

In the Lafayette locker room, the sense of relief was palpable. Navy had come into their place and been a play or two from winning the game. It had taken everything that Ciosici, Ehlers, Whitfield, and Bieg had to win the game. And there had been key contributions from Worthington, Burke, and Frank Barr.

A few yards down the hall, the Navy people were stunned. They had thought they were going to win the game coming in and had been convinced they were going to win at halftime. Savane's opening

18

SINGING UP A STORM

AFTER one week of league play, two teams were undefeated. Lafayette was no surprise. The other was Lehigh.

Neither team had played twice, since Lafayette had the bye on the first night of league play and Lehigh, after beating Army, had it on the second night. Both teams had games against the same nonconference team, Pennsylvania, on their off-night.

The Quakers had come to Stabler Arena on the first weekend of the conference season. While the Lehigh women played on and on (two overtimes), most of the Lehigh players watched the tail end of the Tampa Bay Buccaneers playoff victory over the Washington Redskins. Fifteen miles down Route 22, Tim Bieg, the consummate Redskins fan, was howling with anger. None of the Mountain Hawks were quite as upset.

Sal Mentesana killed the time waiting for the women's game to end by making conversation with Carolyn Schlie Femovich, who had become the Patriot League's executive director in August after seventeen years in the athletic department at Penn. The Patriot League offices are located in Bethlehem, a few minutes from Lehigh, so this was a perfect night for Femovich: a short drive to see her old school play one of her new schools.

Femovich, who had started her career as a coach at Gettysburg College, was telling Mentesana how much she still loved the game, even after years as an administrator. Mentesana shook his head and laughed. "I used to love the game, too," he said. "Then I got into coaching."

The atmosphere in Stabler was different than it had been earlier in the season. Lehigh had won two straight games — against Albany and Army, a hot streak in the context of the recent past — and a number of Penn fans had made the one-hour trip from Philadelphia, swelling the crowd to 2,089 — more than double the norm. The delay put everyone on edge — especially Jared Hess.

This was the night Hess and his father and two uncles were scheduled to sing the national anthem. Hess and Mentesana had talked for two years about the possibility of the four of them singing. Now, it was about to become reality. A few minutes prior to game time, Paul Duke, who had recruited Hess during his final year as Lehigh's head coach and was now an assistant at Penn, noticed Hess pacing up and down. "I'd never known Jared to get that tight before a game," he said later. "Then someone told me he was singing and I understood."

Hess loved to sing. The main reason he went to church every Sunday was to sing. The interesting thing was that he could quite literally be a choirboy and never be teased about it by his teammates.

"No one teases Jared about stuff like that," center Sah Brown said. "We all admire him too much."

There was absolutely no question about who the captain and leader of the Lehigh team was: Hess. That wasn't a knock on the other seniors, it was just testimony to how much Hess was respected. One night, after a bad loss and a Mentesana postgame tirade, Zlatko Savovic was sitting in front of his locker sulking about playing poorly when the team came together in the middle of the room for their postgame huddle. Hess never raised his voice, but said very clearly and firmly, "Zo, get up here." Savovic jumped into the huddle.

College had changed Hess. He had been shy and quiet when he first got to Lehigh, unsure of his role on the team. He didn't drink, not because he thought there was anything wrong with it but because he couldn't stand the taste of alcohol. He didn't curse — at first. By his senior year, the occasional angry profanity would slip out. When it did, it usually got people's attention.

Hess had counseled Sah Brown repeatedly on the need to be more aggressive and more consistent. The coaches had done the same thing, but it was different coming from a teammate. Brown's full name was Sah-u-Rah (pronounced Sa-oo-rah), an Egyptian name which means Sun God. His father had traveled in Egypt in his twenties and had become fascinated by all things Egyptian. As a result Sah and his two sisters all had Egyptian names.

Brown was still learning to play the game, even though he was a college junior. He was six-ten now, exactly a foot taller than he had been as a high school freshman, when he hadn't been good enough to start on the ninth-grade team at Holy Trinity High School on Long Island. He had been a six-three sophomore who played on the JV; a six-six junior who was sixth man on the varsity; then a six-ten senior who averaged 8 points and seven rebounds a game.

Because he was six-ten, slender (205 pounds), and had good grades, he attracted some attention from colleges in spite of his lack of experience and meager numbers. He had opted for Lehigh because he thought he needed to go to the best school possible since he didn't figure he had much future as a professional basketball player. His first two years had been a roller coaster. Even before he got to Lehigh, he had gone through the trauma of seeing his parents split and then divorce.

"I left home just when they were splitting up," he said. "It left me feeling as if I couldn't go home, because my home wasn't what it had been when I left. Either way, whichever parent I went to see, I was going to feel bad. I just took the easiest way out and didn't go home very much at all. It wasn't until last summer that I got to the point where I could deal with it all. Even then I only went home for two weeks."

Brown had played limited minutes as a freshman and a sophomore but was now the starting center as a junior, a role he was slowly adapting to. It wasn't easy. Although Hess's Mennonite background meant he was a practicing pacifist, he had a competitive streak in him that made him a hard-nosed basketball player. Brown's nature was gentle, and he had trouble adapting his personality to deal with the intensity of Division I basketball. There were occasions when he looked like a legitimate player. He had developed a fifteen-foot jump shot, and when he was playing with confidence he was quick and smooth around the basket. But at other times he looked lost, getting pushed around by bigger, meaner big men.

Against Penn, Brown found himself matched against Geoff Owens, a six-eleven senior who outweighed him by a good twenty pounds. Even though he had a good game shooting the ball (four-of-five), he had terrible trouble keeping Owens from dominating him inside and was in foul trouble all night. That meant that six-ten freshman Matt Crawford, who was even skinnier than Brown, had to come in and try to contain Owens. Owens ended up with 19 points and eleven rebounds and the only reason he didn't score more than that was that he was a miserable five-of-fourteen from the foul line.

Even so, Lehigh had a chance to win the game. Both teams shot horribly in the first half, especially Penn, which was eight-for-thirty and zero-for-eight outside the 3-point line, which was where the Quakers normally hurt people. Lehigh was a little better (ten-of-twenty-six) and led, 21-19, at the break.

"The good news is that we're ahead, fellas," Mentesana told the players. "The bad news is we can't expect them to shoot this poorly in the second half, even though I think our defense has had something to do with their shooting."

Although he said nothing about it to the players, Mentesana was very concerned about the officiating. Most of the officials who work in the Patriot League also work in the Ivy League. The crew on this game was a good one: Rich Giallella, Michael Brophy, and Adam Brick. They were all experienced officials who had worked in the two leagues for several years. That was what concerned Mentesana. "Those three guys can't help but think we're not good enough to beat Penn," he told his coaches.

He was especially concerned about Hess, who was being guarded very tightly by Penn's talented freshman Koko Archibong. Archibong and Ugonna Onyekwe were the heart of a tremendous freshman class Fran Dunphy had brought in. They were not "Ivy League–type athletes," in the vernacular of coaches, meaning they both clearly had the physical skills to play in a more prestigious basketball league. But both were excellent students. Archibong's dad was a Columbia graduate, and Onyekwe, who was the son of Nigerian diplomats, had chosen Penn over Princeton and Cornell.

Mentesana had already screamed at Brophy once when Archibong collided with Hess as he was releasing a 3-pointer and there was no whistle. Hess had shot one-for-five in the first half and Mentesana wondered if singing the anthem had distracted him. "I think it has a lot more to do with Archibong than the anthem," Glenn Noak suggested.

The second half began well when Steve Aylsworth made a quick steal and layup to extend the lead to 23-19. But Penn started dumping the ball into Owens on every possession and neither Brown nor Crawford was strong enough to keep him from getting to the basket. Owens wrapped up a 9-point Penn run by missing two free throws, then jumping over everyone to tip in his own miss. That made it 28-23, and Mentesana was red-faced, screaming at the officials that Owens had been over the back.

A moment later when Giallella ran past the bench, Mentesana was all over him. "You guys did a great job in the first half, but now those other two guys know who's supposed to win the game and they're calling it that way."

The insult was pretty direct, but Giallella let it go, in part, no doubt, because Mentesana had questioned the integrity of the *other* two officials (a veteran coach knows that this is always a smart move) but also because officials in the Patriot League are far more lenient with coaches than officials in the big-time leagues.

There's a reason for this: television. In the big-time leagues, just about every game played is on TV someplace and many of them are on national TV. Officials know this — some of them spend a good deal of time preening in front of the mirror before they take the court — and most of them are very determined *not* to be shown up by coaches. The way to do that is to T a guy up who is getting in your face. In the ACC, Mentesana's rant to Giallella would almost undoubtedly have earned him a technical. If that hadn't, then his reaction to a foul called on Anson Ferguson a minute later probably would have: "Anson, how dare you guard somebody. Don't you guys [the refs] worry about a thing, I'm going to admonish him for that!"

If that didn't do it, then his final salvo would have clinched it: "Why don't you guys just go home. We'll call our own and send you the money."

In the Patriot League, where games are rarely on television, and when they are, almost always to only a handful of places, the egos of most officials aren't at the same level as in the big-time leagues. In Mentesana's case, he could get away with a lot because what he said was almost always funny and because the officials knew him well enough not to take it personally.

Through all of Mentesana's jawing with the officials, the game stayed close. Owens kept scoring, but he and his teammates kept missing free throws (they made thirteen-of-twenty-five in the second half) and Lehigh didn't go away. Penn was only leading 45-42 with under five minutes to play when Michael Jordan, who had put the dagger into Lafayette's back earlier in the week, did the same to Lafayette's archrival. He made a free throw, then (naturally) missed one. But Owens tapped the ball back and Jordan promptly drained a three that pushed the lead to 49-42. Lehigh hung in until the end, Aylsworth hitting a 3 to cut it to 57-54 with seventeen seconds to go, but Penn's Matt Langel, fouled with nine seconds left, made both shots, and the final was 59-54.

No one on the Lehigh side was sure how they were supposed to feel. On the one hand, they had played a good team to the wire and hadn't quit when they fell behind. On the other hand, Penn had given them every chance to win with poor free-throw shooting and mediocre 3-point shooting.

"We're getting better, guys," Mentesana said. "You beat two teams you should have beaten [Albany and Army] and almost beat a good team. Now, we go on the road in the league [to Colgate] and we'll find out how much progress we've really made. Don't get down about losing tonight. But don't get too up about staying close, either. This is Division I basketball. We aren't about moral victories. We're about winning games."

One hundred and fifteen miles to the northeast, at Army, they weren't about moral victories either. In fact, they were heartily sick of them.

The Cadets had played well twice after the January opening loss to Manhattan, losing close games to Quinnipiac and Columbia. The Columbia game had been especially tough to take because they had led almost the entire game, going up 41-34 with just over seven minutes left. Columbia rallied to lead 44-43, but Seth Barrett got fouled and drilled two free throws with thirty-three seconds to play. Up 45-44, Army had to dig in and get one last stop. But point guard Derrick Mayo penetrated for Columbia, appeared to have gone too far under the basket, and then, at the last possible second, flipped a blind pass over his shoulder to a wide-open Mike McBrien for the winning layup.

It was the kind of play you might expect in an NBA game, but you certainly didn't expect it in a Patriot League–Ivy League game. Whether it had been by luck or design didn't matter. The Cadets had believed they were going to win the game. Instead, they were saddled with a ninth straight loss.

"All I can say, fellas, is if you keep producing efforts like that, eventually we're going to see results," Harris said, so hoarse at the end his voice was just about gone. "You made some critical mistakes, but we're a hell of a lot closer to where we want to be than we were a week ago."

When Harris met with his coaches, there was little anyone could say. "The effort's there," Marty Coyne said.

Harris nodded. "The effort is always there. The problem is, effort's not enough."

It wasn't enough at Lehigh, especially once the Mountain Hawks adjusted to stop Spatola. The loss there sent them home to face Colgate. On the surface, the timing couldn't have been worse. The Red Raiders were coming off their embarrassing loss at home to Holy Cross. What's more, their worst loss a year earlier had been in Christl Arena. Trailing by 17 at halftime, Army had rallied for a 73-66 victory.

"It was impossible for us to lose that game," Pat Diamond remembered. "It was the weirdest game I've ever been in. We're up seventeen at halftime and everyone's saying, 'We can't lose this game.' I mean, give them credit because they never die, but that never should have happened."

Emmett Davis agreed. On the endless bus ride back he handed out pads and pencils to each player and demanded they write down three things they could have done better so that Colgate could have won the game. Then he made them watch the tape. The bus trip lasted, by most player estimates, two weeks.

Colgate's disaster was Army's moment of glory. The joy in the locker room was such that some players cried, thrilled and amazed at what they had done. A year later Seth Barrett remembered walking out of the locker room, the last one to leave, and looking around the almost empty gym thinking he never wanted to leave, that he just wanted to sit in the stands all night and re-create the game in his mind. "It was one of those nights you didn't want to end," he said. "I can never remember a feeling like that in all the years I've played basketball. Pure, absolute joy, accomplishing something no one thought you could accomplish."

There were not a lot of people at West Point who thought the Cadets could accomplish a similar victory in 2000. Already there were whispers on the post that the team wasn't going to win another game. There were even some people who thought that Harris's job might be in jeopardy. He was only in the third year of a five-year contract and anyone who knew anything about basketball knew how difficult a climb he faced when he took the job. But the firing of football coach Bob Sutton in December after seventeen years at the school — with a year left on his contract — had put everyone in the athletic department on edge. Rick Greenspan, the new athletic director, was all business, and had been given a mandate by General Daniel Christman, the school's superintendent, to rebuild the athletic department.

Sutton's firing, with Christman's approval, made it clear that no one was completely safe. Harris was a graduate, he had the support of the school's best known graduate, Mike Krzyzewski, and he had the respect and support of his players. Sutton had been national coach of the year in 1996 after going 10-2. That hadn't given him a lifeline.

Harris heard the same whispers everyone else heard. But he wasn't really that concerned. He had talked to Greenspan often enough to believe that Greenspan understood that Army basketball was going to be a work in progress for a while and that a lot had to change to get it to where Harris wanted to see it. His concern, for the moment, was winning a game. Any game.

Even on a Saturday night, Christl Arena was 80 percent empty.

Once again, Army played well in the first half. Michael Canty was finally coming out of his post-Christmas funk, and Jonte Harrell, who could be stunningly good at times and equally bad at others, was having one of his good nights. Colgate, having watched the tape of the Lehigh game, was doing everything it could to deny Chris Spatola the ball, reminding Harris again how tough it was to build your team around a five-foot-ten-inch guard.

Army scored the last 7 points of the half, spurred by a Canty 3, to lead 28-25. Once again, Colgate was getting very good play from Pat Campolieta and Jordan Harris and very little from everyone else. Pat Diamond picked up two fouls in the first three minutes and didn't play the rest of the half.

But two straight steals by Campolieta early in the second half seemed to turn the game around. First he fed Marques Green for a layup, then Harris, who dunked to make it 35-33, Colgate. Campolieta scored a few seconds later on a post-up move and Harris called time to calm things down. It worked. Army came back to lead, 40-39, but then Colgate took control of the game, steadily building the lead. When Campolieta, who would finish with a game-high 17 points, hit a jumper in the lane, it was 53-43 with 5:38 left.

"I remember looking up and thinking we're in serious trouble," Canty said. "For us, coming from ten down isn't easy."

More like impossible. Somehow, though, they rallied one more time. Backup center Charles Woodruff, a slender sophomore who looked as if he could be blown away by a gust of wind, kept taking the ball to the basket and scoring. Joe Clark, whose shooting woes had gone past the critical point, finally made a 3. When Canty made a 3 with 2:38 to go, it was 55-52 and the Colgate players had that look teams get when they can't believe a team hasn't gone away yet.

Spatola made two free throws to cut the lead to 1, then Woodruff made one-of-two with forty-seven seconds left and it was tied at 55. Colgate called time, to set a play. But Devin Tuohey forced a pass inside and Army had the ball back with seventeen seconds left. Harris wanted a shot for Spatola, but the ball was knocked loose and out of bounds with two seconds left. Harris called time and set up a shot for Canty, figuring Spatola would be the decoy. But the inbounds pass was knocked away.

One second left. Now it was Davis's turn to call time out. The ball would be coming in from just in front of the Army bench. Harris changed tactics. He made Canty the inbounder and called for him to drop the ball in to Woodruff in the low post. But Davis had anticipated that and had dropped a second defender into the post in front of Woodruff. Canty spotted Spatola sprinting around a screen at the top of the key and curling toward him. He flipped the ball to him and Spatola turned and in one motion fired from twenty feet.

Swish.

Army had won, 58-55. Spatola disappeared from view, buried by his teammates. The Colgate players felt like they were watching a rerun of an awful movie. Losing to Army once was horrifying, but twice? Blow a 17-point lead at halftime and then blow a 10-point lead in the last 5:30? They had scored 2 points in that last 5:30. "We did everything we could to lose the ball game," Davis said. "Against Army, you can't let up even a little because they won't. Intellectually you know that, the kids know that, but sometimes you just don't do it." He forced a smile. "The kid hit a tough shot."

The kid had done just that. He had hit the biggest shot anybody had hit at Army in a long, long time. "All of a sudden all the work seemed to have meaning," said Jonte Harrell. "January is such a long month around here, first with the military intersession, then the weather, then starting classes again, you need something. We finally got it."

While the Colgate players headed for their bus, knowing they were facing a 155-mile trip that would feel like a 15,500-mile trip, the Army players celebrated. The postgame pizzas had never tasted so good.

"All the work, all the frustration, all the losing," Spatola said. "You put up with it for moments like this. I'll remember this night as long as I live."

There had been 681 people in the building. No TV. No newspaper outside the Hudson Valley would give the game more than two paragraphs. None of that mattered to the Army players. For them, it wasn't about the glory. It was about the moment. There would be few that would match this one.

19

SEARCHING FOR RESPECT

THE dawning of the new millennium had not exactly brought joy and rapture to the basketball players at Bucknell.

They had returned from their sojourn in Arizona — where they had split two games — and started the New Year with a trip to northern Virginia to play George Mason. A year earlier, when the Patriots (the team, not the league) had been champions of the Colonial Athletic Association, they had needed overtime to beat the Bison in Davis Gym. This time, they led the whole game en route to a 69-58 victory.

The Bison went home for an easy victory over Division III Haverford but then managed to lose their final preconference game to Cornell. This was a shocker to Pat Flannery, his staff, and the players. Losing to Princeton was one thing, but Cornell was a second-division Ivy League team, a team that had needed overtime to beat Army on its home court.

The loss to Cornell reinforced a concern Flannery had been quietly voicing to everyone since preseason practice: the strength of this team was its maturity, not just in terms of playing time but as people. The five seniors were all well-grounded young men, good students — Valter Karavanic, Dy Cameron, and Brian Muckle had all made the dean's list for first semester and would graduate with GPAs well into the 3s, and Dan Bowen and Shaun Asbury were solid students, too — who would all flourish in the postgraduate world. Each of them was articulate, polite, well-read, exactly the kind of young man you would hope your daughter would bring home.

None was likely to tear up a locker room in disgust over a loss. None was likely to get in a teammate's face if he wasn't producing. None was likely to trash-talk an opponent or play mind games or try to intimidate someone.

Which was exactly the problem.

When Flannery looked at the league's other two top teams, the teams that had been to the NCAA Tournament in the recent past, he saw teams with an edge. Stefan Ciosici and Brian Ehlers might not be big talkers, but there was no doubting that they would rip your heart out to win a basketball game. Even though the Bucknell seniors were all good players, no one was likely to describe any of them as an "assassin," the way Chris Williams admiringly described Ehlers. Navy seemed to play with a collective chip on its shoulder, as if the basketball court was the place where they took out the frustrations of academy life. Sitapha Savane and Williams never seemed to shut up, yelling at each other, their teammates, the officials, and opponents.

Flannery saw none of that in his group. He saw competitors, kids who listened well and badly wanted to win. But the very perspective that was going to make them all successful in life beyond Bucknell seemed to prevent them from taking a last-chance-or-die approach to this season.

For Flannery and his coaches the challenge was to find a way to get their players to a different emotional level. The good news was that they never panicked in a game — that had helped them rally from 17 points down to almost win at Penn State — but that was also the bad news. Some situations call for panic.

Flannery had been talking to the seniors since the previous spring about making sure they didn't walk away from their final season with the same empty feeling they had all felt after the 4-point loss to Lafayette in the championship game at the end of their junior season. He talked constantly about "the promise we made to each other," and he met often with them to reinforce that promise.

The Cornell loss was a true downer and dropped them to 7-6 after the 5-1 start going into league play. Then came the Dan Bowen–less loss to Navy. Keeping the game close without Bowen was a very small bright spot on an otherwise gloomy night. None of the seniors had ever lost to Navy at home. This was not what they had in mind to start their final conference season.

With Bowen back and playing in his air-conditioned sneaker, they took a lot of their frustrations out on Holy Cross three nights after the Navy game. Ralph Willard had been afraid that his team might hit a wall in this game. The Crusaders had needed just under six hours to get home from Colgate on Wednesday night in the snow, arriving back on campus at about 4 A.M. Thursday. Then on Friday, they were all back on the bus for another six hours–plus en route to Bucknell.

"This kind of scheduling doesn't make sense," Willard said. "We're supposed to be an academic league; why not make a schedule that makes sense academically? We should play Thursday–Saturday or Friday–Sunday so that teams that have long trips don't go all the way back to campus and then turn around and make another trip right away."

His idea made sense. The Ivy League has always played Friday–Saturday to minimize missed class time. It is able to play back-to-back nights because the second game of a trip is always played close to the first: Princeton to Penn (or vice versa) is under an hour; Harvard to Dartmouth is less than two hours; Brown to Yale is about an hour. The only trip that can be difficult is Cornell to Columbia, which is about four hours if the roads are clear.

Friday–Sunday would make even more sense because it would give teams time to travel on Saturday, get to where they're going in plenty of time to practice and rest, then play on Sunday afternoon, and be home in plenty of time to get a good night's sleep before class on Monday.

That was not the way it was done in the league in 2000. So, Holy Cross arrived in Lewisburg tired, and no matter how much Willard tried to tell his players they needed to play just as hard as they had at Colgate, there was a sense that their work for the week was done. By contrast, Bucknell was rested and angry coming off the Navy loss. The result was predictable: The Bison led 21-1 and cruised to a 69-44 crushing. Flannery was relieved, but knew the victory wasn't as impressive as it appeared to be in the next day's newspaper because of the mitigating circumstances.

"Iona will tell us more even though it's a nonleague game," he said. "We only have two days to get ready, and they have talent. Let's see how we handle that."

Iona was a talented team, as it would prove by winning the Metro Atlantic Athletic Conference Tournament in March to reach the NCAA Tournament. The Gaels were coached by Jeff Ruland, who had been a superstar at Iona under Jim Valvano in the late 1970s, leading the school into the NCAA Tournament three straight years. In Ruland's senior year, Iona had been the last team to beat Louisville, the eventual national champion, crushing the so-called Doctors of Dunk by 17 in Madison Square Garden.

Ruland had gone on to a career in the NBA, which had been cut short by injuries, before returning to Iona to get his degree and to be an assistant coach. When Tim Welsh had left after a successful run to take the Providence job in 1998, Ruland had become the head coach. If nothing else, at six-eleven, weighing close to 300 pounds, with a black goatee, Ruland had to be the most physically intimidating coach in the country when he got up to berate a referee.

Iona has always taken players whose academic numbers might not indicate that postgraduate work is in their future. Ruland, who hadn't come terribly close to a degree during his first stint at the school, was fully aware of the academic differences between his team and Bucknell's. Watching the teams warm up, he noted Valter Karavanic's smooth lefty release.

"Wasn't he an academic All-American or something last year?" he asked Bucknell assistant Terry Conrad.

Conrad nodded. "Yeah. He's got a three-point-eight GPA in chemical engineering."

Ruland laughed. "I've got some guys on my team who want to be engineers," he said. "Train engineers."

The cerebral approach that the Bucknell players took to basketball was once again in evidence that night when the players turned in their scouting reports to the coaches. At the bottom of the question page, believing that emotion would be critical to the outcome of the game, Conrad had written: "How many charges will you take to win this game tonight? How many loose balls are you going to get?"

Karavanic hadn't answered the questions. When Conrad asked him later why he hadn't responded, Valter shrugged and said: "I thought the questions were rhetorical, Coach."

This was one night when the players had the answers the coaches really wanted. Karavanic, who had snapped out of a shooting slump by making five 3s against Holy Cross, came out firing again: a 3, a pull-up twelve-footer, and another 3 before the game was eight minutes old. Bucknell jumped ahead, 18-13. Flannery had decided after the Cornell game to make more use of his bench, in part because the freshmen had to get some experience, in part to keep the starters from wearing down.

He had four different freshmen on the court before halftime: the guards Chris Zimmerman and Dan Blankenship, six-six swingman Boakai Lalugba, and six-ten Brian Werner, who was the team's most rapidly improving player. Werner hit a putback to up the margin to 33-26 with 3:10 to play, and then Karavanic capped off a superb half by taking a Zimmerman pass and burying one more 3 just before the buzzer to make it 38-30 at the half.

Naturally, everyone knew the job was far from done. Still, Flannery felt good about Karavanic's revived shooting and the play of the freshmen. He also knew Iona was too talented to just go away. "He [Ruland] is in there right now giving them hell for being behind a Patriot League team," Flannery told the players. "Let's keep him pissed off."

They did. Iona crept to within 3 at 49-46 with thirteen minutes left but never got closer than that. After Flannery ripped into them for playing laid-back basketball during a time-out, the seniors took over the game. Karavanic made a pretty steal and fed Bowen for a layup. Then Muckle made a steal for another layup to make it 55-47, and Ruland called time.

Carl Danzig said it best for everyone as the Bucknell huddle broke: "Do not let up!" he bellowed.

The final was 73-67. Every time Iona tried to make a move, Bucknell had an answer. It was easily the most satisfying victory they'd had since the comeback from 17 down at Mount St. Mary.

"That's the way we play, guys," Flannery said in the postgame din. "You bring that intensity every night for forty minutes and I promise you we're going to get where we want to go." He looked at Bowen and Muckle, who always sat side by side in the front of the room when he spoke. "You guys know exactly where that is, don't you?"

They nodded. They did. It was right in front of them every day on an orange piece of paper taped over each player's locker:

- Get better every day.
- Patriot League Regular Season Champions.
- NCAA Tournament.

It was right there in black and orange. Every day.

There were no lofty goals posted in anyone's locker at Holy Cross. It wasn't that Ralph Willard didn't believe in goals or in writing things down. He just thought his team's focus needed to be more narrow. His last words before every game were the same: "Whatever we do," he would say, "let's make sure we come back in here a better basketball team than when we went out."

One week into Patriot League play, even the always-demanding Willard would be forced to admit that his team had lived up to that credo a lot more often than not. The Bucknell game had been more an aberration than a setback.

Now, though, the Crusaders faced a crucial week if they were to make themselves any kind of factor in the league during Willard's first season. They would host Lafayette on Wednesday, Navy on Sunday. The league's two best teams. At home.

"Guys, these two teams are where we're trying to go," Willard told the players before the Lafayette game. "Let's see just how close we are to that level."

Two of Willard's wounded would be back for this game: Jared Curry had tested his back briefly at Bucknell. He had felt some soreness, so Willard yanked him after seven minutes, seeing no reason to risk further injury in a game that was already lost. Fortunately the back hadn't stiffened and he was in uniform for Lafayette. So was Ryan Serravalle, who had missed ten games since hurting his knee against Boston College. Juan Pegues was still wearing an eye patch after his collision with Curry's elbow in December. And Patrick Whearty's elbow was getting no better. The coaches were almost convinced he wouldn't play again before the end of the season.

Once upon a time, the presence of the defending league champion in the Hart Center would have guaranteed a good-sized crowd. Not anymore. Standing on the floor watching a few fans trickle in during warm-ups, Roger Breslin shook his head. "It hurts to see how little people care around here right now," he said.

Breslin had been the point guard on Holy Cross's last championship team, the 1993 group that had won the Patriot League Tournament and had finished 23-7 after losing to Arkansas in the first round of the NCAA Tournament. That senior class had been Holy Cross's last scholarship class before the post–Father Brooks return to scholarships in 1998. Breslin had come back to Holy Cross as an assistant in 1996 and was the only one of Bill Raynor's assistants retained by Willard. He was fiercely loyal to the school and the players. Seeing the building so empty, especially when the team had been playing well despite the injuries, bothered him.

"Down in that end zone," he said, pointing to the empty bleachers at Lafayette's end of the court, "we used to have a bunch of students just like Lafayette's Zoo Crew or Bucknell's Sixth Man. They called themselves "The Hart Attack," and they would go crazy the whole game. Now, we've got nothing like that. The kids are back in school this week, but there won't be two hundred of them here tonight. Maybe not even a hundred."

In fact, the only thing in the building that night that made anyone think about a Hart Attack was a scary moment a few minutes before tip-off when Patrick Butcher, who had been Holy Cross's timekeeper for years, felt faint and briefly collapsed behind the scorer's table. An EMC unit was called. Butcher was conscious and talking by the time he was carried out, and he proved to be fine when he got to the hospital. But the incident shook everyone up.

The attendance turned out to be a whopping 714. The masses who stayed away missed a very good basketball game. The only thing positive about a slew of injuries for a team is that they force backup players into expanded roles and, sometimes, a player finds himself given the opportunity. For Holy Cross, the loss of the Wounded Four had done just that. Walk-on guard Guillermo Sanchez and freshmen Brian Wilson and Tim Szatko had been pushed into the starting lineup and all three of them were gaining confidence with each game.

Sanchez had played high school basketball at Cardinal Hayes High School in the Bronx. Unrecruited by Division I schools, he had come to Holy Cross on an academic scholarship and had played on the JV team as a freshman. Like Chris Spitler three years earlier, he had asked for a varsity tryout as a sophomore and had made the team. The injuries had made him a starter and he had made the most of that, making a number of key plays and becoming one of the team's best rebounders from a guard spot. He'd had ten rebounds in two games — including Colgate — and nine in another. He had gone from a walk-on to someone who was being asked to play more than thirty-five minutes a night.

Wilson was less of a surprise because he had been recruited as a scholarship player. Like Sanchez, he had been a National Honor Society member in high school and he had been scheduled to back Serravalle up at the point guard spot and play some at the shooting guard position. That had all changed when Serravalle and Curry went down. Wilson had also played a critical role in the Colgate win, with 15 points.

Those 15 points had matched Szatko for high scorer that night. Szatko was a classic Midwesterner, a six-eight kid with a big smile and a hearty hello for everyone he met. His father, Greg, had been a defensive lineman on Notre Dame's national championship football team in 1973, and Tim had been set to go to Notre Dame as a recruited walk-on until Willard had called in midsummer to see if he would be interested in coming to Holy Cross on a full scholarship.

A recruited walk-on is a player that a big-time school wants to have come but isn't quite willing to risk a scholarship on. If the family can afford tuition — as Szatko's could — he is encouraged to come to school, be a part of the team, and, if he plays well enough, he may become a scholarship player as a sophomore or junior. Given the Szatko family ties to Notre Dame — "We lived and died with the Irish every Saturday," Szatko said — this seemed to make sense.

Holy Cross had recruited Szatko earlier in the year but his grades and SATs had been borderline. During the coaching change, no one had bothered to find out if Szatko could or could not get admitted to school. Willard, with a scholarship to give during the summer, had seen Szatko on tape. When admissions told him that, yes, Szatko could get into school, he had called and asked Szatko to at least visit. Szatko visited, liked the school, liked the idea of a full scholarship and a chance to play right away, and changed his mind about Notre Dame.

The new Notre Dame coaching staff, led by Matt Doherty, was not at all happy with Willard or Holy Cross. But Willard had done nothing wrong. Since Szatko was a walk-on at Notre Dame, he hadn't signed a letter of intent, and if Holy Cross was willing to offer a full scholarship, Szatko was entitled to change his mind.

Szatko's decision had paid off for him and for Holy Cross. He had a good jump shot almost to the 3-point line and the size to score inside. He was still learning to play and still made the kind of mental errors most freshmen make, but he was progressing. At the moment, school was a lot more difficult for him than basketball, but he was getting better there, too.

Coming off the emotional victory over Navy, Lafayette may not have been ready for the intensity Holy Cross was bringing to the floor most nights. The first half was dead even for sixteen minutes, until the Leopards got hot and Josh Sankes got to the foul line late in the half. After Brian Ehlers had made two free throws to put Lafayette up 31-29, Sankes was fouled. With Willard screaming at him from the bench to remember his latest drill — "Turn your wrist, Josh!" — Sankes missed the front end of a one-and-one. Mick Kuberka made a layup to make it 33-29. Sankes was fouled again. Again Willard screamed about the wrist. Again he missed. Brian Ehlers and Brian Burke then hit 3s to close out the half. The run was 10-0.

Willard wasn't down during the break. His team had produced twenty-one deflections in the first half. That was on pace for 42, seven more than the 35 needed to have a chance to win, in the Hubie Brown vernacular. He knew how hard they were all trying, so he didn't jump them. Five minutes into the second half, with the lead at 51-36, he did. "You're playing like five scared little puppies out there!" he screamed. "Just play."

They did. Spitler — yes, Spitler — beat Ehlers off the dribble, got fouled, and made two free throws. That seemed to ignite the Crusaders. Curry scored twice, then Wilson scored on a drive, and suddenly it was 55-48. They chipped the lead all the way to 65-61 before Tim Bieg made a critical play for Lafayette with less than three minutes to play.

Fran O'Hanlon called time after a Szatko basket had cut the margin to 4 with 3:13 to play. Out of the time-out, Bieg came off a screen for a 3 — and missed. But before any of the Holy Cross players could make a move for the basketball, Bieg ducked under several players and rebounded his own miss.

"Aaah!" Willard screamed in frustration. "Guys, you've got to rebound the ball!"

Too late. Lafayette ran some more clock down, and Ehlers was fouled going to the basket and made both shots with 2:27 left. The rally had been stemmed. The final was 77-70.

"That's a pretty good team," O'Hanlon said afterward, impressed by Holy Cross's young players and by how hard they had played. Sankes, even with three-of-nine free-throw shooting, had finished with 15 points and twelve rebounds. Wilson had 17, Szatko 13. Brian Ehlers had saved the day for Lafayette with 28 points.

Willard knew his team had given him everything it had. He also knew that staying at that level, game in and game out, would not be easy. "I owe it to them to not go easy on them," he said. "There are a hundred different excuses for them to go out and lose every night, especially with the injuries. I know that. But I can't let them know I know that."

For the long term, the most encouraging aspect of the Lafayette game had been the play of Serravalle and Curry. Each had looked healthy and not all that rusty. Willard decided to start Curry against Navy in the small forward spot. He had started James Stowers there against Lafayette hoping to give Stowers a mental boost. Classes had started on Monday and already Willard was beginning to see a blank look on Stowers's face that told him he was worrying about school. He had finished first semester with a 3.6 GPA, but now, with the academic finish line in sight, Willard knew he was capable of obsessing about it.

Serravalle would come off the bench against Navy only because Willard didn't have the heart — yet — to sit Sanchez, the logical candidate to come off the bench once Serravalle was restored to the starting lineup.

Navy was coming to town rested — the Midshipmen hadn't played in a week — and angry, since the last time they had played had been against Lafayette. Unlike the Lafayette game, which had been played in a near-empty gym, there would actually be a good-sized crowd for Navy, although it had little to do with basketball.

In early December, Worcester had been sent into a state of collective shock when six firefighters died in a warehouse fire accidentally set by some homeless people who had taken refuge from the cold in the empty building. All the Holy Cross players and coaches vividly remembered the day because the Hart Center parking lot, which is at the top of Mount St. James, affords one a panoramic view of downtown Worcester. As they walked into practice that day, they could clearly see the warehouse on fire, the smoke blurring the rest of the city skyline.

Among the fund-raising efforts put together on behalf of the firefighters' families was one led by Bob Cousy, who had lived in Worcester throughout his life. The Navy game was turned into an official fund-raiser. Tickets, normally $5, cost $15. Cousy and a number of other local sports heroes, including ex–Celtics star Dave Cowens, Hall of Fame New England Patriots offensive lineman John Hannah, ex–New York Mets pitcher Ron Darling (who had grown up nearby), and ex–Red Sox catcher Rich Gedman, hosted a pregame reception that cost $100 to get into.

In all, 2,173 showed up on a dreary, snowy afternoon, about double the normal crowd. The ceremony honoring the firefighters was scheduled for halftime of the women's game, in part to let the celebrities make an early exit if they wanted to, but also because at Holy Cross a large chunk of the crowd comes for the women's game. When the Worcester Fire Brigade Pipe and Drum Corps played "Amazing Grace," the Hart Center was amazingly quiet.

The easy thing to think at that moment was how unimportant basketball is. Except that on this day, basketball raised $40,000 for six families in need of help and comfort.

Willard was aware of the emotion in the building and of his players' awareness of what had gone on. Most of them had arrived in time to watch the halftime ceremony. He urged them in his pregame talk to use the emotion in a positive way, to be aware of the larger than usual crowd. "You played your hearts out on Wednesday," he told them. "Do that again and we'll win this game."

As against Lafayette, Holy Cross was able to hang on with a more talented opponent throughout the first half. The main reason was Josh Sankes, who, in spite of his free-throw shooting problems, was becoming more of a force with each passing game. Earlier in the week, his father had thanked Willard, not for making Sankes a better player but for making it possible for him to enjoy basketball again. "I'm not sure any of us thought that was possible," Gary Sankes said.

"If I was really a miracle worker, he'd make his free throws," Willard said.

Sankes was all over the boards in the early going, but Navy's game plan — go right at him with Sitapha Savane and try to get him in foul trouble — was working. He picked up his third foul with 5:38 left and had to come out. Still, Holy Cross hung in and trailed 26-19 at halftime. Willard was pleased with the defense but felt his players were tight on offense.

"Fellas, it's a basketball game, that's all it is," he said during the break. "Try to have fun out there. The only guy I see who is having fun out there right now is Spitler. The rest of you look like it's life and death. You know better than that. You saw what life and death is about at halftime of the first game. This isn't that way."

The irony of Willard using Spitler as the team's role model wasn't lost on anyone — including Spitler. "Coach and I usually have a love-hate relationship," he said later. "I love him. He hates me."

That wasn't true. As tough as it was for him to reconcile himself sometimes to the fact that someone with Spitler's talent was important to a team he was coaching, Willard couldn't help but respect

Spitler's work ethic and desire, his willingness to do anything to help the team win. Late in the first half he had stepped directly in front of Savane and taken a charge. That was typical.

Willard decided to start Spitler in the second half, hoping he could provide some energy — some fun — for his teammates. Naturally, when Frank Mastrandrea saw that Spitler would be starting the second half, he said exactly two words: "Phase three."

Phase three started out well enough. Sankes scored twice, then Curry made a steal and scored to make it 29-26. But after Navy's John Williams answered with a 3 to boost the margin back to 32-26, Sankes got an elbow up as he tried to turn on Savane in the post. The whistle blew: it was Sankes's fourth foul, a questionable one in that the contact didn't move Savane an inch and that Sankes was clearly just trying to establish position.

No matter. He came to the bench and, for all intents and purposes, Holy Cross's chances to win went with him. Navy went on an 18-4 binge to stretch the lead to 50-30. Sankes came back in just long enough to pick up his fifth foul. Willard tried man-to-man to pick up the tempo, but that was playing into Navy's hands. The final score was an embarrassing 81-49. Even so, with seventeen seconds left, Spitler took another charge. Even the players on the Navy bench shook their heads at that one. Down 32 and he takes a charge.

"It's the only thing I do well," Spitler explained.

For Navy, the victory was cathartic. It got the bad taste of the Lafayette game out of their mouths and left them 2-1 in league play with three of their six road games behind them. They had not looked at Holy Cross as any kind of gimme win, especially after looking at the tape of the Lafayette game.

For Holy Cross, it was the first blowout loss they had suffered to a team the players and coaches had thought they could compete with. Willard again talked in the postgame about having fun on the court.

"Look at Savane on tape sometime," he said. "The guy is playing as hard as anyone out there but he's having fun. He enjoys making plays, he likes the competition, he's not afraid to fail. Some of you guys are afraid to fail."

He looked at Stowers, who had played as if in a trance until hitting two late 3s long after the game had been decided. "James, when you came back it was to help us out but it should also have been to have fun," he said. "You know better than anyone in here there's more important things in your life than basketball, so come out here and enjoy it. Relax. All of you need to relax."

He called them into their huddle for their postgame prayer. When Willard prays he almost sounds as if he is leaving a message on God's answering machine. He began by asking for remembrances of the six firefighters and their families. Then he added: "In the future, if You could perhaps provide us with some clarity on how to be consistent at both ends of the floor, it would be a great help to all of us. Amen."

20

THE RIVALRY

THE minute he walked into the locker room following the Holy Cross game, Don DeVoe went straight to the blackboard in front of the room. He erased all the matchups and pregame instructions that had been scrawled all over the board and in large block letters wrote one word: "ARMY."

He congratulated his players on how well they had played in the second half, told them it was a win they could be proud of, and reminded them they would play Holy Cross again so they need not gloat when the media — in the Patriot League that usually means no more than a half-dozen reporters — asked them about the game.

Then he turned and pointed at the board. "We all know what's next, guys," he said. "We all know the emotional level this game will be played on. It's just not like any other game."

Army-Navy is arguably the best rivalry in all of college sports. The football game still draws most of the attention because it is played every year before a sold-out stadium on national TV, but for the athletes who compete in other Army-Navy games, winning and losing means every bit as much as it does to the football players.

The Army-Navy basketball rivalry had lost some luster in recent years because of Navy's total dominance. Once, it had been the other way around. Bob Knight was 6-0 against Navy and Mike Krzyzewski was 4-1. Paul Evans had turned those numbers around when he became Navy's coach in 1980, winning seven straight times against Army. Pete Herrmann had then extended the streak to ten when he succeeded Evans. But even then, the games were close. The three Navy teams that went to the NCAA Tournament with David Robinson as the starting center beat Army by scores of 48-47, 55-52, and 58-52.

The two schools were playing in different leagues during that period, Navy in the Colonial Athletic Association and Army in the Metro Atlantic Athletic Conference. When both decided to join the Patriot League in 1990 it meant that they would be playing at least twice a year and occasionally three times if they were to meet in the conference tournament. That meant that the games would be a little less urgent since they would occur more than once a year.

That certainly wasn't going to sully a rivalry like Army-Navy in the grand scheme of things. The importance of the rivalry was underscored in 1992 when Army beat Navy twice. If a 6-22 record didn't get Pete Herrmann fired, losing to Army twice surely did.

DeVoe arrived the next season, and what had been a relatively even rivalry — Navy led 38-34 up until that point — became completely one-sided. During his first seven seasons the margin ballooned to 54-35. In seventeen games, DeVoe lost just once to Army — in the 1996 Patriot League Tournament, a defeat that still galled him four years later — and most of the games were one-sided. In 1998–1999 the scores had been 81-67 and 81-46.

No one was more aware of this than Pat Harris. When he thought of Army-Navy games, he still pictured the old Army and Navy field houses, games played in front of packed houses and Army winning. He had been 3-1 as a player against Navy. It was all different now. Both teams played in relatively new buildings and Army was struggling to try to compete with Navy.

Army-Navy I for the 1999–2000 season would be played at Navy. Each year, one of the two games was designated as the A*-N* game, which made it the official Army-Navy game. The winner got a giant trophy — "The Alumni Trophy" — and, far more important, the right to place an N* or an A* on their uniform. In 2000 the second game — at Army — was the designated trophy-star game.

To the Army players, that really didn't matter. They were fully aware of the one-sided nature of the rivalry in recent years. They knew that a victory would go a long way toward wiping away the specter of a 3-14 record. They also knew just how difficult it would be to beat Navy, especially in Alumni Hall.

The first problem for the Cadets had nothing to do with Navy. A major winter storm swept through the northeast from Maine to Virginia on Tuesday, January 25, icing roads and making travel virtually impossible. Harris and Athletic Director Rick Greenspan waited until late in the day, hoping the weather would clear, before they finally called Navy to say they couldn't make it down that night. If the weather cleared — as it was supposed to — the next day, the Cadets could probably make it down in time for the game but the last thing Harris or Greenspan wanted was to have their teams (the women were, of course, playing too) sitting on a bus for five hours — or more if the roads were still slick — and then jump right into uniform for one of the biggest games of their season.

Jack Lengyel, the Navy AD, was loath to postpone the game because, as one might expect, ticket sales were considerably higher than for most regular season games. Lengyel had been close friends with Al Vanderbush, Greenspan's predecessor at Army, who had retired in June. Like Lengyel, Greenspan was his academy's first AD who was not an academy graduate. One of the reasons Army had decided to go the "civilian" route was the success Lengyel had enjoyed as Navy's AD. Greenspan was nothing like Vanderbush. He was aggressive and blunt and he and Lengyel had already clashed on a number of issues during the football season. When Greenspan called Lengyel to tell him there was no way for Army to get to Annapolis on Tuesday night and the game needed to be postponed for twenty-four hours, Lengyel wasn't pleased.

"Can't you drive around the storm?" he asked Greenspan.

"No, Jack, we can't," Greenspan answered. "We'll get down there, if we can, on Wednesday and we'll play Thursday."

Lengyel sighed. He knew this was one argument he couldn't win — or really make with much enthusiasm. If Army had been flying, it might have been able to get in late Tuesday after the snow stopped or first thing Wednesday morning. But Army wasn't flying. This was, after all, the Patriot League.

"We'll see you Thursday," he said finally.

Unfortunately for Army, the snow did stop. The Cadets made it to Annapolis without incident. For an Army-Navy game, even in basketball, it isn't just a matter of transporting the teams. Cheerleaders travel, as do the pep bands, as do a selected group of cadets and midshipmen.

The crowd in Alumni Hall, even with the still lousy weather, even with the postponement, was a very respectable 3,689. The athletic department people at Navy were disappointed because the new academy commandant, Sam Locklear, a decided nonjock, had not ordered the midshipmen to attend the game. The entire Brigade is required to attend every home football game, a fact that causes considerable grumbling within their ranks — especially if the team isn't playing well. At Army, the Corps of Cadets is not required to attend every home football game, but they are "strongly encouraged" to do so and not allowed to leave the post until after a game is over. Most go to the games.

"Mandatory fun" is the term used by the mids to describe football games and pep rallies they are required to attend. Most years the commandant will only require that they show up for one basketball game — the Army game. But Locklear had decided against that, much to the dismay of the basketball people. Quite a few of the mids did show up, but there was no doubt that all 5,710 seats would have been full if the commandant had given the order.

Those that came enjoyed themselves. Harris's pregame message to his players was direct and forceful: "The time has come to draw a line in the sand," he said. "You have to go out there tonight and tell Navy they can't cross any goddamn lines on you and if they do, they'll have to pay for it." He pointed in the direction of the court. "That's Navy out there. Navy. I am sick and tired of coming down here and losing to these SOBs. Let's draw the line right here."

Harris didn't really think the Navy people were SOBs — except when he had to compete against them.

His approach to Navy was similar to his old coach's approach. In 1986, before Duke played Navy in the Eastern Regional Final of the NCAA Tournament, Mike Krzyzewski had talked to his players about the Midshipmen.

"I want to tell you something right now," he said. "There is no group of college basketball players that I respect more than the guys sitting in that other locker room right now. None of you can know how hard they've worked or what they go through every day. It's impossible for you to understand how extraordinary it is for them to be playing in this game. I respect every single one of them because I do understand what they go through. If they weren't great people they couldn't survive at Navy.

"But let me tell you one more thing: if you don't go out there and kick their ass, don't even bother coming back in here. You won't be able to look me in the eye. Because they're Navy. I'm Army. I don't lose to goddamn Navy. You guys have to do that for me today."

Krzyzewski meant every word he said. Duke won the game 71-50.

Harris didn't have the personnel that Krzyzewski had on that afternoon fourteen years earlier. He had two freshmen — Michael Canty and Adam Glosier — trying to guard an all-league junior, Chris Williams, and an all-league senior, Sitapha Savane. One look at the matchups on the board in the Army locker room was a clue to how tough the evening was going to be.

Down the hall, DeVoe's mission was to remind his players how much Army would want to beat them, how much emotion and intensity they would bring to the game. "There's going to be a lot of adrenaline out there," he said. "This is Army-Navy. Don't get caught up in anything."

Army led the game once, 6-5, after a pretty pass from Chris Spatola to Glosier with 15:18 left in the first half. Even then, Harris knew his team was in trouble. Navy's defense was so quick and aggressive that the Cadets were starting their offense forty feet from the basket. That wasn't going to work for very long. Navy scored the next 14 points to blow to a 19-6 lead. It was 32-20 at halftime only because Spatola made an off-balance 3 at the buzzer to get it that close.

Navy was getting great play off the bench from three freshmen: Jason Jeanpierre, Francis Ebong, and Scott Long. All three had gone to the Navy Prep School and had clearly benefited from the experience. A fourth prep schooler, Jamie Nero, who was now a sophomore, was someone Harris had recruited, since he had grown up near West Point. "He's twenty-five pounds heavier now than when we recruited him," Harris said to his coaches. "You don't think their prep school program is a little better organized than ours?"

The second half was no better for Army. The closest the Cadets got was 32-22 when Matt Rutledge hit a short bank shot. After that the lead just widened and widened, to 76-49 at the finish. DeVoe played the last five players on his bench during the last three minutes, but none of them was a bad player. In fact, Harris probably would have loved to have had any of them on his team.

The nature of the rivalry was never more evident than in the meaningless final minutes. Harris, who rarely got angry with Spatola, because he knew how hard he played, yanked him for taking bad shots. The midshipmen were on their feet screaming for more while the cadets who had made the trip gamely stood and joined the cheerleaders in the traditional "USMA-rah-rah" cheer. Looking at the scoreboard, it sounded rather hollow.

With nine seconds left and Navy leading 76-48, freshman Kyle Barker — the only non–prep school freshman on the Navy team — was called for a foul on Andy Stenoish. Sitapha Savane, who had come out of the game with seven minutes left after scoring 18 points on eight-of-nine shooting, couldn't resist yelling at referee Joe DeMayo about the call from his seat on the bench.

"That wasn't a foul!" he said. "There was barely any contact!"

DeMayo turned around, looked at Savane, and pointed up at the scoreboard. "Sitapha," he said. "Look at those numbers and be quiet."

Savane smiled. "Got you," he said.

As is always the case when Army and Navy play, both alma maters were played when the game ended, the players standing at attention throughout both of them. At Navy, "Blue and Gold" is played at the conclusion of every basketball game, which sometimes makes the players a little bit nuts — especially after a loss. At Army, "Alma Mater" is only played after Navy games.

For the Army players, those extra moments on the court were torture. All they wanted to do was get off the court and hide someplace.

Losing was bad enough, being blown out in a game that ceased being close after ten minutes was humiliating. "I can't tell you," Pat Harris said to his players, "how sick this makes me. I just want to go somewhere and get sick."

When he heard the final score later that evening, Harris's old coach had a similar reaction. "Losing to Navy that often and by scores like that is embarrassing," Mike Krzyzewski said. "I would have lost my mind if it had been that way when I was coaching there."

Krzyzewski did not, by any stretch of the imagination, blame his ex–point guard for Army's woes. He saw the problem as going way beyond the control of Harris or anyone sitting in the basketball coach's office.

"The whole culture has to be changed," Krzyzewski said. "Somewhere along the line a decision has been made way up the line that it's okay to lose in basketball. There's no way that twenty straight losing seasons [actually nineteen out of twenty] would be accepted in football. There would be four-star generals in the Pentagon demanding that something be done. That doesn't happen in basketball.

"If you want to compete with Navy, you have to do more than hold spirit rallies and make everyone shout out, 'Beat Navy!' You have to put some bullets in the gun before you go into battle. Right now, they're telling Pat and his players to go take the damn hill without any weapons. Then, when they get killed trying to do it, they say they failed because they didn't take the hill."

Specifically, Krzyzewski believed the Army needed to stop telling Harris no while the Navy was telling Don DeVoe yes. Example: Army's prep school has had the same coach, John Pike, for sixteen years. He and Harris have a relationship that is, at best, civil. Harris, like Krzyzewski, believes in man-to-man defense. The first time he saw the prep school play in 1999, the team was playing zone some of the time and zone-trapping at other times. How, Harris wondered, was that helping the prep school players prepare to play man-to-man defense at West Point.

DeVoe's relationship with Walt Ayers, his prep school coach, was entirely different. They talked often, and players coming into the

Navy prep program have run offenses and defenses similar to Navy's and have been on a weight program similar to Navy's. "He's terrific," DeVoe said. "He's an important ingredient in our success."

Harris can't — and won't — say the same thing. In fact, after he was quoted in a story in the *Middletown Times Herald Record* as saying, "We need to have a solid prep school program. I think it needs to improve. That's an important year," Pike stopped speaking to him. But according to people at West Point, government service rules make it impossible for Pike to be transferred to another job.

"You see, that's the whole problem," Krzyzewski said. "The easy way out is to cite rules. Do you want to make things better, give a guy a chance to succeed, or do you want to cite rules?"

There's more. Navy's players are excused, during season, from some ceremonial and drill duties; they are given the opportunity during the off-season to get time in the weight room. Harris is trying to get changes made at Army that will allow that to happen. There is also the matter of how basketball is currently viewed within the ranks at each academy. Although football players still carry more weight at Navy, the basketball players are viewed with a certain amount of respect because of the success the team has had under DeVoe. Other midshipmen understand that most basketball players come to the academy because it is their best basketball opportunity and they deal with the military aspects of academy life as a by-product.

At Army, the same is true of most basketball players — Seth Barrett being a notable exception. But when freshman Michael Canty was asked by a squad leader why he came to West Point and answered, "To play basketball, sir," he became a pariah within his squad. The correct answer would have been, "To serve my country, sir," even if it was not an honest answer.

"You see, a good squad leader would have been proud of Canty for telling the truth," Krzyzewski said. "Aren't Cadets told to never lie? I had a similar experience at the end of my junior year. I was called in by my TAC [Tactical Army Commander] and told that I was under serious consideration to be a company commander as a senior. I told him, 'Sir, I'm going to be captain of the basketball team. I have one more year to play basketball in college and I would really like to focus

as much time and energy as possible on that.' He went nuts, screaming and yelling at me. What he should have said was, 'Mike, I respect
that. But I would also like it if you found a way to be involved with
your company, too, in some kind of leadership role.' Then, if I don't
respond to that, I'm the jerk."

Krzyzewski says he had advantages that Harris doesn't when he
coached. Many of the men (Army was all men until 1976) he had
gone to school with were back at West Point as teachers or TACs or in
administrative jobs. He used them to round up support for his basketball team. "Guys would bring their company to games," he said.
"Or their classes. They would have a party before or after for the
group. Anything to make going to a basketball game fun."

Of course, the games were more fun back then because Army was
winning. Krzyzewski thinks another way to change the culture of losing is to be bolder and more creative in recruiting. "I'm not saying
just go take guys who play good basketball," he said. "You can't do
that. But why not, as a school, go to the twenty-five biggest cities in
the country and find inner-city kids who are valedictorians and saluta-
torians in their class. Or class presidents. Regardless of their SAT
numbers, they're clearly leaders. Army is about finding and teaching
leaders. Accept twenty-five a year. Some may be athletes, others
won't be. Some may flunk out, others will be great officers. Take some
chances, but take chances on kids who have proven they have some
guts and desire already. Don't just look at numbers. My last captain,
Matt Brown, finished in the bottom ten in his class and now he's a
battalion commander. There's more to this than numbers."

The basketball numbers in recent years have been stark and ugly.
Krzyzewski the alumnus hates what has gone on. "Can Army win
again? Yes. But it has to have a plan that comes from the top, that
gives the coaches a realistic chance. They haven't done that for a long
time. Someone has to say that losing is unacceptable and let's find
ways, within the parameters that make West Point West Point, to
make things better. Pat Harris isn't going to flush Army's values any
more than I would have. But he's human like everyone else. If you
don't give him a fair chance, he's going to eventually lose his enthusiasm. I had things a lot better than he did and at the end of five years I

was exhausted. Recruiting was hard, retention was harder, and winning got tougher and tougher. There's never an easy day when you're the Army basketball coach."

Harris would certainly agree. Late in September, he returned to West Point after three straight weeks on the road recruiting. It was late on a Sunday night and he flew into Newark Airport and took a cab back to West Point to pick up his car. He had left it in a parking area up above Michie Stadium because the lot where the coaches normally park is used on football Saturdays for school officials and military brass.

He walked to the spot where he left his car and found the spot empty. He had been towed. When Harris called to find out why he had been towed, he was given a litany of reasons, none of which made sense to him. At two o'clock in the morning, he had to call his wife for a ride home.

There is never an easy day as the Army basketball coach.

21

GETTING TENSE

THE first round of conference play finished up on the night of February 2 with Navy playing at Colgate, Holy Cross at Lehigh, and Bucknell at Lafayette. Army had the bye that night, having reached the midway point of the conference schedule with a 1-5 record after a loss at Holy Cross the previous Sunday. That victory pushed Holy Cross to 2-3 going into the Lehigh game. The Mountain Hawks were 1-4, having dropped four straight after their opening win over Army. They were tied with Colgate, whose only victory had been against Lehigh. Still, Emmett Davis felt as if his team was making some progress after the disastrous start against Holy Cross and Army. The Red Raiders had played well in losses to Lafayette and Bucknell.

Clearly, this was a two-tiered league. The three top teams were Lafayette at 5-0 and Navy and Bucknell at 4-1. Navy's only loss was at Lafayette and Bucknell's only loss was to Navy. It appeared likely that the Big Three would stage their own race for first place while the Little Four fought it out for fourth.

Returning to Lafayette was an emotional experience for all the Bucknell players and coaches. They had all replayed their last appearance in Kirby Arena in their minds dozens of times. Then, the Patriot League championship and an NCAA bid had been at stake. They had led the game throughout the first half and looked like they were going to take a 7-point lead into the locker room, before Tyson Whitfield tossed in a seventy-five-foot bomb at the buzzer to cut the margin to

4. The gym exploded, Lafayette got a huge lift, and Bucknell never really recovered. The Leopards ended up winning, 67-63.

"Right there," Brian Muckle said during pregame shootaround, pointing to a spot near the top of the key. "That's where he was when he took the shot." He shook his head, still not believing eleven months later that it had gone in.

That game had been talked about among the seniors and coaches at length. Now the Bison were coming back to Kirby feeling good about themselves. They had won five straight since the loss to Navy and were still discounting that game because of Dan Bowen's absence. Lafayette was also on a five-game winning streak, having beaten everyone else in the Patriot League. The win at Colgate the previous Saturday had been predictably difficult (64-58), given that Colgate had beaten the Leopards twice the previous season.

Although Lehigh and Lafayette have been rivals for a lot longer and are only about fifteen miles apart, the basketball rivalry between Lafayette and Bucknell had become a lively one. The schools are separated by about two hours of Pennsylvania interstate and have played basketball against each other since 1915. Often they recruit the same players. They were now also bonded by the insistence on the part of their administrations that they would not follow Holy Cross and Lehigh down the slippery slope to athletic scholarships.

"I'm dead set against it," Lafayette president Arthur Rothkopf said that night a couple of hours before tip-off. "I just don't think it's right to single out athletes for special financial treatment. And, at least right now, we're competing quite well without athletic scholarships."

Unlike many of his presidential brethren, Rothkopf could not be accused of being a pointy-headed academic who had no understanding of the real world of Division I athletics. He was a graduate of Lafayette (Class of '55) who had gone on to Harvard Law School and had then practiced law in Washington until George Bush made him General Counsel of the Department of Transportation. He had become Deputy Secretary of DOT in 1992 and had come back to Lafayette as president in 1993. "The offer sort of came out of the blue," he said. "But I thought I would try it and see how it worked out."

It had worked just fine, although continuing questions about the future of Lafayette athletics had been a major issue. In 1998, Lafayette had undertaken a painstaking study of the entire athletic department. The overriding question was simple: Where should Lafayette be competing athletically? There were some faculty members convinced that a small academically minded school like Lafayette belonged in Division III. There were some alumni who thought athletic scholarships in basketball were the only way to remain competitive. The school compromised and ended up changing nothing. It would be Division I in basketball with need-based scholarships and Division I-AA in football.

Rothkopf was fully aware of the pressure on the school to keep up with the Holy Crosses and the Lehighs. "For the moment, I'm not having that much difficulty, because we're at the top of the league," he said. "I'm fully aware of the fact that if we were to lose our coach, things could change. And if they did change, the pressure would grow. I know that losing put a lot of pressure on Father [Bernard] Reedy at Holy Cross after John Brooks retired. Father Brooks was very powerful. He could handle that sort of thing. His successor wasn't likely to wield that kind of power."

Rothkopf knew that his counterpart at Bucknell, William (Bro) Adams was leaving at the end of the school year to become president of the University of New Hampshire. Adams had been as adamant about athletic scholarships as he was. The new president might not see things quite that way. "Time will tell," Rothkopf said. "I understand you can't do something like this unilaterally. I sincerely hope it doesn't come to that."

Almost no one in the building that night was concerned about the question of scholarships, although Fran O'Hanlon *was* tempted to bring it up to Pat Flannery before the game just to distract him. It was interesting to note that when the ten starters walked onto the floor they carried with them a combined GPA of 3.2. The lowest GPA in the group was 2.6, the highest 3.8. There were not a lot of college basketball games being played around the country that night where those numbers would apply to anything except assists or rebounds.

And, as Rothkopf pointed out, both teams were very competitive at the level they were being asked to compete on. Without scholarships.

This was Bucknell's first look at the renovations to Kirby Field House. The Bison were just about as impressed with the locker rooms as Navy had been. "It looks like they built them with jockeys in mind," was Don Friday's comment. Most of the Bucknell players chose to sit in the hallway before they gathered for their pregame talk rather than in the cramped locker area. The best locker room in the building belonged to the referees. It was about the same size as the vistors' locker room and only needed to house three occupants a night.

The game wasn't very different from the one the teams had played for the Patriot League championship. The gym was very much alive, a sellout crowd in place, the Zoo Crew back — though still not in the same numbers as a year before. Nonetheless, it was a superb basketball atmosphere, and the game lived up to it.

"Hey, guys, if anyone wants to give up his sneakers tonight, I'll take them," Flannery said before the game. "These are the nights you play basketball for."

The tension everyone was feeling was evident from the start. Down 9-2 early, Fran O'Hanlon pulled every starter except for Ehlers. Lafayette rallied and went up 30-17. "Hey, guys, if you aren't going to play defense, this is going to be a very long night," Flannery railed in the huddle. Bucknell responded with a 10-0 run to close the first half, leaving O'Hanlon shaking his head at halftime and asking his players, "What are you guys afraid of? Quit playing scared!" Both coaches were all over the officials from the beginning, neither of them pleased with any call that went against them.

"It's the kind of game that's fun to be a part of," Tim Bieg said later. "You know the other guys are a lot like you. They work hard at school, they're good guys, they're smart, all of that. And for forty minutes you try to rip each other's hearts out."

Bieg was the least likely looking heart ripper on the court. Although he had reached legal drinking age on New Year's Day, he still had a number of years of being carded to look forward to, since he looked closer to sixteen than twenty-one. The only things about him that were big were the pronunciation of his name and his heart. He was generously listed at five-eleven, 185 (especially the 185), and had curly black hair that tended to run amok on him if he let it get at all long.

At Camden Catholic High School in the Philadelphia suburb of Haddonfield, New Jersey, Bieg had been recruited more for baseball than basketball. He was an excellent infielder, who hit .463 as a junior, and since he had both the grades and the board scores, several Ivy League schools expressed serious interest in him as a baseball player. One school saw him primarily as a basketball player: Lafayette.

Like Brian Ehlers, Bieg is a sports junkie. His entire family lives and dies with Notre Dame football, and Bieg is obsessed with the Washington Redskins, a fact that causes him to receive considerable grief from his teammates, especially those from Philadelphia. "I just remember watching them beat the Dolphins in the Super Bowl [1983] when I was very young and thinking they were great," he said. "Ever since then, I've rooted for them."

As a senior, Bieg's plan was to go someplace and play both basketball and baseball. The Ivies — Dartmouth, Princeton, Penn — all told him he could walk on for basketball if he wanted to, as long as it didn't interfere with baseball. Lafayette took the opposite approach: you can play baseball when basketball season is over. Bieg played his senior basketball season not sure what he wanted to do. He knew Lafayette was a very good school, but the Ivies were the Ivies. Then, fate intervened to help him make his decision: he broke a foot at the tail end of basketball season, wiping out baseball. The Ivy League schools didn't disappear, but they weren't quite as enthusiastic since they didn't have a chance to see him play as a senior and because they didn't know how the injury might affect his future.

Lafayette never backed off. Bieg was convinced he could play Division I basketball. He chose Lafayette.

"As important as players like Stefan [Ciosici] and Brian were for us, we really started to come together as a basketball team when Timmy took the point," Fran O'Hanlon said. "He's one of those guys who makes everyone else better, and just as important, he almost never tries to do too much. He knows his limitations better than anybody."

That's not to say that Bieg's freshman year was easy. The academic transition was tougher than the basketball transition. Then he got sick during Christmas break and spent most of it in his dorm room, miserable, lonely, and homesick. He wasn't quite sick enough to go home but he was sick enough to feel awful. Eventually he was diagnosed with mononucleosis and he did get to go home for a little while.

He recovered and ended up starting twenty-one games that season. The mono pretty much ended his thoughts about playing baseball. "I was behind in everything when I came back," he said. "College is hard. Playing for Coach O is work. By the time basketball season was over, I just wanted to crawl away and get some rest."

He had the prototype point guard's personality: outgoing, a leader, someone everyone on the team enjoyed being around. Ehlers loved to play practical jokes and leave everyone wondering who did it. Bieg was the locker room trash-talker. He critiqued everyone and everything from the coaches' fashion sense to teammates' haircuts. Naturally, he got it right back in return. O'Hanlon was probably harder on him when things went wrong on the court than on anyone, for two reasons: he knew he could take it and he knew he would understand what needed to be done to correct it.

His importance to the team was perhaps best understood by listening to opposing coaches talk about him in pregame scouting reports. Don DeVoe was direct: "This guy makes their team go, guys," he said. "We get to him, we get to their whole team. Cut off the head and the body dies. He's their head. Let's cut it off and watch the body die."

That, of course, was easier said than done.

Most nights, Bieg was content to get the ball to his team's scorers: Ciosici inside, Whitfield outside, Ehlers anyplace. But when defenses geared to stop the scorers and gave him extra space, he was capable of taking advantage, as he had proven so graphically at Penn when the defense had left him alone early in the second half and he had drilled three straight 3-pointers. The second half began with Bucknell determined to cut off Ehlers, who had scored 13 first-half points. Bieg hadn't scored in the first twenty minutes, but when Bryan Bailey left him to double Ehlers the first time he touched the ball, Ehlers quickly reversed the ball to Bieg, who let a 3 fly right away and bottomed it.

"No margin for error with those guys," Flannery said later. "You go to double someone inside or outside and Bieg will kill you."

Or rip your heart out. Whatever was necessary.

Lafayette kept trying to make Bucknell go away in the second half. The Bison would have none of it. Both teams were doing a good job of shadowing the other's best 3-point shooter: Whitfield would finish the night three-of-thirteen, Karavanic four-of-fourteen. Others picked up the slack. Bucknell couldn't stop Ehlers; Lafayette couldn't stop Dan Bowen. A Brian Burke 3 with 11:21 left stretched the lead to 52-42, and Kirby was a cauldron of noise.

But Shaun Asbury, the only nonstarter among the five Bucknell seniors, came off the bench to bring his team back into the game. Asbury was another Philly kid, and he had been recruited by Lafayette. But he had found Bucknell's campus more appealing and had decided to go west. Finding playing time had always been a struggle for him. Someone had always been ahead of him in the rotation. Now, as a senior, he had extended his shooting range and had found a comfortable and important role as the team's sixth man. In a 77-second stretch, he hit three straight 3s, single-handedly producing a 9-0 run that put the Bison right back into the game.

Bucknell took a brief lead at 57-56, but Lafayette went on a 10-4 run, keyed by a Bieg (and big) 3 to lead 66-61. Again, Bucknell rallied. Bryan Bailey's two free throws cut the lead to 70-68 with just under a minute left. O'Hanlon was convinced that Rob Worthington had blocked the shot cleanly that led to the free throws, and screamed uncharacteristically at Joe DeMayo about it.

"No way, Joe!" he yelled. "No way! That was all ball and you guys know it!"

DeMayo, like O'Hanlon a Philadelphia kid who had known him forever, walked directly at O'Hanlon, staring at him, whistle in his mouth, his message clear: DON'T make me T you up at a moment like this. O'Hanlon got the message and calmed down.

Down the stretch they came. After Bowen made a 3-point play to cut the margin to 72-71 with twenty-seven seconds left, Bailey tried for a steal on the inbounds. The ball came loose for an instant. The

Bucknell bench was on its feet. But Bailey had bumped Burke just enough for the whistle to blow. Now it was Flannery's turn to rail to no avail.

Burke, who was in the middle of a streak in which he would make forty-nine straight free throws, made two. Bowen promptly answered with twelve seconds left, and it was 74-73. Bucknell pressed. Bieg broke long and Worthington tossed a strike worthy of Joe Montana to him. He caught the ball in full stride, took one dribble, and was fouled by Bailey, who was almost stride-for-stride with him.

Bieg went down hard, more from his own momentum than the foul. It was Bailey's fifth foul. He immediately went over, helped Bieg up, and made sure he was okay. Bieg said he was fine, but he looked a little bit shaky. There was no way he was coming out with nine seconds left. Flannery took the full thirty seconds he was allowed to sub for a fouled-out player to give Bieg some time to think about the free throws he faced.

The first shot spun out. Bieg backed away from the line, angry with himself. Then he drained the second. O'Hanlon used his last time-out to make sure his players were where he wanted them on defense. With Bailey out, Flannery had Chris Zimmerman on the point. His job was to get the ball into the hands of one of the scorers and let them create a shot of some kind. Flannery didn't care if it was a 2-point shot to tie or a 3-point shot to win, just as long as it was a good shot.

Zimmerman quickly got the ball to Shaun Asbury on the left wing. Asbury had shot the ball too well for the defense not to come out on him. He head-faked, dribbled the ball into the lane, and drew a crowd of defenders. Alertly, he pitched the ball to Karavanic on the right wing as the clock ticked under two seconds. Karavanic caught the ball, gathered himself, and stepped into his lefty jumper. He was a half step outside the 3-point line as he left his feet. Everyone in the gym was standing as the ball left his hand.

The Lafayette players held their breath. Later, in the locker room, O'Hanlon would tell them that they had played "hope defense" on the last possession. "You left a guy open and hoped he would miss," he said.

Their hopes were answered. The shot hit the front rim and bounded in the air and away from the basket. Karavanic slumped to the floor in disgust as the buzzer sounded. The Lafayette players were more relieved than thrilled. They had escaped on their home court by a margin of about two inches. They knew they still had to go to Davis Gym on the final weekend of the season, so this was not a moment to jump up and down and celebrate. They lined up to offer condolences to the Bucknell players, each of them offering an extra pat on the back or the back of the head for Karavanic. Any competitor could understand how awful the moment was for him.

"Don't you dare feel bad about that shot, V," Flannery said in the locker room. "That shot didn't lose the game. You made plays that gave us a chance to win. You all did. We also made plays that lost the game; all of us, everyone in here. That's the way the game is. But you know what's great about the game? We get another shot at these guys. We still have a long way to travel before this journey is over. Remember that."

They remembered. But they all knew they had just had a great shot at those guys. And now they had to go to Navy, a place where they had rarely had any luck in the past.

"All I can say is that we're due to have one go our way," Dan Bowen said. "I just hope it's sooner rather than later."

It wasn't sooner. In a sense, the timing for the rematch with Navy — which would kick off round two of conference play — seemed perfect. The first half had ended with Lafayette at 6-0; Navy at 5-1 (loss to Lafayette); and Bucknell at 4-2 (losses to Lafayette and Navy). No one else in the league was at .500. Holy Cross and Lehigh were 2-4 after Lehigh had killed Holy Cross on Wednesday, and Colgate and Army were 1-5. Colgate had played well against Navy at Cotterell Court on Wednesday but the Mids had squeezed out a 69-65 victory.

Even though the game had been close, the Midshipmen had come out of it feeling very good about themselves. The Colgate trip was never an easy one, and they had played the game with Sitapha Savane hobbling on an ankle he had turned late in a victory two days earlier over William and Mary. In fact, in the closing seconds, as Chris Williams and Jordan Harris had waited at the scorer's table to report in, Williams couldn't help but chortle a little bit.

"Damn, Jordan, we're beating you up here," he said. "We're going to kill you when you come to Navy."

That wasn't for another couple of weeks. Before that, the Mids had back-to-back games with Bucknell and Lafayette to deal with. Savane's ankle felt fine by the time the team got home from Colgate, and Saturday, February 5, dawned bright and sunny for the afternoon game with Bucknell. The whole team felt very confident. Four of their six league road games had been played, and the only two that were left were at Army and Lehigh. The next five games were in Alumni Hall. They wouldn't play on the road again until the last week of the regular season.

Don DeVoe had a feeling that his team was on the verge of becoming very good. Some of the issues that had concerned him in the preseason had gone away. The once Restricted Nine had seemed to grow from their experience, and there was no question about the leadership that Savane and Jeremy Toton were providing. Reggie Skipworth, who had struggled early at the point guard spot, was becoming more and more confident with every game. The up-tempo was working, and the freshmen, notably Jason Jeanpierre, were playing better with each passing game.

Perhaps most amazing of all, Robert Reeder was making free throws.

Reeder was the team's workhorse, the guy who did most of the dirty work inside at both ends of the court. He played so hard that he always looked worn out when he came to the bench, but he never played worn out. Reeder got banged up so often, catching elbows, diving on the floor, going after rebounds and loose balls, that his nickname was "Bobby Bleeder." He had been allowed to grow a goatee for several games to hide stitches he had taken on his chin after catching a Francis Ebong elbow in practice. "I'm trying to convince them to leave the stitches in for a while," he said. "I like not shaving."

If Savane and Toton were the team's vocal leaders, Reeder was the quiet leader, the guy who led by example. He was from California, having grown up just outside Los Angeles, and had never found the academy as taxing as most others did. His grades were solid and he had never been in even a little trouble until the night of Chris Worthing's birthday. He was as calm as his counterpart at the other forward spot, Chris Williams, was hyper. When the team left the locker room, the players had gotten into the habit of forming a circle and screaming things at one another to get themselves excited before they went on the court, yelling different rap lyrics as they did. Reeder just hung back, like the big kid in the schoolyard who doesn't engage in little-kid games, and waited until they finished.

He had enough confidence in his place on the team that he didn't feel the need to participate in something that clearly wasn't him. And the others respected him enough that they didn't mind at all. "In his own way, Bobby's the most irreplaceable guy on our team," Savane said. "There's no one else who can do the things he does for us."

Bleeder, er, Reeder, always guarded the other team's best inside player to start the game, making life easier for Savane. He picked up big rebounds, was an excellent interior passer, and almost never took a bad shot. And now, he was making free throws. That was important to DeVoe, who had worried early in the season that he would be unable to play Reeder down the stretch in close games because of his foul-shooting troubles.

That wasn't a problem against Bucknell, not because of Reeder's improved free-throw shooting, but because the game was never close. Navy was dominant from the start, jumping the Bison at both ends of the floor. By halftime, the lead was 37-23. Flannery wasn't sure whether to be angry or stunned. He tried challenging his players at halftime, telling them he expected to find out what kind of men they were in the second half.

In a funny way, he did find out. But not the way he wanted to. Navy was on one of those rolls that can make a good team look bad, a tough team look soft. The Midshipmen pushed the lead to 30 — 68-38 — midway through the second half. The easiest thing for Bucknell to do at that point would have been to fold up completely. The game was clearly lost. They had already had a brutal week with the last-second loss at Lafayette.

Instead, the Bison made a remarkable run, actually getting the lead to 9 late in the game. Navy certainly let down a little with the huge lead, but Bucknell never stopped playing. The final was 75-61, a respectable margin, given what the score might have been.

That was hardly soothing to Flannery. He was angry, confused, and frustrated. "I'm telling you something, guys, I will not let this season get away from us," he said. "There is too much at stake right now and we've all worked too hard to accept that kind of performance. We're going to come to practice Monday and I swear to God anyone who hangs their head or doesn't listen or isn't absolutely ready, I'll toss you in a second. I'll play all the freshmen if I have to. Whatever it takes, I'll do it. All I ask is the same from you."

Down the hall, they were as exuberant as Bucknell was depressed. Until DeVoe said four words: "Lafayette is next, guys."

They had wanted to beat Bucknell. They were *living* to beat Lafayette. DeVoe didn't have to say another word. The game wasn't for four days. Navy was ready to play right then and there.

22

THIS ISN'T OVER

NAVY'S one-sided rout of Bucknell made it pretty clear that first place — and the crucial top seed for the tournament — was almost certainly going to come down to the Midshipmen or Lafayette. Which meant that Lafayette's trip to Annapolis on February 9 was, without question, the most critical game left on the schedule.

A Lafayette victory would all but wrap up first place for the Leopards. They would have a two-game lead in the standings, and even if Navy somehow caught them and tied for first place, they would have the tiebreaker by virtue of having beaten Navy twice. A Navy victory would make everything even. Each team would have one conference loss, and they would be 1-1 against one another.

The Yard rarely buzzes about a basketball game. Each Monday during football season the midshipmen are all given buttons with some kind of slogan for that week's game: "Ground the Falcons" or "Sting the Jackets." The best one is the last one, which simply says "Beat Army." There are no such buttons during basketball season, no mandatory pep rallies, no bonfires, no send-offs or middle-of-the-night welcomes.

But there was very clearly a sense of something special in the air on the day of the Lafayette game. It started at breakfast, when Sitapha Savane spoke emotionally to his fellow midshipmen about the importance of the game and the need for their support that night. Don DeVoe showed up at lunch to give a similar talk, and then Savane spoke *again* — because Superintendent John Ryan told him to speak again.

Ryan was an old basketball player, who sat in the first row at every home game and often shared his opinions on the officiating with the officials. Rarely did he stand up to say, "Nice call, Ref." (Who does?) Earlier in the season, Athletic Director Jack Lengyel had expressed concern to DeVoe about the fact that his occasionally salty language in the huddle could be heard in the stands by, among others, the Supe. The next time DeVoe saw Ryan, he apologized to him for his language, telling him he would try to be more careful about it in the future.

"Don," Ryan answered, "just keep winning."

The Mids had been winning a lot. They had come a long way since the pre-Thanksgiving redemption, winning sixteen of eighteen games. The easy win over Bucknell had sent their confidence soaring, and even the calmer people on the team had a real good mad on for Lafayette, which had now won the team's last three meetings.

"Can you believe they bus down here the day of the game?" the usually reasoned and reasonable Jimmy Allen said at pregame meal. "They think they don't need to be rested to beat us. We'll just see about that."

Actually Lafayette's travel plans had nothing to do with their self-confidence and everything to do with budget. By busing on game day rather than the night before, the school saved about $1,000. "We do stop to eat," Fran O'Hanlon said, smiling.

The trip took just over three hours nonstop. The players went to morning classes, then the bus left around one o'clock. With a stop to eat, they arrived at Alumni Hall a little more than two hours before tip-off. The day was about as nice as you could ask for in February, temperatures rising into the fifties, the afternoon sun glinting off the Annapolis harbor and the Severn River. It was a reminder to everyone that the finish line was in sight. The regular season would end two weeks from Sunday and the conference tournament would begin six days after that.

O'Hanlon was fully aware of the fact that the Midshipmen were lying in wait for his team. He knew how narrow the escape had been twenty-four days earlier in Easton, and he knew how well they had played against Bucknell. He was a little bit concerned that the string of successes his team had run up against Patriot League teams — they had now won eighteen of twenty conference games dating back to 1998–1999 and nine in a row — might make them a tiny bit lax in their approach. Even when challenged — Navy, Bucknell — they had managed to escape.

The blackboard in the Lafayette locker room was a little more crowded than normal that night. O'Hanlon had written down the usual litany of O-keys and D-keys, but the items under "They" went on at more length than usual. The last three items were less technical and more to the point than O'Hanlon was accustomed to being:

- *Are Sneaky.* It was meant as a compliment. Navy played smart, aggressive basketball. Like a lot of teams — including Lafayette — the Mids knew how to move on screens without getting called and how to bang on people inside without being blatant about it.
- *Have won 16 of 18.*
- *Have a lot of pride/Believe they are the best.*

The last two were meant as a warning. This was a good team, with a chip on its shoulder where Lafayette was concerned. They were still angry about losing in Easton and didn't just want to beat the Leopards, they wanted to hammer them. This was evident a few minutes later at the other end of the hall when Savane gathered his teammates in a circle before they took the court. Every basketball team says something when it puts its hands together in a huddle. Some will say "team"; others will say "family." Some "pride"; others "play hard." It is nothing more than a ritual coaches and players use to remind themselves of some theme on a regular basis. As the Navy players put their hands together, Savane — as always — stood in the middle. "On three," he said. "Bust their chops!"

That was Navy's theme for the night.

This was one evening when Alumni Hall was anything but a mausoleum. Although the commandant still wasn't ordering the Brigade out in full, Captain Bruce Boles, who was the o-rep for the basketball team, and Captain Corky Gardner, the football team's o-rep, had both ordered their battalions out. Since there are six battalions at the academy, that meant at least a third of the Brigade would be at the game. There were probably close to 1,500 midshipmen in the stands, and the crowd was just under 4,000. What's more, they were loud right from the beginning.

As always seemed to be the case, Lafayette started slowly. It was 10-2 after three minutes and 17-4 after a Reggie Skipworth 3 less than five minutes in. This was really no different from the start of the game in Easton, except that Lafayette didn't have the aid of its crowd to will it back into the game. Another 3, this one by Jason Jeanpierre made it 22-10 — the exact score Navy had led by in the first game.

The game was rough on both sides. Chris Williams sent Bieg flying as he tried to fight around a screen early, and Stefan Ciosici and Savane were at war in the middle. Savane had been convinced after the first game that Ciosici had intentionally leaned back on him in the low post so that his bulky knee brace would cut his knee. Ciosici had been equally convinced that Savane was trying to push against his bad knee every chance he got.

Both were wrong. But it didn't matter. They both believed the other was guilty.

Lafayette cut into the margin — again, much like the first game — getting to within 33-26 when Brian Burke made two free throws with 5:35 left. Then Chris Williams picked up his second foul a moment later in a shoving contest with Burke and left the floor screaming at official Reggie Greenwood that he had missed the first shove.

But this time, the Mids didn't give ground at the end of the half. Reeder, always there when he was needed most, tipped in a Chris Williams miss, and John Williams hit a bomb to make it 38-26. Reeder and Chris Williams each made baskets on pretty back-cuts, and the margin at the half was 44-31. The lead had been down to 6 at the half the first time the teams played.

O'Hanlon was clinical for most of halftime. His coaches reminded him that a number of shots had gone in and out that could have made the game considerably closer. They certainly weren't out of it down 13. Everyone in both locker rooms agreed that the old adage about the first five minutes of the second half being key would be especially true in this game. DeVoe's final words in the huddle before the start of the second half were direct: "Let's show them right now we're going to win this basketball game. No messing around."

They didn't mess around. Lafayette was an experienced team that did not panic. Ciosici and Brian Ehlers knew they had to bring their team back, and both came out firing. But Navy answered everything. Ciosici scored, Savane matched him. Ehlers hit a jumper, John Williams swished a 3. Ciosici scored again inside; Jeremy Toton, finally back from the ankle injury he had suffered in late December, rebounded a miss, was fouled, and made both free throws.

For eight minutes they more or less traded baskets, which wasn't doing Lafayette much good because the clock was ticking and the lead was still 59-43 after Savane tipped in a Reeder miss. Lafayette set its offense and the ball swung to the corner. Jason Jeanpierre, the quickest player Navy had, moved to double-team and slapped the ball loose. It looked as if it would go out of bounds, but Jeanpierre, who had a remarkable knack for saving balls that were going out, leaped across the end line and made a spectacular play: he grabbed the ball in midair, and in one motion turned and threw the ball downcourt to Chris Williams, who was streaking toward the Navy basket.

The entire crowd was on its feet, knowing a big-time slam dunk was coming to cap off the play as Williams closed in on the basket. Lafayette freshman Greg McCleary was desperately chasing him. McCleary was six-five, a kid who had grown up in the same West Philadelphia neighborhood that O'Hanlon was from. He was a typical O'Hanlon player: tough and competitive on the court, polite and gentle off the court. He had missed ten games because of a stress fracture in his leg and had only returned a game earlier. The only reason he was in the game at that moment was because O'Hanlon was deep into his bench looking for a way to turn things around.

McCleary knew Williams was going to go up and slam the ball and that the crowd was going to go crazy. His job, as he saw it, was to prevent the dunk from happening one way or the other. As Williams went up, McCleary leaped into the air behind him, reached out with both arms, and took Williams down. His intent wasn't to injure, it was to prevent the dunk. But the contact was substantial and Williams went flying. His head caught the corner of the basket stanchion, and he rolled over, blood gushing from his forehead, writhing in pain. Navy trainer Loren Shipley was out of his seat sprinting toward Williams even before the officials signaled for him.

If McCleary had been more experienced he might have done the smart thing and tried to make immediate amends, checking to see how Williams was, telling the other Navy players that he hadn't meant to injure him. But he was a scared freshman in a hostile environment, so he did nothing. When a couple of the Navy players accused him of a dirty play, he just stared at them until Ciosici pushed him back in the direction of the Lafayette bench. Boos were raining down from all corners of the building while Shipley and DeVoe checked on Williams.

The blood made the injury look worse than it was. Williams never lost consciousness and Shipley had him up in a few moments. He headed to the locker room. McCleary had been properly called for a "hard foul," which meant Navy would shoot two free throws and then get the ball out of bounds. John Williams came in to shoot the free throws for Chris Williams and made them both.

It was here that O'Hanlon made a rare coaching mistake. The best thing he could have done at that moment for McCleary and his team was get McCleary out of the game. The kid was freaked out and the booing was merciless. But the street kid in O'Hanlon tended to come out at moments like this. For one thing, from the angle he had at the far end of the court, it looked to him like McCleary had gotten his hand on the basketball and the hard foul should not have been called. Later, when he saw the play on tape from a better angle, he realized the call was correct. In fact, he was disturbed enough by what he saw on the tape that he asked McCleary if he had meant to hurt Williams. McCleary told him absolutely not and O'Hanlon took him at his word.

"I told him that I believed him and I hoped it was true," he said. "Because we don't play that way. Greg isn't that kind of kid. But seeing the tape gave me a different view than what I had during the game."

At that moment, O'Hanlon was feeling very put upon: his team was down 18, he thought perhaps the officials had overreacted on the call, and he was completely convinced the crowd — especially the mids — was overreacting. So he left McCleary in the game.

"I wasn't going to back down to the crowd," he said. "I figured, let them boo all they want. We aren't responding to what they want to happen."

What they wanted to happen did happen. McCleary stayed in, and Lafayette, completely out of character, became unglued. Reeder hit a ten-foot jumper off the ensuing inbounds pass to make it 63-43. Then, at the opposite end, he took a charge from Ciosici and came up screaming in Ciosici's face. If that reaction didn't tell O'Hanlon how intense the situation was, nothing would. Reeder was, without question, the least likely of the Midshipmen to do any trash talking.

The Navy bench was as hot as the crowd. Even before Williams was on his feet, assistant coach Mark Alarie, whose nature was quiet and calm away from the basketball court, was walking down the bench saying, "He [McCleary] can't get away with that." He looked at Jeremy Toton. "When you're in, make sure he knows that's unacceptable."

Alarie, like everyone else from Navy, was as upset about Mc-Cleary's reaction to the play as the play itself. On the court, the carnage continued. McCleary caught a pass on the wing, the boos rained down, and he traveled with the ball. Savane scored at the other end. By now O'Hanlon was convinced that the officials were as unglued as his team, and he was screaming at them to get control of the game. Navy scored the game's next 14 points after the takedown, the lead going from a surprising 16 to a mind-boggling 30 at 73-43 with nine minutes still left in the game.

Still O'Hanlon left McCleary in the game. Toton came in, and almost immediately he and McCleary were tangled up. Toton knocked McCleary down, then helped him up, patted him on the back, and said softly, "That's just the beginning, pal." Seconds later, the two players had to be separated under the basket. The officials, who *were* doing a good job trying to maintain control, called technicals on both. Then, and only then, did O'Hanlon get McCleary out of the game. He understood that the Navy players weren't going to let this go and he didn't want a full-scale riot in a game that was over.

Shortly after McCleary came out, Chris Williams came back to the court. He had changed uniform jerseys, from number 33 to number 32, because 33 was soaked in blood. He had four stitches on his forehead, far less than anyone would have thought when he first went down. He returned to the game to a thunderous ovation and went right to the basket the first two times he touched the ball, as if to prove to everyone including himself that he was bloodied but not beaten. He was fouled on both plays and made all four free throws.

The final was a stunning 94-66. There were very few words exchanged during the postgame handshakes. When Williams and McCleary came to one another, there was a brief handshake. McCleary said nothing. Williams looked at him for a moment, waiting to see if he would say something. When he didn't, Williams turned and screamed at him, "This isn't over. We'll see you again. This is not over!"

For most people, the incident overshadowed the fact that Navy had dominated the team that had dominated the Patriot League for most of two seasons. Trailing by 16 before the incident, Lafayette still had a puncher's chance to rally, but there had been no indication up until then that it was going to happen. The incident had turned what was looking like an easy Navy victory into an ugly rout.

O'Hanlon had a lot on his mind in the locker room. The most important thing was for the players to recognize what had happened. "They just took this league to a new level, fellas," he said. "They raised the bar. If we want to go back to the NCAAs we're going to have to become a lot better team than we were tonight."

The good news was that they were angry, embarrassed. Ehlers later called it the worst night of his basketball career. There were no excuses — that's not Lafayette's way anyway — because Navy had flat-out kicked their butts and they knew it.

O'Hanlon's other concern was the aftermath of the incident. Even though he hadn't seen the tape yet and wasn't clear on what had happened, he sat down alone with McCleary after the rest of the players had left the meeting room. He knew McCleary was shaken by what had happened and he wanted to calm him down.

"It looked like you got the ball," he said.

McCleary shook his head. "No, Coach, I didn't. It was a foul. But I wasn't trying to hurt him."

O'Hanlon understood. Even though he would go back to McCleary later after seeing the tape to be absolutely certain, he had assumed McCleary's intent had not been to hurt Williams. He wasn't that kind of kid.

"If you get a chance at some point," he said. "Tell him that."

McCleary nodded. Later, he and Pat Brogan went looking for Williams, but Williams had already left the locker room. O'Hanlon stopped in the Navy coaches' office on his way out. Nathan Davis was the only coach in the room.

"How's Chris?" he asked.

"He's okay, Coach," Davis said.

"I'm sorry he got hurt," O'Hanlon said, meaning it.

"Thanks, Coach. I'll tell him."

The fences weren't mended, but at least the pieces were starting to be picked up.

Around the league, the McCleary-Williams takedown was little more than a footnote to the final score. No one had dreamed that anyone could beat Lafayette by 28 points. This was, after all, a team that had lost at Villanova by 4, at Georgia Tech by 11, and at Penn by 4. This was a team many had thought would go undefeated in conference play. Now, even though the teams were tied for first place with one loss apiece, the sense was that Navy had become the favorite to win the conference title.

Navy's win also brought up the issue of the conference tiebreaker. There was, after all, a pretty good chance both Navy and Lafayette would win out and finish 11-1. The most serious challenge for either team would come on the last day of the regular season, when Lafayette played at Bucknell. Navy's toughest remaining game would probably be at home on Valentine's Day when it played Colgate. In three games against his old boss, Emmett Davis was 0-3, but the total margin of victory was 12 points.

If the two teams did tie at 11-1, the top seed for the tournament would be decided by the computerized RPI rankings. Everyone remembered that two years earlier when Navy and Lafayette had tied for first, all of the tiebreakers had been exhausted and the top seed had been decided by a coin flip. Navy had won the coin flip and had opted for the chance to play the final at home. Lafayette had gotten the first round bye as the consolation prize. Both teams had made the final, and Navy had won in Alumni Hall.

That spring, the coaches had decided that the top seed was too important to be decided by the luck of a coin flip. They needed to find another method to break a first-place tie. They had finally settled on the RPI, which ranked all 318 Division I teams based on a computerized formula that took into account wins and losses, strength of schedule, and opponents' strength of schedule. It was a complicated system that no one completely understood. But the way it worked, a team could actually win a game and go down in the rankings because of the opponent's ranking. It was far from perfect and did not take into account margin of victory. As far as the computer was concerned, there was absolutely no difference between Navy's 28-point win over Lafayette and Lafayette's 6-point win over Navy.

Still, the coaches agreed it was better than a coin flip. The morning after Navy-Lafayette II, for the first time all season, players and coaches began asking about the RPI ratings. Lafayette had been a few spots ahead of Navy going into the game. Afterward, Navy jumped in front: the Mids 134, Leopards 138. There were now two races to pay attention to.

23

MIDDLE OF THE PACK

THE last place the Holy Cross basketball team wanted to be on Saturday, February 12, was Easton, Pennsylvania. Timing is everything in both life and basketball and playing a good team coming off an embarrassing game is just not something anyone wants to do. Nonetheless, the schedule called for the Crusaders to show up on an unseasonably warm and pleasant afternoon at Kirby Arena to play a Lafayette team still smarting from the clocking it had taken at Navy three days earlier.

"Given the way the season has gone, this is nothing," Ralph Willard said, laughing, when the scheduling misfortune came up.

Willard was laughing, but he wasn't kidding. Holy Cross 1999–2000 was a cross between the '62 Mets (40-120, baseball's all-time worst record) and *The Bad News Bears* — the early part of the movie. The injuries were a big part of the story, but not the whole story.

A few examples: Three days after the loss at home to Navy, the Crusaders were scheduled to play at Hartford. Much like the Yale trip, this was a simple day trip. Instead of making the bus trip and then eating as they had done at Yale, the team ate their pregame meal in the student cafeteria. As soon as they were finished, everyone piled on the bus, which had been parked right outside, to make the sixty-mile trip to Hartford.

More as a reflex than anything else, assistant coach Roger Breslin said to the driver as they were pulling out of the parking lot, "You know how to get there, right?"

"Absolutely," the driver replied. "Been to UConn dozens of times."

Breslin started to sit back in his seat, then bolted straight up. "UConn?" he said. "We aren't going to UConn. We're going to the University of Hartford."

The driver shook his head. "That's not what my instructions say. They say we're going to UConn."

By now, Breslin was standing next to the driver, who showed him the instructions. Sure enough, they were for a trip to UConn. Very clearly, on the top of the page that the driver handed to Breslin, it said, "Women's ice hockey trip to the University of Connecticut at Storrs."

Breslin didn't know whether to laugh or cry. "Uh, driver, we've got a little problem here."

"What is it?"

"You see anyone on this bus who looks like a women's ice hockey player?"

The driver stopped and looked in his mirror. "Guess not."

The bus was turned around and driven back up the hill to the Hart Center while Breslin tried to explain what was going on to the less-than-pleased Willard. Sure enough, when they pulled up to the door, there was a second bus and a number of unhappy-looking female hockey players waiting there. The second driver had noticed that no one getting on his bus looked like a men's basketball player and had refused to allow the hockey players to board, insisting he was waiting for the men's basketball team.

"Why don't you just take the women to Storrs and we can go on the bus we're already on to Hartford?" Breslin suggested.

Nope. The drivers had to follow their orders. And so, the basketball players all got off the first bus, all their equipment was unloaded, and they and the equipment were loaded onto the second bus while the hockey players and their equipment were loaded onto the first bus. Thirty minutes after they were scheduled to leave, the Crusaders were on their way to Hartford.

"The only thing that would have made it better," Sports Information Director Frank Mastrandrea said later, "would have been if

Roger hadn't said anything to the guy and we had pulled up to the hockey rink in Storrs."

Holy Cross won that game and then beat Army three days later, 52-42, in a game that made Wagner-Lehigh in November look like a Lakers-Celtics playoff game.

Three days after that, Holy Cross went to Lehigh to complete the first round of Patriot League play. Holy Cross was 2-3 in the league, Lehigh 1-4, having not won a league game since the opener against Army. This time the bus driver knew that he was supposed to be driving the Holy Cross men's basketball team to a game at Lehigh. That was the good news. The bad news was that he had no idea how to find Stabler Arena. He ended up driving in circles around downtown Bethlehem, until he finally turned down an alley and found himself behind a car that was stuck on an ice patch.

Breslin and Mastrandrea were designated to push the car off the ice, no doubt because Breslin was held responsible for the fact that they were behind the stuck car and because Mastrandrea, who has a law degree, was deemed the most expendable person on the bus. The car was freed, the bus moved on, and, eventually, the driver found Stabler.

Which proved to be a mistake, because Lehigh dominated the game and won, 64-57. Mastrandrea's explanation the next day: "We played forty minutes of Army basketball."

Mastrandrea had a copy of Army's "40 minutes" poster. He couldn't resist the one-liner. He would pay for it later. Spitler Phase Three was in full bloom by now. He started against Lehigh, played thirty-four minutes, and scored a career-high 15 points.

When not making On the Road movies, the Crusaders continued their habit of hurting one another. Patrick Whearty actually felt well enough to practice one afternoon. Ten minutes into practice, Tim Szatko caught him with an elbow in the mouth. Five stitches.

Practice injuries happen. So do game injuries. Guillermo Sanchez broke his nose diving for a loose ball in the Army game. He was out-fitted with a mask designed to protect the nose and allow him to play. Holy Cross came home to play Colgate after the Lehigh game. Jared Curry had been forced to sit out the Lehigh game because his back had flared up on him again, but Juan Pegues had finally returned, playing seven minutes.

Curry was back for the Colgate game and Willard put him back in the starting lineup. As the lineups were introduced, the Holy Cross bench players formed an alleyway for the starters, the way most teams do when the starters are introduced. Curry, all enthusiasm and energy, made his way through the alley, high-fiving his teammates on either side of him. Somehow, as he turned to high-five Sanchez, he caught him right on the nose with his elbow, shattering the mask. Sanchez looked as if someone had turned a blood faucet on inside his nose. Trainer Anthony Cerenduolo had to take Sanchez back to the locker room, stanch the bleeding, and reset the nose.

Only at Holy Cross could a player be injured during the introduction of the starting lineups.

One other player, though not injured, was also missing. On the morning of January 24, the day after the Navy game, James Stowers had come to Willard's office. Classes had been underway for a week and Stowers was already feeling his insides churning. Basketball vs. school loomed again as an issue for him, and it was already making him feel uptight.

Willard had sensed the problem even before Stowers came to see him. He had tried everything he could to convince Stowers that basketball could be fun, that it didn't have to be deadly serious, that it could be a release from his schoolwork rather than a burden. Before Stowers left the locker room after the Navy game, he had reminded Willard that he had a late class on Wednesday that would mean he would miss pregame meal before the trip to Hartford. He and Willard spent several minutes discussing logistics and what would be done if Stowers missed the bus because the class ran late.

"We'll get you there, James," Willard said. "Let us worry about it."

Stowers nodded and headed into the cold winter night. Willard looked at his assistant coaches and said softly, "I'm not sure that kid will ever play for us again."

His instinct proved correct. Even though he knew the team could use Stowers's shooting touch and his experience, Willard made no attempt to talk him out of his decision. "The last thing I wanted," he said, "was for the kid to be miserable. I had a tough time with basketball my senior year, too. I understood."

Through it all the Crusaders somehow stayed competitive. They lost by 3 to Colgate — the fastest-improving team in the league — and then by 6 to Bucknell in a game they led until the last two minutes. It actually looked as if Holy Cross would win the game when Chris Spitler — yes, Chris Spitler — bombed a 3 to make it 44-39 with 3:25 left. But Valter Karavanic and Dan Bowen hit 3s for Bucknell, and the Bison rallied late to win.

All of which brought Holy Cross into Lafayette with a 2-6 conference record, an 8-14 overall mark. Lafayette was 6-1, the one shaped in their minds like a black eye, and 15-6 in all games. Fran O'Hanlon had told his team that if it wanted the top seed for the Patriot League Tournament it was going to have to play with a lot more emotion and intensity than it had shown at Navy.

"I think we'd gotten just a little bit on cruise control before that game," he said. "You forget sometimes that these are kids. They've played very well against good teams outside the league, and they've been winning consistently inside the league. Sooner or later they were going to stumble. I just don't think any of us thought it would be such a complete pratfall."

It was almost as if the loss to Navy had rekindled interest in the team on campus. The students had pretty much been on cruise control, too, taking the team's success for granted. To be fair, none of the undergraduates had been on campus when the team was 2-25. The worst record the seniors had endured had been the 11-17 when Ehlers and Homer had been freshmen. Then it had been 19-9 and 22-8. Most of the students were accustomed to good teams by now.

The Navy loss seemed to have them wondering. Kirby was just shy of a sellout (3,218) and the Zoo Crew was back, if not in force, at least in voice. Pegues and Serravalle were both back in the starting lineup for Holy Cross. Curry was out once more with his back miseries.

The game began predictably — with Sankes missing two free throws. What was amazing about Sankes was how well he had played in spite of his free-throw shooting problems. He had already set a school record for blocked shots in a season and was routinely reaching double figures in points and rebounds almost every night. This game would be typical Sankes: forty minutes played; 18 points; ten rebounds; two-of-five from the foul line and three blocks. Willard was concerned, because he knew Sankes was wearing down playing so many minutes every night, but he didn't think he had any choice but to keep playing him. Sankes never complained. That wasn't his nature, but even if it had been, he was enjoying basketball so much that it wouldn't have occurred to him to complain.

Holy Cross hung in the game for seventeen minutes, trailing 26-20, before Lafayette blew it open the last three minutes of the half with a 9-1 run that made the margin 35-21. Even on a day when Ehlers shot the ball poorly (three-of-fifteen) the Leopards had too many different weapons for Holy Cross. Tyson Whitfield, the team's mad bomber, had 19 points, Stefan Ciosici 15, and Brian Burke came off the bench to chip in 13 in seventeen minutes, hitting three-of-three from 3-point range. Left open even a little, Burke was almost automatic from just about anyplace on the floor. Whitfield didn't even need to be open. His release was so quick that he could catch and shoot anytime he wanted to do so.

Holy Cross stubbornly hung around for most of the second half, actually drawing to within 66-60 on a 3-pointer by Szatko with 2:34 to go, but Lafayette methodically put the game away at the free-throw line. The final was 77-66.

Willard knew his team had given him everything it had. He knew the players were tired, that the injuries and the schedule — not to mention the bus drivers — had worn everyone down as the season progressed. But he didn't want them to give in to the mental temptation to accept defeat. He lectured them on their mistakes and then he appealed to their pride.

"That team didn't take us very seriously today," he said. "I don't think anyone in this league really respects us right now. And maybe that's with good reason. But I want to tell you something, fellas, it's going to change. Our day is coming. You know that, I know that. I want all of you to remember games like this. Remember guys smiling at you on the court. Don't lose that thought.

"But that's down the road. I don't want to wait that long. Spit's gone next year. We still have things we want to get done with him in this room. It isn't easy, I know that. Josh, I know you're tired. I know it isn't fair to ask you to play forty minutes. But that's the way it is right now. We've only got a few games left, but we can still make something special happen this season. You aren't that far away, because you've all worked so damn hard all year. Just keep working hard and something good will happen."

Willard didn't know it, but something good had already happened. He had passed, without quite understanding it, into Spitler Phase Four: You understand how lucky you are to coach someone like him.

Fifteen miles down the road at Stabler Arena, Colgate and Lehigh tipped off in The Battle for Fourth Place about twenty minutes after Lafayette and Holy Cross finished their game.

Both teams came into the game feeling pretty good about themselves: Colgate, after losing close games to Lafayette and Navy to finish the first half of league play at 1-5, had started the second half by winning at Holy Cross and then bombing Army (67-51), avenging the two first-half losses that had ruined the month of January. Lehigh had also won two straight conference games, the win over Holy Cross followed by a second victory against Army. That put the Mountain Hawks in fourth place in the league at 3-4, followed by Colgate at 3-5.

But Emmett Davis was feeling a lot more confident than Sal Mentesana. In between Army on Sunday and Colgate six days later, Mentesana had scheduled a game at Brown. He had wanted to play the game in December before league play began, but the only time Brown could schedule it was in February. So his team had made the six-hour bus trip to Providence, had lost a close game, and had lost Jared Hess, who had injured both his left ankle and his left shoulder when he was hammered going to the basket late in the game. The game had been rough throughout, and the team had returned home at about four A.M. Wednesday, exhausted, bruised, beaten, and with its captain and leader out indefinitely.

"Not a great piece of scheduling right there," Mentesana said.

The Colgate game was a 5:30 tip-off, because it was on Patriot League TV. The school had also put together a number of kids' promotions for the game, which had swelled the crowd to more than 2,000.

"A perfect night for us to go out and lay an egg," Mentesana said.

The egg was a mutant. Part of the credit had to go to Colgate, which was confident and came out making shots from everywhere. Less than five minutes in, it was 13-3. Then it was 21-6. Pat Campolieta was running rings around the Mountain Hawks, scoring every time he touched the ball. Mentesana kept trying different players and different defenses. Nothing worked. If freshman Matt Logie, who would finish with 16 points, hadn't shown up, Lehigh might have been shut out.

It was 38-22 at halftime. "I'm not sure I've ever felt this helpless in a game," Mentesana said to his coaches. "I'm not sure there's anything we can do to turn this around."

Across the hall, Hess, in street clothes, was lecturing his teammates, trying to tell them that if they clamped down on defense, they could make it a ball game. The looks in their eyes told him he wasn't getting through. He was so frustrated he wanted to go off in a corner and cry. Six days earlier, after the Army game, they had been one game under .500 in the league and headed in the right direction. Now they were spiraling again.

The second half was no different from the first. The closest Lehigh got was 38-24 when Fido Willybiro opened the half with a short jumper. Colgate answered that with a 15-4 run to make it 53-28. The rest of the night was extended garbage time. The game was so sloppy the last ten minutes that Glenn Noak leaned back in his seat next to Mentesana at one point and said, "This looks like a summer-league game."

Mentesana shook his head in disgust. His favorite phrase when he is angry with a player is "I can't play him." He had said that about every player on his team — except Logie — at some point during the game.

"Are we allowed to practice here after a game?" he asked as the final minutes wound down.

Jeff Wilson shook his head. "Against the rules," he said.

"What if we go to the CYO?" Mentesana said, half joking.

The evening — from Lehigh's point of view — was summed up with a little more than four minutes left with Colgate leading 57-33.

Logie took a 3 and was hammered by Jim Detmer as he released the ball right in front of Mentesana.

"That's a foul!" he screamed — correctly.

Referee Kevin Quirk simply shook his head and said, "No, it's not."

Mentesana couldn't take that answer. "Hey, Kevin, believe me, I want to get out of here at least as much as you do," he said. "But you still have to do your job!"

Quirk was doing his job — trying to get the game over as quickly as possible.

The final was 65-43, and in truth, it wasn't that close.

Colgate had now won three straight games. It was 4-5 in the league, 11-11 overall, and was on a roll. Lehigh was back to square one. At least that's the way it felt.

"I wish I knew what you guys were afraid of," Mentesana said. "You went out there with fourth place in the league on the line, which around here means something, and you backed down right from the start. I don't mind losing, I can handle losing. But this wasn't 73-71 at the buzzer because they make a play. This was an embarrassment right from the start. I know he's [Hess] out, but that's not an excuse. We have to stop making excuses around here. I'm sick of making excuses."

Emmett Davis didn't need any excuses at that moment. He and his players had come a long way from that horrible night four weeks earlier when Chris Spatola had made the 3-pointer at the buzzer to drop the Red Raiders to 0-2 in league play.

After a second straight miserable bus ride from West Point to Hamilton, Davis had turned the game tape over to Pat Diamond the next day and suggested the players go through it without the coaches. Every once in a while a team needs to hear a voice — or voices — other than that of their coach. There's a tuning out that occurs at different times during a season, especially when things haven't been good and the coach has been on them. Davis thought his team had reached that stage.

He felt good about leaving the team in Diamond's hands under almost any circumstances. As the only senior, having been through the real-life traumas of Adonal Foyle's battles with Jack Bruen, Bruen's illness and death, and the coaching changes that had followed, Diamond had matured into someone who was almost half player, half coach. Everyone on the team looked up to him and respected what he said. He wasn't the team spokesman by virtue of being a senior or having the title of captain, he was the team spokesman because everyone listened to him.

The players-only meeting/tape session proved to be a turning point. Not only did Diamond reinforce the need not to get discouraged by two bad games, the star sophomores Pat Campolieta and Jordan Harris both made a point of letting the others know that the efforts against Holy Cross and Army weren't satisfactory. All of them had to recommit to working hard in practice, to playing every possession on defense hard. They all knew that the offense might malfunction on some nights but there was no reason not to play good defense.

It was especially important for Campolieta to be outspoken and emotional. There were times when Davis sensed he wasn't completely there mentally in practice. "He understands the game so well that sometimes he gets bored," Davis said. "Whatever we're going over, he already knows it. I know when the game starts he'll be all there, so it's not a problem for him. But the other guys can't afford to be that way."

Campolieta pledging to bear down every day had meaning for the other players. As much as they looked to Diamond as a person, they looked to Campolieta as a player. That was less true of Harris, only because his physical gifts were so remarkable no one in the room could relate to them. Campolieta beat you with his head and heart as much as with his body.

The turnaround hadn't come overnight. It had been more of a steady progression. A slow start against Lehigh, but a strong finish. A solid win over a Dartmouth team they had lost to in the season opener. Then three straight losses to the league's elite: Bucknell, Lafayette, Navy. But playing the latter two tough at home had set the stage for the three-game winning streak against the league's bottom three: Holy Cross, Army, Lehigh. Those two streaks were a pretty good summation of where Colgate was: well behind the top three, well ahead of the bottom three. They owned fourth.

"Now we really get to find out how much progress we've made the last couple weeks," Davis said. "We're four and five in the league and we've got the big three left to play."

It was Monday morning, February 14 — Valentine's Day. Colgate had bused from Lehigh to Navy on Saturday night and would make the six-hour bus trip back to Hamilton after the game that night. Gail Davis had made the trip — in the car with their two boys, who were two and a half and almost six months — stopping along the way to see her parents. For Emmett Davis, returning to Annapolis was always fun and emotional. It had been his home for twelve years, it was the place where he had met Gail (she had been an assistant coach for the Navy women's team), and it was a place where he still had many friends and still owned a home.

"Last year was a lot tougher," he said. "Walking back into Alumni Hall, seeing Coach DeVoe on the other bench, seeing all those kids who I had recruited and coached. It was very emotional for me. Now I'm a year removed from it. I've coached against them three times, I'm closer to my kids at Colgate, and it's become home now. I still root for them when they aren't playing us and I still have feelings for the kids I worked with, but it isn't as acute as it was a year ago."

Even so, it was different from your average road game. As Davis and his team finished their morning shootaround, DeVoe walked into the gym. "Hey, Emmett, when you're done, come into my office," he said. "I've got presents I need to give you for Gail and the kids."

For the record, DeVoe had not shown up bearing gifts at any of the other morning shootarounds that season.

Davis's players were fully aware of his feelings for Navy. In fact, they had been a little bit dubious when Colgate had hired a Navy guy. When Adonal Foyle first heard that Colgate had hired a Navy assistant, his eyebrows went up. "Put it this way," he said, "it gave me pause."

Even Diamond, whose older brother was at the academy, wondered about it. "At least at first I did," he said. "I mean, we were so used to hating those guys. But then you think about it: They've been the most successful program in the league. We all know what a great job Coach DeVoe has done. We figured if Coach Davis was a part of that, he must know what he was doing."

They had all gone through the adjustment from Bruen's occasionally intense personality, offset often by a laid-back jocularity, to
Davis's always intense personality, occasionally offset by jocularity.
Davis brought with him DeVoe's belief in man-to-man defense and a
mixture of his offense and some of the offensive principles he had
learned years earlier under Paul Evans. Almost all of Colgate's calls
were identical to Navy's.

"It's almost like a scrimmage when we play," Davis said. "We know
all their sets and calls, they know all ours."

Davis felt good about his team's chances to pull an upset. Like
everyone else in the league, he knew how well Navy was playing. It
had now won eight straight games since the loss at Lafayette. But he
thought his team was better than it had been when it had lost to the
Midshipmen twelve days earlier. The reason the teams were playing
again so soon was logistics: Colgate had asked Navy and the league
if it would be possible to play Navy out of the normal scheduling
order so it could break up the 325-mile bus trip, at least in one
direction.

Davis was 0-3 against his old school, but each game had been close.
He had no reason to believe this game would be any different. His
final locker room comment to his team was direct: "We've been close
against these guys three times," he said. "Let's get it done tonight. We
don't want close, we want a win. Close means nothing."

Like DeVoe, Davis always writes offensive and defensive goals on
the corner of the board before his final pregame talk. He had written:
"Gate — 60s, Navy — 50s." Down the hall, DeVoe's numbers were:
"Navy — 80s, Gate — 50s."

DeVoe must have known something. As it was now in the habit of
doing, Navy came out flying at the start. It was 10-2 after a Reggie
Skipworth 3 and Davis was already calming his troops. "We started
just like this down here last year, guys," he said. "Don't get flustered."

It didn't help that Diamond picked up two quick fouls trying to
guard Savane, who had become an almost unstoppable force inside. It didn't help that Navy looked to be playing six-on-five most
of the time. DeVoe brought freshman Kyle Barker, who had played
very little early in the season, off the bench early and he promptly
buried a 3. Navy looked capable of fielding a freshman team —

Scott Long, Jason Jeanpierre, Francis Ebong, Quintrell McCreary, and Barker — that would be competitive with a lot of teams in the league.

Colgate simply couldn't get into the game at either end of the floor. The lead built to 17-4, then 30-8. Davis kept trying to call time-outs to stop the avalanche, but it wasn't helping. At halftime it was 37-18.

During the break, Diamond apologized to the team for getting in foul trouble, acting as if he had somehow been singularly responsible for the margin. Everyone knew better. Davis reminded them they had been *up* 16 at Lehigh at halftime and hadn't thought the game was over. That meant this wasn't over.

Unfortunately, he was right. Navy just kept coming in waves (appropriately enough). It was 77-33 when DeVoe went to the deepest depths of his bench and backed off his defense a little. By then, Davis was screaming at his players to not look at the scoreboard and just play. That was easier said than done.

Even Chris Worthing, who had never completely gotten over the aftermath of August 26 and had been through a season so frustrating that he would end up trying out for the football team in spring practice, had a moment to remember. Late in the game, he made a steal and went in for a flying, windmill dunk that would have merited 10s across the board in the NBA slam dunk contest. It was the kind of move that had caused Doug Wojcik to trek to Kansas over and over in the winter of 1997 to recruit Worthing.

"Sportscenter," he screamed in the locker room later. If the game had been on TV, the dunk would most certainly have made Sportscenter. But, as is the case more often than not in the Patriot League, there was no TV. Worthing had to settle for knowing that a crowd of 1,758 in Alumni Hall had whooped it up along with him.

The final was 81-47 — that close only because Colgate's reserves managed to score the last 10 points of the game.

"My God," Davis said to his assistants before talking to the team. "We came close to being down fifty."

He was more awed than anything else. He had known after seeing the Lafayette score that Navy was playing at a new level, but he hadn't expected anything like this. He didn't even have a desire to scream at his players. He knew they were just as shocked as he was.

After home games, the Navy assistant coaches traditionally head to Riordan's to rehash the evening and, after a victory, to enjoy what they have just witnessed. Davis had been a part of many of those postgame sessions. He remembered one in 1997 when the Midshipmen had hammered Adonal Foyle's last Colgate team, 79-56. As the evening wore on, Davis had informally tracked the progress of the Colgate bus as it headed north and west.

"They should be passing through York about now."

An hour later. "Bus is on I-81 approaching Harrisburg."

And then: "Scranton looms."

Now, Davis would be on the highway while the Navy assistants sat at Riordan's and monitored his trip.

"Well," he said with a grim smile. "I guess what they say is true: what goes around, comes around."

Light snow was starting to fall. "Probably sixty in Hamilton," he said. He looked into his car, where Emmett Jr. and Shane were sleeping peacefully. It had been an embarrassing loss. It would be a long trip home. He could handle it.

FAREWELLS

WHILE Navy was in the process of destroying Colgate, Lafayette was struggling through a 71-69 victory at Stony Brook. The game had been scheduled as a homecoming for Brian Ehlers, and the brutal traffic the team encountered en route was blamed solely on Ehlers.

"I told them I don't live that far out," Ehlers said. "When they scheduled the game, I don't think they realized how far east Stony Brook is."

Exit 62 of the Long Island Expressway to be precise.

Navy's dismantling of Colgate, combined with Lafayette's difficulty in putting away Holy Cross at home and Stony Brook on the road, added to the consensus around the league that, even though the two teams were still tied for first place, Navy had become the number one league team. Both schools were now following the RPI rankings closely, since that appeared the likely tiebreaker. With the regular season beginning to wind down, Navy was at 131, Lafayette at 141.

Conference play in the Patriot League seems to come and go in a heartbeat, because each team plays only twelve games over seven weeks and because the conference tournament begins while most of the big-time leagues are still completing their regular seasons. That means mid-February has just passed when teams start playing their last home games.

Navy was the first league team to complete its home schedule. Strangely enough, the Mids had played their first three conference games on the road and would also play their last two on the road. In between, they had played six of seven at home. In all, the Mids played sixteen home games. Everyone else in the league played twelve or thirteen.

Like Navy, Lehigh would hold Senior Day on Saturday, February 19, even though the Lafayette game was not its home finale. Navy, three days later, would be the finale, but Lehigh decided to honor the seniors before they played their archrivals rather than before the Navy game.

Navy came into its last home game rested, since it had played Colgate on Monday, and rippling with the confidence that comes with hammering opponents game after game. "We had gotten to the point," Chris Williams said later, "where the starters felt as if we had let everyone down if we didn't have the subs in the game with ten minutes left."

Holy Cross had no such luxuries. After losing at Lafayette, the Crusaders had gone to New Hampshire and beaten a truly awful team, 73-53. "Darkest gym I've been in, and I coached a lot of years in high school," Ralph Willard said. "A shot would go up and you really never knew for sure whether it went in or not."

Enough had gone in (apparently) for the Crusaders to get to 9-15. They now knew that both Jared Curry and Patrick Whearty were not going to play again before season's end. The bright spot in that scenario was the fact that freshmen Tim Szatko and Brian Wilson had received extended playing time, and although they had experienced the ups and downs any freshman goes through, both had emerged as better players.

The one constant all season had been Josh Sankes. But now even he was hurting, with a sore back. It didn't keep him from playing, but it had to be monitored and watched. Sankes had first hurt himself taking a charge in practice. Willard couldn't get on him for trying to take a charge but he couldn't resist jokingly saying, "See what happens when you try something you aren't used to doing?"

On the surface, Holy Cross was nothing more than fodder for a Saturday afternoon party honoring Sitapha Savane and Jeremy Toton. A crowd of 3,585 had turned out, expecting to see another in the Midshipmen's continuing series of romps. In five league games at home, Navy was 5-0 with an average victory margin of 25.6 points per game. The closest anyone had come to them had been Bucknell, which had lost 75-61 after trailing by 27 midway through the second half. There was also the memory of the teams' meeting in Worcester, which had been close for about twenty-five minutes before Navy had blown to an 81-49 win.

And so, as is often the case when everyone expects a one-sided contest, the game was anything but one-sided. The second half of the first Navy game had been a genuine aberration for Holy Cross. The Crusaders had given up 80 points or more in three of their first four games. Since then, Navy had been the only opponent to hit the 80 mark. Holy Cross played good defense. Offense was another story: only once had the team scored 80 points in a game (in December, against Northeastern) and it had scored less than 60 points on thirteen occasions.

The Crusaders were good field, no hit.

The Navy game was no different. The Crusaders did something that teams never do to Navy: they hammered them on the boards. Every pregame scouting report done on the Mids emphasized rebounding. It was a point of great pride with DeVoe that his team was always one of the leaders in the country in rebounding margin, because rebounding is the product of three things: size, desire, and a willingness to give up your body. What the Midshipmen lacked in size, they always made up for with their desire and willingness to give up the body.

"If you can't rebound with them, you can't beat them," Fran O'Hanlon always told his players. "Keep them off the boards and you take away their number one weapon."

Holy Cross was able to do that all afternoon, and it made life difficult for Navy. Unaccustomed to a close game, the Mids were tight and uptight. DeVoe started Toton in his final home game but angrily yanked him when he tried an open 3-pointer from the top of the key with Navy clinging to a 22-19 lead.

"Jeremy, what are you thinking?" he demanded.

"Coach, I'm sorry," Toton said, "but I was open."

"Of course you were open!" DeVoe yelled. "They want you to take that shot. We're not here to give them what they want!"

But they did for most of the first half. When Ryan Serravalle buried a jumper at the buzzer to give Holy Cross a 28-24 lead, there were some seriously unhappy campers walking down the hall to the Navy locker room.

"Lehigh," trainer Loren Shipley said softly, raising the ugly specter of the tournament debacle of a year ago.

DeVoe was clearly thinking the same thing. He was all over the players during the break. "They are kicking our ass mentally," he said. "They're playing smart, we're playing dumb. They're on the boards, we're not. They're getting calls because they're playing harder than you are."

Someone handed DeVoe a first-half stat sheet. He glanced at it, then came to a number that clearly stunned him. "*One* offensive rebound?" he said. "Are you guys goddamn kidding me? You know that's unacceptable."

The first ten minutes of the second half were much like the first half. The best news for Navy was that Sankes picked up his third and fourth fouls on back-to-back possessions, both times on the offensive end of the floor. At Holy Cross he had picked up his fourth foul trying to get offensive position, and his departure had pretty much marked the end of the game. Not this time. Szatko and Juan Pegues were still controlling the inside and when Serravalle weaved through the defense for a layup, Holy Cross led 41-36 with 10:48 to go.

"Oh jeez, it's Lehigh all over again," moaned Athletic Director Jack Lengyel.

It was as if Lehigh was an invisible six-foot rabbit lurking at the end of the Navy bench.

But this Navy team was better than that Navy team had been. It had a better bench and more shooters. Jason Jeanpierre came in and hit a baseline jumper. Then Chris Williams made a steal, and his layup tied the game at 41. Willard called time to calm his team and Navy's crowd. His message was simple: "Keep fighting. Change nothing."

But Navy finally had momentum. The run reached 16-0 and the Holy Cross drought stretched to more than seven minutes before Guillermo Sanchez hit a jump shot. By then, it was 52-43 and the game was finally in hand for Navy. The Crusaders actually had one more run left in them, cutting the lead to 57-51 with Szatko on the line and 16 seconds left. But he missed both free throws and Chris Williams sealed the verdict by making one at the other end. The final was 58-51.

Willard didn't know whether to be overjoyed or depressed. He was amazed and impressed by his players' heart and their lack of quit. Everyone else in the league had been blown out by Navy in this building; there was no reason for them not to do the same thing. There wouldn't even have been any shame in it. But they had out-rebounded a great rebounding team 49-33 and had held them to 39 percent shooting. Savane, who had routinely been scoring 20 points a game in under 30 minutes, had been held to 9 points in 37 minutes by Sankes. Chris Williams had missed 8 of 12 free throws.

All of it — except the Williams free-throw shooting — was a credit to Holy Cross. It also meant that the game had been there to win. And it hadn't been won.

"If you can bring that kind of desire and toughness to the rest of the season, we will make some noise, I promise you that," Willard said. "We have two games left (Army and Lehigh) and if you play the way you did today, we'll win them both. Then we'll see what kind of damage we can do in the tournament."

As Willard spoke, Navy was conducting its senior ceremony. Unlike most teams, Navy honors its seniors after their last home game. This is a tradition that SID Scott Strasemeier had stolen from Indiana, where Bob Knight has always held his senior ceremony after the final home game has been completed. There was some risk in this approach, because the ceremony could lose a good deal of starch if the game was lost. Indiana had only lost once on Senior Day during Knight's tenure — in 1985 — and Knight had refused to return to the floor with his two seniors, Uwe Blab and Dan Dakich, that year. Strasemeier, who is one of those Indiana graduates who believe the chair that Knight threw years ago got exactly what it deserved, still liked the idea of holding the ceremony after the game, regardless of the risks.

After a win, it worked quite well. DeVoe spoke at length about how far Toton and Savane had come as basketball players and as midshipmen. He talked about Toton's selflessness and said there was no doubt in his mind that Savane should be the Patriot League player of the year.

Both players got emotional when it was their turn to speak. Toton talked about the tough times, the frustrations, but how he had gotten through it thanks to his teammates and his best friend: Savane.

Savane was suprised how emotional he found himself getting, first when Toton hugged him at the end of his speech, then when it was his turn to talk. He had witnessed other Senior Days and thought they were kind of overblown. "I'm not too sentimental," he said later. "I thought it was just an American thing, you know, let's all say good-bye and have a good cry. I was surprised when I found myself having a good cry."

Toton made him cry first. "Thanks for doing that before I have to talk, Jeremy," he said. Then he too talked about all that had gone on in four years, the mistakes he had made, the lessons he had learned. Neither player used notes, as seniors at big-time schools often do when asked to talk. They didn't need them. They spoke their minds and from their hearts. The whole place was standing and cheering when they were finished.

"One last thing," Savane said. "This was *not* our last home game. We'll be back here for the Patriot League championship game."

Navy was now 20-5 — DeVoe's fourth 20-win season in eight years at the academy — and 9-1 in the league, with Lehigh and Army left to play. Everyone was convinced they would be back in Alumni on March 10 for the league title game.

"Maybe if we do that," DeVoe told the crowd, "we'll get some mids to want to come out and watch us play."

They introduced the four Lehigh seniors before the start of the Lehigh-Lafayette game that night. Which was a good idea for two reasons: Lafayette went on to win the game and Fido Willybiro wasn't around for the finish.

The game was typical Lehigh-Lafayette. Lafayette had won the last seven times the teams had played, dating back to O'Hanlon's first season at Lafayette. Neither Mentesana nor any of the seniors — Willybiro, Steve Aylsworth, Jared Hess, and the injured Pete DeLea — had ever beaten Lafayette. But they had been achingly close on a number of occasions, even the previous year when they had lost the game in Stabler 73-70. That game said a lot about the rivalry: a 6-22 team taking on a 22-8 team and the game had been decided in the final minute.

This game started out to be Lehigh's moment. With what was by far the largest crowd of the season — 3,221 — making a lot of noise from the start, Lafayette jumped to a quick 9-2 lead. But then Lehigh — specifically Aylsworth, the noted Lafayette killer — got hot. The Mountain Hawks led, 37-25, with under four minutes left in the half, before a 10-2 Lafayette run closed the gap to 39-35 at halftime.

The game was still tight, with just under twelve minutes left, when one play turned it around completely. With the game tied at 49, Frank Barr caught the ball in the low post and backed in on Willybiro. Giving away seven inches, Willybiro did everything he could to push Barr away from the basket. For his efforts, he was rewarded with a foul call by referee Jim Haney. Already frustrated by the pushing and shoving with Barr, then getting the foul called, Willybiro lost it for a second, throwing an elbow at Barr's head.

Haney was looking right at the play. As soon as Willybiro swung the elbow, he was gone — automatic technical, automatic ejection. Barr plays as hard as anyone, but proving that he was true to the Christian teachings that are so important to him, he literally turned the other cheek.

Haney, who grew up in the Lehigh Valley and still lives there, often works games in the big-time leagues. But he willingly takes Patriot League assignments in order to cut down on his travel schedule. Throwing Willybiro out of a Lehigh-Lafayette game, especially with the score tied, disturbed him.

"I had no choice," he said. "I was almost hoping Barr might retaliate so I could call something on both of them. But he just walked away from it. I know Fido's a good kid and he just lost it for an instant. But the rules are clear. Sal was screaming that it was retaliation, but it wasn't. I was looking right at the whole play."

Mentesana was furious, Willybiro was gone, and Lehigh was unhinged. Lafayette got five points out of the play — one-of-two free throws by Barr, two by Brian Burke for the technical, and a jump shot by Ehlers on the ensuing inbounds. The game went from tied to

54-49, and Willybiro, who had been having an excellent night with 11 points and seven rebounds, was banished to the locker room. Lafayette dominated the last ten minutes, cruising to a 77-63 win.

There was certainly no guarantee that Lehigh was going to win the game, but Mentesana was as close as he gets to speechless about what had happened. "I'll even go so far as to say that Lafayette probably would have figured out a way to beat us because they're that good a team," he said. "But that call ended the game. It wasn't fair. There should have been another way to handle it."

Haney wished that there was. "If I let it go and then there's a brawl a minute later, who's to blame for letting it happen?" he said. "I've known Sal since we were kids. I love the guy. But it wasn't a debatable call."

The win left Lafayette tied with Navy at 9-1 in the league with one week left in the regular season. Bucknell was third at 6-3. Then came Colgate at 4-7, Lehigh at 3-7, Holy Cross at 2-8, and Army at 1-9. Navy's lead in the now all-important RPI was nine spots — 134 to 143. And counting.

25

FAMILY FEUD

IT all began innocently enough. Fran O'Hanlon was sitting in his office on the morning of Tuesday, February 22, working on his Thought for the Day, a quote he always put on the daily practice plan for the players to see. Most either glanced at it or giggled at it. Only Nate Klinkhammer took the time to learn it. If the Lafayette players suspected O'Hanlon might be in the mood to quiz them on it, they would run to Klinkhammer and say, "Klink, quick, what's the thought?"

O'Hanlon had just found a lengthy one: "Nature is at work, character and destiny are her handiwork. She gives us love and hate, jealousy and reverence. All that is ours is the power to choose which impulse we shall follow."

O'Hanlon was admiring his own handiwork when the phone rang. It was Corky Blake, the Patriot League beat writer for the *Easton Express-Times*. Blake knows and understands the league as well as anyone, having covered it since its inception. He was working on a story for the weekend on the tiebreaker, how the rule change had come about two springs earlier, and how the coaches felt about the RPI, which Blake believed was full of fatal flaws that rendered it almost as unfair as a coin flip.

O'Hanlon was aware of all this. He didn't disagree with anything Blake was saying, but still thought it was better than the coin flip, even if Lafayette did end up losing the tiebreaker to Navy. He was certain, he said, the Mids would opt for the home court in the final, just as they had done two years ago, and give Lafayette the first-round bye once again.

"Fran," Blake said. "You're missing something here. There is no option anymore. They win the tiebreaker, they get everything."

No, no, O'Hanlon insisted. That's not the way it works. The winner gets to choose one or the other. It doesn't get both.

"Fran," Blake said, "you better read the Patriot League rule book."

O'Hanlon hung up with Blake and went and found a rule book. There it was, clear as could be, on page 23: "In the event of all tie-breakers failing to break a tie, the RPI rankings will be used to determine the bye and any home-court advantage."

O'Hanlon was stunned. "I had no memory of ever voting for that," he said. "I thought when we voted to use the RPI, it was with the understanding that whoever won on that basis would get to choose home court or the bye."

Don DeVoe remembered it the same way. "It never occurred to me that it wasn't a choice," he said.

In fact, earlier in the year DeVoe and his staff had actually discussed which option they would choose in that situation. Assistant Coach Nathan Davis had raised the possibility of choosing the bye because a semifinal against Bucknell would probably be more difficult than a semifinal against whoever finished fourth. DeVoe had shaken the suggestion off. "You've got to get that final game at home," he said. "Check out league history, it's the difference maker. If we can't beat Bucknell on a neutral site [Lafayette] then we're not good enough to get where we want to go anyway."

Now the rules said there was no choice to be made. In the old days, when the coin flip was still an option, the rule had said that if the tie was broken without a flip — by head-to-head record or by records against other league teams — the winner would get both home court and the bye. Only in the event of a flip was there a split. O'Hanlon and DeVoe had both assumed that the split remained in place when the RPI replaced the flip. Not so.

The only other league coaches who had been at that meeting were Sal Mentesana and Pat Flannery. Pat Harris hadn't yet been named the coach at Army in May of 1998; Ralph Willard was still coaching at Pittsburgh; and Emmett Davis was one of DeVoe's assistants at Navy.

Mentesana, who had technically been in charge of the meeting, initially thought that the vote had been to give the RPI winner everything. But when Blake asked him about it on that Tuesday afternoon, his memory wasn't clear. "I may have to go try to find my notes," he said. Only Flannery remembered voting to give the RPI winner everything. "I thought when we decided to take luck out of it, we also took the split out," he said.

The person who was least happy about the whole flap had to be Carolyn Schlie Femovich. She had still been an administrator at Penn when all of this had occurred. Now she was being bombarded by calls from Lafayette and from the media — especially those who covered Lafayette — wanting to know what she intended to do about the situation.

"There's nothing for me to do," Femovich said. "There's a rule book and I've got to follow what's in it."

She was, of course, right. All of which made the Lafayette people that much more crazy.

"This isn't going to just go away," O'Hanlon said. "This isn't what we voted for. I'm not letting it go."

O'Hanlon is a man of his word. Which meant it was going to be a long week for Carolyn Femovich.

On the night O'Hanlon received the news about the tiebreaker, Pat Harris sat in the coaches' lounge off the Army locker room, talking to his assistant coaches. The last thing in the world he was concerned about was a Lafayette-Navy tiebreaker or the RPI rankings.

All he wanted to do was beat Holy Cross.

And for the first time in several weeks, he had some hope.

Six days earlier, in a season filled with valleys, Harris had reached a personal low. His team had lost at Lafayette 69-43 in a game blown open by a 20-2 Lafayette run in the first half. But that had not been what made Harris most miserable. He knew Lafayette was a very good basketball team, one capable of getting on a shooting roll that would make it tough for his team to compete. But on two occasions during the game, he had seen what he believed were plays that bordered the line between aggressive and dirty: a Stefan Ciosici elbow in Adam Glosier's back, and a Reggie Guy elbow aimed at Michael Canty.

In neither case had anyone on Harris's team responded. "They backed down," Harris said. "I can live with us being beaten by superior talent. I can't live with us being out-toughed, with guys running away from someone coming after them. You have to stand up for yourself; you have to stand up for your teammates. No one did either."

The next afternoon Harris walked into the locker room at West Point carrying two pictures with him. Both had been hanging behind his desk. One was of Seth Barrett jostling with Duke's Elton Brand for rebounding position. The other was of Joe Clark releasing a jump shot that looked like it had been taken off a clinic tape. His form was perfect. Without even seeing the result, there was almost no doubt the shot had gone in.

It was time, Harris told the players, for what he called a "Go to Jesus Meeting." Everyone needed to look inside, look at himself, and look around the room with one notion in mind: this isn't good enough.

He started by replaying the two plays from the previous night. How, he asked, could any of you accept that? How can we allow that to happen? What, he demanded to know, are you afraid of? The only thing to be afraid of was losing and they were already doing that: nine in a row; 19 of 20; 21 of 24 for the season.

"Fellas, let me ask you a question," he said, standing in the middle of the room, between the two rows of lockers and directly in front of a third row. "How many of you would describe yourselves as being passionate about basketball?"

Almost every hand in the room went up.

"Okay then, let me ask you this: Last Sunday, when we had the day off after the trip to Bucknell, how many of you came up here on your own to shoot?"

This time, two hands went up.

"You see, fellas, passion for something means doing it when you don't have to. In fact, real passion means doing it when it isn't easy.

When I was a kid, I used to shovel snow off the schoolyard court near my house so I could shoot. I was passionate about the game — for better or worse.

"I know it's not easy here. I know the demands that are made on you guys. But if you're truly passionate, you have to figure out ways to make yourself better. You don't accept losing, you get really pissed off at it. And if someone swings an elbow at you, you make the sonofabitch pay for it. That way it won't happen again."

He held up the pictures of Barrett and Clark.

"What happened to these two guys?" Harris asked, showing each player his picture. "What happened to the Seth Barrett who weighed a rock solid 242 and wasn't the least bit afraid of Elton Brand? Where did the Joe Clark who had perfect shooting form go? I know you guys are better than what you've been showing because I've seen it. I've got the evidence right here in my hands. These pictures are staying down until we find this Seth Barrett and this Joe Clark again. I know they exist. But we've got to find them again, somehow, some way."

Harris had gone into the season conservatively figuring that his two juniors would produce about 25 points and 12 rebounds a game between them. At that moment they were producing just about half of that: 12 points and 6 rebounds. Both had been taken out of the starting lineup. Harris didn't question their effort or desire, he just thought that each, in his own way, had talked himself out of being the player he could be or should be. He was hoping to shock them back into being themselves.

Harris talked for several more minutes before he and his coaches left the room. He told them to take all the time they needed to talk to one another, to tell each other what they were really thinking, and, if they had any problems with anything he had said, to come and tell him. The players spent a full hour in the locker room. They talked about backing each other up more; about sticking together; about the need to get Clark's and Barrett's pictures back on Harris's wall.

"Mostly," said Chris Spatola, "we talked about being sick of losing, about how we were too willing to accept it. It was the best meeting I've been a part of in two years."

Two nights later, playing an Albany team that had dominated them at home, the Cadets built a 10-point lead in the second half and won,

52-45, their first road win in more than a year. They outrebounded the Great Danes 46-27, with Jonte Harrell and Adam Glosier each coming up with 14. It was the best confidence boost possible because it was proof that digging down and playing forty minutes of Army basketball could work.

It was into this atmosphere that Holy Cross arrived at Christl Arena. The Crusaders hadn't won a league game since their last game against Army on January 30. But they were feeling pretty good about themselves because they had played both Lafayette and Navy close and had beaten New Hampshire in between. Willard knew that a win — any win — would be a boost for Army's confidence, and he warned his players to expect Army to come after them.

"Right now they're sitting at the other end of the hall thinking they have a great opportunity to beat you," he told his players. "Let's get that idea out of their heads right away. Let's make it clear we're the better team and we've come here to get a win and get out of here. Okay?"

They nodded. Willard felt good, because they had practiced very hard the day before the bus trip down I-84 and across the Newburg Bridge to the banks of the Hudson. He knew that both teams had fragile egos — especially on offense — and a good start by his team could knock Army backward in a hurry. The Crusaders then caught a huge break early when Spatola picked up two quick fouls and had to come out after two minutes with the score tied 4-4. Juan Pegues promptly hit a three to put Holy Cross up 7-4, and it began to look like it would be another long night for Army.

Only it didn't continue that way. Jonte Harrell, who had been mired in a shooting slump, hit a three pointer. Then sophomore Jerry Crockett, in for Spatola, hit a three — his fourth of the season — and Army had a lead, 10-7. Joe Quinn subbed for Crockett and *he* hit a three — his fifth. By now Willard was rolling his eyes. He had mentioned Quinn and Crockett on the scouting report as "two little guards who play a little bit." That had been accurate. Now, each had shown he could shoot a little bit, too.

The Quinn three made it 17-10. Then Seth Barrett came in and started to look like the Seth Barrett who had been on Harris's wall. When he went over the entire Holy Cross front line to rebound a miss and score, Willard was off the bench screaming, "Would somebody please box out!"

Joe Clark came in. He also hit a three, meaning that four Army players — none named Spatola — had hit threes in the first half. The Cadets led 24-16 at the break.

The only question in the Holy Cross locker room at halftime was who was angrier, Willard or Chris Spitler. Willard couldn't believe they were allowing themselves to be outhustled by Army at both ends of the floor. The deflections — nine — were telling. Spitler sat in the back of the small room, head buried, while Willard talked. When Willard mentioned that the team had played harder in practice on Monday than it was now playing in the game, Spitler picked his head up.

"Why do we kill each other in practice every single day and then come into a game and let them jump all over us?" he screamed. "This is ridiculous. We need to go out and kill *them!*"

Willard let Spitler's words hang in the air for a moment. He knew the rest of the team would listen because it was unlike Spitler to get angry with anyone other than himself. They were all sitting up now, alert, listening. He went through Army's sets one more time and warned them to watch for Spatola to come out shooting at the start of the second half. He decided to start Spitler in the second half. "Let's see if he can give us a boost," he told the coaches.

Army was almost brimming with confidence. As they came to the bench to start the second half, Assistant Coach Marty Coyne pointed to the Holy Cross bench and said, "They just aren't having any fun playing against you right now."

Before the second half was five minutes old, Willard had spent three time-outs trying to regroup. Nothing was working. Josh Sankes looked sore and weary inside. Army kept hitting threes. Michael Canty stole a pass from Spitler and fed Charles Woodruff for a layup. Willard took Spitler out, started to say something about the pass, and then saw the pained look on his face. "Good hustle," he said. Spitler buried his head in a towel.

It was a romp, an out-and-out stomping for Army. Three days earlier, facing the hottest team in the league, Holy Cross had led Navy 41-36 with 10 minutes left in the game. Now, playing 1-9 in the league Army, the Crusaders trailed 41-28 at the 10-minute mark. It only got worse. The biggest lead was 19, the last time at 56-37 with 2:27 to go. After that, Harris had the rare pleasure of clearing his bench. The final, with Holy Cross scoring the game's last six points, was 60-48.

Willard was stunned. It was the first time all season that he had honestly felt that the opponent had beaten his team because it wanted to win the game more. This had nothing to do with injuries or travel troubles or lack of talent. Army had played harder. It had, as Frank Mastrandrea was reminded at the finish, played forty minutes of Army basketball.

"That was a complete and total disgrace," Willard said in the locker room. "I want everyone on the bus in five minutes. There is absolutely nothing to be said about this right now. And I don't want to hear a single word on the bus ride home. I don't want to hear anyone *breathing* loud. No one is entitled to talk about anything."

He started to walk out. Bravely, Ryan Serravalle said very softly, "Coach, we didn't pray."

Willard paused for a moment. "After that performance," he said, "you don't deserve to talk to God."

Needless to say, the feeling in the Army locker room was 180 degrees different. "How good does it feel?" Harris asked rhetorically. "That's what can happen when you go out and play with confidence and get after a team the whole game. I'm proud as hell of all of you."

The locker room was crowded with celebrants. One of them was the school's new commandant, Eric Olson, who had played lacrosse in his undergraduate days at West Point. He went around the room, player to player, saying the exact same words to each one:

"Good win. On to Navy."

At Army, that's the way it is. A win is nice. But it's always on to Navy.

Senior Night at Lafayette was a little different than at the other schools, because everyone knew the game would not be the last appearance in Kirby arena for the four seniors. Since the first two rounds of the Patriot League Tournament would be played there, Lafayette would play at least one more home game and could play as many as three — if it hosted the final — before the white uniforms would be put away for good.

Even so, Fran O'Hanlon was a little bit concerned that the game against Colgate might be emotional for the players. Stefan Ciosici and Nate Klinkhammer had both come back from season-ending injuries the previous year to play again. Brian Ehlers had come a long way from the days as a freshman when he couldn't finish practice to be the league's player of the year. And, even though Mike Homer's career hadn't panned out the way he had hoped, he had grown a lot during his four years at Lafayette and had given a lot of thought to what it would mean to not be a basketball player anymore.

"There's no feeling quite like putting on a uniform with a bunch of guys you feel so close to and then going out and playing in front of a crowd," he said. "You can play rec-league ball the rest of your life and it will never feel the way it feels to play college basketball. I'm ready to move on with my life, but I know I'll miss it."

Homer's degree would be in art. Ehlers's in business/economics, Klinkhammer's in biology, and Ciosici's in biology and German, the double major being a requirement for him to receive a fifth year of financial aid. As each senior was introduced, his major followed his name. In the ACC or the Big East, it's usually points per game. In fact, at one Big East school — Georgetown — the majors of the players are kept a strict secret. They aren't mentioned in the media guide and you aren't supposed to ask what they are.

Any concerns O'Hanlon had about his players being too emotional about Senior Night faded fast. He started Klinkhammer and Homer, and on the game's second possession, Homer made a steal and went the length of the court for a layup, getting a standing ovation from the Zoo Crew for his effort. It was 20-7 after eleven minutes and 40-16 at halftime when Tyson Whitfield banked in a 30-footer at the buzzer.

Emmett Davis went off on his team at halftime. "You know why that last shot went in?" he screamed. "Because you let them get started! You didn't fight at all. Why isn't there any fight in you on the road? That's inexcusable! You give them forty points in a half? They are *not* that goddamn good!"

He walked out of the locker room, slumped against a wall, and said, "They're playing pretty goddamn well."

They were. The minislump brought on by the Navy loss had passed. The spark had returned, perhaps brought on by the controversy over the tiebreaker. The final was 92-51. Everyone got to play for Lafayette. The seniors lingered when the game was over, taking pictures in uniform with friends and family.

Down the road, Navy had beaten Lehigh just about as easily, 89-53. Navy and Lafayette were both now 10-1 in the league. Navy would finish the season on Saturday at Army. Lafayette would conclude on Sunday at Bucknell. The final weekend would decide a lot.

26

AND THE WINNER IS . . .

THE final weekend of the regular season lined up this way: Navy at Army, noon on Saturday. There would be no senior ceremony because Army had no seniors. Not even a manager. At seven o'clock that night Lehigh would be at Holy Cross. Senior Night would be Chris Spitler Night. Rumor had it there were so many Spitlers on the road from Buffalo to Worcester that extra tollbooths had to be opened on the New York State Thruway. Finally, on Sunday, Lafayette would be at Bucknell at four o'clock for what would probably be a tense, important game and an emotional day for the seven departing seniors — five players, two managers. Colgate had completed league play at Lafayette and would finish the regular season with two nonleague home games.

The standings looked this way: Navy and Lafayette were 10-1. Bucknell was locked into third place at 8-3 and Colgate would finish fourth at 4-8, because even if Lehigh, which was 3-8, won at Holy Cross, Colgate would win that tiebreaker because it had beaten the Mountain Hawks twice. Holy Cross was 2-9 but could still jump over Lehigh into fifth with a victory because it had a win over Colgate. Army was also 2-9. If it somehow beat Navy and Holy Cross beat Lehigh, Army would be the fifth seed because it would have a win over Navy, something neither Holy Cross nor Lehigh could claim.

In short, everyone playing except for Bucknell had something at stake in terms of seeding. And Bucknell wanted a win as badly as anybody, to make a statement and because of Senior Day.

As much as Pat Harris hated losing to Navy, he felt Don DeVoe had built a program that was a benchmark for his own. He had gone so far as to call DeVoe the day after the game in Annapolis to ask him how he handled things like the prep school, weight training, and finding free time for individual work for his players. It was that model that he had presented to Rick Greenspan when he and his boss had discussed what needed to be done to turn the program around.

Harris had received his all-league ballot that week. He had voted for Sitapha Savane as player of the year and for DeVoe as coach of the year. "His team was picked second or third and they've played the best basketball of anyone," he said. "He deserves it, but I bet he doesn't get it because there's a bias in this league against Navy."

Harris knew some of that bias existed because Navy had been good and some of it was because of Navy's perceived advantages. But he also believed some of it got back to attitude. "Last year we had the ball on a possession up here and I got up and told Joe Quinn to take the ball straight to the basket. He did, and Skip Victor [then a Navy senior] came over and blocked the shot. Fine. Good play. But then he turns to me and says, 'Coach, don't ever send someone in here again.'

"I was pissed. I just didn't think someone from Navy should speak to someone that way. I know no one from Army would get away with it. I said something to Don about it after the game. He didn't say anything, but later, Doug Wojcik came to the locker room to apologize."

All of which left Harris dealing with a conundrum. He liked DeVoe and his staff, he respected Navy. And he wished like hell he had more kids with in-your-face instincts. As long as they knew where to draw the line. "On the one hand, I want a couple of real MFs," he said. "You need them. On the other hand, I'm not sure I can coach kids like that or that they'll make it at the academy."

As always, Army-Navy produced Christl Arena's largest crowd of the year: 3,172. Although the entire Corps wasn't called out, one regiment was and it was placed strategically behind the benches to make sure the CBS-TV cameras had a clear shot of enthusiastic cadets making the place look close to full. The game was on CBS because Navy Athletic Director Jack Lengyel had negotiated a clause into the Army-Navy football contract several years earlier that required the network to televise one Army-Navy basketball game each year. Of course, Lengyel couldn't control how many markets CBS actually showed the game in, and in this case, the answer was seven: New York, Baltimore, Washington, Albany, Salisbury (Maryland), and Norfolk and Richmond (Virginia).

"That's seven more markets than we would be in without the contract," Army Sports Information Director Bob Beretta said.

True. And the CBS banner looked very good right up near the front of each school's media guide every year. Nowhere in those pictures was an asterisk that said, "Seen in seven markets." All it said was CBS.

Since this was the N*-A* game, the brass from both schools was out in full force. Everyone from Navy was brimming with confidence. Everyone except DeVoe, who had his team up at 7 A.M. because the only time to get into Christl for a shootaround was at 7:30 and he was taking nothing for granted. "My guys are used to being up at that hour," he said. "Why not take advantage?"

Nonetheless, his belief in the difference between the two teams was apparent when he wrote his numbers in the top right-hand corner of the blackboard: "Navy-80s, Army-40s." When Savane gathered his teammates around him for their final word, the three words he asked for in unison were "Blow Them Out."

Harris and his players knew they needed something approaching a perfect game to have a chance. "Beating Navy is a very difficult thing for anyone in this league to accomplish right now," he told his team. "Their record speaks to that. The road to the NCAA Tournament in the Patriot League still leads through Navy. But remember this: there is nothing better, no better feeling than beating Navy. You have to go out there today and be better than your best."

They certainly tried. Chris Spatola opened the game with a three, and five minutes in it was 10-2, Army. Christl was actually rocking. No one was reading a schoolbook. "It's funny," Savane said later, looking back on that early Army burst. "That was the first time I ever really felt the Army-Navy rivalry, because they were really after us. They were knocking us down and going at us full force. It was very, very intense. I remember saying to Jeremy [Toton], 'So this is how the football players feel.'"

That feeling lasted most of the first half. After Navy had worked its way back to a 20-16 lead, Joe Clark buried a three to make it 20-19. Then two things happened that Army simply couldn't afford: first, Barrett, who had played with the kind of fire Harris had been pleading for all year, picked up his second foul. Worse than that, a few seconds later, Spatola and Jason Jeanpierre chased a loose ball down. Spatola knew Navy was going to get possession — Army had lost the ball in the frontcourt and it had gone into the backcourt — but he wanted to be certain the lightning-quick Jeanpierre didn't beat him to the ball and end up with a layup. Both players dove for the ball and Spatola got a hand on it to stop the play. But he came up limping in pain, having rolled his ankle.

With Barrett and Spatola out, Navy quickly scored the next six points. After team doctor Dean Taylor looked at the ankle and confirmed that it was sprained but not broken, trainer Ian Wood taped it tightly, allowing Spatola to hobble back into the game. Taylor warned Spatola he was going to be very sore by game's end. He knew he had to say it. He also knew Spatola would ignore him.

By now, though, Navy had control. DeVoe kept bringing in fresh, talented players and Army was wearing down. It was 30-21 at halftime. Marty Coyne shook his head sadly when the coaches met to talk: "They go to the bench and they're just as good," he said. "We go to the bench and we're struggling to survive."

In the locker room, Barrett was pleading with his teammates. "If you've ever dug down, dig even deeper now," he said. "This can get done, but only if we're willing to die to do it."

They were willing, but not able. Navy was relentless, getting the ball inside to Savane, getting solid play inside and out from Chris Williams, and getting points from six different players off the bench. The lead built steadily to 55-31. Army kept trying right to the finish but there was no question which team was superior. The final was 65-47.

As soon as the final notes to "Blue and Gold" faded, the Midshipmen raced to their locker room to celebrate. They had finished 11-1 in the league. Coming into the weekend their RPI margin had been 125 to 146. "That's it, you guys have done it," DeVoe told them. "We'll be the number one seed in the tournament and we'll have the bye and home court advantage. You earned it. I'm proud as hell of you."

The only person in the room who wasn't beaming and celebrating was SID Scott Strasemeier. He was the team's computer geek, the RPI-ologist so to speak. "Army's rated very low in the RPI," he said softly. "We'll go down, even winning. And Bucknell is actually ranked higher than Lafayette right now [143 to 146] because they played such a tough nonconference schedule. I'm not saying we won't get it, but if Lafayette wins . . ."

He didn't finish the sentence. He just hoped the celebration wasn't premature.

The announced attendance at the Hart Center that night was 1,104. Not counting people named Spitler it might have been closer to 104.

He had never planned on being the center of attention at his final home game. In fact, the thought had never really occurred to him. When he had made the team as a walk-on sophomore, there had been three recruited players in his class: James Stowers, Tony Gutierrez, and Malik Waters. He had never known from year to year if he had a spot on the team. Now, he was Senior Night.

Ralph Willard had seen Stowers earlier that day. He had gone into the weight room to ride a stationary bike for a while and there was Stowers, finishing a workout. He walked over to his ex-coach with a wide grin on his face.

"Coach," he said, "I'm killing 'em in class."

Willard gave him a high five. "I couldn't have been happier for the kid," he said. "He decided what he wanted and he went out to get it. Good for him."

Spitler had wanted to play basketball. Like Mike Homer, who had thought a lot about the life-changing notion of never putting on a real uniform again, he was fully aware of the fact that a phase of his life was coming to a close. "I will be the king of rec-league players," he said. "They'll have to drag me off the court someday. But I know it won't be the same as this."

No, it wouldn't be. Thirty minutes before tip-off, Spitler found out he was starting, which surprised him. The game was important to the Crusaders. After all the work they had done and all they had overcome during the season, a loss would leave them tied for sixth place with Army. A win and they would tie Lehigh for fifth and be the fifth seed in the tournament. A game with Colgate — a team they had beaten once — was a lot more appealing than a game against Bucknell.

But starting Spitler was hardly a stretch. He had started four games during the season and the second half against Army based on merit, not being a senior. Willard's theme for the game was direct: Pride and Payback. They owed Lehigh one for the game in Bethlehem four weeks earlier. They owed themselves one for the game at Army four days earlier.

Knowing that most of the living Spitlers on the planet (okay, twenty-two in all) would be in the building, Frank Mastrandrea had outdone himself in writing the Senior Night introduction for Spitler. A simple recounting of the three phases of Spitler might have sufficed, but Mastrandrea wrote an ode to a walk-on, chronicling Spitler's career.

Some excerpts (the entire text is on file at the Library of Congress): "He has appeared in 61 career games, starting 16 [now 17] times. A 78 percent free-throw shooter, he has averaged 3.2 points per game and scored in double figures five times. . . . After serving as a seldom-used reserve for the first half of his sophomore season, he earned a starting assignment at Bucknell and scored 11 points. He then started eight of the last nine games that year, and has played an important role on the team ever since. . . ."

Still more: "In a game at Lehigh last season, he hit a pair of free throws with just eight seconds left, to preserve a four-point Crusader victory. . . . This season he had a career-high seven assists against Northeastern, and scored 12 points in the win over Sacred Heart. Against Lehigh, he hit four-of-six from three-point range and scored a career-high 15 points. . . .

"Beyond the numbers, though, this Crusader has become a Hart Center favorite for his scrappy play and boundless enthusiasm. And while he may have walked *on* the team three years ago, tonight he walks *off* the court with our respect and appreciation.

"Ladies and gentlemen, the six-one guard from North Buffalo, New York . . . number 11, Chris Spitler!"

Everyone was standing and there were some wet Spitler eyes. The players on the Lehigh bench were standing and applauding, too, because Sal Mentesana had brought his team back to the court (perhaps unaware of the length of the introduction) for the ceremony. "It's the right thing to do," he said. "We're in the same league, why not show some respect for them and for him. Kids like him are what's right about the game anyway. I'm glad to do it."

It was one of those nice moments in college basketball. On a day when Duke Coach Mike Krzyzewski had to plead with his student body not to taunt St. John's guard Erik Barkley, who was one of a number of big-name players being investigated by the NCAA, the Lehigh basketball team was more than happy to stand and clap for an opponent.

Then the Mountain Hawks went about the task of trying to ruin the evening for him. Jared Hess, finally healthy after missing four games because of the injuries he had suffered at Brown, started the game with a three. Matt Logie then made one and Hess hit a jumper and a three before the game was four minutes old. Lehigh led 11-7. But the Crusaders came back. Proving there was some kind of karma in the air, Josh Sankes, Spitler's best buddy, hit two straight free throws to put Holy Cross ahead, 15-14. They went back and forth until halftime, back-to-back threes by Ryan Serravalle and Brian Wilson giving Holy Cross a 32-28 lead.

Mentesana was incensed with the officiating, specifically the fact that Holy Cross had shot 15 free throws, his team zero. Sankes had returned to normal after his first two, missing four in a row. Otherwise, the margin might have been much wider. Three minutes into the second half, Eddie Lacayo was fouled going to the basket by Tim Szatko and went to the line. As he did, Mentesana stood up and said, "Well, it only took twenty-three minutes for us to get to the line."

Much to his surprise, that crack earned him a technical foul. Mentesana shook his head and said, "If I got a T for that, watch what comes next."

For the rest of the evening he and officials Paul Smith, Bill McCarthy, and Michael Brophy jawed at one another. The game was rough and the officials were calling almost everything. The two teams shot a combined 57 free throws in the second half — 37 by Holy Cross. At one point, Mentesana got truly angry and ordered his players not to defend. "Everyone back up into the paint," he yelled. "Don't guard anyone. We're having a *protest* possession."

It had to be an NCAA first. A team boycotting defense on its coach's orders. Naturally, Holy Cross threw the ball away.

Holy Cross made a total of six field goals in the second half — including one during an 11-minute stretch — but still pulled away in the last 10 minutes, thanks to all the fouls. Spitler's only two points of the night came — naturally — at the foul line. With the game still close — 42-40 — and 12:12 left, he made both ends of a one-and-one to up the lead to four. An 11-2 run shortly after that put the game away.

Willard took Spitler out with 18 seconds left. He got one more ovation and hugs up and down the bench. The final was 72-57. Mentesana was still angry about the officiating — "Talk about three blind mice," he cracked — but angrier with his team. "They played with more heart, more guts, and more courage than you," he said. "That's why they won. We've now got five days to turn this thing around and figure out how to beat Bucknell. The talent to do it is in this room, but not playing like that."

The win made Holy Cross 10-17. On the outside, looking at the record, it would not appear that very much had changed in a year. The Crusaders had been 7-20 a year earlier. But on the inside, everyone knew what had gone into those ten wins, that the players had, almost every night, done the one thing Willard always asked them to do: come back to the locker room a better team than when they left.

And they had gotten Spitler a win on his last night as a player in the Hart Center. An hour after the game ended, he was still in uniform, posing for picture after picture with family and friends.

"I don't think he's ever going to take the uniform off," Kevin Spitler said, watching happily as his younger sons picked their big brother up for one more picture.

There is an NCAA rule that requires student-athletes to return their game uniforms at the end of a season. Three years after Holy

Cross grudgingly gave Chris Spitler a uniform, no one at the school was inclined to ask him to give it back.

The opening words of the game-day press release put out by the Lafayette sports information department for the Bucknell game spoke volumes about the mood at Lafayette: "A game that many coaches and players thought would have seeding significance for the Patriot League Tournament will only feature a battle for respect. Lafayette, which is tied atop the Patriot league standings with Navy at 10-1, has already been 'assured' of the second seed in the tournament due to the final tiebreaker [RPI] . . ."

Take that, Patriot League.

Fran O'Hanlon was still seething about the nonsplit after the RPI tiebreaker had been decided. He had called it a joke in print and had decided to start his second five in the Bucknell game, forcing Jack Corrigan and Kelly Tripucka, who would be calling the game on Patriot League TV, to address both the issue and his anger even before tip-off. After all, how else would they explain the presence of Brian Ehlers, Stefan Ciosici, Tyson Whitfield, Tim Bieg, and Rob Worthington on the bench?

The entire Patriot League office was in Davis Gym on a gray, rainy Sunday afternoon, and Carolyn Femovich was still being peppered with questions. Behind the scenes, Lafayette Athletic Director Eve Atkinson had asked (in no uncertain terms) for a conference call the next morning among the seven athletic directors to revisit the issue.

Of course, there was still the not-so-small matter of Lafayette beating Bucknell. If the Bison were to win the game, the entire issue would be moot. Lafayette had won in Davis a year earlier only after Brian Muckle had missed two free throws with nine seconds left and Brian Ehlers had hit a runner at the buzzer for a 66-65 victory. A similar type of game seemed likely.

The Lafayette players weren't nearly as uptight about the tiebreaker issue as the coaches and administrators were. When O'Hanlon told Ehlers during the team's morning shootaround about his plan to start the second team, Ehlers just nodded. He then told the other starters what was happening on the bus ride back to the hotel. They wondered what the big deal was, but didn't question the move.

"We just wondered how long he'd keep us out," Tim Bieg said.

"Thirty seconds," O'Hanlon said. "Maybe a minute. I'm just making a point."

The only point Bucknell wanted to make was that it was not third fiddle in the league behind Lafayette and Navy. The outcome of the game would not change Bucknell's tournament seeding, but a win would certainly give the team a confidence boost. Beyond that was wanting to send the seniors out with a victory in their last game in Davis.

The building was packed, hot as always, and brimming with anticipation as the teams warmed up. Someone had hung a sign on the far side that said, "Mrs. Muckle is the best," a tribute to the fact that Jean Muckle was about to watch the 113th game of her son's 113-game Bucknell career. At the other end of the spectrum were Valter Karavanic's parents. They were about to watch their son play for the second time in his Bucknell career. Valter had taken the money he had made working at an engineering company during the summer and flown them in for the week.

Flannery had helped him coordinate the trip, but had been very careful about his involvement. Bucknell could help the Karavanics find a hotel room, but they couldn't help them get a discount on the room. NCAA rules. There were about 106 other possible violations associated with a kid paying his parents' way to see him play his final two home games. It was almost a sure bet that if someone from Bucknell bought the Karavanics dinner, the NCAA posse would ride into Lewisburg. In the meantime, AAU coaches and street agents and shoe salesmen were running amok and no one was doing anything about it.

With seven seniors, the ceremony would take several minutes. O'Hanlon and Flannery agreed to a four-minute warm-up period afterward so everyone wouldn't be cold and tight from waiting during the ceremony. Each senior received a long, lingering ovation after PA announcer Greg Mascara introduced them. The seven introductions combined were about as long as Mastrandrea's ode to Spitler, but each prominently mentioned everyone's major. They would all graduate in May. In fact, the five players had a combined GPA of 3.3 — led by Karavanic's 3.8.

When Karavanic and his parents were introduced, the three of them walked on court with their arms around one another. It was all too much for Valter, who buried his face in his mother's shoulder. For a coach, this is the danger of a pregame ceremony. Emotions tend to run very high. The four-minute post-ceremony warm-up was important for the Bison as much to cool their emotions as to get their bodies warm.

The score was 1-0 Bucknell when O'Hanlon ended his protest 61 seconds into the game by sending his starters to the scorer's table. A few seconds later Karavanic hit a three to make it 4-0, but then Lafayette began to take command of the game. The usual suspects were at work: Ehlers, Bieg, and Whitfield all hit threes. Burke came back off the bench to hit a three and Rob Worthington, who seemed to come up with a key bucket in every game, rebounded a miss to make it 24-18, Lafayette. Flannery called time. By now, he was pouring sweat and he had to scream to be heard over the noise. O'Hanlon sensed a chance to break the game open. "Keep the pressure on them right now," he implored. "Let's widen the lead by halftime."

They did. Bucknell was cold and Lafayette's matchup zone was pushing them outside their shooting range. Whitfield and Ehlers were unstoppable at the other end. Whenever the defense came up to stop them, they put the ball on the floor and got into the lane. The Bison were used to this from Ehlers but this was a new dimension of Whitfield. The longer he played without the back miseries that had short-circuited his first two seasons, the more confident he became. An Ehlers 10-footer late and a follow shot by Frank Barr pushed the halftime margin to 39-23.

The Bucknell locker room was in a state of shock. This was not the way the script was written. They had shot less than 30 percent for the half. Lafayette wasn't going down to a team shooting under 30 percent. Flannery appealed to their pride, reminded the seniors what this day meant, how long they would remember it, and pleaded with them to keep their poise and rally.

They managed to score the first five points of the half to cut the margin to 39-28. But every time they seemed ready to really bring the crowd into the game, Lafayette came up with a response. A Bryan Bailey jumper made it 44-32. Then, in 90 seconds Ciosici scored inside and rebounded a Bieg miss to score again. Brian Ehlers stole the ball and fed Whitfield for a layup. It was 50-32 and Flannery was frantically calling time out.

By now, about 100 members of the Zoo Crew who had been able to buy tickets had stopped trading barbs with their Bucknell counterparts — the Herd — and were happy to simply chant, "We Want Navy." Those words were darts through the heart to Bucknell. They had become an afterthought.

Bucknell had one last rally left. Down 20 with six minutes left, the Bison actually got the lead to 66-57 when Karavanic made the last three of his home career with 1:26 left. But it was too late. Lafayette made eight straight free throws down the stretch, and the final was 74-59. Flannery waved the white flag with 36 seconds left, taking the seniors out for one last ovation. It was warm and sweet, but for the seniors, there was a feeling of emptiness. They had been through too much together for this to be their last memory of Davis. That's often the trouble with competition: the other guy has a script he wants to follow, too.

Lafayette's victory made it official: the Leopards and Navy were tied at 11-1. The new — and most meaningful — RPI would be calculated overnight. The Lafayette players, like everyone else, assumed Navy would still be in front.

"I don't mind the idea of going down there again," Rob Worthington said, sitting in the now-empty gym, waiting for the bus home. "I think we'd all like another shot at playing in their place. We've got something to prove down there."

Ciosici nodded. "I don't care where we play them," he said. "I just want to be sure we get to play them again. Anyplace, anytime."

Chris Williams was awake the next morning before dawn. Like everyone else at Navy — and Lafayette — he hadn't slept too well, wondering what the RPI numbers would look like in the morning. Finally, at 5 A.M. he rolled out of bed and turned on his computer. He was about to click on to the RPI to see if the updated rankings were on-line when he noticed that he had an instant e-mail message waiting for him. He was a little bit surprised because he had checked his e-mail just before going to bed.

The message was from Sitapha Savane. It was short and direct: "Can you believe this shit?" was all it said.

Attached to the message was the new RPI. The 129th-ranked team was Lafayette. The 131st-ranked team was Navy. Williams stared at the computer screen for several seconds, not believing what he was seeing. "Oh my God," he thought. "Oh my God."

Savane and Jeremy Toton had been up an hour earlier than Williams. They had seen the rankings before anyone else. Scott Strasemeier's fears had been realized. The win over Army had dropped Navy six spots. Beating Bucknell — which was ranked 150 spots higher than Army — had jumped Lafayette 17 spots.

"I think we had all planned on playing the final at home," Savane said. "Now, it was looking like we were going back to Lafayette. I think it rocked us. All of a sudden, everything was different."

When the athletic directors convened by phone that morning, Eve Atkinson still had to push her proposal that the top seeds split the home court and the bye. The vote was 7-0 to ignore what was written in the rule book and do just that. Perhaps the other ADs couldn't resist the irony that, after a week of complaining, Lafayette would now get less than it would have gotten if it had said nothing. Everyone insisted they were just doing what they thought was right.

And so it was that Navy got the bye after Lafayette opted to open the tournament against Army, knowing that if it reached the final it would be playing in Kirby. The tournament would begin on Saturday morning at eleven — seventh-seeded Army vs. number one seed Lafayette.

Now Navy was the aggrieved party. "Something this important shouldn't be decided in the boardroom," Don DeVoe said after hearing about the conference call and vote.

Actually, what was truly important — home court — hadn't been decided in a boardroom. It had been decided inside a computer.

27

THREE WINS TO THE PROMISED LAND

POSTSEASON play in college basketball unfolds in stages. While many of the power leagues are concluding their regular seasons, a number of smaller leagues are beginning their conference tournaments. These are, in most cases, the "one-bid" leagues, so-called because, almost without exception, only the winner of the conference tournament will qualify for the NCAA Tournament. On a very, very rare occasion a one-bid league might get a second bid if it has a dominant regular season champion that somehow fails to win the conference tournament. More often, though, that regular season champion will find itself with a consolation bid to the National Invitation Tournament. To teams in the power leagues NIT has come to stand for the "Not Invited Tournament," because being in the NIT means you were not invited to the NCAAs.

The Patriot League is a prime example of a one-bid league. Not only has there never been a second Patriot League team invited to the NCAAs, there has never been a Patriot League team invited to the Not Invited Tournament. Even before the seven teams gathered at Lafayette to begin the conference tournament, everyone in the league was trying to figure out a way to end that streak. Navy came into the tournament with 22 wins, Lafayette with 21. If they met in the final, both teams would have 23 wins. That sort of record, one would think, should merit serious consideration from the NIT, which was more than willing to take any team from the ACC, Big East,

Pac-10, Southeast Conference, Big Ten, or Big 12 that had an overall record of .500 — no matter how pathetic that school's nonconference schedule might be. The NIT was about names, not merit or achievement.

Scott Morse, Lafayette's SID, found that out when he placed a call to his ex-boss, Walt Hameline, the athletic director at Wagner. Hameline was a member of the NIT executive committee. "Everyone on the committee has been getting calls telling us we should take Lafayette or Navy," Hameline told Morse.

"Well," Morse said. "Will you?"

"We're a lot more likely to take Princeton," Hameline said. Princeton had finished second behind Penn in the Ivy League.

"Princeton?" Morse said. "We beat Princeton — *at* Princeton!"

"I know," Hameline said. "But they're Princeton."

So much for an NIT bid.

No one came to Easton on the afternoon of March 3 thinking about the NIT. Everyone, from Navy and Lafayette to Lehigh and Army, was dreaming about the NCAAs, about sitting in a room together on the night of March 12 while their name went into the 64-team bracket on national television.

"Fellas, we're three games from the NCAA Tournament," Pat Harris told his Army team. "I shouldn't have to say another word."

The tournament would begin on Saturday morning with a triple-header: Army-Lafayette; Lehigh-Bucknell; Holy Cross–Colgate. The winners of the first two games would play one semifinal on Sunday, the winner of the third game would play Navy. Then Sunday's winners would get to sweat for five days until ESPN told them they could play the championship game.

First, though, everyone gathered for the annual awards banquet or, as Pat Diamond might have put it, the annual hate-in. There wasn't a lot of love lost when the seven teams arrived for the Friday night dinner. The Lafayette people and the Navy people were still sniping at one another over the RPI affair. The Lehigh people were upset because the local media had sided with Lafayette on the issue. The Colgate folks were unhappy because everyone else in the league was balking at the notion of playing the tournament in Hamilton in two years. And so on. That and the fact that many of the players sharing tables would be playing against one another the next day did not make for the most convivial atmosphere.

The league liked to make players from different teams sit together. Tables were designated by class: seniors, juniors, sophomores, freshmen. That meant, like it or not, you had to talk to players from other teams. This was actually a good idea because it reminded the players that the other guys really were a lot like them.

"If they held the dinner after the season, people would probably have a lot more fun and relax," Stefan Ciosici said. "But when you're playing the next day, it's kind of tough to loosen up and enjoy yourself."

That was true. Logistically, though, this was the only time when all seven teams would be in the same place. Most of the TV leagues don't even bother with banquets. They know the coaches and players would whine too much about it, so they don't make the attempt. No doubt some coaches and players would demand appearance fees.

The awards announcements were predictable in that almost everyone was unhappy about something. Pat Flannery couldn't believe Brian Werner didn't make the all-rookie team. Ralph Willard was stunned when Josh Sankes made only second-team all-league. Sal Mentesana thought Jared Hess should have been on the second team.

The three big awards of the evening were rookie of the year, player of the year, and coach of the year. No one was surprised when Tim Szatko of Holy Cross won the rookie award. He had been forced into a starting role because of the injuries and had improved steadily during the season. Don DeVoe did win coach of the year, in spite of Pat Harris's prediction that he wouldn't be given his due. The vote, in fact, was unanimous, a tribute to how well Navy had played down the stretch.

The one award that there was doubt about was player of the year. There were two clear candidates: Sitapha Savane and Brian Ehlers. Each had been the leader of a team that had tied for first place. Their numbers were similar: both had averaged more than 17 points a game. Savane had a higher field-goal percentage — not surprising since he played in the low post — and Ehlers had a higher free-throw shooting percentage. Savane had more rebounds; Ehlers more assists. Savane had been a dominant defensive player inside most of the season.

In truth, there would have been nothing wrong with naming them co–players of the year. Both were deserving. Each league coach had a vote, and they were not allowed to vote for one of their own players. Fran O'Hanlon voted for Savane; DeVoe for Ehlers. They canceled each other out. That left it up to the other five. Harris and Emmett Davis voted for Savane. Flannery and Willard voted for Ehlers. All four men said the decision was difficult but, when they got right down to it, clear cut.

That left one conflicted coach: Mentesana. "I honestly and truly wrestled with the decision," he said. "To me, Ehlers was always the guy who was the difference maker for Lafayette at the end of close games. They needed a play, they looked to him. But Savane was so good defensively this year, and he never seemed to miss a shot. I hated the idea of not voting for either one of them."

Finally, Mentesana cast his ballot for Ehlers. "In the end, I just didn't want there to be a perception out there that in a close vote the guy from Lehigh voted against the guy from Lafayette. Maybe that wasn't fair to Sitapha, I'm really not sure. But I just couldn't pull the trigger and then wonder myself if I was somehow being unfair to Ehlers."

What Mentesana should have done was split his vote. That would have left him with a clear conscience and the league with co–players of the year. Instead, after all the other awards had been announced, Ehlers was introduced as player of the year for the second straight season. At Lafayette, this was a popular decision. The looks on the faces of the people from Navy made it apparent they weren't nearly as happy.

"Patriot League politics strikes again," DeVoe said the next morning.

This time, he might have had a point.

The newly christened Kirby Sports Center had never looked better than it did the next morning when a sellout crowd began arriving early since the home team was playing in the opening game. With the new annex and a paint job and cleanup for the tournament, the building practically sparkled. The curtain that was normally pulled across the area behind the basket for home games was gone, replaced by a bleacher for extra seating.

There is always an extra buzz on the first day of a conference tournament. Before the first game tips off, everyone still has hope. Basketball lore is full of stories about teams seeded at the bottom of their league pulling upsets, even reaching the NCAA Tournament. In nine years of Patriot League play, the seventh seed had upset the second seed on opening day no fewer than four times — including the Lehigh upset of Navy one year earlier that the Mids still weren't 100 percent over.

Army's only two victories in the conference tournament had come as a seventh seed. In 1995, the Cadets had upset Bucknell when a brilliant little shooting guard named Mark Lueking had gone off for 43 points. A year later, they had shocked Navy, the only time in 20 games that a Don DeVoe–coached Navy team had lost to Army.

Along with the feeling of hope that pervades a building as a conference tournament begins, there is also a palpable sense of ending. Seven teams were in Easton on Saturday morning. By nightfall on Sunday, five of them would be packing their uniforms up for the last time. Every senior who stepped onto the court did so knowing it could be for the last time.

In a one-bid league, every tournament game becomes a crucible. The loser's season is over and the seniors' basketball lives will come to an end. Most college basketball players have played the game their entire lives, have spent countless hours working on their games, thinking about the game, dreaming about the game. For most Patriot League seniors there is no thought of the NBA. A very few get the chance to play overseas for a few years. For most, this is it.

The contrast between the Patriot League Tournament atmosphere and the atmosphere at a TV league tournament is striking. In the TV leagues, more than half the teams know they will play postseason. Some leagues will send nine or ten teams to the NCAAs and the NIT. And, even among the handful of teams who won't play postseason, most of the players are convinced that their basketball careers will continue beyond college. The number of seniors in the TV leagues who walk off the court after their team loses in a conference tournament believing that their basketball career has just ended can probably be counted on one hand. The number of Patriot League seniors who walk off after losing in the conference tournament *not* knowing that their basketball career has just ended is smaller than that.

Alex Morris, a one-time Army point guard, may have described one-bid tournament basketball better than anyone. "Every game is a forty-minute season," he said. "Because your whole season rides on that forty minutes. Nothing that has happened before matters. You can have twenty wins or two wins and all that matters is what happens in that forty minutes. Because that's what you're going to remember when all is said and done."

The Navy seniors, Class of '99, could certainly attest to that.

Every one of the senses is keener during a one-bid conference tournament. Coaches are jumpier, players are more eager and more nervous all at once. Even the media can feel the extra electricity in the air. There is no such thing as a routine game once the tournament begins, regardless of the final score.

The opening game almost always matches the team with the least to lose — the last seed — against the team with the most to lose — the top seed. This was especially true of Army-Lafayette. To begin with, Army had no seniors. Deep down, Pat Harris knew some of his players would not be back next season. Some would return to their companies to focus on academics. Some would be recruited over — he hoped — because Army needed to go out and find better players. But none were absolutely playing their last game. They didn't know for sure and he didn't know for sure.

By contrast, Lafayette was playing on its home floor in front of its home fans. Everyone was expecting a showdown with Navy the following Friday. There might be some nervous moments in a semifinal the next day against Bucknell, but the Bison had been beaten easily the week before at Bucknell. The Army game should be a walkover. Anything but that would make everyone extremely nervous.

All of which made Fran O'Hanlon a semiwreck Saturday morning. "Everyone keeps coming up to me and saying, 'No problem today, Coach,'" he said with a smile. "I'm glad it's no problem for *them*."

O'Hanlon knew his team was a lot better than Army's. He also knew that Navy had been a lot better than Lehigh. And he knew the Cadets would come out and attack, especially on defense, for the entire game. This late in the season, coaches didn't just worry about winning, they worried about how they won. He wanted to stay healthy, no bangs on Stefan Ciosici's knee, no stiffening in Tyson Whitfield's back. There was no margin for error anymore.

Harris had decided to change his team's defensive approach. He wasn't going to double-team Ciosici in the post. Instead, he wanted to focus on Whitfield and Brian Ehlers, trying to deny them the ball on the perimeter at all costs. If Ciosici scored 40, so be it. He believed his only chance was to keep Whitfield and Ehlers from burying his team from the outside.

Remembering that it was in this building that he had sensed his team backing down, both physically and mentally, three weeks earlier, he reminded his players to take Lafayette's attitude toward them personally.

"They chose to play you," he said. "They could have taken the bye and they took you. Show them that they made a mistake. Don't take any crap off them. Someone shoves you, shove back."

O'Hanlon had nothing negative to say about Army. Instead, he offered a simple warning. "This is a new season today," he said. "Right now, our record is the same as Army's."

The toughest thing about playing Lafayette for Patriot League opponents is the number of weapons the Leopards have available to them. There is never anyone on the floor who can be guarded loosely. With the Cadets trying to clamp down on Ehlers and Whitfield, Tim Bieg opened the game by making a three. Then Ciosici, using his fifty-pound weight advantage on Charles Woodruff, posted for an easy basket inside.

Army got the ball to Harrell, who scored on a short jumper. Then Adam Glosier, who had started every game as a freshman, produced a pretty pass inside to Woodruff for a layup. It was 5-4 four minutes into the game and O'Hanlon, feeling that extra level of pressure, was climbing all over the officials about illegal screens. In a regular season game, he probably would have said nothing. Or he might have made one comment. Now he was practically out on the court, demanding that they watch for movement when the Cadets set their screens.

No margin for error.

Harris noticed O'Hanlon's complaints. Naturally, it concerned him. He was convinced — as is every other coach at the bottom of any league — that the officials called games the way they *thought* they were supposed to go. "Officials always tell me how impressed they are with how hard we play," he had said before the game. "I always say, 'Oh yeah, then why won't you give us a call every now and then.'" With O'Hanlon on the officials, Harris was convinced they would eventually give in to his demands and begin blowing the whistle in Lafayette's favor.

The next whistle didn't bother Harris. It was on Ciosici, who had jumped out to try to block a Chris Spatola three-point shot. In the scouting report, O'Hanlon had written in bold letters *Do not foul* next to Spatola's name. Ciosici was so wound up to finally play in the Patriot League Tournament after a two-year wait that he mind-blocked and jumped right at Spatola.

Spatola made all three shots to cut the Lafayette lead to 11-7. "Stefan," O'Hanlon barked. "What did we say about fouling him?" Ciosici nodded. He understood.

The first thirteen minutes were like that for Lafayette. Army was doing what it did best: playing tenacious half-court defense and getting just enough offense to hang around. Barrett scored twice. Joe Clark made a three. Mike Canty stole a careless Bieg pass and laid the ball in to cut the lead to 23-19. O'Hanlon called time and lit into his players.

"You have to use your heads out there, guys," he said angrily. "You're just running up and down the court thinking they're going to go away. They won't unless you make them."

Slowly, Lafayette made them. As had been the case all year, Army's inability to generate offense with any consistency was its eventual undoing. Spatola had to leave with foul trouble again and the Cadets hurt themselves by making just three of seven free throws in the last few minutes of the half. By the intermission, the lead was 41-30.

That didn't mean O'Hanlon felt safe. His halftime talk was as intense and angry as it had been all year. He sensed that his team was on a little cruise control and he didn't like it. It was okay for the fans to be talking about playing Navy in the final. It was up to the players to keep their minds in the present and focus on the job at hand.

The message got through. Lafayette came out and scored the first 12 points of the second half. It was 53-30. Game over. Army wasn't capable of rallying from that far behind. Still, the Cadets weren't about to stop competing. Harrell and Whitfield collided and came up jawing at one another. Then Rob Worthington took off on a fast break with Charles Woodruff in pursuit. Woodruff took him down and Ciosici took exception, shoving Woodruff as he and Worthington untangled. Harrell jumped in and began shoving Ciosici, and there was a lot of pointing and shoving as the officials and other players closed in.

O'Hanlon sensed disaster. Bob Patey, the lead official, had quickly called technicals on Ciosici and Harrell for jumping into the fray. Ciosici was still angry and trying to get at Harrell or at Woodruff or at anyone in black. A second technical would mean ejection. That wasn't going to affect the outcome of this game, but an ejection would automatically mean a one-game suspension, meaning Ciosici would sit out the semifinals. O'Hanlon grabbed Ciosici from behind and pulled him away, telling him to calm down. Bieg was right behind him. "Don't do something stupid!" he yelled at Ciosici. "Get ahold of yourself. We don't need that."

Ciosici calmed down. Harris was on the floor demanding to know why Harrell had been given a technical when Ciosici had been the first one to jump in between Woodruff and Worthington. More than anything, he was exorcising some frustration. The teams managed to get through the last 10 minutes without any further incident. Taking no chances — and not needing to — O'Hanlon kept Ciosici on the bench the rest of the game. The final was 71-45.

Harris didn't wait long to begin talking to his team about the future. He thanked his players for the way they had approached the season; for their willingness to work and listen; for their resilience through a long winter. "There's an old basketball saying, fellas," he said. "It goes like this: teams are made from October to March, players are made from March to October. You guys need to start working very soon with October in mind. You have to come back stronger. You have to come back better shooters. You have to come back with more confidence. You have to get *better*. The only way we get better is if you get better.

"And if this season has done nothing else, it should have told us that we must get better. Our goal is to be back in this tournament a year from now and win it. Start working toward that goal right now."

Things move very quickly during a tournament. As soon as Army and Lafayette had cleared the floor, Bucknell and Lehigh took their place. The players had been waiting upstairs in the locker room areas until word came up that the first game was in the final minute. They then made their way down the steps and through the public hallways that led to the gym and onto the court.

Both teams had been through soul-searching weeks after ending the regular season with disappointing losses. Pat Flannery had again told his seniors that they needed to play with more emotion, that this was the time when they needed to play with an abandon that he felt had been lacking at key moments during the season. "We're out of next times, guys," he told them. "Next time is the last time."

Sal Mentesana had gone a step farther than Flannery. On Thursday he had brought the team into the green room, the locker room in Stabler normally used by the officials, and had everyone sit down for a talk. He began by showing tape of the game they had played at Bucknell on February 16. It had been perhaps their worst performance of the season, a game in which they had trailed 43-18 at halftime. The miracle of the evening was that Mentesana didn't land back in the hospital.

He went through the tape in great detail, showing them how poorly they had listened that night, how unfocused they had been — especially on defense, where Bucknell got one open shot after another. Mentesana talked about his belief that the players lacked the three P's — poise, purpose, and passion. He spoke about each player individually, asked each one what he thought his game lacked. Then he asked Jared Hess, as the captain, to speak.

Quiet as he is most of the time, Hess is passionate about basketball. He had been through four years of bad basketball — 24 wins and 85 losses — and he had reached the point where he was sick of losing and sick of hearing excuses. "We talk and talk about getting better," he said. "When does the time come when we stop talking and just go out and *do*?"

There ended up being no practice that day. They spent four hours in the green room, talking and shouting, sometimes crying. As Flannery had said to his seniors, they were out of next times. There wasn't a player in the room who had ever beaten Bucknell. In fact, the losing streak against the Bison was nineteen.

"I don't know about the rest of you," Hess said, "but I am damn sick and tired of losing to Bucknell."

Strangely enough, even though the seventh seed in the tournament had won in the first round four times, the sixth seed never had. But Lehigh was clearly ready to play from the beginning. Bucknell had prepared for the possibility that Mentesana might go back to the zone he had unveiled a year earlier against Navy, but that wasn't in the plan. The plan was to be aggressive, to use the bench to try to wear the Bison down, and to make sure freshman Matt Logie, who had been the other serious candidate for rookie of the year along with Tim Szatko, got the chance to shoot the ball from outside.

Throughout the first half, Flannery's last words to his players seemed to hang in the air near the Bucknell bench: "Don't let these guys think they have a chance. You can be the bulldozer or the pavement. Let's run them over early."

That wasn't happening, and with each passing minute, one could feel Lehigh's confidence slowly growing. The Mountain Hawks' offense was predicated on hitting from outside — which they did. Eighteen of their first 26 points came on threes, culminating when Logie hit one from outside just as Valter Karavanic piled into him. The four-point play put Lehigh up 26-20, and Flannery's voice was starting to get shrill on the sideline.

Bucknell righted itself after that play, scoring the last nine points of the half to lead 29-26. The half ended with Brian Muckle blocking a Hess jumper out of the corner. That sent Mentesana into a tizzy, because the play had been run wrong. "Why don't you listen?" he yelled as the players headed up the stairs to the locker room. "Plays like that are how you lose games, not how you win them."

Behind him, assistants Jeff Wilson and Glenn Noak sensed their boss's frustration. The team had played good basketball for sixteen minutes and then mentally checked out for four. "Whether he's right or wrong to be angry doesn't matter," Noak said. "A screamfest isn't going to get this done right now."

Wilson nodded. Then he repeated what Noak had said to Mentesana before the coaches went into the locker room to talk to the players. "I know, I know," Mentesana said. "I'm trying. It's just that when the chance is there . . ."

Flannery knew the chance was there and it had him pacing up and down in the bathroom area outside his locker room. "Same thing," he said. "Same thing. They're the aggressors. Why? Why doesn't this group understand what's at stake now?"

He decided to keep his cool with the players. They had finished the half well. They needed to make some adjustments defensively to get out on Lehigh's shooters more aggressively. The only time he raised his voice was when he looked at the stat sheet and saw that Dan Bowen hadn't committed a foul. To some, this would be a positive. To Flannery it was a sign that Bowen was playing soft on defense. That might have been a little unfair: Bowen had scored 14 points, while his counterpart, Sah Brown, had scored four. But Flannery was searching for fire. He didn't want a close game. He didn't want Lehigh thinking this game was Navy all over again.

But this wasn't destined to be an easy day for Bucknell. There was no early second half burst to get the game under control. Instead, leading 38-35, the Bison suddenly went ice cold. They went five and a half minutes without a field goal, during which Lehigh put on a 12-4 burst to take a 50-42 lead. Now a nervous game had become a crisis game. Bowen understood. During a time-out he yelled at his teammates that enough was enough, it was time to get going. Dy Cameron backed him up. "They're talking trash on us," he said. "It's time to shut them up."

Bowen scored twice. It was 50-46. Hess went to the basket and went up. Muckle went up with him. A clean block? No. A foul on Muckle. Flannery was all over referee Peter Palermino. "That stinks!" he screamed. "That just stinks."

Palermino walked over so he could get close enough to Flannery to be heard without raising his voice. "Pat, enough," he said. "This is too close a game. Don't make me do something."

Flannery sat down and said to Don Friday, "Why do I yell at him — that's the stupidest thing I can do."

At that moment, Fran O'Hanlon, sitting across from the Bucknell bench on press row, stood up and left. He was supposed to be scouting his next opponent along with his assistants but he didn't want to watch the last few minutes. "I knew that, either way, someone I like was going to be heartbroken," he said. "I knew one group of kids was going off the floor crying. I didn't want to watch it."

While Flannery was jockeying with the officials, Lehigh's bench was sticking a dagger into his players. Bobby Mbom — the six-foot-five-inch, 260-pound sophomore known as "The Beast" — was pushing Bucknell's inside players around. On one possession, he went to the basket and missed, rebounded and missed, then rebounded again and scored. Eddie Lacayo took a perfect pass from Steve Aylsworth, scored, and was fouled. The free throw made it 58-47.

The clock was under five minutes. The foul on Lacayo's basket had been committed by Karavanic — his fifth. He left the game, knowing his career might be over, with one point. The only field goal he had made all day had come while Muckle was being called for a foul away from the ball, wiping out the shot. He sat on the end of the bench, his head in a towel, not believing what he was seeing.

Things were becoming desperate for Bucknell. Lehigh was running the clock on every possession and spreading the floor, which made it difficult for the Bison to guard them. Aylsworth could see a look creeping into the eyes of the Bucknell players that he recognized because he had seen it a year earlier in the eyes of the Navy players.

"In both cases the notion that we might stay with them for a while had occurred to them," he said. "But the notion that they could actually lose the game had not. Then it hit them like a ton of bricks."

On the flip side, the Mountain Hawks had gone from hoping they could win to believing they could win. During a time-out with the lead 61-52, Mentesana wondered if the players might be tiring. The gym was hot and the pressure hotter.

"Would you like to go to black [zone] for a couple of possessions?" he asked in the huddle.

"NO!"

They didn't need rest. Adrenaline was coming out of their pores at that stage. The huddle around Mentesana was so tight you couldn't have run a piece of string through it. This was the kind of game that makes March so special in college basketball. These were kids who had been to hell and back throughout the winter, who had spent four hours in a room together two days earlier trying to figure out how to be better than they had been, rising to a new level.

Of course in every March success story someone has to be the foil. Looking at the Bucknell bench in the final minutes brought to mind the old *Peanuts* strip in which Linus is explaining at length to Charlie Brown how thrilling it was to see his favorite football team throw a 90-yard touchdown pass on the last play of the game to pull out an amazing victory, with the crowd going wild and all the players jumping joyfully on one another in the end zone.

"It was amazing, Charlie Brown, it was just amazing," Linus reports.

At which point Charlie Brown looks at Linus and says, "How did the other team feel?"

What Lehigh was doing was amazing. Bucknell was the other team.

The Bison tried to rally. Bryan Bailey made a three-point play to cut the margin to 65-60 with 1:40 still left. They fouled Aylsworth right away. He made both free throws. Then Bailey missed inside and Brian Werner fouled out going for the rebound. Lacayo made two more free throws and the margin was back to nine, 69-60. Lehigh was just too solid. The guards, who hadn't been able to get the ball across midcourt against Wagner in November, broke through Bucknell's pressure every time.

Dan Bowen, who never stopped grinding, scored his twenty-fifth point of the day and the last basket of his career with 30 seconds left, making it 71-62. Zlatko Savovic immediately broke the press and fed Lacayo for a layup with 23 seconds left. Bailey tried one last jumper. Savovic rebounded with 15 seconds to go.

Flannery jumped off the bench. "Don't foul," he ordered. "Back off."

He knew the game was over. There was no sense lengthening the torture for his players, and there was no reason not to let Lehigh enjoy what it had done in the final seconds. Some coaches will call time out trailing by 12 with five seconds to go. Flannery was about to suffer one of the most painful losses of his career. But he was going to do it with dignity and class.

The Lehigh players also showed class. When the buzzer went off, they celebrated briefly, but then, seeing the looks on the faces of the Bucknell players, they stopped and lined up to shake hands. Perhaps there is no love lost among Patriot League players, but there is certainly an understanding of how the other team feels. Only when they reached the locker room did the Lehigh players let loose with joyful hugs while Mentesana told them how proud he was of the way they played.

Flannery needed several minutes to compose himself before he faced his players. There really wasn't very much he could say. Their final record was 17-11. They had worked hard, they had been competitive. They were a credit to the school. The seniors had won 64 games and had never given Flannery a minute of serious trouble.

And yet, this would be their last memory of college basketball. They had come to Easton planning to play two games, hoping to play three. They had played one. Now, the emotion Flannery had been searching for all season came out. Now, they cried. It was as if they had never believed it could end this way and now it had.

There was absolutely no point in telling them why they had lost or what they had done. So Flannery didn't. Instead, he thanked the seniors for everything they had done. "We'll miss all of you," he said.

Emmett Davis had poked his head out of his locker room door at the precise moment that the Bucknell players were walking, heads down, to their own locker room a few feet down the hall. As soon as he saw them, Davis froze for an instant and then ducked back inside. He had just sent his own players downstairs to warm up. The last thing he wanted was to try to think of something to say to Flannery and his assistants as they walked by. Because he knew there was nothing he could say at a moment like that.

Neither Davis nor Ralph Willard knew quite what to expect from their teams in the last of the first-round games. Colgate had peaked in the Lehigh game three weeks earlier and had then lost four of its last five games to finish the regular season 12-15. Willard's team had won its last regular season game — against Lehigh — but was still hobbling. Sankes's back was now so bad that he hadn't practiced on Friday.

At pregame meal, Willard had talked to his team about attitude. He knew that their mental approach in terms of effort had been great all year, but he still thought they were a long way from where they needed to be in terms of self-belief. "You have to go in to every game honestly believing you can win," he said. "We still have a ways to go with that."

In the locker room, he brought up Lehigh as an example of what could be done if a team believed in itself. The Lehigh celebration could be heard in the adjoining locker room as he spoke.

The atmosphere in Kirby for this game would be a lot different than it had been at eleven o'clock in the morning, five and a half hours earlier, when Lafayette and Army had tipped off. Some of the Lafayette fans had hung around for Bucknell-Lehigh. Now, most of them had gone off to have dinner and the place was less than half full. Which meant that it felt like most of the games Holy Cross and Colgate had played during the regular season.

Willard sensed he was in for a long day when Sankes had to come out after four minutes to have his back worked on. By then, Diamond had gone outside and drained a three. There was no way Sankes could chase Diamond on the perimeter — back or no back. It was 9-2 until Tim Szatko hit a three. Sankes came back, laboring, but willing to try. Both teams were laboring on offense — which wasn't surprising. Neither had been a consistent offensive team all season but both worked like crazy on defense. It was 18-18 at halftime.

This was a game that was about survival. Both teams — and their coaches — knew that the chances for either one to beat Navy the next day were slim. The Midshipmen had practiced earlier in the day and were now spread out in the half-empty bleachers watching the game. But even if winning only extended the season by one game, everyone wanted that chance. No one wants a season to end. Each team had one senior — Diamond for Colgate, Chris Spitler for Holy Cross.

Each had thought long and hard that day about the fact that they might be going about their pregame rituals for the last time. Diamond had gone so far as to ask Davis for permission to speak to the team before the game. He had then read his teammates a short story he kept on his desk about what a father says to his son before his first game. The theme was direct: effort matters more than winning. Diamond had more control over what would ultimately happen in the game because he was on the court for most of the afternoon. Spitler was spot-subbing behind Ryan Serravalle, Brian Wilson, and Guillermo Sanchez, so his minutes were limited.

Early in the second half, Diamond and Sankes got tangled up and began barking at each other. This was uncharacteristic for both. They were both competitive, but mild mannered by nature. Juan Pegues picked up a technical for getting in the middle of the fracas and jawing at Diamond. The technical proved to be part of a 7-0 run that put Colgate ahead for good. Holy Cross kept creeping back: it got as close as 40-38 with 7:22 left on a Serravalle jumper, but Colgate had just enough to stay ahead.

The Crusaders' last gasp came after Sankes scored a three-point play in true Sankes fashion: he missed the back end of a two-shot foul and then rebounded the miss and dunked. That made it 45-41. Sankes would finish the game four-for-11 from the foul line, meaning for the season he had shot 120-for-256 from the line, a percentage of 41.6. This was remarkable for several reasons: first, it was evidence of how hard Sankes had worked to become an offensive force that he had been to the line that often. Beyond that, though, was this: in 27 regular season games, he had missed 129 free throws. Lafayette — as a team — had missed 127.

There was 5:15 to go when Sankes dunked, but Holy Cross simply had no offense left after that. Szatko missed a jumper and Sankes fouled Diamond trying to get over his back for the rebound. Diamond made both shots. Spitler was fouled, but missed the front end of a one-and-one. Jordan Harris took a pretty pass from Pat Campolieta, scored, and was fouled.

Colgate's lead reached double digits. It was over. With a little more than a minute left and the Red Raiders leading 56-43, Willard put Spitler back in one last time. Spitler checked in, looked up at the clock and the score, then dug down in a stance and chased Devin Tuohey, who was killing clock on the perimeter. A few seconds later, Serravalle fouled out, fouling to stop the clock. Spitler ran across the court to pat him on the back.

The seconds ticked away. Brian Wilson hit a three with six seconds left to cut the margin to 58-49. The ball came inbounds. Willard had ordered no fouls. The clock hit zero. Spitler bent over, grabbed his shorts, and stared at the floor. Around him, the handshake line was forming. Pat Diamond came and found him. He leaned over, put his arm around him, and told him how much he had enjoyed competing against him. Senior to senior they hugged briefly, Diamond knowing this moment would come for him soon enough.

In the quiet of the Holy Cross locker room, each of his teammates came to Spitler one by one for a hug. No one said anything. No one needed to. Willard didn't linger long on the game. "Chris," he said softly, "I want you to know what a pleasure it's been to coach you. I would wish you good luck, only I know you aren't going to need any. You're going to be great, whatever you do, wherever you go."

Spitler looked up from the spot on the floor he had been examining very closely. His mouth was dry. There was a lot he wanted to say, a lot he was thinking about. "Thank you," he said. Then he buried his head again. He had known all along that this moment would hurt. He just hadn't known how much.

28

UH-OH, IT'S LEHIGH

LEHIGH'S victory over Bucknell changed the tone of the semifinals. Everyone had been expecting a tight Bucknell-Lafayette game followed by a less tight Navy-Colgate or Holy Cross game. By winning, Lehigh had made virtually everyone that much more certain that Lafayette and Navy would be playing in the final.

All of which terrified Fran O'Hanlon. He knew his players had been expecting to play Bucknell. The good news was that the upset had been pulled by Lehigh, and it was almost impossible for Lafayette to overlook Lehigh under any circumstances because of the nature of the rivalry. Additionally, the last meeting between the two teams had been extremely tight until Fido Willybiro's ejection.

Lehigh was just having fun. As difficult as the past two years had been, they had managed to come into the tournament and ruin someone's March. In doing so, they had proven to themselves that they hadn't been delusional when they thought they could be a good team. They had given themselves something to take away from the season that could make them feel proud.

"Of course, there's always going to be a part of you that says, 'Why now? Why not sooner?'" said the always thoughtful Jared Hess. "But I guess now is better than never."

After their victory on Saturday, the Lehigh players had come up with a new slogan for themselves: "Uh-oh, it's Lehigh." And so, when Sal Mentesana finished his initial pregame talk on Sunday, they gathered in a circle, and instead of mouthing the ritual "team" or "family," they put their arms around one another and began rocking back and forth screaming "Uh-oh! uh-oh! uh-oh!" at the top of their lungs. Mentesana and his assistants watched with a bemused look on their faces.

"Whatever works," Mentesana said.

Mentesana's theme for the day was simple: don't be satisfied. One win was nice, but it wasn't the goal. The chance to make the final had been there a year ago and they hadn't been able to make it happen. This time, he said, let's make it happen.

"I don't want this to be the last day of our season," he said. "I want to go to practice tomorrow, then get on a bus Tuesday and go some-place and play the final Wednesday."

Someone pointed out as the players left the locker room that the final was on Friday.

Mentesana shrugged. "What do I know about when the final is?" he said. "When we get there, I'll worry about it then."

Everyone in the Lafayette locker room knew exactly when the final was, down to the minute. To emphasize that they needed to keep their minds on the semifinals before thinking about the final, O'Hanlon had written what he called the "current" Patriot League standings on the board in the front of the locker room:

Lafayette 0-0
Lehigh 0-0
Colgate 0-0
Navy 0-0

No doubt Freud would have had a field day with figuring out why Navy just happened to be last. But O'Hanlon's point, which he had made the day before, was direct: your twenty-two victories don't matter right now any more than their twenty losses do. The next forty minutes matter.

Kirby was more than jammed. PA announcer Jim Finnen had to make several announcements to get people out of the aisles, notably in the Lafayette student section. The Zoo Crew was making a belated comeback now that things were getting truly serious. Mentesana was mildly concerned that his team might be spent after Saturday, but as soon as he walked into the gym and felt the atmosphere he knew that wasn't going to be a problem. Steve Aylsworth had a look on his face that told Mentesana that he — and everyone else wearing brown — was ready to play.

Except during the first five minutes. Lafayette, the notorious slow starter, roared out of the blocks, jumping to a 9-1 lead. Mentesana called a quick time-out to try to slow the momentum down. It worked. Hess hit a three, then Logie hit one. Matt Crawford, the rail-thin freshman center, came off the bench to make several good plays inside.

O'Hanlon was exasperated. He thought the officials were letting Lehigh get away with moving screens. He wasn't happy with his team's shot selection. In other words, he was coaching a favored team in a difficult game.

And there was also the matter of Aylsworth. The little Lafayette killer was up to his old tricks. With Lafayette leading 15-12, Aylsworth had the ball out front. The Leopards trapped him as the shot clock wound down. Aylsworth squeezed himself through the trap, got to the foul line, lost his balance, and, as he was going down, flipped an underhanded 15-footer that went in.

The crowd screamed in amazement, delight, and horror — depending on who you were. A few seconds later the Lafayette bench was screaming in horror because the shot had been put on the board as a three-pointer. Aylsworth's foot had been on the foul line as he leaned in and released the shot. Somehow the officials had gotten confused and thought his foot was on — or just outside — the three-point line.

"When the Lafayette bench objected, Bob Adams, the lead official, consulted with his partners, Jeff Plunkett and Bill Laubenstein. No one was certain what had happened. The two coaches were called to the scorer's table.

"We're going to check the tape," Adams said. Since the game was on TV (Patriot League) the officials were allowed, by rule, to check the TV tape if they were unsure whether a shot had been a two or a three.

"Don't bother with the tape," Mentesana said. "It was a two."

"We're going to check the tape," Adams said.

Mentesana was amused, since he knew that Aylsworth was nowhere near the three-point line. O'Hanlon, already uptight in a 15-15 game, just paced. The tape, naturally, confirmed what everyone knew. The score was changed to 15-14, and Aylsworth, hardly daunted, fed Willybiro for a layup, then squeezed inside again for a layup to put his team ahead 18-15.

Lafayette's problem certainly wasn't lack of effort. A moment after Aylsworth's layup, Ehlers chased a loose ball into the press table, dove full length for it, and saved it back inbounds. He ended up spread-eagle across the table. He jumped up, limped for a couple of steps, and then ran down the floor to get back into the play.

"It hurt," he said later. "But what was I going to do, stop playing? Couldn't do that."

No one was going to do that in this game. Lafayette tied the game at 20. Aylsworth nailed another three. Bieg answered at the other end to tie the game again. That started a 9-1 Lafayette run to end the half. The Leopards had started the half and ended the half with 9-1 binges. Normally, that would be enough to kill Lehigh. Instead, the halftime lead was 29-24.

Mentesana was as calm at halftime as he had been all year. "You can do this, fellas," he said. "If nothing else, that should be apparent. Just keep your head. They'll make runs because they're a good team. They've already made a couple and we're still right there."

At the other end of the hall, the Lafayette coaches were hoping Lehigh would go away in the second half the way Army had — but they weren't counting on it.

"How could they have even thought about giving Aylsworth three on that shot?" Assistant Coach Mike McKee asked.

"Should have given him four for degree of difficulty," O'Hanlon said with a tired laugh.

Coaches always have a gut feeling about a game once it starts. In his coach's gut, O'Hanlon knew this game wasn't going to be easy.

What helped was that he had a mature team. Being in a tough game didn't faze them. They understood what was at stake but they weren't yelling at each other in the locker room. Like their coach, they stayed calm even in stressful moments.

The stress kept on coming in the second half. Lehigh's three seniors were not ready to go home yet. Hess hit a jumper; Willybiro was fouled rebounding a miss by Frank Barr and made two free throws to tie the game at 31. Lafayette crept ahead by five again, Aylsworth came back with a three, then fed Matt Logie for another.

With Lehigh attacking on the perimeter defensively and Ehlers struggling with his shot, someone had to take up the slack for Lafayette. Someone did: Ciosici. On Friday night, Ciosici had been selected second-team all-conference. In a sense, that was an achievement, given the severity of his knee injury and the struggles he had gone through to come back. But it was difficult, having been called up two years earlier as player of the year, to be called up with the other second-teamers and then listen as the first team was announced.

Throughout the season, whenever his knee hurt, whenever he felt he couldn't do the things he had once done, whenever he was frustrated to find himself on the bench again in foul trouble, Ciosici had pushed himself to keep going with one thought in his mind: the celebration he had watched in street clothes. He had stood there by the Lafayette bench, unable to even take part in the postgame party as a fan because of fear he could redamage his knee. All year long, that memory had pushed him.

Now, with the team in trouble and Ehlers having a tough day, Ciosici dug in and became Lafayette's main man again. After a Logie three had put Lehigh up 38-37, he rebounded an Ehlers miss and scored. Then he demanded the ball in the post and scored. Thirty-five seconds later, he scored again on the same drop-step move. After a Brian Burke three, he took a pass from Burke at the foul line, faced the basket, and drove past Sah Brown for a layup. In all, he scored eight points during an 11-1 burst that opened a 47-38 Lafayette lead.

Mentesana had to call time. "They get every damn call," he said, starting to get upset. Then he caught himself. "Okay, let's all of us keep our composure. There's lots of time. Keep running our offense and we'll start to make shots."

To the amazement of most in the crowd, they did just that. The seniors again made plays: Hess, a three; Aylsworth, a rebound put-back; Willybiro, the same thing.

The game had now become an absolute battle, the kind of game where every single possession is hugely important and every play matters. The tension in the building was almost unbearable. None of the players were talking to one another, that would take too much energy. The coaches were almost reduced to spectators because there was little they could say. The players knew what had to be done. Every player dug into a stance on defense each time. Every missed shot produced a war inside for the rebound.

This was one of those games worthy of all the cliches associated with college basketball. It had everything: intensity, atmosphere, effort, and stakes that were precious to everyone on the floor. "It's the kind of game you love being part of," Tim Bieg said, "*after* it's over."

With 6:33 left and Lafayette leading 52-48, Bieg missed a free throw. Ciosici somehow got his hand on the ball and back-tapped it. Bieg leaped for it, took one dribble to free himself, and drained what should have been a back-breaking three to make it 55-48.

Lehigh didn't blink. Hess caught the ball on the wing, drew the defense, and reversed the ball to Aylsworth, who drained another three. Then Lacayo found Hess in the corner and he hit a three. It was 55-54. Ciosici got trapped with the ball and Hess stole it from him. He took off the length of the court and dunked with 4:52 to go. Remarkably, Lehigh led, 56-55. Up in the corner of the stands, someone in the Lehigh band was standing up, holding a sign that said, "We Believe."

At that moment, they weren't the only ones.

Now, it was O'Hanlon's turn to call time to calm his troops. "Just run your offense," he said. "Do that, we'll get a good shot."

The shot they got really wasn't that good. It was Bieg shooting a three with six-foot-five-inch Scott Taylor right in his face. If Ehlers is the Silent Assassin, Bieg is the Baby-Faced Killer. He rainbowed the shot — making his coach proud, no doubt — over Taylor and drained it. Now, Lafayette was up, 58-56. Lacayo tied it again at the other end as the clock ticked under three minutes.

TV took a time-out. In the huddle, Mentesana drew the play Lafayette would run: a screen for Ehlers that would set him up to shoot or drive. Lafayette ran exactly that play, and Ehlers, a miserable one-for-nine to that point, still made the shot, an off-balance runner. Seconds later, he stole the ball and took off. Aylsworth chased him, reached in from behind, and stole the ball back. For once, Ehlers's poker face cracked. He was convinced he had been fouled.

Aylsworth came right back the other way, went to the basket, and scored his 17th point of the game. It was 60-60.

The clock was under two minutes. Again, O'Hanlon wanted the ball in Ehlers's hands. He caught the ball at the top of the key with Hess right in front of him. He dribbled left, then right, and pulled up just inside the foul line. Hess went right up with him. The ball cleared Hess's hand by an inch. It dropped through the basket as Hess collided with Ehlers. The place was crazed. Ehlers made the free throw.

"That's why he's the player of the year," Mentesana said later. "He's their fifth gear."

The clock ticked down. With under a minute to go, Logie, who had been defended well most of the day, rushed a long three. It hit the front rim. Reggie Guy, in the game for defense, rebounded it and was fouled with 38 seconds to go.

But Guy missed the front end of the one-and-one and Lehigh came down, still trailing by just 63-60. This time, Hess fired a three with Ehlers flying at him. The shot rimmed out and Nate Klinkhammer, also in for defense, rebounded. Again, Lehigh fouled. Twenty-one ticks remained. Klinkhammer had been to the foul line only four times all season. The gym was as quiet as it had been all day as he stepped to the line.

The shot rimmed out. Lehigh had one more chance, except that Ciosici had somehow gotten inside everyone and, for the second time at a critical moment, back-tapped it to a teammate. This time it was Ehlers. Hess fouled immediately with eighteen seconds to go. Ehlers made one of two but that was enough to make it a two-possession margin, 64-60. Rushing, Hess fired one more three. It hit the rim and bounced to Reggie Guy. This time he made the two foul shots with seven seconds left.

It was 66-60. Lehigh was finally finished. Aylsworth charged across midcourt and fired one last meaningless shot. As he released the ball, he pitched forward trying to get momentum behind the shot and ended up flat on his face. The buzzer sounded with the shot in the air. The Lafayette players had their arms in the air in relief and celebration.

Someone was reaching down for Aylsworth, pulling him to his feet. Aylsworth looked up, expecting to see a teammate. Instead, he saw Tim Bieg.

Bieg helped him up, then wrapped his arms around him. "I just want you to know how much I respect you," Bieg said in his ear over the din. "You're an unbelievable competitor."

"So are you," Aylsworth said, returning the hug. "If basketball has to end, I'm glad it ended in a game like this."

Everyone from Lehigh had a strange sense of joy mixed with their sadness at that moment. Aylsworth, Hess, and Willybiro all wanted to keep playing. But if they had to stop, this was a game they could walk away from with their heads up. The memory would have some sweetness to it.

"I could not be more proud of you if you had won the game," Mentesana told them. "That's a very good basketball team in there and you were every bit as good. You were one shot, one box out, one play from winning. You four seniors, all I can say to you is thank you. You went through four tough years and you never quit. We *are* going to win here, and when we do, you guys will be a big part of that because of what you did. You have my respect and you have my love."

They cried when Mentesana finished, tears for what might have been and, for the seniors, for what was no more. They hugged each other, proud and sad all at once. Athletic Director Joe Sterrett, who almost never comes into the locker room after a game, came in after this one to thank the players for their effort.

"It's good to see tears in there," he said. "That game was worth crying over. We haven't been in a lot of those the last few years. That's the way you want a team to feel when it loses. I wish we had won, but I feel great right now."

In a sense, everyone felt great. Lafayette was obviously thrilled to advance — to survive — and knew it had won a superb basketball game. Ciosici had finally come all the way back to being the Ciosici of 1998: 18 points, 16 rebounds, and two crucial back-taps that didn't show up in the statistics. Ehlers, on "the worst day of my life as a basketball player," had still made the two biggest baskets of the game.

Brian Burke had chipped in 10 critical points and Bieg, at war with Aylsworth all day, had 14 and three assists. Lehigh's three seniors had scored 40 of their 60 points.

As Aylsworth said, if basketball had to end, this was the way to go out. They had squeezed everything they had to give out of themselves. They had forced a class team that had come into the game with 22 wins, to reach deep within itself to find a way to win. They had made it clear to everyone in the building that a college basketball game didn't have to be on CBS or ESPN to be a classic.

No one who played in the game was going to be an NBA draft pick. That didn't matter even a little bit.

Navy-Colgate almost had to be an anticlimax after Lehigh-Lafayette. Almost half the crowd left, taking a lot of the electricity that had been in the building with them.

Colgate made it a game for ten minutes. A Jordan Harris three nine minutes in sliced an early Navy lead to 17-16 and Emmett Davis was up encouraging his players to stay after the Midshipmen. The problem was there were just too many of them to stay after. Don DeVoe kept going to his bench for fresh troops. Davis was already hamstrung by Pat Diamond's early foul trouble and the Navy bench began wearing the Red Raiders out.

Demond Shepard made a steal and scored. Josh Hill, who had barely played in the last month, stole the ball and slammed home a dunk. Jason Jeanpierre nailed a three. Navy went on an 18-2 run over nine minutes and the lead at halftime was 37-21.

Davis didn't know what to say. He raged at them for letting Josh Hill make plays against them. "Josh Hill's not any good!" he screamed. "He can do exactly one thing: play hard. And you guys let him make plays because you won't play as hard as him!"

Davis knew his players were giving him everything they had. Like Willard, he was obligated to stay on them until the finish even when he knew they were outmanned, as they surely were now. "Make one run," he pleaded. "Do that, get it close and they may get nervous. They're over there expecting to blow us out."

He was right about that. DeVoe's numbers on the board had been Navy — 80s, Colgate — 50s, and the last ten minutes of the half had reinforced that notion. "Build the lead every five minutes," DeVoe said. "Do *not* go backwards."

They didn't. Chris Williams started the second half by stuffing a Devin Tuohey jumper and going the length of the court for a layup. The lead built to 45-25. The crowd thinned. The lead got to 26. Davis went to a full-court press and was rewarded with a quick 6-0 burst. But that was as good as it got for the Red Raiders.

Diamond fouled out with 7:51 left and came off to a warm ovation from those left in the stands — including the Navy fans. He spent the rest of the game urging his teammates to try to find one last push. It wasn't there. The final was 82-56. In the locker room, when Davis started to talk about how much Diamond had meant to the team, he never quite finished. Diamond walked over and hugged him. Then everyone in the room hugged him.

When the buzzer had sounded a few minutes earlier, Davis had shaken hands quickly with the Navy coaches and made a fast exit. The Navy assistants were surprised and wondered if he had thought they had poured it on a little at the end. DeVoe had played the end of his bench, but those players had still been chasing Colgate hard in the final minutes.

Davis was a little bit hurt, but it didn't keep him from walking down the hall after he had talked to his team to congratulate everyone from Navy again and to have a few words with the players he had once coached.

He had a small smile playing on his lips as he walked back to have a final talk with his players. "It's my fault," he said. "I recruited too damn well when I was there."

He was joking. But no one from Navy would have contradicted him.

29

ALL OR NOTHING

IN the TV leagues, the conference tournament semifinals are played the day before the final. TV may dictate a starting time, but it doesn't dictate a four-day wait to play the game.

In the Patriot League, as in many one-bid leagues, the final is played when ESPN says the final will be played. It is a part of Championship Week, an ingenious creation of Tom Odjakian, who was ESPN's college basketball programmer from 1982 to 1996, when he left to become associate commissioner of the Big East.

Odjakian is a Lafayette graduate, Class of '76. As such, he has a warm spot in his heart for the smaller schools in Division I. He knew full well that his job was to get as many Indiana–North Carolina and Duke-UCLA matchups on ESPN as he possibly could. But he was always looking for ways to give the smaller schools a moment in the limelight.

"I was looking for a way to get Lafayette's league on TV," he said. "I couldn't go in and say, 'Hey, let's do the Patriot League championship game because my school's in the league.' So, instead, after we started doing a couple of championships, I went in and I said, 'Let's televise *everyone's* championship game.'"

And so, in 1993, Championship Week was born. In the first year, Bucknell and Holy Cross played the final in Davis Gym.

Holy Cross won 98-73. That was the last time the visiting team had won the final.

Odjakian's idea took hold. Championship Week grew in scope with each passing year until it reached the point where if a league wasn't part of Championship Week, something was very wrong.

The Patriot League championship game had been slotted at 4:30 on Friday afternoon every year since 1995. That meant it came right after an ACC quarterfinal game and right before *Sportscenter* and two more ACC quarterfinals. In all, not a bad spot to be for a league looking for exposure.

To a college basketball team, playing on ESPN is the ultimate. Whatever one might say about the massive collective ego of those who run the network, ESPN has done a fabulous job of marketing itself through the years — especially to college kids. Even though the NCAA Tournament is televised by CBS, it is ESPN that college basketball players watch all the time. To them, ESPN *is* college basketball. There are teams in the TV leagues who will play on ESPN six, eight, ten times a year. To those players, being on the network isn't that big a deal — although they are always aware of being on, especially when Dick Vitale is doing a game and they will actually mug and preen for his benefit.

In the Patriot and other one-bid leagues, there is one ESPN shot a year — courtesy of Tom Odjakian.

"When you talk about playing on ESPN, it's exciting," Tim Bieg said. "But once the game starts, other than the fact that there's a banner on the scorer's table that says ESPN on it, it's just like any other game."

The excitement was in the anticipation. Being in the championship game, one victory away from the NCAA Tournament, was always a big deal. But playing the game on ESPN, seeing the production truck roll up outside the gym with the familiar logo on it, knowing your friends and relatives around the country would be able to watch the game — Patriot League TV didn't penetrate too many markets — added to the package. Technically, Navy had been on network TV when it played Army, but the players knew how many cities the game had actually been on in. And CBS wasn't ESPN. In the Lafayette media guide, each player had been asked the question, "What would your *Sportscenter* highlight be?"

Sportscenter wasn't on CBS.

The Patriot League championship game wasn't going to bring Dick Vitale to town. It would bring Beth Mowins and Bob Wenzel to town. Mowins was a Lafayette graduate (Class of '89) who had played on the basketball team. A lot of her ESPN work, especially when it involved men's basketball, was as a sideline reporter, the person who had the thankless job of breathlessly asking a coach at halftime, "What do you think your team needs to do in the second half to win?" (The answer, by the way, is always, "Execute better than we did in the first half.") But for Championship Week, with ESPN announcers trekking to far-flung venues around the country, Mowins moved up to play-by-play.

Wenzel did most of his work on ESPN-Plus, the pay-per-view arm of the network that televised a lot of regional games, which could be picked up for an extra few bucks. He had coached, with a good deal of success, at both Jacksonville and Rutgers and had become a successful money manager who lived in Florida after leaving Rutgers in 1997. If Mowins and Wenzel had been sent to the Big East Tournament 60 miles away in Madison Square Garden, they would have gotten a lot of funny looks from everyone from coaches to players to security guards. In Kirby Sports Center, they were the king and queen. There was nothing the people from Lafayette and Navy couldn't — or wouldn't — do for the folks from ESPN.

For the players, the toughest part was waiting four days to play. A normal tournament builds to a climax. Each game is supposed to be a little tougher, but you get into a playing rhythm with each passing round. Lafayette had reached an emotional peak in surviving the Lehigh game. Perhaps if the final had been played a day later, the Leopards would have been drained and would have had a tough time with a well-rested Navy team. In a situation like that, the bye really could make a difference.

Sometimes, though, a team that just barely wins its semifinal carries the emotion of that victory over to the next day. Tournament history is rife with stories of teams that looked dead and buried in a semifinal, rising to win and then killing someone in the final. One of the great examples of that was the 1987 North Carolina State team that needed two overtimes to beat a seventh-seeded Wake Forest team in the ACC Tournament semifinals on Saturday. A day later, the Wolfpack beat a top-seeded North Carolina team that was 16-0 in ACC play entering the final.

But it wasn't that way in the Patriot League. Navy went home after beating Colgate in the semifinals and everyone went to class on Monday morning. The Lafayette players were also in class. The only difference was that the Lafayette players kept hearing people ask, "You think you have any chance to beat Navy?" A year ago, the Bucknell game had been looked upon at Lafayette as a coronation — and had turned out to be an extremely tough game. Now everyone wondered if the team was going to get blown out again by Navy.

The way life had changed at Lafayette since O'Hanlon's arrival was perhaps summed up best by the advance story on the championship game written by freshman Chris Reich in *The Lafayette*. The story began this way: "There are many intrinsic rights that students inherit upon arriving at Lafayette College: Among these are the right to a diet consisting of cereal, spaghetti, and flo-yo; the right to a run-in with campus security at some time or another; and the right to watch the men's basketball team play in the Patriot League Tournament Finals every year."

This was Lafayette's third straight championship game. That meant that only those in the senior class remembered what it was like *not* to be in the championship game. Friday would be the last day of class at both schools before spring break. For Lafayette, the timing was perfect because their students would hang around to watch the game. For Navy, it meant the only midshipmen available to make the trip to Easton were the 112 mids who were on restriction and not eligible to leave the Yard on spring break.

Navy made the trip back to the Lehigh Valley on Thursday night. It was the fourth time in eight weeks that they had checked into the Holiday Inn Bethlehem. "Home sweet home," Loren Shipley said as the bus pulled up to the front door. The Mids had stayed at the Holiday Inn for the game at Lafayette, for the game at Lehigh, and for the tournament the previous weekend.

"If you drive eighty miles an hour the entire way, it takes three hours to get here," Don DeVoe said. "If you drive fifty, it still takes three hours."

If Navy had an advantage being on the road, it was that the team was strictly in basketball mode once it left Annapolis. All the rituals were the same: practice, bus to the hotel, go to sleep, wake up and eat, go to shootaround, eat again, rest, meet in the hotel, take the bus to the gym. The only change DeVoe made was moving the pregame meal from the normal four hours before tip-off to four and a half so the hotel would serve breakfast food. After noon, it wouldn't.

"We've had good luck with breakfast food," he said. "Let's stick with it."

Lafayette had no game-day shootaround because the players were in class. Tim Bieg came in to shoot on his own around lunchtime looking bleary-eyed. "I had a test last night," he said. "International Trade Relations. It was long and it was hard. I'll be fine for the game. A little adrenaline will kick in, I won't even remember taking the test."

Adrenaline was everywhere on the picturesque little campus. One of the athletic department secretaries walked down the hall carrying a doll dressed in Navy blue with the number 55 on it. It was a Sitapha Savane doll and it was full of pins.

The Leopards did eat pregame meal at their usual time, the difference being that the cafeteria was close to full at 12:30 instead of being empty the way it normally was at four o'clock, the pregame time before night games. Bieg and Ehlers were being trailed by a local camera crew as they went through the day.

The big story wasn't about the players. As he walked out of the cafeteria to where his car was parked, Fran O'Hanlon noticed a problem on his Jeep: a flat tire. "One way or the other," he said, "this is an omen."

O'Hanlon always goes home after pregame meal to see his family and change from sweats to a jacket and tie. There was no time to wait around for help, so he left the car with a manager and got a ride home.

After pregame meal was over, most of the players went back to their rooms to try to lie down and rest for a while. Stefan Ciosici had gone to a biology class and a German class before pregame and was planning to take a nap before heading over to the gym at about three o'clock. He went back to his room, stretched out on his bed, and tried to sleep for about twenty minutes. It was no use.

"I was completely wired," he said. "More wired than I've ever been before a basketball game in my life. I realized I had been waiting two years to play in this game — the championship game, against Navy. The '98 game had been the biggest disappointment of my basketball career. The only way to put it behind me was to play in it again and win it. All I could think about was getting on the court and going at it with Savane."

Ciosici finally got up, got dressed, and walked over to the gym. It was still more than two hours before tip-off. He walked up to the locker room, punched in the combination, and went inside. He put on his uniform and his sweats and then sat there by himself thinking about what was to come.

When his teammates began trickling in, he went downstairs to shoot by himself. Even though the gym was slowly starting to fill up, no one was going to bother him. He wanted to be alone with his thoughts until the last possible moment. He knew, one way or the other, this would be the last time he played in this gym wearing a uniform. He wanted to be sure it wasn't the last time — period — that he played wearing the Lafayette uniform.

By three o'clock most of the participants were in the building. The players were working their way into uniform and would join Ciosici on the floor to do some pregame shooting, since they had the luxury of not dealing with another game being played beforehand. The three referees were in their locker room, just as nervous, in their own way, as the players.

For a second straight year, Frosty Francis, the league's officiating supervisor, had assigned the same three men to the championship game: John McDonell, Fran Connolly, and Joe Pescitelli. Like all referees, the three of them worked several leagues, but all worked a lot of games in the Patriot League and the Ivy League. They understood what the game meant to the players and the coaches, and as a result, the game had great meaning to them, too.

Officials always hold a pregame meeting in their locker room. They go over basics: positioning, getting subs in and out of the game, making sure to get the right shooter on a foul, how to administer a technical if there is one, what to look for from each team and from each coach. McDonell, who was the lead official, had made up a separate list for this game of things to go over in addition to the normal checklist.

The first thing he had written down in capital letters on his list was: "CANNOT OVERSTATE THE IMPORTANCE OF THIS GAME." He knew, and he wanted to remind his partners, that the two teams had been working for six months for the chance to play in this game. There is no consolation prize in the Patriot League. Or, as Chris Williams had put it, "This isn't YMCA ball. They don't give everyone a trophy."

McDonell knew that tempers might be short, especially early. He knew the coaches might be a little bit hyper. "They're both good guys," he said. "They'll both listen to you if you talk to them. Let's make sure we give them a chance to get things out a little bit when they're upset with a call." In other words: let's not give anyone a quick T.

McDonell was also very aware of Ciosici and Savane. "Let's try to get that under control right away," he said. "The first ninety seconds is crucial. Let's try to keep them off each other and, if we can, do it without the whistle. If there's a train wreck, there's no choice, we call it because we don't want it going the other way either and things getting out of control. But if we can, let's let them know we're watching, we want everything clean but we're going to let them play basketball. The best thing we can do is keep each team's five best players on the court if we can."

They talked about the crowd, which McDonell thought would help. "It'll be loud, so we should be able to run up and down and just work the game," he said. They were aware of the Zoo Crew, but expected no problems from them. They talked about how to deal with a last-second shot. This was a concern. The only game clock in the building was the one directly overhead. This was a problem for the players at the end of a half and a game, but also a problem for the officials because only one of them — the official under the basket — would have a clear view of the clock. That meant if the game came down to one shot, he would have to make the call on a shot that might or might not beat the buzzer. The luxury of going to the TV tape if a final call was in question was there (due to an NCAA rules change at midseason after several controversial endings), but McDonell was hoping they wouldn't need to do that.

"Let's remember one thing," McDonell said finally. "These are good kids who are good basketball players. We owe it to them to do everything we can to let them decide the outcome."

Connolly had one final thought. "Let's do such a good job that Frosty brings us all back next year," he said. "I like this assignment."

Something was bothering Jeremy Toton as the teams warmed up. In the pit of his stomach, he wasn't 100 percent certain that his younger teammates were completely ready for what was to come. Sure, they had played at Lafayette before. They had dealt with loud crowds. But not a crowd quite like *this* in a game quite like *this* with so much at stake. At pregame meal he had warned them to be ready for an atmosphere unlike any they had ever experienced before.

"After a little while it won't matter," he said. "But be prepared for a lot of emotion early. This isn't just another game."

All the upperclassmen on both teams had been in this game before. They knew what winning felt like. The Lafayette seniors and juniors also knew what losing felt like. They had also experienced this game on the road — at Navy in '98. No one from Navy had ever played this game anyplace but Alumni Hall.

"On Sunday, when we were waiting for the Lafayette-Lehigh game to end, some of the guys started saying they wanted Lafayette to win," Toton said. "They were saying, 'It won't be the same beating Lehigh at home as it will be beating Lafayette at their place.' My attitude was, the goal is to get to the tournament. I'll take Lehigh at home in a heartbeat."

That wasn't what they had, though. They had Lafayette and a wound-up crowd of 4,122 — 600 over capacity — that wanted to prove once and for all who was King of the Patriot League.

There was another factor: February 9. While Chris Williams might still be carrying a grudge against Greg McCleary for the takedown foul that had caused his four stitches, the entire Lafayette team was carrying a giant chip on its shoulder dating back to that game.

It wasn't personal at all. In fact, it was directed more inward than outward. They were a proud team that had been humiliated on that night and they weren't about to forget. Brian Ehlers had vowed to Ciosici and Bieg on the bus ride home that night that there would be another chance to play Navy and they would atone for what had happened. The coaches had reminded them about it constantly since then and so had their fellow students. In a sense they were in an ideal situation: playing at home with a roaring crowd behind them, believing *they* were the underdog.

Both coaches were convinced their players were ready. Both believed the game would be decided by one play or two at the very end. The last hour before tip-off was the most difficult: killing time, wondering if everything to prepare had been done. Nathan Davis tried to lighten things up in the Navy locker room when the team came upstairs after its initial warm-up. Straight-faced he went to DeVoe and said, "Ehlers twisted his ankle pretty bad. Don't think he'll be able to play."

DeVoe was so wired he didn't even crack a smile. "Yeah, right," he said.

Each coach had a final message for his players once they had gone through the matchups. DeVoe's was direct: "Want It More!" He was convinced that was what the game would come down to because the teams were that evenly matched. O'Hanlon's was more philosophical: "Set your goals higher than ten feet."

They came down the steps, Navy in the old section of the building, Lafayette in the new, and walked into a cauldron of noise. Other places in college basketball seat a lot more people than Kirby does, and anyone connected with a big-time program would no doubt look at Lafayette-Navy as a less-than-worthy warm-up for the real basketball that would be played later in the month. After all, the winner of the game would go into the NCAA Tournament as nothing more than low-seeded first-round fodder for some power school.

And yet, this setting, these stakes, and the players who would compete for those stakes represented everything that remains right in a world gone wrong. For Lafayette and Navy *this* was the national championship game. This was the game they would all remember forever, win or lose. This was the game they had put in countless hours in the weight room, in meetings, in practice, in their waking dreams, to play in. There wasn't an NBA scout within miles of the place and there wouldn't be any agents lurking around the locker rooms to glad-hand anyone when it was over. None of the players had been sent to jock-sniffing prep schools to get their grades or SAT scores up to NCAA minimum standards. There wasn't a single PE or general studies major in the bunch, and the closest thing any of them had to an entourage was the band of Nate Klinkhammer buddies who had started calling themselves the "Nate 'Colonel' Klinkhammer Club."

This was college basketball. It wasn't pros-in-training. There were real students on the floor, many of whom had actually been in class a few hours earlier. Try to imagine a coach in one of the big-time leagues being told that one of his players had to be in class a few hours before the biggest game of the season. Do not imagine too vividly — you might not be able to stop laughing.

And so, after the starters had been introduced, they lined up on court, exchanging handshakes, nodding politely at one another, each of them tingling with anticipation. McDonell got the signal that ESPN was out of commercial. He stepped into the center jump circle, softly murmured, "Good luck, guys" to Ciosici and Savane, and, at 4:36 on a cool, breezy March afternoon, he tossed the ball into the air to begin a game they all knew they would remember forever.

Savane, always the quicker jumper, tapped the ball to Chris Williams. Fran O'Hanlon whipped his jacket off — as always — Don DeVoe began screaming a play — as always — and they were, at last, playing basketball.

As planned, Navy went right to Savane. He turned on Ciosici in the post, had to adjust his shot in midair to get it over him, and missed badly. The officials watched closely. There was contact, but no foul. Their whistles were silent.

After a Lafayette turnover at the other end, Navy again set its offense. Reggie Skipworth tried to go crosscourt to John Williams, but Tim Bieg, a long way from his International Trade Relations test, stepped into the passing lane, stole the ball cleanly, and went the length of the court for the first points of the game. It was 2-0 after 51 seconds. Navy tried to go back to Savane, but the ball was knocked away. Lafayette, looking to run, sprinted back and Tyson Whitfield went to the basket, under the basket, and reversed the ball in. It was 4-0. Chris Williams missed a three and Rob Worthington followed a Whitfield miss. The game was three minutes old and Lafayette led 6-0. Navy had two turnovers and four missed shots. The noise level was so high that if you turned to the person sitting next to you and screamed you still could not be heard.

Sitting in his usual seat on the end of the Lafayette bench, Pat Brogan's eyes were lit up like Times Square. His gut was telling him something he would never voice at this stage of any game, something he almost didn't want to acknowledge to himself: We've got them. It wasn't the 6-0 start, it was the body language of the two teams. Lafayette looked coiled, ready to spring on every play. Navy looked tight, almost stiff in the way the players were moving. Savane hadn't looked uncomfortable shooting the ball for two months. Now, he looked off balance, awkward.

"And," he said later, "we were on the boards. You take it to Navy on the boards, you beat them. We were all over the boards."

Navy finally scored when Chris Williams was fouled rebounding a Savane miss and made two free throws. Bieg promptly nailed a three, then stole a Jeremy Toton pass and fed Whitfield for a layup. It was 11-2. Savane missed his fourth straight shot and Frank Barr, giving Ciosici a quick breather, scored to make it 13-2. The game wasn't yet five minutes old but Navy had already been staggered. When the first TV time-out mercifully stopped play, the Midshipmen came to the bench looking stunned.

DeVoe knew at that moment that he had a problem. He'd seen the deer-in-the-headlights look he was getting in the huddle before, but not anytime lately. His players had been rocked by Lafayette's intensity and by the crowd's response to that intensity. He was afraid to kill them at that moment because they might fold. So, he soothed. "Guys, we're in great shape," he said. "Five minutes in. Good start for them but so what. Keep running our stuff and we're fine."

Briefly, they seemed to find their balance. Jason Jeanpierre came off the bench and, as he had done throughout February, he provided an instant spark. He hit a jumper for Navy's first field goal of the game. Then, a minute later, he hit a three and the gap was 15-9 with

13:47 to go. The game seemed to be settling into the kind of fight everyone had anticipated. Lafayette had surged on emotion early, now Navy had settled down and settled in.

Ehlers missed a shot at the other end and Jeanpierre rebounded. He turned to pass to Demond Shepard, who was in at the point guard spot, and threw the ball directly to Brian Burke, who had stepped in between the two Navy players. Burke caught the ball cleanly at the three-point line almost as if it was a feed from an assistant coach during a shooting drill. In one quick motion he launched his textbook jump shot (O'Hanlon had commented that morning that he would bet his life on winning every single game if he could get Burke 30 good shots), and the ball was through the basket almost before Jeanpierre realized what had happened.

Just like that, Navy's slowly building momentum disappeared. No one in the gym could know it at the time, but Burke had just made the game's biggest play with 12:16 left in the first half. The lead went to 18-9 and Lafayette's confidence came right back. A little more than a minute later, Robert Reeder picked up his third foul — with DeVoe trying to get him out of the game after his second foul — and things kept sliding downhill for Navy.

Ehlers and Bieg hit back-to-back threes to push the margin back to 26-13. Navy kept trying to rally as DeVoe tried one combination after another, but the closest it could get was eight at 33-25. And whenever Navy did start to make a move, Lafayette had an answer; specifically, Ciosici had an answer. He was everywhere: stuffing Savane on defense, rebounding every miss, scoring in the post. During one time-out DeVoe yelled at Savane to stop letting Ciosici kick his butt. Savane nodded. On the next possession, Ciosici rebounded a miss, scored, and was fouled by Savane. DeVoe could not believe what he was seeing.

With the final seconds ticking down at the end of the half and Navy looking to get to the locker room without any further damage, real disaster struck. O'Hanlon called a 30-second time-out to set up a final play with the lead at 40-28. The ball ended up in the hands of Whitfield, a player who had never really hurt Navy in the past. That all changed on one play. With Jeanpierre guarding him, Whitfield took the ball on the left side, well beyond the key. He drove right and pulled up, Jeanpierre right with him, for a tough, twisting three. He had missed all six of his threes until that moment.

This time, the ball bottomed the net just as Jeanpierre landed with his right foot underneath him, screaming in pain. He had already had trouble with the foot earlier in the year and now he had twisted it underneath him. The clock hit zero and Lafayette raced from the court, leading 43-28. The Navy players trudged slowly to the stairs — except for Jeanpierre, who was still down and being looked at by Loren Shipley.

Lafayette had played an almost perfect half. The Leopards had completely blunted Navy's two main weapons, Savane and Chris Williams, holding them to four and five points each. The most important and telling statistic, though, was the rebounding. Lafayette had 26 rebounds. Navy, always so proud of its rebounding, had 16. Lafayette had 12 offensive rebounds.

DeVoe was beside himself at halftime. Just as Pat Brogan's coaching instincts had told him early that Lafayette was ready to play, his instincts told him that even though 15 points was a far from insurmountable lead, this wasn't his team's day.

He pointed to the words he had written in the middle of the board: "Who Wants It More!"

"Right there, guys, that's the story," he said, pointing to the words. "There is absolutely no question right now who came out here wanting this game more. I mean, that team has absolutely kicked your ass in every possible way. Sitapha, you've made Ciosici look like a three-time goddamn All-American so far. I don't know what you expected coming into a championship game on someone else's floor, but you were certainly not prepared for what we're facing out there. Guys, we either get it together right away or this is a twenty-five-point loss."

DeVoe and his assistants walked into the hallway so they could go into the adjacent locker room to talk among themselves. Jeanpierre was stretched out on a training table in the hallway, lying on his back while Shipley wrapped his foot.

"What's it look like, Ship? DeVoe asked

Shipley shook his head. "Done for the day."

DeVoe patted Jeanpierre on the arm, then walked into the empty locker room. "Well, guys," he said, "the one guy who gave us some offense in the first half is done for the day."

DeVoe stared at a stat sheet for a moment. "Look at the rebounding," he said. "Can you believe those numbers? We haven't blocked out yet. This has all the makings of a forty-point loss."

Jimmy Allen spoke up. "Coach, when we played them in the championship game two years ago we were *up* fifteen and they tied the game in the second half before we went on and won."

"I know, Jimmy," DeVoe said. "We've got a lot of guys in there, though, who don't know what just hit them."

He wasn't wrong. As soon as the coaches had left, Savane and Toton had started circling the room, trying to lift everyone's spirits. They all knew they had been outplayed and outworked. "We've got plenty of time," Toton said. "We just need to hit a couple of shots to get our confidence back and do a better job on defense. There's no rush, no need to panic."

Heads started to come up. The coaches returned. DeVoe let them know what he thought about the rebounding statistics. Then he went over what he thought needed to be done to turn things around. "Get the ball to 55," he said. "That's still our game. He makes a couple, that opens things up for everyone else. But don't come out bombing threes, thinking that's how we have to come back. Because it's not. It's not our game."

DeVoe brought them together one more time. "Guys, if we don't play right now," he said, "we're looking at an eighty-point loss." That may have summed up how DeVoe felt: in twelve minutes, his prognostication had gone from a 25-point loss to an 80-point loss.

O'Hanlon's only job during the break was to convince his players they were only halfway there. Coaches hate halftime when they have a big lead. They want to keep playing. O'Hanlon could do nothing more than warn his players to expect Navy to come out with the same kind of fire they had thrown at the Mids in the first half.

It never happened. The run that seemed inevitable never developed. Skipworth opened the half with a drive to cut the margin to 43-30, then Ciosici went right at Savane and dunked over him. Whitfield hit a pair of threes. Ehlers scored. Bieg made another steal for another layup. It was 57-36. Ehlers drove the lane and he and John Williams collided. Williams came up bleeding. This was nothing like Chris Williams–McCleary. It was a fluke elbow in the wrong place. But it took ten stitches to close the gash on top of Williams's head. Seconds later, almost as if to make sure Navy's nightmare would be complete, McCleary scored on a drive.

DeVoe tried everyone in a Navy uniform except the restrictees — and he may have been tempted to suit them up. "Why," he pleaded during one time-out, "can't we fight these guys? Where the hell is our desire?"

At 68-44, he took Savane and Chris Williams out. Both thought they were being rested until after the TV time-out that would come at the eight-minute mark. They rested a lot longer than that. Both were struggling, the game was out of control, and DeVoe saw no reason to put them back in.

"At first I thought, 'Okay, I need a breather,'" Savane said. "Then as the clock went down and down, I realized he wasn't putting me back in. I sat there and thought to myself, 'No way this can be happening. The story doesn't end this way.'"

But for Navy and Savane the story wasn't going to have a happy ending. The lead got to as high as 78-51 before O'Hanlon, not wanting to pour it on, but not wanting to declare victory too soon, began subbing liberally. He got Mike Homer and Klinkhammer in while the Zoo Crew chanted, "It's all over," and waved car keys at the Mids.

Ehlers came out first — to a standing ovation.

Then Ciosici came out and it felt like the roof might come off the place. The entire Lafayette bench was waiting for him. Finally, two years later, he had exorcised his Navy demons, his championship-game demons. Even O'Hanlon let go a little bit, high-fiving Ciosici as he came to the bench, then hugging him.

It ended with the Lafayette subs dribbling out the final seconds under orders not to shoot the ball. There was no need for further humiliation. The final was an astonishing 87-61. At only one point — 15-9 with the ball — had there been any sense that Navy was going to make it a game. Then Jeanpierre had thrown the ball to Burke, and his three had proven to be the final nail — a nail hammered with more than thirty-two minutes left in the game.

When the buzzer sounded, the first person on the court was Stefan Ciosici. He was right in the middle of the joyous Zoo Crew, arms in the air, tears in his eyes. The whole thing felt remarkably familiar to him, and as the hugs and the high fives and the net cutting went on, it occurred to him that he had lived this moment before — hundreds of times — lying on his bed, dreaming it over and over, knowing he couldn't feel complete as a basketball player until he was out there on the court with bedlam breaking loose all around as he and his teammates and his classmates celebrated being Patriot League Champions. Now, he didn't have to dream it anymore. Finally, he had lived it.

The Navy players shook hands and offered congratulations and tried to get off the floor as quickly as they could. Jeremy Toton didn't want to cry until they were in the locker room, but he didn't make it. The tears began coming in the handshake line and he was crying almost uncontrollably by the time they hit the steps. They trudged up the steps and into the locker room. They were starting to sit down when Scott Strasemeier, the SID, came in, a stricken look on his face.

"Coach," he said quietly, "they want you back downstairs for the awards ceremony."

"What?" DeVoe said. "No one told us that."

"I'm sorry," was all Strasemeier could say. "I guess they forgot."

For a split second it seemed possible that DeVoe wouldn't make his team go back downstairs to be part of Lafayette's victory party. But he set his jaw and nodded his head. "Fine," he said. "Let's go back downstairs, guys. They kicked our ass, we can at least show some class and take it like men."

When they were a little slow responding, he got angry. "Come on, let's move!" he barked. "We haven't moved all day, we can at least move now!"

They went back down the hall and down the steps, Jeanpierre helped by Mark Alarie because he was on crutches. When they walked back into the gym, the Lafayette fans stopped celebrating and turned to applaud them.

"That might have been the worst moment of all," Chris Williams said. "They were almost pitying us because they had beaten us so bad.

I know the gesture was a good one, but it hurt like hell hearing polite applause."

Savane was more blunt: "We didn't go up there to make them happy," he said. "And we ended up making them ecstatic. I felt sick."

They had to endure the announcement of the all-tournament team. Savane and Williams both made it. When Carolyn Femovich handed them their trophies, they looked at them as if they had poison ivy on them. Williams gave his to his parents, wanting to get it out of sight. Savane put his under the bench and left it there. Later, when he went to leave the locker room, someone told him not to forget his trophy — which was sitting next to his locker. He left it behind again. When the bus got back to Annapolis, one of the managers said, "Sitapha, your trophy." This time Savane left it on the front seat of the bus. Finally, a week later, walking through Alumni Hall, Savane was stopped by equipment manager Dion Harris. "Hey, Sitapha, I've got your trophy in my office, when are you going to pick it up?"

"Damn thing grew legs," Savane said.

Finally, they were allowed to escape to the locker room. DeVoe didn't spend long telling them what had gone wrong. They already knew and it wasn't going to do any good to go over it now anyway.

"It was an awful day, guys," he said. "You can't come into a championship game like that, not ever. That team was primed and ready for you and they played a great game. But we're better than that. We all know that. I don't want you to forget what you accomplished this year. You were 0-3 and you came back to win twenty-three games. That's a hell of an achievement."

He paused and looked at Savane and Toton. Savane was stone-faced, Toton red-eyed. "You two guys gave us great leadership," he said. "After that night in August, you were both terrific. I'm proud of both of you and I thank you from the bottom of my heart."

He talked for a few more minutes and then wrapped up. "When you talk to the media," he said, "let's show class. Give them the credit they deserve. And you know what? I hope they play like this next week, because if they do, they may scare someone. They're worthy champions, guys, worthy champions."

Down the hall, the champions were making plans for Sunday night, when they would gather to watch the announcement of the NCAA pairings, knowing their name would show up on the TV screen at some point.

"I thought we'd win," O'Hanlon told his players. "But I never thought we'd win like that."

Neither did anyone else.

30

WORTHY CHAMPIONS

FOR the Lafayette players, the only difficult thing associated with the victory was waking up the next morning on an empty campus. Everyone had cleared out after the postgame parties on Friday night and now they faced several days with the campus to themselves.

"Actually, it isn't so bad," Tim Bieg said. "It's a lot easier than right after Christmas when the weather is awful and you think the season's never going to end. Now, we've got decent weather and we're getting ready to play in the NCAAs. You can't complain about that."

Especially when the alternative would be to be in Navy's shoes. The Mids had returned home to an equally vacant campus. Some would go home for spring break, others wouldn't. Chris Williams had been faced with a decision a week earlier: make a plane reservation when he could get a cheap fare or not make one. He didn't make one, and after the loss found himself with ten days to do nothing in Annapolis. "Depressing,' he said, "to say the least."

The coaches had told the players who were leaving to make sure to check in Sunday night just in case the NIT called to extend a bid. Everyone knew it was a long shot, especially after the way they had performed on national TV on Friday, but Don DeVoe was still holding out some hope.

"If they look at the record at all we should have some chance," he said. "We won twenty-three basketball games. Shouldn't that count for something?"

It should, but with the NIT it doesn't. TV ratings count. Filling a building counts. Being a name counts. And so, on Sunday night when the NIT bids came out, Rutgers, at 15-15, got a phone call. Penn State, at 15-15, got a phone call. South Florida (South Florida?), at 17-14, got a phone call. No one called Navy. DeVoe got the official word shortly before midnight that his team's season was over.

"The perfect end to a perfect weekend," he said.

By then, Lafayette knew where it was going: Buffalo, as a number fifteen seed, to play the number two seed in the East, Temple.

No one was terribly surprised. The players had been combing the Internet even before they had played Navy, reading all the mock draws put out by the so-called experts. Almost every scenario had the Patriot League winner as a fifteenth seed. Most had them staying in the East — though a couple had them out West. If they stayed East, they would have to go to Buffalo, because Duke was locked in as the number one seed in the East and would be sent to nearby Winston-Salem to play. That meant the number two seed had to go to the other regional site, and that would mean Buffalo, if Lafayette was, in fact, number fifteen.

Fran O'Hanlon had studied the sixty-four-team field and had concluded that his team would be ranked ahead of seven teams. That would mean being a fifteenth seed. He was holding out hope that the tournament committee would find an eighth team to put the Leopards in front of and make them a number fourteen seed — which would mean playing a number three seed — but he didn't think it was likely.

As the players gathered on Sunday evening in the Limburg Theater on the basement level of the school's union building, O'Hanlon smiled, thinking about what was to come.

"The worst-case scenario for me is playing Temple," he said. "And I'm thinking that's who we're going to play."

The reason O'Hanlon considered Temple a worst-case scenario had nothing to do with the quality of the team. The Owls were outstanding. But so was St. John's, the other likely number two seed in the East. Either way, Lafayette would have a very difficult game. What bothered O'Hanlon about playing Temple was his relationship with the coaching staff. O'Hanlon had worked at Temple for a year with Coach John Chaney and they were still friends. Chaney's longtime assistant Dean Demopoulos was one of his closest friends in the business.

"At least we won't have any trouble getting tape on them if we play," he said.

A big-screen TV had been set up in the theater for the occasion. The local media was out in force, TV crews, radio reporters, all the print people. The *Philadelphia Inquirer* had sent a reporter. It wasn't quite as thrilling as it had been a year earlier when it had all been new, but it was fun.

The players sat in the front rows of the theater munching on pizzas while the TV crews set up to tape them watching TV. Everyone was speculating back and forth on where they might go, whom they might play.

"I'd like to go to Tucson," Brian Burke said. "Getting on an airplane makes it feel like a bigger deal."

Someone asked Stefan Ciosici what he thought of the whole thing. "I have no idea," he said. "It's all still too confusing to me to figure out."

Ciosici had been voted MVP of the Patriot League Tournament, absolute proof that he had come all the way back — and at just the right time. He had celebrated that night by taking his girlfriend and another friend to dinner and ordering the first beer of his life. "Didn't like it," he said. "I went back to soda right away."

Once the pairings show began, it didn't take long for the Leopards to find out where they were going. The East Regional went up first. Sure enough, Duke was number one, heading for the subregional in Winston-Salem. Bonnie Bernstein, who was reading off the bracket for CBS, went through the other seven teams that would be in Winston-Salem along with Duke. When she moved on to the Buffalo subregional, everyone leaned forward in their seats.

Since the number two seed is always placed at the bottom of the bracket, that matchup went up last. "And, Temple," Bernstein intoned, "is the number two seed in the East, with Coach John Chaney seeking his first trip to the Final Four. The Owls will open play on Friday in Buffalo against Lafayette, the Patriot League champion."

There were no cheers or high fives when they saw the pairing. Just a low buzz. It was about what they had expected: Buffalo — which meant a homecoming for sophomore forward Mick Kuberka — and Temple, which meant a lot of questions for O'Hanlon about his relationship with Chaney.

They sat and watched the rest of the brackets go up. Hofstra was the number fourteen seed in the East, slotted to play Oklahoma State in the first round. Penn, which had beaten Lafayette at the buzzer in the Palestra, was the number thirteen seed in the East — meaning the committee ranked the Quakers at least five slots higher than the Leopards. One of the other fourteenth seeds was Iona, the same Iona that Bucknell had beaten easily in January.

Clearly, the committee hadn't done Lafayette any favors. But then the committee never does the Patriot League any favors. The odds were good — almost overwhelming in fact — that "Patriot League winner" had been written into the fifteenth slot in the East bracket even before Lafayette had played Navy. The odds were equally good that the ten committee members hadn't even bothered to watch the game. They were probably being wined and dined by CBS and too busy to watch a game involving two teams already locked into a fifteenth seed.

No one from Lafayette was complaining about the draw. For one thing, there was no point. For another, they were neither that surprised nor that disappointed. Brian Burke wouldn't get to fly to Tucson, but he would get to play against his father's alma mater. Tom Burke had gone to night school at Temple for twelve years while he was raising his family. There were other connections: Ciosici had played summer-league ball with Pepe Sanchez, Temple's star point guard, and Lynn Greer, their 3-point shooting specialist. Reggie Guy had played against senior guard Quincy Wadley growing up in Harrisburg.

But the most significant connection was the one between the coaches. Within minutes of the draw announcement, O'Hanlon was telling Chaney stories. The one that said the most about Chaney — and about O'Hanlon for that matter — concerned a game of noontime hoops that had taken place in Temple's old gym, McGonigle

Hall, years earlier. It was three-on-three half-court and, in a close game, Chaney was trapped in the corner with the ball.

"Time out!" he screamed.

"Time out?" O'Hanlon responded. "You can't call time out in half-court. There's no such thing!"

"It's my gym and if I want to call time out, I'll call time out!" Chaney yelled back.

The two of them ended up nose-to-nose, screaming at each other about whether a time-out was allowable in three-on-three hoops. (No one else on the planet can ever recall someone trying to call time out in a game of three-on-three but it *was* Chaney's gym.) When the game ended — each coach claims his team won — O'Hanlon stomped out of the gym without another word to Chaney. A couple of days later, he returned to Europe to play and coach, and it was almost a year before he was back at Temple again.

When he did get back there, he went down to the basement — the dungeon as Chaney calls it — and popped his head into Chaney's office.

"Hey, John," he said.

Chaney looked up, saw him, and leaped up from his desk, screaming, "Time out!"

The two of them broke up laughing.

That's what made the matchup difficult for O'Hanlon. If almost anyone else — other than perhaps Penn — was playing Temple, he would root for Temple. Now, he had to figure out a way to try to beat his old friend.

A lot of people were quick to point out that Temple might be a good team to play, since Lafayette often used the matchup zone defense that Chaney had made famous. "We see it every day in practice," Tim Bieg said.

"What they see in practice and what Temple will be doing are two very different things," O'Hanlon said. "We play the matchup pretty well. They invented the damn thing."

The team could have flown to Buffalo, since the NCAA picks up expenses for the teams. But it would have meant flying a puddle jumper to Newark, then changing planes to fly to Buffalo. Given the dicey weather and the need to change planes, the players, presented with the option, voted to go by bus. Even Brian Burke.

They left on Wednesday morning, accompanied by a local camera crew that would chronicle their every move for a thirty-minute TV special to air in the Lehigh Valley on Thursday night. The sports anchor for Channel 69 was Jeff Fisher, the voice of Lehigh basketball on the radio. But he was very comfortable around the Lafayette program, having grown up going to Lafayette games. If there had been any doubt in the Lafayette camp about Fisher, it had been put aside when he had shown up on the air the night before the Navy game wearing a Zoo Crew T-shirt.

The trip took about six and a half hours including a stop at a Ponderosa, where everyone gorged on the all-you-can-eat and salad bar fixings. They were assigned to stay in Buffalo in a hotel called The Pillars, which was relatively new and had good-sized rooms. It was also surrounded on all sides — or so it seemed — by hospitals.

When they arrived in Buffalo it was snowing. It snowed all day Thursday but stopped on Friday. The temperature was balmy — in the twenties — with the windchill factor making it feel a lot colder. Even so, a brave group of seven players — Tim Bieg, Brian Burke, Stefan Ciosici, Rob Worthington, Mick Kuberka, Scott Gearhart, and David Bonney — took advantage of the chance to go to Niagara Falls on Thursday. It was snowing and freezing, but spectacular. The only one who had any trouble was Bieg: unafraid to take a charge from players twice his size, Bieg was afraid of heights.

The Leopards had picked up another camera crew when they arrived at Canisius for practice on Thursday morning. ABC News had a producer named Tom Johnson, who was a Lafayette graduate. He had convinced the powers that be at *World News Tonight* that the story of a little school with no athletic scholarships and — unlike the Ivies — very little reputation nationally was worth sending a crew to Buffalo for. As he ran practice Thursday morning, O'Hanlon was miked.

After practice, they made their way through the snowy streets to the Marine Midland Arena — which would actually be given a new corporate name the next day, just in time for national TV exposure — to go through their shootaround and press conference. This is all ritual: one hour on the court, spend some time with the CBS announcers — Ian Eagle and Jim Spanarkel — press conferences for players and the head coach to follow. O'Hanlon teased Eagle mildly about his comments in the Buffalo paper regarding the extra research he would be doing in case the game turned into a blowout.

After the press conference, O'Hanlon and several of the players did several minutes apiece with the ABC crew. Then it was back to the hotel.

O'Hanlon was eager to get back because his wife, Nancy, had been fighting a serious tension headache for a week and he was concerned about her. He had brought Tim, his seven-year-old son, to practice to make life a bit easier for Nancy, leaving her with only six-year-old Grace. By the time O'Hanlon got back to the hotel, Nancy was in enough pain that Dawn Schleiden, the team's trainer, thought it was worth getting her to one of the nearby hospitals for a CT scan if only to make sure nothing serious was going on.

The players who hadn't gone to Niagara Falls holed up in their rooms watching first-round tournament games being played at other sites. That was when the phone calls from "Mike Ericson of the *Buffalo News*" started. "I didn't even know until later that I got the name of the newspaper right," Ehlers admitted. He had sensed at practice that morning that everyone was a little tight, and thought maybe a good mystery would take everyone's mind off the pressure. Ericson placed calls to several players, asking if they could come to the lobby for photos. He even called assistant coach Mike Longabardi, trying to find out what the coaches thought was the key to beating Temple.

Then, to throw people off the scent, Ehlers claimed that Ciosici, his roommate, had gotten one of the calls. He and Ciosici suspected the prankster was Burke.

They met to go through tape one more time in O'Hanlon's room at nine o'clock. O'Hanlon was tired, but relieved because the CT scan had shown nothing. Nancy was feeling a little better and finally getting some rest.

"There isn't much new we can show you on this tape," O'Hanlon said as the players sat in front of him one more time. "There isn't that much to prepare for. They're like a Mack truck. They're going to try to run you over. Think about this for a minute — what do you think

Temple is saying about Lafayette right now? They're saying, 'Let's pound them right from the start; end this thing early and get them out of here.' They were up 34-4 on St. Bonaventure last Saturday night. I'm sure you guys saw what St. Bonaventure did against Kentucky today (the Bonnies had led the game late before losing in double overtime), so that's how dangerous Temple is.

"This will not be a pretty game. They dribble, dribble, dribble, and beat you up in the half-court game. We have to run when we can but make sure we always get back."

He showed them Temple's offense and defense for a few minutes and reminded them that there would be no margin for error against this team. "We've got six games to play, guys," O'Hanlon said, talking pie-in-the-sky. "But we have to get through this first one and it's going to take a great effort to do that."

If they did get through the first one, they would become the story of the tournament. Every single one of them knew that. And every one of them went to bed that night believing it was possible.

There were hints right from the start that Friday might not be a very good day.

When they returned to Canisius for shootaround at ten o'clock, the bus was abnormally quiet, almost as if the game was fifty minutes rather than five hours away. As the players were warming up, Brian Burke teased Tim Bieg good-naturedly about his somewhat timid performance at Niagara Falls.

Bieg almost always takes as good as he gives. Now he whirled on Burke. "You always want to put the knife in, don't you?" he snapped.

Bieg had been cut up a whole lot worse on previous days. But on those days he hadn't been about to face Pepe Sanchez, arguably the best point guard in the country, in front of a packed house and a good-sized TV audience.

Then came shooting drills. A lot of shots seemed to come up short. Often when shooters are nervous their shots are short, because they aren't following through or bending their knees, or because they're thinking too much rather than just using the shooting motion that is second nature to most good players. Of course, the old show business saying goes that a poor dress rehearsal means a good opening night. And there was no question that, playing in the NCAAs, the Leopards were a part of show biz.

They went back to the hotel for pregame meal. O'Hanlon collected some food to take upstairs to Nancy, who didn't feel well enough to come down and eat. Mike Longabardi and Mike McKee left early for the arena to scout Oregon–Seton Hall. Traffic in Buffalo had come to an almost complete halt. When they finally got inside the arena, Longabardi called back to the hotel to tell O'Hanlon that the bus should probably leave earlier than he had planned.

Everyone in the Lafayette party was hoping Seton Hall would win the opening game. Coach Tommy Amaker's top assistant was Rob Jackson, who had been with O'Hanlon during his first two years at Lafayette and had played a role in recruiting most of the upper-classmen, most notably Ehlers, Mike Homer, and Tyson Whitfield. O'Hanlon and Jackson were still close friends and it was hard for O'Hanlon to even watch the game because it made him nervous.

He paced up and down in the hallway while the players dressed, then walked in to write his game keys on the marking board. There was almost nothing in his keys that the players hadn't seen all year. Transition D always came first under D-keys. Under O-keys, where he normally would write "Good decisions," O'Hanlon had written "Good QUICK decisions." That was testimony to the level of competition they were facing. O'Hanlon knew that the pace of this game, not so much up and down the floor, but in the quickness and intensity Temple would bring to bear on every possession, was going to be different from what his players were accustomed to.

At the bottom of the board he wrote what any coach would write at a moment like this: "Stay poised." There were a million reasons not to stay poised and this was a game in which they couldn't afford to be anything but poised for forty minutes.

Once O'Hanlon had walked them through the keys and Pat Brogan had gone through the matchups one last time, they turned the TV back on to watch the end of Oregon–Seton Hall. They were all standing when Rimas Kaukenas hit the shot that sent the game into overtime. "Sit down and relax, fellas," O'Hanlon told them.

As much as he wanted to get the game started, he was happy that Seton Hall still had a chance. He walked out to the court and watched the first four minutes of the overtime before walking back — waylaid briefly by the eagle-eyed security guard — to rejoin his team. After Shaheen Holloway's scoop shot at the buzzer had won the game for Seton Hall, O'Hanlon gathered the players around him for a few final words.

As he did, the door burst open and a CBS camera crew bustled in. In return for its billions, CBS essentially has carte blanche to go where it wants when it wants. A boom mike hovered over O'Hanlon as he told his team to make the day one they would be happy to remember the rest of their lives.

Then they headed to the court. This was an entirely different setting than seven days earlier at Kirby Sports Center. The place was huge and filled to the brim. The building noise during warm-ups gave them all tingles. They knew they had a job to do, but they couldn't help but feel thrilled to be where they were, to have earned the right to be in this arena on this day even if almost no one gave them any chance to win.

There wasn't a player at the other end of the court who didn't dream about being a pro when he left college. If past statistics were a measure, perhaps one of every three would leave with a degree.

No one watching the game cared about any of that. They didn't care about Temple's graduation rate or Lafayette's. They didn't care if Ciosici was a double major if he couldn't produce a double-double (points and rebounds) against the Owls. Already there were arguments going on in the media room about how Temple would match up in a regional final against Duke.

Nine minutes into the game, Temple led 17-12. Lafayette had gotten off to its normal (the Navy game aside) awful start, trailing 9-2 before an Ehlers 3 seemed to get their legs under them. They chipped to within 12-9 on a pretty Bieg-to-Ciosici pass, and then after a Quincy Wadley 3, Burke answered with a 3 of his own. They were into the game and in the game.

Great teams have a way of slicing you up so that you don't even know how severely you're hurt until you look down and find yourself covered with blood. Kevin Lyde dunked. Keaton Sanders posted up and scored. Ciosici missed two free throws. Greer buried a 3. Boom. The lead jumped to 24-12. Ciosici stanched the wound briefly with a layup off a Burke pass. Lyde dunked. Greer hit two free throws. Greer buried another three. Not a fast-break basket to be seen. No major Lafayette errors. But a 14-2 run. It was 31-14 and Lafayette was drowning in its own blood. The lead actually reached 19 before Tyson Whitfield nailed a 3. But Wadley ended the half with a bank shot that hit high on the glass and dropped through at the buzzer, making it 38-20.

If the Leopards had needed something approaching a miracle prior to tip-off, they were now in need of direct divine intervention. The closest thing to anything heaven-sent in Buffalo were the wings at the Anchor Bar (the place where Buffalo wings had been invented). For one brief moment, down 45-31, there was a ray of second-half hope. But it disappeared as fast as a Buffalo summer once Whitfield missed the 3 that could have sliced the margin to 11.

The last few minutes were difficult. They knew they were going to lose and that the margin was going to be ugly. They had to wait out the TV time-outs — two minutes and forty seconds during the NCAAs so CBS could make its money back — and the fouls and the clock stoppages. At 4:55 P.M., the clock hit zero. Temple 73, Lafayette 47. They had finished 24-7, a record they could certainly take pride in. That wasn't on their minds during the postgame handshakes. Later, they would think about the twenty-four wins. For the moment, the loss hurt. It had to. They were competitors. They had come, as O'Hanlon said so often, not to participate, but to compete.

Ciosici took it harder than anyone. Ehlers was saddened, but understood that the moment had to come and when it did he was glad it was in an NCAA Tournament game. Homer walked out the locker room door wearing his team-member pins from the practice day and the game day. A final souvenir.

O'Hanlon, his voice as soft as ever, told them how much he had enjoyed coaching them. "You came to practice with a great attitude every day," he said. "Every one of you has been a pleasure to coach." He paused. "Seniors, all I can say is thank you. We all know the effort you put into this."

He was dry-eyed, but emotional. There was no talk about next year. He knew this wasn't the time. This was a moment to celebrate what they had done, not to speculate on what they would do next.

"What you've done these last two years will always be a part of Lafayette," he said. "Don't ever forget that. You made history."

Most in the media would write that day about Temple's easy victory, about Pepe Sanchez's fifteen assists and about Mark Karcher's five 3-pointers. After O'Hanlon and Ciosici and Ehlers waited fifteen minutes in the holding room while reporters peppered Chaney with questions about what it would mean to him to make the Final Four, the Lafayette representatives walked onto the podium.

As they did, the room looked as if a bomb threat had just been phoned in, deadline-pressed writers scrambling for the exits. A grand total of fourteen writers, among the more than three hundred accredited for the regional, sat and listened as O'Hanlon and his players talked.

All of which was understandable. Temple was the story. Lafayette would get its four minutes of fame on *World News Tonight* that evening. They were The Little Team That Couldn't. In reality, though, they were a team that very much could. And did.

There was certainly no shame in losing to Temple. The Owls were a lot bigger, a lot faster, a lot more basketball-tested. A lot more everything. Knowing that they practiced at five o'clock every morning, O'Hanlon had thought for one brief moment after the draw was announced that his team might have a chance.

"If they put us in the game that starts at ten o'clock we might have a chance," he said. "They might be tired."

They hadn't been tired. They had been too good. Which, in the end, was really okay. They should have been too good. Basketball was what they did. It was their life. For the players from Lafayette, like their brethren around the Patriot League, basketball had great meaning. It was an important part of their lives. Every one of them loved to play and compete.

But they all knew it was only a part of who they were. And in the not too distant future, it would be a part of what they once had been.

"I know I'll miss it a lot," Mike Homer had said. "I'll always love this time in my life. I'll love having been a basketball player. But I'll be ready to move on. Endings are always sad. But they lead to beginnings."

The players in the Patriot League understand that. Basketball is not a continuum. It is a lengthy interlude.

Rob Worthington's bold, shock-the-world prediction, made in the quiet of the Canisius gym, never came true. But in the grand scheme of things, that shouldn't matter. The Patriot League schools all do things the right way in a college basketball world gone very wrong.

They deserve to be cheered, regardless of any final score.

EPILOGUE

TEMPLE and Duke never did meet in the East Regional Final. Temple was upset in the second round by Seton Hall and Duke was beaten in the round of sixteen by Florida. The national championship was won on the night of April 3 by Michigan State with more than 41,000 people watching in a corporate-named dome in Indianapolis and millions more watching on TV.

Michigan State was an unusual national champion in this era: most of its star players were seniors. In fact, the Spartans' 63 percent graduation rate in the 1990s was by far the highest for any national champion since North Carolina won the title in 1993. Florida, the runner-up, was more typical. It was a team built around freshmen and sophomores, and rumors circulated throughout the weekend that at least two of them would leave school at the end of the season. Sure enough, two of them did. But no matter, Coach Billy Donovan was given a new contract, worth more than $1 million annually — in base salary — for getting the Gators to the final.

Florida's graduation rate in the 1990s for basketball players was 33 percent. Which hardly matters.

Three days after Michigan State won the title, Stefan Ciosici and Sitapha Savane were among a group of about eighty players invited to the Portsmouth Invitational, an annual four-day basketball camp for college seniors hoping to be spotted by pro scouts. Portsmouth is not a cream-of-the-crop camp. Almost no one who expects to be an NBA lottery pick plays there. Most of the players are those hoping to get noticed by someone so they might be drafted late, signed as a free agent, or — more likely — have a chance to play overseas.

Savane and Ciosici fell into the latter category. Ciosici had already turned down a chance to join a U.S. Basketball League team, the Pennsylvania Valley Dogs, at the end of the college season. He had told the team he would play the last month of their season — beginning May 21 — after he had graduated. "Too much work," he said. "Double major." Brian Ehlers, who had been drafted by the league's Long Island team, was making the two-hour drive to play for the team on weekends. "Not as much work," he said, smiling. "Not a double major."

Shortly after arriving in Portsmouth, Savane and Ciosici passed each other in the hallway. "My first thought was, 'Oh God, not you,'" Savane said. "I kind of gave him one of those macho head nods and just kept moving."

The next night, going through a buffet line at dinnertime, Savane spotted Ciosici sitting at one of the tables eating quietly with a couple of other players. "It was time to stop acting like a baby," Savane said. "I went over and sat down with them."

Within minutes, he and Ciosici were trading stories about travel in the Patriot League, outrageous calls, things their coaches had said, other players in the league, balancing schoolwork with travel — especially now with graduation closing in.

"Really good guy," Ciosici said later. "It was fun talking to him, especially since we have so much in common."

"All the time we spent talking, he never once brought up the championship game," Savane said. "Not even jokingly. Class act."

They talked a number of times over the next couple of days and ended up on opposite sides in the championship game of the tournament on Sunday afternoon. Early in the second half, Ciosici got hit with a couple of calls he didn't like and started jawing with one of the officials. Sure enough, he got hit with a technical foul.

Ciosici was really angry. Walking down the court, he was still pleading his case to the referee. It was then that Savane walked over to him. "Don't let it get to you," he said quietly. "You get thrown out now, it'll look to the scouts like you're some kind of bad guy or hot-head. Doesn't matter that you're right. Cool it."

Ciosici nodded. And listened. And was grateful to his new friend.

Savane's team won the championship game. "I would trade wins in a heartbeat," he said, thinking back to that March day in Easton.

Throughout the 1999–2000 basketball season, anything and every-thing with the Patriot League logo on it had the words "10th Anniver-sary" above the words "Patriot League."

The question as that tenth anniversary season moved along was whether there would be a fifteenth anniversary — or, for that matter, an eleventh. "Grow or die," Alan Childs, the league's first executive director, said. "That's the way college athletics is today."

Carolyn Schlie Femovich walked into a very difficult situation when she became the league's executive director in August 1999. She had a league that was a hybrid: two military academies that granted govern-ment scholarships, two schools that were giving out basketball schol-arships, and three clinging to the notion of financial-need only. She also had a seven-team league at a time when the NCAA was saying that beginning in 2002 a league would need a minimum of eight teams to receive an automatic bid to the basketball tournament.

Throughout the winter, the rumor mill was rife. Half the league was convinced Holy Cross was leaving. "They didn't hire Ralph Willard for all that money [a reported $200,000 package] to play in the Patriot League," Navy athletic director Jack Lengyel said repeat-edly. According to those in charge, that's exactly what they did, al-though they were certainly aware of the league's perilous position.

While Lengyel was wondering about Holy Cross, he was being wined and dined by officials in Navy's old league, the Colonial Ath-letic Association. Having lost East Carolina, the CAA was down to eight teams. It wanted Navy and Delaware to come in together, al-lowing them to expand north with two schools that played good basketball and had solid academic profiles. Lengyel held the CAA at bay, wondering how Femovich's efforts to convince American Uni-versity to leave the CAA for the Patriot League would play out.

In the end, Femovich won her battle with CAA commissioner Tom Yeager. American agreed to join the Patriot League for the 2001–2002 season. The school did so after the Patriot presidents agreed to allow them to keep athletic scholarships, not only in basketball but in many nonrevenue sports. The presidents had no choice. Grow or die. They chose to grow, even if the school involved met only two of the league's original tenets: student-athletes representative of the student body? Yes. Presidential control? Yes. Financial-need scholarships? No.

There was little doubt that American would be a factor in the league from the start. In the spring, the school hired a big-time coach, Jeff Jones, who had taken Virginia to five NCAA Tournaments. What's more, the league decided to move the conference tournament to a permanent off-campus site in suburban Washington in 2002, AU's debut year.

"Anything else we can do to help?" wondered Lafayette Coach Fran O'Hanlon.

O'Hanlon was also a news-maker in the spring. Having won forty-six games and gone to back-to-back NCAA Tournaments at a non-scholarship school, his name was mentioned in connection with several jobs, most notably Siena. After interviewing at Siena and being offered a five-year contract that would have paid him about $150,000 a year, O'Hanlon decided to stay put. Lafayette had sweetened his package to within shouting distance of the Siena offer (about $125,000 a year) and had finally given him money for a second full-time coach. In 1999–2000 Lafayette had only one full-time assistant: Pat Brugan. Mike McKee, the number two assistant, was paid a part-time salary of $6,000. O'Hanlon said that had to change. It did.

"I really like it at Lafayette," O'Hanlon said when the Siena romance was over. "If I ever leave, I want it to be for my last job. I looked at Siena and I didn't see my last job. In fact, this could be my last job."

Perhaps, perhaps not. If Lafayette, Bucknell, and Colgate ever went to athletic scholarships, O'Hanlon might well stay put. But as long as the unbalanced playing field continued to exist, he had to consider other offers. And, if the LaSalle job were to open as many think it may at the end of the 2001 season, he would be a prime candidate. Being a Philadelphia boy, he might choose to go home.

The other six league coaches were all staying where they were. Don DeVoe's name surfaced in the mix when the Houston job opened, but he wasn't leaving Annapolis for Houston. DeVoe did admit to continued misgivings about Navy's Patriot League presence. The CAA flirtation was dead as soon as American bolted that league for the Patriot League. That wasn't where DeVoe would have wanted to go in any case.

"Big East," he said. "If it were my choice alone, that's where I'd go. If we were in the Big East we would recruit a higher-quality athlete and we could still bring in good students. My attitude is why not be the best you can possibly be. The way to do that would be to join the Big East."

The reason the Big East was on DeVoe's mind was that Lengyel had talked at different times about the football team joining the Big East if and when Navy decided it needed to be in a football conference. And DeVoe was certainly correct that a switch to the Big East would give Navy a higher basketball profile. But there is absolutely no way that Navy could compete in the Big East without compromising its standards. Already the school loses a couple of players a year to "nobody," simply because the player doesn't want to make a commitment to the military.

Jimmy Allen, DeVoe's top assistant, was talking to Colgate Coach Emmett Davis one spring day about the players Navy had lost during the year who had a choice between Navy or nobody and had chosen nobody. Davis had been there, done that in his Navy days. "I'll never schedule nobody," Davis told Allen. "Because by now, they've got a hell of a team."

The point is this: in the Patriot League, the Navy system works. Sending players to the prep school for a year, recruiting good students who will be disciplined enough to survive at the academy and play for DeVoe, has made Navy a force in the league. In the last seven years, Navy has been the Patriot League rep in the NCAAs three times and lost the championship game on two other occasions. The first thing DeVoe's coaches tell recruits nowadays is, "Come here and you'll have a chance to play in the NCAA Tournament."

Playing in the Big East might sway a player or two from nobody to Navy, but it isn't going to change the mind of anyone with NBA aspirations, because of the school's military commitment. And there is nobody playing serious minutes in the Big East who doesn't come out of high school — or junior college — without NBA aspirations. DeVoe isn't wrong to dream, to want to shoot higher. But changing leagues isn't the way to do it.

DeVoe's counterpart at Army, Pat Harris, would be very happy to get his program to the point where it could compete in the Patriot League. To him, the Big East is something to watch on television. Period.

Harris spent a good part of the spring trying to convince Rick Greenspan, his athletic director, that Mike Krzyzewski was right about the need to change the basketball culture at Army in order to win with any consistency. One winning season in twenty years, and none in fifteen, would seem to be a strong indicator that changes are needed. Since Krzyzewski's departure in 1980 the academy has chosen to change coaches (five times) in its search for success. It has hired Army grads, non-Army grads, young coaches, not-so-young coaches, loud coaches, not-so-loud coaches. None have succeeded. After a while there should be a message: changing coaches isn't what's needed. Changing the culture is.

That would mean making the kind of commitment to basketball players that the academy often makes to football players. It would also mean straightening out the problems that existed between Harris and the prep school and working on making the academy a better place to be a basketball player.

Two freshmen had started for most of the season for Army: Michael Canty and Adam Glosier. Harris knew both had thoughts about leaving the school. He knew it was imperative that good young players stay in the program, and he tried very hard to convince both Canty and Glosier that the worst year of their West Point lives was now behind them.

He batted .500. Canty, despite some difficult moments in the spring, decided to come back. Glosier did not. "I just don't see myself as a cadet," he told Harris. To Harris, this was a major loss. Glosier had made tremendous strides during the season, becoming the team's most consistent rebounder and inside defensive player. Harris had no doubt that his offensive game would improve as he matured. Now he was gone.

The good news was that Harris and his staff believed they had come up with an excellent recruiting class. Unlike Navy, which had the luxury of sending most recruits to prep school for a year, Army had to bring its best players directly to the academy if they were ready academically. The quality of Army's recruits got the attention of other coaches around the league. "Best recruiting class they've had in years," Navy assistant Jimmy Allen said.

Even so, Harris still needed his two returning seniors, Joe Clark and Seth Barrett, to come back from disappointing seasons if Army was to show serious improvement. If they didn't, the Cadets would again be terribly young, and, especially at Army where life is so tough for plebes, that's never a good thing.

"I just hope they understand how tough the job is," Mike Krzyzewski said. "Pat's got two years left on his contract. When he took over, it was a seven-year project. They need to realize that up there."

Bucknell, which had been the league's most experienced team, would go into 2000–'01 as one of the least experienced. Five seniors graduated, leaving Pat Flannery with one player, Bryan Bailey, returning among his top six. But Flannery had high hopes for three freshmen, Brian Werner, Dan Blankenship, and Chris Zimmerman, and was bolstered by the notion that Jake Ramage and Pete Santos would both be back after missing the year with injuries. For the first time in five years, Flannery was bringing in a large freshman class — six players.

"After a while you realize that at Bucknell, you bring in six kids, you aren't likely to end up with all six of them playing as seniors," he said. "Some kids decide they just want to be students, others don't develop. We were lucky with this year's senior group. There were six of them as freshmen, and five of them were contributors as seniors. That's unusual."

Emmett Davis also brought in six players at Colgate. He only lost one senior, Pat Diamond, but, like Pat Harris, he lost a key player to transfer. Jordan Harris decided at the end of his sophomore season that he was capable of competing in a league at a higher level than the Patriot League. On sheer physical talent, this was probably true. Everyone who saw him play agreed that Harris had physical gifts not normally seen in the Patriot League. But he had hardly been a dominant player. He finished the season averaging 14 points and seven rebounds a game.

He was the last player selected for the all-league second team. In other words, he had a very good sophomore season that probably should have led to first-team all-league status as a junior. He was Colgate's second-best player behind Pat Campolieta. And yet he believed he belonged in another conference, someplace out west closer to home. Davis was disappointed to lose a player as talented as Harris, but wasn't stunned when it happened. "He had talked about it at the end of his freshman year," he said. "I think it's a mistake, but I'm not the one who has his ear right now."

Davis had scheduled November games at Arizona State and Northern Arizona for the specific purpose of giving Harris a chance to play close to home. Now the Red Raiders would be making the trip without Harris.

Lehigh brought in its second class of scholarship players, most notable among them a shooter from Connecticut named Alex Jensen. He was expected to step into the spot vacated by Jared Hess, and he and Matt Logie were expected to give the Mountain Hawks consistent offense. Sal Mentesana was also convinced that Zlatko Savovic and Matt Crawford would be ready to play a lot more minutes as sophomores.

The captain would be Eddie Lacayo, who hadn't started for most of the season but who had become one of the team's emotional leaders down the stretch. Lacayo and Hess both gave intense speeches at the team banquet, Hess talking not what might have been but what, in his opinion, should have been. Lacayo followed, and insisted that the things that hadn't happened for Hess, Steve Aylsworth, and Fido Willybiro would happen under his captaincy.

"It didn't start out to be an emotional evening," Mentesana said. "But it ended up that way. When I got up to talk, I got very emotional myself, thinking about what the seniors had gone through."

Holy Cross had no banquet, so Chris Spitler didn't get to give a farewell speech. That was fine with Spitler, who was preparing for graduation and life in New York as a carefree bachelor with a hotshot internship on Wall Street. "I'm not sure how my basketball skills will transfer," he said. "I'm pretty sure that if someone drops a pencil and I dive on the floor for it, people aren't going to pat me on the back and say, 'Way to hustle, Spit.' But you never know."

Spitler wasn't the only person from Holy Cross heading for a job in finance. Roger Breslin decided at the end of the season that he wanted to try life without coaching — at least for a while. On Ralph Willard's staff, Breslin had felt a little bit like the old man who outlives his friends. He knew that Willard was doing what needed to be done to get the program turned around, but he never felt completely comfortable with the new regime. He left coaching to take a job in Boston with a financial management firm.

Holy Cross would miss Breslin. It would also miss Chris Spitler. Navy would miss Sitapha Savane and Jeremy Toton. Lafayette would miss Stefan Ciosici, Brian Ehlers, Mike Homer, and Nate Klinkhammer. Lehigh would miss Steve Aylsworth, Jared Hess, Fido Willybiro, and Pete DeLea. Colgate would miss Pat Diamond. And Bucknell would miss Dan Bowen, Dyrika Cameron, Valter Karavanic, Brian Muckle, and Shaun Asbury.

All made contributions to their schools as basketball players. But all were not just basketball players. They were true student-athletes. No term is misused more often in athletics today, but in the Patriot League it still has meaning. The seventeen members of the Class of 2000 in the Patriot League came from diverse backgrounds. They were from New York and California and Indiana and Senegal and Croatia and Romania — among other places. Some were far more successful as college basketball players than others. A couple would try to continue playing basketball for a while longer. Most would leave the game behind. But they all had one thing in common soon after they finished playing college basketball.

They were all college graduates.

ACKNOWLEDGMENTS

THE best part of writing a book for me is writing the chapter that bears the heading "Acknowledgments." The reasons for this are simple: first, it means I've finished the book. Second, it gives me a chance to thank people I have spent a lot of time with while doing my research. Often, these are people I either did not know or knew just a little when I began the book but who, by the time I am finished, have become good friends. In the case of this book, the list is fairly lengthy.

It is only right that I begin with the players. Not only are they what the book is about, more than anyone they made the winter of 1999–2000 great fun for me. Some whom I interviewed at length didn't get nearly as much attention as they deserved in the final manuscript. All were, without exception, patient and forthcoming and giving of their time and their stories. I want to thank the seventeen seniors in particular: Stefan Ciosici, Brian Ehlers, Mike Homer, Nate Klinkhammer, Sitapha Savane, Jeremy Toton, Shaun Asbury, Dan Bowen, Dyrika Cameron, Valter Karavanic, Brian Muckle, Pat Diamond, Steve Aylsworth, Pete DeLea, Jared Hess, Fido Willybiro, and last, and certainly least, Chris Spitler (just joking, Chris).

Others who were generous with their time: Chris Williams, Robert Reeder, Chris Worthing, Joe Clark, Seth Barrett, Chris Spatola, Jonte Harrell (who is forgiven for growing up a North Carolina fan), Michael Canty, Frank Barr, Tim Bieg, Tyson Whitfield, Brian Burke, Reggie Guy, Rob Worthington, Pat Campolieta, Jordan Harris, Devin

Tuohey, Sah Brown, Bobby Mbom, Zlatko Savovic, Bryan Bailey, Jake Ramage, Chris Zimmerman, James Stowers, Tony Gutierrez, Josh Sankes, Juan Pegues, Jared Curry, Ryan Serravalle, and Tim Szatko. A number of managers went out of their way to help, notably Patrick Maloney, Terron Sims, and Sam Feeney.

The coaches could not have been more cooperative, allowing me the kind of access I needed, never once blinking at my presence even in moments when the presence of an outsider was no doubt awkward. So, I thank Fran O'Hanlon, Don DeVoe, Pat Flannery, Emmett Davis, Sal Mentesana, Pat Harris, and Ralph Willard, with an extra dose of thanks to Willard who paid me a high compliment when I thanked him for putting up with my presence all season. "John," he said, "you were completely innocuous." Thank you, Ralph.

Assistant coaches in the Patriot League are brutally underpaid and this year they had to deal with me in addition to their usual headaches. Thanks to all of them: Pat Brogan, Mike McKee, Mike Longabardi, Jimmy Allen, Tom Marryott, Nathan Davis, Mark Alarie, Terry Conrad, Don Friday, Carl Danzig, Rod Balanis, Dennis Csensits, Kevin Curley, Roger Breslin, Kevin Nickelberry, Sean Doherty (yes, you, Sean), Sean Conrad, Jeff Wilson, Glenn Noak, Chris McNesby, Al Keglovitz, Marty Coyne, Andy Johnston, Denny Carroll, and Chris (The Jinx) Beal.

SIDS: Scott Morse and Phil LaBella; Scott Strasemeier and Stacy Michaud; Todd Newcomb; Bob Cornell; Glenn Hofmann, Chris Blake, and Jim Marshall; Bob Beretta and Mike Albright; and Frank Mastrandrea, who introduced me to Chris Spitler and convinced me to get satellite TV. One out of two isn't bad. Mastrandrea must also deal with his own personal God on the issue of his banishment of the Holy Cross cheerleaders from the team bus at the Patriot League Tournament. If God accepts bringing them a plate of cookies as an excuse, I will too.

Staffers at the seven schools: Bruce McCutcheon, Anthony Wilson, Bonnie Luke, Judy Campbell, and Dawn Schleiden at Lafayette; Gene Taylor, Captain Bruce Bole, Admiral Tom Bates, Eric Ruden, Dion Harris, and the inimitable Loren Shipley at Navy; Kelli Sheesley, Scott House, and Tiffany Lebengood at Bucknell; Chris Marshall at Lehigh; Jon Terry, Brian Hogaboom, Michael (Bill, Jim,

Bob) Lawson, Mady Salvani, Ian Wood, Bill Schutsky, and, naturally, Gene Uchacz at Army — not to mention Drs. Bob Arciero and Dean Taylor and my hero, Dick Hall. And, at Holy Cross, Anthony Cerunduolo, Chris Janush, John Butman, Naveen Boppana, and Lillian Williams.

Athletic Directors: Eve Atkinson, Jack Lengyel, Brad Tufts, Mark Murphy, Dick Regan, Joe Sterrett, and Rick Greenspan.

Patriot League staff: Carolyn Schlie Femovich, who had no idea that I was part of the package when she took the job and might have seriously reconsidered if she had; Grace Calhoun; and Dave Sherman.

Special thanks also to Alan Childs, the league's first executive director; Father John Brooks, Dr. Peter Likens, and Tony Maruca, who helped bring the league into existence; and to current Presidents Arthur Rothkopf, John Ryan, Dan Christman, and recently departed President William (Bro) Adams.

Non–Patriot League SIDS, who went out of their way to accommodate me even though the project had nothing to do with their schools: Mike Cragg at Duke; Mike Sheridan at Villanova; Pete Moore at Syracuse; Scott Selheimer at Delaware; Tim Bennett at Yale; Jim Englehardt at George Mason; and Jerry Price at Princeton. Special thanks to Penn's Shaun May, who not only put up with me on multiple occasions but rescued me after I cleverly left my computer in the Palestra one winter night.

All my books desperately need good pictures: Phil Hoffmann worked extremely hard to provide them.

As always I owe my agent, Esther Newberg, special thanks for standing behind a book like this (even if she still thinks Cornell is in the Patriot League) and to her assistants, Jack Horner and Amanda Wilkins.

I rarely use the word *blessed* — except when discussing my children — but I have been seriously blessed to have Michael Pietsch as my editor at Little, Brown and Company for — can you believe it, Michael? — six books. He is everything you could want in an editor: open-minded, a good listener, patient. Not the fastest reader that ever lived, but no one's perfect. He is also good at hiring assistants and did wonderfully when he brought Lauren Acampora and Ryan

Harbage on board. The other Little, Brown person who has somehow steered through six books with me is Holly Wilkinson, who is one of those people who can find the nugget of good that exists in everyone — even me.

Extra credit and thanks to Bill Brill, always a friend, but for this book more than that since he was the one who spent hours and hours researching graduation rates nationally. Thanks also to the Lehigh flash himself, Rick Eskin, and, as always, to Norbert Doyle, believed to be the only man ever recruited by every school in the Patriot League.

Friends: Keith and Barbie Drum; Tom and Jill Mickle; Bob and Annie DeStefano; Jackson and Jean Diehl; Steve Barr and Lexie Verdon-Barr; Tom and Jane Goldman; Peter Gethers and Janis Donnaud; Bob Edwards, Ellen McDonnell; David Maraniss, Bob Woodward, Terry Hanson, Dave Kindred, Hubert Mizell, Len Shapiro, Mike Purkey, Jim Frank; Dick (Hoops) Weiss, Tony Kornheiser (yes, him); Ken Denlinger, Mark Maske, Richard Justice, Steve Berkowitz, Bob Socci, Beth Shumway, Erin Lassen, Beth Sherry, Joe Valerio, Dick Schaap, Mike Lupica, Bob Ryan, Bill Conlin, Michael Wilbon, George Solomon and Shelly Crist, who for some reason remains married to Jason.

Swimming friends: Jason Crist, Michael Fell, Wally Dicks (The Relay); Tom Denes, Jeff Roddin, Clay Britt, Doug Chestnut, Penny Bates, Barbara Clifford, Carole (Princess) Kammel, Kevin Morrissey, John Craig; and from days gone by Ed and Lois Brennan. Basketball friends: Mike Brey, Tommy Amaker, Mike Krzyzewski, Gary Williams, Billy Hahn, Jimmy Patsos, Dave Dickerson, Bob Bender, Dave Odom, Chuck Swenson, Jack Kvancz, Jeff Jones, Rick Barnes, Dick Vitale, and Tom Konchalski. Basketball icons: Red Auerbach, Morgan Wootten. Official cartoonist of my life: Zang Auerbach. Golf types: Colgate grad David Fay, Chris and Laura Smith, Tom Meeks, John and Kitty Morris, Mark Russell, Jon and Martha Brendle, Lee Patterson, James Cramer, Glenn Greenspan, and the always kind and gentle Frank Hannigan. Ex-golf type who actually showed up at Army three different times: Wes Seeley.

Special thanks to Olga Rivera, who is largely responsible for Brigid and her parents surviving the first two-and-a-half years of her life.

I always leave my family for last because they always mean the most: Mary, Danny, and Brigid, who deserve better than they get. And Dad, Margaret, Bobby, David, Jennifer, Marcia, Kacky and Stan, Annie and Greg, Jimmy, Brendan, and fabulous parents-in-law, Arlene and Jim.

The other great thing about writing acknowledgments is that putting the names on paper brings back a lot of fond memories. The memories of this book will stay with me a long time. I thank everyone involved for that.

— John Feinstein
Bethesda, Md.
June 2000

INDEX